Principles
of
Bank
Operations

Revised Edition

Principles
of
Bank
Operations

Harold Wallgren

American
Institute of
Banking

American
Bankers
Association

Previous editions published in
1956 and 1966

Third Printing, February 1976

0525

Printed in the
United States of America

Contents

Preface

Principles of Bank Operations is designed to provide for beginners and newcomers in the banking field a broad overview of the nature of commercial banking activities. Like its predecessor, it holds to the theory that banking students should not only be familiar with what banks do in performing their many services, but should be equally conversant with the basic principles that impel them to seek certain objectives. Therefore, the *what* and *why* of banking are stressed rather than the *how*, or the specific techniques by which the objectives are reached.

This particular textbook must meet the needs of a uniquely diverse group of students. They come from small banks and large banks; from unit banks, branch banks, and centralized main offices; from country towns, suburban complexes, and metropolitan cities scattered over every section of the United States. Students come armed with high school diplomas, college diplomas, and master's degrees; with no experience, limited experience, wide experience, and specialized experience.

For these reasons, the approach to the subject must necessarily be flexible and adaptable. It can neither be too profound nor too superficial. It must deal with what students encounter in banking today and yet not close its eyes to what *might be* tomorrow. In the search for the constants, it must deal with the past, yet not dwell on what is obsolete. It may look to the future with high hopes and expectations, yet it dare not attempt to predict the course of future events.

The author is indebted to a select and very competent group of reviewers who patiently read the manuscript and offered many helpful and constructive criticisms and suggestions. To George E. Bloeser, a member of the Institute's Executive Council, and Assistant Vice President of United California Bank, San Francisco, California; Sidney Goldstein, Vice President of American National Bank and Trust Company, Chicago, Illinois; John J. McCaffrey, Assistant Vice President of State Street Bank and Trust Company, Boston, Massachusetts; and Dr. Weldon Welfling, Professor of Economics and Finance, and Head, Henry Payne McIntosh Division of Banking and Finance, Case Western Reserve University, Cleveland, Ohio, sincere thanks are due, not only for the quality of their comments, but for the promptness with which they read and responded as separate chapters of the manuscript were submitted to them.

In addition to the above, the author wishes to express his appreciation to his former associates in The Philadelphia National Bank who were helpful in so many ways, particularly to Dr. A. Gilbert Heebner, Executive Vice President and Economist, and George F. Hall, Jr., Senior Vice President, who contributed materially to sections of the text dealing with economics and automation, respectively; and especially to Ms. Margaret Stanley who with incredible patience and perseverance, typed, and retyped, and retyped countless pages of the author's often indecipherable handwriting.

Regrettably, space does not permit individual mention of many others who patiently answered questions, supplied information, read selected portions of the text, offered suggestions, or in general gave welcome and material aid and comfort, as did the most congenial and accommodating staff at AIB headquarters in Washington, D. C.

For any errors or omissions in the text, the author accepts full responsibility.

May 1975   HAROLD WALLGREN

Foreword

From time to time in the history of textbook publishing, a book will emerge as a classic in its field. AIB is proud to recommend to its national audience of bankers, scholars and students this 1975 Edition of the classic work, *Principles of Bank Operations.*

The author, Harold W. Wallgren, is an outstanding authority on all aspects of banking functions and operations. Before retirement, he was Vice President and Cashier, Philadelphia National Bank, Philadelphia, Pennsylvania. He has served the banking industry well. A highly regarded lecturer and discussant on issues facing banking, he has been associated with the Philadelphia Chapter, AIB, for many years and has been active in various capacities for the American Bankers Association. Mr. Wallgren served on the critic committee for the 1956 edition of this work and was chairman of the committee for the 1966 revision. Clearly, this experience has served the American Institute of Banking well, for the authorship of the 1975 edition can be attributed solely to Mr. Wallgren's scholarship and independent effort.

The manuscript received several critical reviews before taking on its final form. As each chapter was completed, it was critiqued carefully by a panel of four reviewers, selected both for their comprehensive knowledge of banking and their degree of acquaintanceship with AIB, its teaching philosophy and student needs.

Members of the review team were:

George E. Bloeser, Assistant Vice President, United California Bank, San Francisco, California.

Sidney Goldstein, Vice President, American National Bank and Trust Company, Chicago, Illinois.

John McCaffrey, Assistant Vice President, State Bank and Trust Company, Boston, Massachusetts.

Dr. Weldon Welfling, Head of the Henry Payne McIntosh Division of Banking and Finance and Professor of Economics at Case Western Reserve University, Cleveland, Ohio.

Mr. Wallgren used the resources of many other experts and authorities for manuscript preparation. The American Institute of Banking is indebted to all those individuals who have contributed to this most important text. It is especially grateful to the author who gave so unselfishly to this effort and to members of the review team who worked most harmoniously with the author in reviewing and developing critiques of the manuscript as it unfolded.

Principles of Bank Operations is the cornerstone of the AIB national curriculum of courses and its readership far surpasses that of any other book published by the Institute. It is probably safe to say that close to a million bankers have read all or parts of the 1966 edition. AIB, therefore, is vigilantly aware of the important role this book plays in the education and training of bankers. We feel that in the Revised Edition, we have achieved a new plateau of excellence for guiding the reader, not only in the understanding of bank operations, but also in the perception of how the banking industry enhances the American way of life.

The book has been completely reorganized in light of the most recent developments in the industry. Some chapters have been added, others expanded, and still others combined as necessary to meet current demands of our reading audience. Through survey methods, AIB students and faculty provided both feedback and input. Consequently, the new book reflects the needs of the users. AIB is proud to introduce this 1975 edition on the occasion of its 75th Anniversary. We hope it will prove to be a hallmark experience for career development in banking.

ROBERT P. CAVALIER, PH.D.
Director of Education & Training

Commercial Banks and Our Monetary System

The Purposes of This Chapter:

1. To explain the economic function of a monetary system.

2. To trace briefly the development of various forms of money.

3. To explain the importance of negotiable instruments in modern monetary systems.

4. To name the traditional commercial banking functions that service our monetary systems.

Banking is a service industry. It does not produce, manufacture, or otherwise process goods, merchandise, or other commodities. Stated very simply, banks deal in money and, in that connection, offer certain related financial services.

Commercial banking provides a smooth and efficient system of making payments to settle all kinds of business and personal transactions. In addition, it is an important part of a financial system which provides funds to manufacturers, producers, users, and consumers, by making loans and extending credit. In short, commercial banks service our

1

monetary system. This is a most important function without which it would be impossible to maintain, let alone increase, the levels of production and consumption in our economy.

Servicing the monetary system of a nation as large and as commercially active as ours requires a fast, effective, and accurate system of operating procedures, supplemented by a competent staff of well-trained personnel. *The purpose of this text is to study the underlying principles and the objectives on which these operating procedures are based.* Our interest lies in what is done and why it is done, rather than how it is done. Technological advances frequently change the specific techniques by which we accomplish our objectives, but the underlying principles as well as the objectives change slowly, if at all, and over much longer periods of time.

Since banks handle money in official form (coin and currency) and all kinds of obligations, undertakings, and claims involving money in paper form (checks, drafts, and promissory notes), it is necessary for the student of banking to acquire a basic understanding of the nature of money in whatever form it takes.

What is Money?

Money, or the love of it, has been described as the root of all evil. It has also been described as the "life-blood" that flows through the veins of our economic system, without which the system would surely collapse. The American economy is a money economy, and everything that moves in commerce or trade is expressed in terms of money.

The purpose of a monetary system is to facilitate the free exchange between buyer and seller of all such items of value, whether they be intangibles such as the wide range of personal services—from performing heart transplants to trimming shrubbery; or such tangibles as manufactured products—from jumbo jet airplanes to roller skates; or raw material—from iron ore to gladiola bulbs. Money is a *medium of exchange* because people who want to exchange what they have to offer (services or tangible assets) first convert those things into money, and then exchange the money for things they need. Money is also used as a means of storing the value of what is sold today, so that the ability to make future payments next week, next month, or next year may be assured. The "money" of any country can be loosely defined, therefore, as a medium of exchange authorized or adopted by its government as the official circulating medium of that country.

2

Development of Modern Monetary Systems

The modern concept of "money" did not develop overnight. Over many, many years and indeed up to the present time, significant changes both in the theory and in the mechanics of monetary systems have taken place. Today there are current expressions of dissatisfaction with present systems, on both the international and domestic scenes. There can be little doubt that change will be the order of the future in monetary systems as in everything else. A brief review of where we have been and how we reached our present state should be useful.

In early days, bartering, that is, the direct trading of an item or items of value for another item or items of value, was the only means of exchanging wealth. The shortcomings of bartering are all too obvious, not the least of which was the difficulty of finding someone possessing the item a prospective buyer needed who was simultaneously interested in the equivalent value of what the buyer himself had to offer. The need for a common denominator of value was evident at an early date, and man experimented for centuries with a variety of media of exchange, including such useful or valuable commodities as salt, cattle, gunpowder, fishhooks, precious stones, and semi-precious stones. Thus the first forms of "money" were available commodities that had universal acceptance in the community.

Commodity Money

Commodity money tended to inspire confidence because it had inherent value, that is, if not used as a medium of exchange, it had its individual value as a useful and desirable commodity. But the inconveniences were insurmountable. Can you imagine the number of fishhooks one would have to offer to purchase a few acres of land or the difficulty of splitting a diamond or a ruby into pieces small enough so that the owner could purchase a half-dozen ears of corn? In time the superior qualities of semi-precious metals, including malleability and divisibility, led to the adoption of metallic coins as the most satisfactory form of commodity money. But even the relative ease with which precious metals can be divided into practical units failed to provide a medium of exchange capable of serving all the needs of rapidly developing societies. In the first place, there simply was not enough to go around. In the second place, as the value of the more complex conveniences of advanced living standards grew, the characteristic of transportability became a problem. Today, it would take unwieldy loads of metallic currency to cover even relatively small business purchases, let alone the purchase of heavy equipment or, say, a computer.

3

Representative Paper Money

As the wealth of nations and their citizens increased, so did the demand for a more sophisticated medium of exchange that could satisfactorily express greater quantities of more costly items. Centuries ago men found the answer to the unwieldiness, the sheer bulk, or the inflexibility that were characteristic objections to the various forms of commodity money. The commodity, whatever it happened to be, was simply deposited with a trusted and respected depository, such as a religious temple, which then issued paper receipts in suitable denominational units. As long as the public had confidence in the depository, it would be willing to accept the receipts as readily as the commodity itself. Thus the receipts could be "spent" as easily as the actual commodity, and with much greater convenience to all concerned. Such early forms of "paper" money have been called *representative money*, since each receipt represented an equivalent quantity of the commodity in storage that could be claimed by simply surrendering the receipt. It should be noted that this type of representative money had 100 percent backing, since the quantity of the particular commodity held in storage by the depository or custodian equaled the aggregate quantity represented by the outstanding receipts.

Credit Money

The transition from representative money to credit money came about gradually, and perhaps inevitably. Over a period of years other less satisfactory commodities were abandoned, and, as the leading nations of the world adopted the gold standard, gold (and to some extent silver) became the basic commodity supporting the paper currencies. It was soon realized that ordinary business and personal requirements made it highly improbable, if not impossible, for all "receipts" or "claims" against commodity reserves to be presented at the same time. Governments began to issue paper currency, redeemable in gold or silver, but in quantities the face value of which far exceeded the value of the gold or silver reserves of the nation. Thus, credit money came into existence with partial "commodity reserves" and was accepted because of the faith and confidence of the citizenry in the fiscal policies of the government and in the financial strength it derives from its power to tax.

Today most nations issue 100 percent credit money, partly because of the relative scarcity of gold, silver, or any other suitable reserve commodity. A nation may hold substantial reserves including gold and the currencies of other nations, but since most governments will not deplete their reserves by redeeming paper currency, even partial backing by such tangible reserves is more a theory than a fact. In this country, while the government owns some 270 million ounces of gold, none is presently earmarked as reserves or collateral for the principal form of paper money (Federal Reserve notes). The United States abandoned the gold standard in 1934, and for about 40 years thereafter, U.S. citizens were not permitted to own monetary gold, but were limited to possession in the form of jewelry, heirlooms, or collector's items. However, since December 31, 1974, American citizens have been permitted to purchase and hold gold bars and wafers.

Nations have experimented with credit money for many years, sometimes with disastrous results. History has taught us one irrefutable lesson: Whatever medium of exchange a nation adopts—commodity money, representative money, or credit money—a monetary system based on that medium can survive only as long as the public has confidence in its ability to express on a reasonably stable basis the value of all other forms of wealth necessary to provide an acceptable standard of living.

Credit money can and in many instances does provide a sound and practical medium of exchange. However, its acceptability by the people depends upon the soundness of the "credit" behind it, which in turn depends on the quality and effectiveness of the fiscal and monetary policies of the issuing government.

Financial Instruments

To bring this brief and admittedly over-simplified discussion of monetary systems up to date, we now must turn to a new monetary element, the financial instrument, another paper device that is centuries old, yet still modern in view of its ever-expanding use in advanced civilizations. The modern check (a financial instrument payable out of demand deposits) is a prime example.

The term *financial instrument* is a broad one that can be interpreted to include any writing having monetary value or evidencing a monetary transaction. For the purposes of this text, we shall confine our discussion to a certain type of financial instrument that qualifies legally as a *negotiable instrument,* a category well-defined in the law, and that includes only orders to pay money (drafts and checks) and promises to pay money (promissory notes and certain certificates of deposit).

A negotiable instrument is simply a piece of paper, whose intended purpose is to transfer money from one owner to another. It is not money in itself, but represents a claim to money. In one sense, a negotiable instrument resembles representative money, because it is redeemable (if honored) on demand or at a specified maturity in official coin

5

and currency. But most negotiable instruments do not bear the seal or the signature of the fiscal officer of a sovereign state. For the most part, they represent the good faith promises, obligations, and undertakings of ordinary citizens and business firms, and as such they more closely resemble credit money.

Negotiable instruments have a decided advantage over coin and currency in that they provide a much safer way of transferring money from one person to another. Official money is, for all practical purposes, unidentifiable. It is true that our paper currency (Federal Reserve notes) has serial numbers imprinted on each bill and an indication of the point of origin. But the average citizen does not keep a record of such identifying characteristics. If money is lost or stolen, the hapless victim has a slim chance of recovery through tracing coin or currency to the finder or thief.

Negotiable instruments, on the other hand, can be identified and traced. They provide a clear record of payments and, in most cases, provide a legal receipt for such payments. They do not pass innumerable times from hand to hand. Particularly when such instruments are collected through the banking system they can be clearly traced from person to person, from start to finish.

The negotiable instrument has become the most important element in modern monetary systems. In this country alone, billions of such pieces of paper are issued every year. Most of them are checks drawn against the demand deposits of commercial banks.

Checks are issued by the purchasers of goods, services, or anything else that is bought and sold, for the purpose of transferring to sellers the agreed-upon purchase price. What is the difference between payment by check and payment by means of official coin or currency? Actually, there is no real difference. Any demand depositor can withdraw all or part of his deposit in cash, thus surrendering his "checkbook money" for coin/currency, and turn the cash over to a creditor. Ordinarily, the creditor would deposit the cash in his checking account, thus exchanging the coin/currency for an equal amount in demand deposits. Obviously, it is much simpler for the debtor to give his creditor a check to deposit. The result is the same, that is, the debtor loses demand deposits and the creditor gains demand deposits, without the inconvenience of the conversion from deposits to cash and back to deposits again.

To the public, money is money whether it is in the form of coin, Federal Reserve notes (currency), or a demand deposit balance in a commercial bank. The depositor in a commercial bank may withdraw coin or currency or both at any time by simply cashing his check, subject only to the limits of his withdrawable credit balance. He may have his currency or coin in any available denominations in whatever proportions suit his convenience. Similarly, by depositing coin and currency, he receives the equivalent value in demand deposits. In either case he is simply exchanging one form of money for another form of money. It makes no difference to a bank depositor, in a monetary sense, whether he has $500 in his checking account or $500 in Federal Reserve notes in his wallet.

It should be noted that the several forms of money (coin, currency, and demand deposits) are interchangeable at the option of the public. Thus, the amount of coin and currency in circulation is determined by the needs and convenience of the public and not by banks or the U. S. mints or the Federal Reserve System. In this connection, it is interesting to note that the ratio of demand deposits to coin and currency in circulation, as determined by public option, is roughly 3 to 1. The exact ratio changes from time to time depending on the public's needs and seasonal influences.

Since a check is supported only by the character and financial responsibility of the person who issues it, it is not surprising that, in certain instances, it is less acceptable than coin and currency when offered in exchange for items of value. Nevertheless, it is estimated that 90 percent of all business and personal transactions, in terms of dollar value, are settled by means of checks. This is convincing evidence that the common check, a form of credit money, is generally accepted every day in exchange for goods or services.

Money Supply

With this background, we can now attempt to offer some general definitions. *Money* can be broadly defined as anything generally recognized and used as a medium of exchange, acceptable in settlement for business and personal transactions or for the payment of debts. *Money supply* or *money stock* can be broadly defined as the amount of money in public hands immediately available for spending. Thus money supply does not include what might be termed "inventory" money, such as coin and currency in bank vaults, uncirculated coin in United States mints, or unissued Federal Reserve notes.

In more technical terms *money supply* can be defined in several ways, but a commonly accepted definition, known to economists as M_1, includes only the following:

1. Demand deposits, *adjusted* (which means all accounts subject to check except domestic interbank deposits, United States government deposits, and items in process of collection) , and

2. Coin and currency *in circulation* (which means outside of the

7

Treasury, Federal Reserve banks, and the vaults of commercial banks).

This definition is the most suitable for the purposes of this text, although it is relatively narrow in scope in that it does not include savings accounts or other readily available assets or claims that could be converted to purchasing media on demand or on very short notice. But M_1 is an effective gauge of the amount of money in the hands of the public apparently intended for immediate spending purposes.

With our active money supply consisting of demand deposits, plus coin and currency, it is interesting to note that our banking system supplies the vast bulk of our money. Commercial banks supply all of the demand deposits, and Federal Reserve banks supply our paper currency in the form of Federal Reserve notes. The United States Treasury supplies only the coin (through the United States mints), which is roughly less than $3\frac{1}{2}$ percent of the total. On the other hand, demand deposits of commercial banks constitute about three-fourths of our present money supply.

The Monetary Role of Commercial Banks

It would be impossible at this time, and probably at any time in the future, to define the functions of commercial banks in precise terms. In this world of ours, change is inevitable, and banking has had to adapt to meet the ever-present challenges of a far from static society.

In the areas of finance and monetary mechanisms, the changes that have taken place over the years have at times been startling and drastic. Curiously enough, however, the services that were rendered by ancient banks bear a striking resemblance to the basic services rendered by our modern banks. Centuries ago, "banks" accepted various forms of wealth for protection and safekeeping. The deposited wealth in one way or another could be transferred to others as a means of making payments and settling debts. And ancient banks used such deposits to finance commerce, agriculture, and governments. These services are readily recognized as what today are called the traditional banking functions, that is, (1) *the deposit function,* (2) *the payment function,* and (3) *the loan or lending function.*

The nature of the banking services related to these functions and the methods employed to offer these services have changed dramatically over the years, and the next few decades may see even greater changes. Yet the basic functions of banking have remained remarkably intact, and, if anything, are even more important and of greater value to society today than they ever were. The "what" of banking has not changed nearly as much as the "how."

8

This chapter attempts to define very briefly a rather complicated story—the development of modern forms of money and claims to money. The development of money is traced through its various stages—from commodity money to representative money to our present form of credit money. Money is simply a medium of exchange, a means of converting the things that people have to offer into something that will be acceptable in payment for the things they need or desire.

By necessity, over the years money has gradually lost its original characteristic of tangible value until it is now largely "faith" money. Yet credit money that is based on the faith of the public in the fiscal integrity of governments can be the basis of a sound and viable monetary system as long as that faith is maintained.

Money is transferred from one party to another party, from debtors to creditors, either by the physical delivery of official coin and currency or by means of financial instruments, which are claims to money, that is, they can be converted into official coin and currency.

The nation's commercial banks play an essential and indispensable role in servicing our monetary system by converting coin and currency into demand deposits and making these two forms of money interchangeable at the option of the public; by collecting financial instruments; and by providing an efficient payments mechanism through the medium of the common check drawn against demand deposits.

Questions Based on This Chapter

1. In what ways do banks service our monetary system?
2. What is money? What purpose does it serve?
3. How does commodity money differ from representative money?
4. What is a financial instrument?
5. Is there any real difference between payments made by check and payments made in coin and currency?
6. "Money supply" can be defined in several ways. What elements are included in what is known as the M_1 definition?

Chapter 2

Negotiable Instruments

Part I: Origin and Characteristics

Purposes of This Chapter:

1. To describe the origin of the "bill of exchange," the forerunner of what is known today as "commercial paper."

2. To explain the nature and general purpose of orders to pay (bills of exchange, drafts, and checks) and promises to pay (promissory notes).

3. To state the qualifications of a negotiable instrument under the standard version of the Uniform Commercial Code.

4. To define some of the terms used in the Code.

In the previous chapter it was shown that a certain kind of financial instrument, namely, *checks* drawn against demand deposits in commercial banks, are used more than anything else as a means of making payments today. The importance of the common check becomes apparent when it is realized that less than 10 percent of business and private money transactions are settled by the use of official coin and currency.

The standard form of a check, when executed and signed, qualifies under our laws as a special kind of financial instrument known legally as *commercial paper.** The Uniform Commercial Code (as had other statutes before it) not only precisely defines the commercial-paper type of financial instruments, but it also spells out in detail the rights, privileges, and obligations of those who become parties thereto, and lays down specific rules relating to the issuance, transfer, negotiation, presentment, and payment of such instruments.

How did this useful piece of paper come into being? And why did the courts of older nations centuries ago focus so much attention on these instruments?

Origin of Commercial Paper

It all began in the days when merchants and traders recognized only one kind of money, the kind one didn't accept on blind faith, the kind people could hold and feel and know the value was there—in short, *hard currency,* gold and silver coins or precious stones. It was one thing to exchange hard currency for commodities in a face-to-face transaction. It was quite another thing to consummate such a transaction when the buyer or seller, as the case might be, lived a few thousand miles and an ocean away! To be sure, there is a substantial element of trust and faith in all business transactions, but there was, and still is, a limit to the amount any businessman was willing to gamble on his ability to judge another man's trustworthiness. After all, it is still customary to request and receive receipts for payments, deposits, and deliveries of any form of wealth.

The progress of civilization was directly responsible for the development of financial instruments. Ancient and modern history records man's thirst for adventure and his desire to probe the unknown and explore the world about him. The early adventurers and explorers were followed by the merchants who, in their constant quest for greater profits, progressively broke down the boundaries of villages, communities, and tiny nations, as they sought trading markets in the far corners of the earth. At first, this was a game only for the bold and daring, for it was a hazardous, risky business. But the rewards were tempting—a way had to be found!

Primitive transportation facilities inhibited constant travel, and merchants soon discovered that the safest and most practical way to deal with a buyer or a seller in a distant land was to have someone on the spot, a neutral agent, so to speak, who could deal with the other

---

* In this text the legal definition of *commercial paper* will be used rather than the popular money-market concept of *commercial paper* as "unsecured short-term promissory notes of business concerns with high credit ratings."

11

merchant on a face-to-face basis. On behalf of his principal, the agent could deliver hard currency in exchange for commodities, or vice versa, and at the same time he could protect the interests of both parties.

The system worked something like this: A merchant in Rome would establish a contact with a trusted merchant in London. He then would ship a cargo of olive oil to the London merchant for sale in the British market. The London merchant might purchase the shipment outright and offer it for sale on his own account, or he might sell the olive oil on behalf of his Italian friend and handle deliveries and receive payments on a commission basis. Either way, eventually the London merchant would find himself in possession of the value of the shipment in pounds sterling that he owed to the Italian merchant. But, instead of having his money returned to Italy by sailing vessel, the Italian merchant would find it more convenient to leave the proceeds of the sale in the hands of the British merchant. At the same time or at a later date, whenever it suited his convenience, the Italian merchant would purchase products in the British Isles for sale in Italian markets. He would make payment for these commodities by instructing his London merchant to use all or part of his credit balance for that purpose. This rather ingenious method had several important advantages. It made unnecessary much of the costly, time-consuming, and risky (in those days) transportation of bullion or other forms of hard currency on the high seas. It avoided unnecessary conversion of British pounds for Italian lire and vice versa. Also, because of its protective features, it made possible a considerable expansion of the volume of international trade.

Instructions to use credit balances for such purposes originated as simple letters of instruction explaining the wishes of the creditor. As time went on, and as the practice became more widespread, the letters tended toward uniformity, unnecessary verbiage was dropped, and the streamlined *bill of exchange* came into being.

Bills of Exchange or Drafts

A *bill of exchange* may be defined as a written order addressed by one party to another party instructing that a payment of money be made to a third party. In the example given above, if the Italian merchant were selling goods to a purchaser in England, he would draw (issue) a bill of exchange addressed to the purchaser instructing him to pay the cost of the purchase to his London friend. The bill of exchange would be mailed to the London merchant together with the merchandise or shipping documents representing title to the merchandise, and the London merchant would be instructed to present the bill of exchange to the purchaser, and on receipt of payment, to deliver to him the merchandise itself or the title documents covering the merchandise.

On the other hand, if the Italian merchant were the purchaser of goods, he could draw a bill of exchange payable to the seller and addressed to the London merchant. Upon receipt of the merchandise or evidence that it had been shipped, the London merchant, following the instructions in the bill of exchange and using funds held for the account of the Italian merchant, would pay the seller. Thus this versatile instrument was and still is used by either a seller or a buyer, in the latter case much as we use checks today.

The term *bill of exchange* is still widely used in international transactions, but today, in domestic transactions, this instrument is known as a *draft*. Thus, for practical purposes, the two terms are synonymous.

A draft is a written instruction issued by one party (the drawer) addressed to and ordering a second party (the drawee) to pay a sum of money to third party (the payee). The drawer, the drawee, and the payee are the principal parties to the instrument, and, in the eyes of the law, each one has separate and distinct rights and liabilities. However, it is possible for a single person to appear in two positions, in which case that person enjoys the rights and must assume the liabilities of both capacities. For example, a drawer may name himself as the payee of his draft.

If the draft is drawn by a purchaser instructing *a bank* to pay the seller, and it is payable on demand, it is called a *check*. Thus, a check is a kind of draft—a demand draft drawn on a bank.

Exhibit 1: Essential Features and Parties Involved in an Order to Pay (Bill of Exchange or Draft)

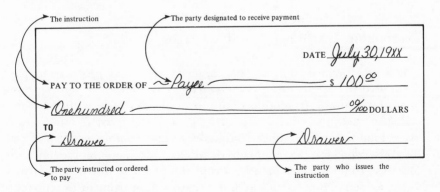

Promissory Notes

Another widely used type of commercial paper is a promise to pay, rather than an order to pay. A promissory note is not addressed to a third party. A promissory note has only two principal parties: the party who makes the promise (maker) and the party to whom the promise is made (payee). Basically, the party who signs a promissory note takes *upon himself* an obligation to pay money to someone according to the terms set forth in the writing. By contrast, the party who signs a draft or bill of exchange *instructs or orders another party* to make payment according to the terms of the instrument, based on an underlying arrangement or a transaction that presumably obligates the party so instructed to comply with the order.

Exhibit 2: Essential Features and Parties Involved in a Promise to Pay

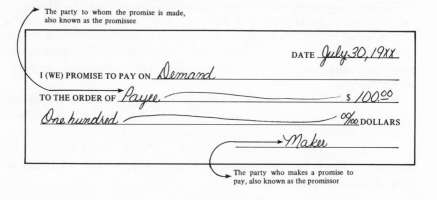

The party to whom the promise is made, also known as the promissee

DATE July 30, 19XX

I (WE) PROMISE TO PAY ON Demand

TO THE ORDER OF Payee. $100.00

One hundred °⁰⁄₁₀₀ DOLLARS

Maker

The party who makes a promise to pay, also known as the promissor

Negotiable Instruments and the Law

These two financial instruments, orders to pay and promises to pay, were used in various forms many years ago as a means of settling business transactions. It soon became apparent that the usefulness and value of these instruments would be greatly enhanced if some means were found to permit their ready acceptance by other merchants and bankers who were not involved in the original transaction. For instance, could a merchant who accepted a financial instrument in payment for something he had sold, use that same instrument as representative money, to pay for something he wished to buy? In other words, could he negotiate the instrument as a *separate* financial transaction, entirely divorced from the original transaction? Put another way, could the person who issued the instrument, dissatisfied for some reason with the goods he had purchased, refuse to honor his obligation in the hands of an innocent third party who acted in good faith and was in no way responsible for the alleged faulty merchandise?

Ancient courts of law frequently dealt with this question as they were called upon to settle differences and disputes between merchants and traders. Over a period of time, the court decisions and the laws they engendered increasingly favored the position that any person who gave value in good faith for a financial instrument would be protected from the consequences of disputes between the original parties concerning the specific terms and conditions of the underlying transaction. Thus the term *negotiable instrument* came into being, and this special type of instrument, specifically intended to provide this protection to subsequent holders, has been carefully defined.

The major purpose of the laws relating to negotiable instruments is to facilitate the transfer of such instruments from one person to another by shielding the party who takes the instrument as transferee, from adverse prior circumstances of which he had no knowledge and over which he could have had no control. But this is not to say that an instrument that does not fall within the legal definition of a negotiable instrument is therefore invalid and unenforceable!

No one is compelled to issue instruments in negotiable form, and if a person chooses not to do so, he will not be subject to the provisions of negotiable instrument laws. He may find, however, that his nonnegotiable draft, check, or note is not as readily acceptable by those with whom he does business. Those who accept nonnegotiable instruments are not without legal rights, but those rights will be determined under the general provisions of contract law rather than under the special laws *that are more favorable to the holders of negotiable instruments.*

Since this nation came into existence as a rather loose consolidation of a number of separate sovereign states, we had our own distinctive legal problems in early days. For many years, our lawyers, legislators, and businessmen had to contend with problems arising from uncoordinated laws, which, although generally based on British common law, seemed to vary in every state of the Union. After a number of partially successful attempts to encourage the adoption of uniform laws covering specific areas, a Uniform Commercial Code was finally approved by the National Conference of Commissioners on Uniform State Laws and the American Law Institute in 1952. The new code adopted the concept that "commercial transactions" is a single subject of the law. It revised and consolidated nine separate "uniform" statutes, including the Uniform Negotiable Instruments Law, into a single statute dealing with all phases of commercial transactions.

The Uniform Commercial Code was adopted by Pennsylvania in 1953 and became effective on July 1, 1954. Since that time, all of our states have adopted at least *some* portions of the Code. Some have adopted the standard version; some have adopted it in modified form; and one state has adopted only certain sections of the Code.

The standard version of the Uniform Commercial Code defines negotiable instruments in Article 3 (Commercial Paper) Section 3-104 as follows:

"1. Any writing to be a negotiable instrument within this Article must
   a. be signed by the maker or drawer; and
   b. contain an unconditional promise or order to pay a sum certain in money and no other promise order, obligation or power given by the maker or drawer except as authorized by this Article; and
   c. be payable on demand or at a definite time; and
   d. be payable to order or to bearer.
2. A writing which complies with the requirements of this section is
   a. a 'draft' ('bill of exchange') if it is an order;
   b. a 'check' if it is a draft drawn on a bank and payable on demand;
   c. a 'certificate of deposit' if it is an acknowledgment by a bank of receipt of money with an engagement to repay it;
   d. a 'note' if it is a promise other than a certificate of deposit.
3. As used in other articles of this Act, and as the context may require, the terms 'draft,' 'check,' 'certificate of deposit' and 'note' may refer to instruments which are not negotiable within this article as well as to instruments which are so negotiable."

While the wording of Article 3 is fairly clear, the drafters of the Code appended a commentary which does much to reveal the *intended* meaning of some of the terms and expressions used. For instance:

"Writing" includes printing or typewriting, in addition to handwriting.

"Unconditional" means that the instrument may not be *subject to or governed by* any other agreement between the parties thereto, although it may *refer* to such an agreement or the underlying transaction merely as a matter of information. "Unconditional" also means that the instrument may not be limited to payment out of a particular fund or source, *except* where the issuer is a government or government agency or where payment is limited to the entire assets of a partnership, unincorporated association, trust, or estate.

An "order" to pay must be a direction to pay and not merely an authorization or request.

A "promise" must be an undertaking to pay and not merely an IOU or an acknowledgment of debt.

"Sum certain" is not an unintentional transposition of the two words, but is intended to mean a sum (of money) which is certain in amount, and not a "certain sum" in the sense of a particular fund of money, which, as indicated above, would violate the "unconditional" nature of the instrument. Also, "sum certain" means that a holder must be able to determine the amount payable from the instrument itself. Thus, a note bearing interest at the rate of 6 percent per annum is negotiable, whereas a note bearing interest "at the current rate" is not.

"Money" means a medium of exchange authorized by a domestic or foreign government. Thus, an order or promise to pay in pounds sterling, francs, or any other recognized currency of a foreign government is negotiable even though payable in the United States. However, orders or promises to pay a specified quantity of a commodity, which has not been officially adopted by a government as a part of its currency, are not negotiable.

"Payable on demand" means payable *upon presentation* to the person primarily liable, and the term includes an instrument payable at sight or those in which no time for payment is stated. The Code (Section 3-501 through 3-503) specifies where, when, and how presentment must be made.

"Definite time" means a time of payment which can be precisely determined from the face of the instrument, although an acceleration clause or an extension clause exercisable at the *option of the holder* does not affect negotiability. Excluded are instruments payable only upon an act or occurrence certain to happen but uncertain as to the time of occurrence, such as "one year after the War" or "three months after my death."

"Payable to order" means an instrument payable to a specified person or to anyone to whom he had transferred or assigned his interest therein.

"Bearer" means the person in possession of an instrument payable to bearer or indorsed in blank.

Other Types of Paper Documents That Can Be Negotiated

As indicated earlier, the term *negotiable instrument* may be applied to writings other than orders to pay and promises to pay as defined in Article 3, the "commercial paper" section of the Uniform Commercial Code. This article does not deal with money itself (coin and currency), nor with documents of title such as warehouse receipts or bills of lading, nor with investment securities. In fact, official money is negotiable, but it is so under statutes other than the Uniform Commercial

Code. On the other hand, the Code separately treats documents of title (Article 7) and investment securities (Article 8), and both documents of title and investment securities can qualify as negotiable under these articles.

Commercial paper came into existence through the ingenuity of ancient merchants and traders who were not willing to limit their merchandising efforts to local communities.

The bill of exchange was the forerunner of our modern negotiable instruments. To be negotiable an instrument has to meet certain legal requirements as set forth in the Uniform Commercial Code. The law is designed to facilitate the transfer of negotiable instruments from one party to another

As defined in the Code, this type of commercial paper includes drafts, checks, notes, and certificates of deposit.

Questions Based on This Chapter

1. Briefly describe the circumstances that led to the development of a "bill of exchange."

2. What is the difference between a bill of exchange and a draft? A draft and a check?

3. What characteristics must an instrument have to qualify as a "negotiable instrument" under the Uniform Commercial Code?

4. Under what circumstances can a "certificate of deposit" qualify as a negotiable instrument?

Chapter 3

Negotiable Instruments

Part II: Rights and Liabilities of Parties

Purposes of This Chapter:

1. To identify the immediate parties to an order to pay and a promise to pay.

2. To discuss the obligations of immediate parties.

3. To explain what is meant by negotiation.

4. To describe the general contract and the warranties of an indorser.

5. To explain the status of a "holder in due course."

The Uniform Commercial Code, as had its predecessor statutes, takes great pains to identify and spell out the rights and liabilities of all parties who handle negotiable instruments in any capacity. Among these parties are those who issue them, those to whom they are made payable, those to whom they may be addressed, those who transfer them by negotiation, those to whom they are negotiated, those who present them for payment, and those who ultimately pay them.

Article 3, Section 3-104 of the standard version of the Uniform Commercial Code refers to two distinct types of negotiable instruments: *orders to pay* and *promises to pay*. Persons who are normally named on the face of the instrument are known as immediate parties, and presumably (but not necessarily) the immediate parties were participants in the transaction or arrangement that caused the instrument to be issued.

There are three immediate parties to an order to pay:

1. The drawer (the party issuing and signing the order) ;
2. The drawee (the party to whom the order is addressed) ; and
3. The payee (the party to whom payment is to be made) .

In the eyes of the law, these three parties participate in distinctly separate capacities. Nevertheless, a single person can and sometimes does serve in more than one capacity.

There are only two immediate parties to a promise or obligation to pay:

1. The maker or promissor (the party who signs and issues a promissory note or a depository bank that engages to repay a certificate of deposit in accordance with its terms) ; and

2. The payee or promisee, to whom the promise is made, or in the case of a certificate of deposit, the party to whom the certificate is made payable.

Liability of a Maker or Drawer

Although the terms *maker* and *drawer* are often used interchangeably, in legal terminology, the person who issued a note or promise to pay is a *maker*, while the issuer of a draft is called the *drawer*.

Both the makers of notes and the drawers of drafts create instruments and, by delivery thereof to the payee, pass them into the general stream of money instruments. It is both logical and necessary that they assume definite liability to those who acquire such instruments as subsequent holders.

The maker of a promissory note or a bank that issues a certificate of deposit with an engagement to repay it, commits himself or itself to pay the instrument according to its tenor, on demand or at maturity, as the case might be. They are primarily liable for the instrument they created, and normally this liability is discharged by payment to the holder upon presentation.

The drawer of a draft similarly is responsible for creating and delivering a financial instrument and becomes primarily liable thereon. If the draft is dishonored upon presentation to the drawee, upon notice of such dishonor, the drawer will be obliged to pay the amount of the draft to the holder.

Liability of Drawee

The drawee of a draft has no control over the issuance of an instrument naming him as drawee; thus he has no liability whatsoever at that point, since no person can be liable on an instrument unless his signature appears thereon. When the draft is presented to him, the drawee may deny liability and refuse to pay the instrument, thus leaving the drawer as the party primarily liable. On the other hand, the drawee may acknowledge his liability by paying the draft, which would have the effect of cancelling the instrument and relieving the drawer and any other party involved of liability for payment.

Liability of an Acceptor

There is yet another alternative available to the drawee of a draft, particularly in the case of a draft payable at a future time. He may acknowledge his liability thereon by "accepting" the instrument, which is normally accomplished by writing the word "accepted" vertically across the face of the draft, indicating or confirming the date payable, and signing his name. Acceptance is the drawee's signed engagement to pay the draft as presented when it becomes due. Thus, by acceptance, the draft (an order to pay) becomes in effect a promise to pay, and the drawee-acceptor replaces the drawer as the party primarily liable on the instrument.

Where the drawee is a bank, it is customary to use the word "certified," rather than "accepted." However, certification of a check is the legal equivalent of acceptance of an ordinary draft. When a bank certifies a check, it acknowledges its liability under the contract with its depositor and becomes primarily liable on the instrument. Where the drawer of the check requests and obtains certification before delivery, he remains secondarily liable for payment, but if certification is procured by a holder, the drawer and all prior indorsers are relieved of liability for payment.

While a certified check is the legal equivalent of an "accepted" draft, there is an important difference between the obligations of the respective drawers. The drawee of a check is a bank, and the instrument must be payable on demand. The holder of a check has the right to present the instrument and demand payment, but the bank is under no legal obligation to certify the check. Certification of a check is a courtesy that a bank *ordinarily* will extend only to its customer, the drawer of the check.

On the other hand, a draft may be made payable at a future date, and the law does not require the holder of a time draft to wait until maturity to discover the intention of the drawee. The holder has the legal right to present the time draft *before maturity* for acceptance, and failure of the drawee to comply is the equivalent of dishonor.

Negotiation

A negotiable instrument is created (issued) by the drawer, maker, or, in the case of a certificate of deposit, by the depository bank, and the payee acquires legal title to the instrument when it has been delivered to him by the issuer. As the original holder of the instrument, the payee may personally present it to the drawee or promissor at maturity and demand payment therefor. In this case, no holder, other than the payee (an immediate party) is involved.

On the other hand, the payee may elect to transfer his rights as owner of a negotiable instrument to another person, who becomes a secondary party, and as such has the same options available to him. In other words, he or any other subsequent holder may present the instrument to the immediate party primarily liable thereon or transfer his rights as owner to yet another party. All such subsequent holders become secondary parties.

Elements of Proper Negotiation

The transfer of a holder's title to and rights in a negotiable instrument is called *negotiation*. Negotiation is a special kind of transfer. If the instrument is payable to order, it is negotiated by delivery and any necessary indorsement. If it is payable to bearer, it may be negotiated by delivery only.

There are two important elements to a "legal" negotiation. The first is *delivery* of the instrument. As indicated above, a named payee does not become the owner of a negotiable instrument until it has been delivered to him by the issuer. Similarly, a transferee does not become a subsequent holder of an instrument until it has been delivered to him by his transferor. The second important element concerns the *intention* of the transferor. Delivery must be accompanied by the intention to transfer good legal title. Instruments that are not intentionally delivered, such as those that are lost or stolen, are not considered to have been legally negotiated.

Indorsements

An *indorsement* is the signature of the payee or of any secondary party, usually inscribed on the reverse side of an instrument by the holder himself or by someone authorized to indorse on the holder's behalf. In certain cases, by agreement between parties, a stamped, printed, or typed indorsement is acceptable, but in a normal negotiation the handwritten signature of an individual is required, whether he signs for himself or in some capacity, such as agent, trustee, executor, or treasurer.

Normally, the purpose of an indorsement, when accompanied by delivery (negotiation), is to transfer to someone else title to the instrument. However, sometimes a person who has no direct interest in the instrument will indorse it for the purpose of lending his name to a party who is directly at interest. In this case, the indorser is known as an *accommodation party,* but he assumes the same liabilities as any other indorser. Also, when an instrument is deposited in a bank, the purpose of the indorsement is not necessarily to negotiate the item but, more frequently, to authorize the bank as a collecting agent to present the instrument, on demand or at maturity, and to receive the amount due thereon on behalf of the depositor.

Liabilities of an Indorser

1. *General contract of indorsers*
Most of us have at one time or another indorsed a check, but not all of us are fully aware of the responsibility and liability assumed by an indorser when he signs his name on the reverse side of a negotiable instrument.

First of all, every indorser of a negotiable instrument engages (legally promises) that if the instrument is dishonored (not paid on proper presentation) and he is promptly notified of such dishonor, he will pay the amount of the instrument to the holder. This is the general contract of all indorsers, which in effect guarantees that the instrument is good for the amount indicated at the time of the indorsement, and that, if it is not, the indorser will make it good.

But even this definite and firm commitment is not the limit of the obligations assumed by the person who simply writes his name on the reverse side of a negotiable instrument and transfers it to another for value.

2. *Warranties of an indorser*
In addition to his guarantee of the ultimate financial worth of the instrument, under the law an indorser must give certain warranties as to its quality. For instance, he must warrant to his transferee and subsequent holders that the instrument is valid, that all prior transfers have been proper, that it has not been altered, that he has a good title

to it, and that his action in transferring the instrument by indorsement is taken in good faith.

In the more specific language of the standard version of the Uniform Commercial Code, Section 3-417 (2), an indorser warrants that:

    a. he has a good title to the instrument or is authorized to obtain payment or acceptance on behalf of one who has a good title, and the transfer is otherwise rightful; and
    b. all signatures are genuine or authorized; and
    c. the instrument has not been materially altered; and
    d. no defense of any party is good against him; and
    e. he has no knowledge of any insolvency proceeding with respect to the maker or acceptor or the drawer of an unaccepted instrument.

These warranties run with the instrument, and any subsequent holder can recover from a prior indorser in the event of a breach of any of the warranties.

Indorsers are liable to each other, both on the general contract and on the warranties, in the order in which they indorsed, which is presumed to be the order in which their names appear on the instrument.

It is important, however, to distinguish between *subsequent holders* of an instrument, and *parties primarily liable thereon* such as a drawer, a drawee, an acceptor, a promissor, or a paying agent. In these capacities, such persons are never holders of the instrument. Their station is, so to speak, at "the end of the line," and their function is to pay or accept the instrument or dishonor it, as circumstances warrant. As such, their position places certain information in their possession that is not normally available to the original payee and subsequent holders. Thus, while the warranties of an indorser as described above run with the instrument to all *subsequent holders,* certain modifications must be made with respect to those warranties as they apply to parties *primarily liable.*

For instance, an indorser warrants to all subsequent holders that "all signatures are genuine or authorized" even though the indorser may not know or be in a position to know or to ascertain that this is true. By the same token, subsequent holders will probably be in no better position to know or acquire such knowledge. Nevertheless, it is logical and equitable to assume that anyone who for value transfers an instrument bearing the forged signature of a maker, drawer, or acceptor, or the forged signature of a prior indorser, should be liable to his transferee and any subsequent transferees for any loss sustained by reason of such forgery.

Similarly, a maker, drawer, or a drawee who pays or accepts a draft is normally not in a position to know that the signature indorsement of the payee and that of other intervening holders are genuine or authorized, so it is equally logical and equitable to require each indorser in turn to give this warranty to those who take the instrument after him, as well as to the party primarily liable for payment (or acceptance).

However, a maker or drawer is required to know and recognize his own signature; a drawee is required to know and recognize the signature of those having the right to draw on him; and a paying agent must know and recognize the signature of his principal. Thus, no indorser is required to guarantee the issuer's signature (that of a maker, a drawer, or a depository bank) to the party responsible for payment of the instrument. The logic supporting this concept is formidable, and this position has been upheld by our courts for more than 200 years since the principle was first established at British common law in 1762.*

The effect of this longstanding principle of law can best be illustrated by an example that should be of more than passing interest to banking students.

A car is stolen, and the thief, forcing open the locked glove compartment, finds a supply of blank checks that bear the imprinted name of the depositor. After forging the depositor's signature, the thief succeeds in persuading a local appliance dealer to accept a check for $225 in connection with the purchase of a portable TV. The dealer indorses the check and delivers it to a wholesaler as part payment for merchandise received. The wholesaler deposits the check and in due course it is presented to the drawee bank, which fails to detect the forgery and pays the check by charging it against the depositor's account.

Eventually, the stolen car is abandoned, recovered by the owner, who then becomes aware of the theft of the blank checks. He notifies his bank and upon investigation the forged check comes to light and is branded a forgery by the depositor. The drawee bank, of course, is obliged to credit the depositor's account in the amount of $225 to reverse its improper debit. Can the bank recover its loss from indorsers by reason of their warranties? The answer is "No!" Under the law, indorsers do not warrant the genuineness of the drawer's signature to the drawee. A drawee bank is expected to know the signatures of its depositors.

In the above illustration, had the drawee bank detected the forgery upon presentation of the item, it would have dishonored the check by promptly returning it to the presenting bank, the last indorser. Assuming that the presenting bank was also the wholesaler's depository bank, it could recover the funds by reversing its credit to the wholesaler's

---

* Price vs Neal 3 BURR. 1354.

account, and the wholesaler in turn could do likewise by reversing its credit to the appliance dealer's account, because under this principle of law, indorsers do warrant the genuineness of *all* signatures, including the drawer's signature to *all subsequent holders*. To repeat what has been said earlier in this chapter, no person acting *in the capacity of* a drawer, a drawee, an acceptor, a promissor, or a paying agent can be properly considered a "holder" of the instrument.

Types of Indorsements

There are four principal kinds of indorsements, each of which serves a particular purpose: (1) indorsement in blank, (2) special indorsement, (3) restrictive indorsement, and (4) qualified indorsement.

1. Indorsement in Blank. An indorsement in blank (also called a general indorsement) consists simply of the indorser's signature on the reverse side of the instrument. If the signature is the indorsement of the payee, it should agree with the name of the payee appearing on the face of the instrument. The effect of a blank or a general indorsement is to make the instrument payable to bearer, and the instrument may be further negotiated by the holder simply by delivery to his transferee.

2. Special Indorsement. A special indorsement names the person to whom the instrument is being negotiated. For instance, a check made payable to George K. Smith might bear a special indorsement reading as follows:

Pay to the order of William Jones
George K. Smith

The indorsement of the designated transferee (William Jones) is necessary for further negotiation of the instrument.

3. Restrictive Indorsement. A restrictive indorsement is one that restricts the transferee in some manner, such as by naming the specific purpose of the transfer or imposing a condition on the transferee. There are several forms of restrictive indorsement, the most common being that used when the holder deposits a check in his bank for credit to his account. Such a restrictive indorsement might read as follows:

for deposit only
George K. Smith

Notice that in this case, the funds represented by the instrument do not pass to the control of another person. The Uniform Commercial Code (Section 3-206) requires the depository bank to apply the funds "consistently with the indorsement," which means, in the latter example given, that they must be placed to the credit of George K. Smith's bank account. Obviously, the funds can then be withdrawn *only* upon the written order of George K. Smith or upon the written order of his duly authorized representative. This is one of the situations in which it is not necessary for the depositor to add his personal signature to the restrictive indorsement. "For deposit only" indorsements may be printed, typed, rubber-stamped, or otherwise inscribed in any legible manner.

Another type of restrictive indorsement, known as a conditional indorsement, subjects the transfer to a specific condition, for example:

```
Pay to the order of William Jones
if repairs to my house are completed
by March 1, 1975
```

George K. Smith

It will be remembered that, as between the immediate parties, a negotiable instrument must be an *unconditional* order or promise to pay. Nevertheless, a restrictive indorsement of a negotiable instrument may contain a condition, as in the example given.

A restrictive indorsement does not prevent further transfer and negotiation of the instrument. Under the Code, the terms of a restrictive indorsement are binding only on the immediate transferee, the first taker of the instrument following such an indorsement. Subsequent transferees (holders) are not required to ascertain that the funds were applied "consistently with the restrictive indorsement" or that a specified condition was met.

4. Qualified Indorsements. The purpose of a qualified indorsement is to *limit* the liability of the indorser. It will be recalled that there are two distinct parts to an indorser's liabilities. First, there is the general contract of an indorser in which he guarantees the financial goodness of the instrument and agrees that if he is promptly notified of dishonor, he will take the instrument from the holder and pay the amount involved. To disavow liability on the general contract of an indorser the words "without recourse" or words of similar import precede the indorser's signature.

However, an indorsement in the form of the above example would leave Mr. Smith liable on all the warranties of an indorser, for which he may be held accountable whether or not the instrument is paid on presentation. To avoid liability on his warranties, an indorser must disclaim such liability by specific agreement with his transferee, and the disclaimer *must appear as a part of the indorsement,* rather than as a separate agreement or understanding.

An indorser who seeks to avoid any of his legal liabilities may find that his intended transferee will rebel and refuse to accept the instrument under such conditions. Except where circumstances clearly justify the use of a "without recourse" indorsement or a disclaimer with respect to warranties, those who accept negotiable instruments for value should insist on the unqualified indorsement of transferors.

Combination Indorsements

Each of the above types of indorsement, which independently serves its particular purpose, may be used in *combination* with another type. For instance, the third example given above to illustrate a conditional indorsement, is actually a combination of a special indorsement and a conditional (restrictive) indorsement. Similarly, a special indorsement can be combined with a qualified indorsement, as:

Pay to the order of William Jones
Without recourse
George K. Smith

Holders in Due Course

It would be advisable to mention at this point that the major purpose of the laws relating to negotiable instruments is to facilitate the transfer or negotiation of such instruments from one person to another by shielding any party who innocently takes the instrument in good faith from adverse circumstances of which he has no knowledge and over which he could have no control. The law accomplishes this very nicely by permitting, under certain circumstances, a subsequent holder of a negotiable instrument to become a "holder in due course"—a status that carries very desirable features.

It is characteristic of negotiable instruments that a subsequent holder, under certain conditions, may obtain title to an instrument with rights superior to those of the named payee, and also superior to those of his transferor, even if that transferor is a thief.

28

The holder of a negotiable instrument acquires these superior rights *only* when he takes the instrument—

1. For value, and
2. In good faith, and
3. Without notice that it is overdue or has been dishonored or of any defense against or claim to it on the part of any person.

Under these circumstances the holder is known as a "holder in due course," and he takes the instrument free from all claims to it on the part of any party with whom he has not dealt. This means that even if the negotiation to a holder in due course is fraudulent or otherwise illegal, such a holder is immune from claims or legal defenses of injured parties. For instance, acquisition of an instrument by a thief is not negotiation because of the obvious absence of intentional delivery. But delivery of that same instrument by the thief to an innocent taker is a valid negotiation.

Further, a holder in due course is immune from contractual defenses of any party to the instrument including those primarily liable thereon, such as want or failure of consideration, non-performance, non-delivery, and others.

To illustrate, suppose Allan selects and purchases from Barker, a jeweler, a diamond bracelet and delivers his check for $5,000 representing payment in full, made payable to the order of Barker. Upon returning to his home, Allan discovers that Barker has fraudulently substituted a paste replica for the genuine diamond bracelet that Allan inspected and intended to buy. Allan immediately contacts his bank and orders payment of his check stopped. In the meantime, however, Barker purchases some genuine diamonds from Cartwright and indorses and delivers Allan's check in payment therefor, which Cartwright accepts and deposits to his account. The check is dishonored by Allan's bank and returned to Cartwright. When Cartwright discovers that Barker has closed his shop and left town, he brings suit against Allan to recover his $5,000. Since Cartwright received Allan's check in good faith, for value, and without any knowledge of Barker's fraudulent conduct, his rights as a holder in due course would prevail, and Allan would be obliged to make his check good by paying the $5,000 to Cartwright.

On the other hand, based on the facts as stated, Allan's defense would be good as against Barker, had Barker brought suit on the dishonored check, or against any taker from Barker who could not qualify as a holder in due course.

If it were not for this protective feature of the law, it would be exceedingly dangerous for anyone to accept any negotiable instrument without thoroughly investigating the original transaction and without taking steps to make sure that all parties to that transaction had completely and satisfactorily discharged their obligations thereunder—obviously a highly impractical if not an impossible undertaking.

It should be noted, however, that even a holder in due course *may* be subject to certain defenses, such as infancy, incapacity, insolvency, and conditions that under state law would render the instrument a nullity.

The holder-in-due-course doctrine has served business and the public well for many, many years. Unfortunately, it has been abused by the unscrupulous who deliver faulty merchandise or perform shoddy workmanship and immediately negotiate checks to others who, under the law, succeed in cutting off the defenses of the victims. For this reason, the doctrine recently has been under attack by those who seek to shield the public from these abuses. Perhaps a way will be found to accomplish this desirable objective without at the same time destroying the effectiveness of negotiable instruments as an important feature of our present monetary system.

The general contract liability and the warranties of an indorser have been firmly established by law and this, together with the holder-in-due-course doctrine, has made possible the widespread use and acceptability of negotiable instruments. For instance, a check or a note is basically a piece of paper; in very few cases is there complete and unqualified assurance of final payment. It is certainly logical to assume that the holder of a dishonored check or note should be permitted to recover the value he has given for the instrument from the person who negotiated the item to him, and that this person should be able to recover from the indorser who preceded him, and so on.

Banks are particularly interested in the liability and warranties of indorsers because of the huge volume of checks they handle daily. When a bank accepts checks for deposit, it extends immediate credit to the depositor's account. Certainly the bank under the law must have the right to reverse its credit by charging or debiting the depositor's account in connection with any item dishonored on presentation or subsequently returned for a breach of the indorsers' warranties.

Presentment, Notice of Dishonor, and Protest

The Uniform Commercial Code carefully spells out the manner in which a negotiable instrument must be presented for payment or acceptance; how, when, and to whom notice of dishonor should be given; and when formal protest of a dishonored item is required.

Presentment

Presentment is (1) a demand for payment made upon the maker, acceptor, drawee, or other payor, or (2) a demand for acceptance made upon the drawee of a time draft on or before the date payable. In both instances, the demand is made by or on behalf of the holder. It is extremely important for the holder of a negotiable instrument to make presentment in the manner prescribed, for proper presentment is necessary to charge (that is, hold liable) parties secondarily liable on a dishonored instrument.

In general, proper presentment for payment or acceptance must be made at the place specified in the instrument or, if not so specified, at the residence or business of the party primarily liable, within reasonable business hours, or if at a bank, during its banking day. Presentment may be made in person, by mail, or through banking channels.

The party to whom presentment is made may insist that the instrument be exhibited or produced for inspection. He may also require reasonable proof (under the circumstances) of the identity of the holder-presenter, or evidence of the authority of the person making presentation on behalf of the holder.

Where an instrument shows the date when it is payable, presentment for payment is due on that date.

An instrument payable on demand must be presented within a reasonable time; however, "reasonable time" is determined by the nature of the instrument, custom and usage, and the facts in any particular case. In the case of an uncertified check drawn and payable within the United States, "reasonable time" for presentment or the initiation of bank collection is presumed to be (1) with respect to the liability of the drawer, 30 days after its date or issue, whichever is later, and (2) with respect to the liability of an indorser, seven days after his indorsement.

An inexcused delay in presentment discharges any indorser, and where the instrument is payable at a bank, if the bank should become insolvent during the delay, a drawer, acceptor, or maker may discharge his liability by assigning to the holder his rights against the drawee or payor bank with respect to the instrument.

Notice of Dishonor

It will be recalled that under his general contract, every indorser engages that if the instrument is dishonored on presentation, *and he is promptly notified,* he will pay the amount of the instrument to the holder.

Notice is normally given by the holder or by an indorser who has himself received notice. Notice by a bank must be given before its midnight deadline (which is normally the banking day following the banking day on which it receives the dishonored item or notice of its dishonor). Persons other than banks must give notice before midnight of the third business day after dishonor or receipt of notice of dishonor.

Where without excuse, notice of dishonor is delayed beyond the time it is due, indorsers are discharged, and, as in the case of delayed presentation, drawers, acceptors, and makers may also be discharged.

Protest

The practice of protesting dishonored items is followed much less frequently today than in earlier times. Actually, this practice is closely associated with the need to give prompt notice of dishonor to parties secondarily liable on a negotiable instrument.

Before the development of our modern systems of communication, transportation, and efficient check collection, there were frequent disputes concerning both presentation and notice of dishonor. Months after an alleged dishonor, a payor might deny that presentation was made, or, if made, that it was properly made. Similarly, while the holder of a dishonored instrument might solemnly swear that notice of dishonor had been promptly dispatched, indorsers might deny with equal force that such notice was ever received or received in time to be considered "prompt." Conclusive proof was difficult to furnish, and conflicting evidence made it impossible to determine the true facts. It should not be hard to visualize the problems that existed when mail was carried by stagecoach or pony express, when it took two weeks for trains to traverse the continent, and when a largely disorganized and haphazard bank collection system was the norm.

The practice of protest furnished a solution to those problems. In the language of the Code, a protest is a certificate of dishonor made under the hand and seal of a United States consul or vice-consul or a notary public, or other person authorized to certify dishonor by the law of the place where the dishonor occurs.

In those days when a negotiable instrument was dishonored, it was customarily delivered by the holder to a qualified official (usually a notary public), who personally re-presented the item and demanded payment. If such a payment was again refused, the official attached to the dishonored instrument a formal statement (sometimes called a *jacket*) certifying that presentment had been properly made and that appropriate notices were prepared and dispatched to all parties to the instrument including all indorsers. Naturally, such a statement by an impartial public officer bearing an official seal constituted prima facie evidence in court and avoided the problem of conflicting testimony.

Today, in the face of modern bank records it is rather difficult to assert that proper and timely presentment was not made or that notice was not promptly received. Therefore, the Code requires "protest" only in the case of a draft that on its face appears to be drawn or payable outside of the states and territories of the United States or the District of Columbia. However, the presenter of any instrument that is dishonored upon presentation may, if he chooses, cause official protest to be made by an authorized official.

Waiver or Excused Presentment, Notice, or Protest

The Code, in certain circumstances, provides for some relief from the above rather strict procedures. For instance, presentment or notice or protest can be waived by any party to be charged. Delay in presentment, notice, and protest is excused when the delay is caused by circumstances beyond the control of the party responsible, and reasonable diligence is exercised after the cause of the delay ceases to operate. Waiver of presentment, notice, and protest may be embodied in the instrument itself, in which case it is binding on all parties, but a waiver written above the signature of an indorser is binding only on that indorser.

There are few adult citizens in this country who have not, at one time or another, found themselves in possession of a negotiable instrument. Anyone who has given more than casual thought to these "pieces of paper" surely must recognize the important and indispensable role they play in our monetary and economic systems.

The laws affecting these instruments are complex, and even the brief discussion in this chapter might seen confusing to some. Nevertheless, thoughtful consideration cannot fail to reveal the logic of the many legal provisions affecting such instruments and the need to define them, to provide for their negotiation, and to define the rights and liabilities of all parties thereto.

Negotiable instruments have served our people and our economy well, and, until we devise a better system, we shall have to live with them. The tremendous increase in the volume of such instruments has presented problems which some refer to as a "paper tiger" that must be tamed. For some years now, thoughtful bankers and economists have envisioned a "cashless" and "checkless" society. There can be little doubt that these dreams will be realized, perhaps sooner than we expect. But whatever form a newer system takes, a new set of laws will undoubtedly be required. We may be able to eliminate intermediary parties altogether and have all payments go directly from the debtor's bank to the creditor's bank. Nevertheless, it is inconceivable to believe that all orders to pay or promises to pay will or can be executed without question in every case. There will be problems, of this we can be sure. The new laws and customs, replacing those of the present, still will have to define rather precisely, the rights, liabilities, and responsibilities of debtors, creditors, and the institutions that handle their financial transactions.

Questions Based on This Chapter

1. At what point does the liability of a drawee commence?

2. As related to checks and drafts, what is the difference between the terms *certified* and *accepted*?

3. What are the elements of a legal negotiation?

4. Name at least three types of indorsements and explain their purposes.

5. What is the general contract of an indorser?

6. In what respects do the warranties of an indorser to subsequent holders differ from the warranties given to parties liable for payment of a negotiable instrument?

Chapter 4

The Commercial Bank and Its Depositors

Part I: The Nature of the Relationship

The Purposes of This Chapter:

1. *To explain the legal nature of a deposit account contract.*
2. *To detail the responsibilities of a depository bank.*
3. *To point out the responsibilities of the depositor.*
4. *To emphasize the advantages of making payments by check.*

The term *financial institution* is a broad one that embraces a wide variety of service organizations, such as commercial banks, savings banks, savings and loan associations, consumer finance companies, and mortgage companies. This text deals exclusively with commercial banks; however, before discussing the nature of the commercial bank/depositor relationship, it would be advisable to point out some of the differences between commercial banks and other financial institutions.

Practically all such institutions are engaged in the business of lending money, and most tend to specialize in catering to the needs of a particular class of borrower. Some, such as savings banks and savings and loan associations, emphasize their facilities for storing purchasing power not currently needed in interest-bearing accounts. These institutions also participate to a limited extent in the payments mechanism by selling money orders or otherwise providing for the payment of debts.

Commercial banks have been referred to as department stores of finance because of the wide variety of services they offer. They make loans in considerable volume, for, rather than tending to specialize, their loan services are designed to accommodate every kind of short- and intermediate-term borrower—from giant multinational corporations to the average individual consumer. Commercial banks also provide facilities for storing purchasing power. They offer savings accounts and savings certificates to individual savers and negotiable certificates of deposit in large denominations to corporations and other large investors.

But there are some significant differences that distinguish commercial banks from other financial institutions. For one thing, under present laws, commercial banks are the only institutions permitted *to accept demand deposits subject to withdrawal by check.* Considering the fact that something like 26 billion checks are issued each year covering approximately 90 percent of the dollar volume of all financial transactions, it is evident that the commercial banking system plays by far the most dominant role in servicing our payments mechanism. In fact, in this respect, commercial banks serve all other financial institutions.

The relationship between a commercial bank and its depositors is intimate and highly confidential and one that imposes important obligations on both parties. From the viewpoint of banks, the responsibility involved in handling the billions of dollars that represent the active and constantly churning working capital of this nation's citizens is not one to be taken lightly or handled carelessly. Similarly, while the making of payments by the quick and convenient method of drawing and signing checks seems amazingly simple, carelessness or negligence on the part of a depositor in the handling of his bank account can produce annoying consequences and at times disastrous results.

The Deposit Account Contract

There is a very definite contractual relationship between a commercial bank and its depositors. Since a contract is enforceable in law, both parties can be held accountable for failure to live up to the expressed or implied terms of the contract. In a legal sense, the relationship is that of *creditor* (the depositor) and *debtor* (the bank), although in some respects, such as in the collection of deposited items, the relationship in most instances is that of *principal* (the depositor) and *agent* (the bank).

Seldom is an attempt made to spell out the terms of the contract in a detailed written agreement. The reason is that most of the financial transactions handled by commercial banks for their customers are governed rather thoroughly by the Uniform Commercial Code, other state and federal laws, the rules and regulations of duly constituted regulatory agencies, and long-established banking customs. Actually, there is little left to be negotiated independently between the bank and its depositors. Where written agreements are used, they deal mostly with the specific nature of the account or with local matters involving individual bank policy with respect to service charges, stop payment procedures, overdrafts, late deposits, and the like. Even in these matters, however, the agreement must conform to applicable laws and regulations.

As we examine more closely the nature of bank accounts, reference will be made to circumstances that could expose the bank, its depositors, or both, to substantial financial losses. The intent is not to magnify potentially dangerous situations or to picture the opening of a bank account as a particularly hazardous exercise. As a matter of fact, thousands of bank accounts are opened throughout the country during every business day, and in the vast majority of cases these prove to be highly beneficial to both the bank (increased deposits) and to the depositor (banking services). Nevertheless, it must be recognized that hazards and pitfalls do exist, and even though they may be encountered with relative infrequency, the penalty for carelessness can be disproportionately high.

It is difficult to think of any human activity that does not require some knowledge, training, or special skills. The process of opening bank accounts is certainly no exception. The objective here is *to impart to those involved in this routine banking function a clearer understanding of the nature of a bank account, to create an awareness of potential dangers that exist, and to explain the techniques required to perform satisfactorily in this area.*

Capacity, Identity, and Authority—The Depositor's View

Generally speaking, a contract is enforceable only if the contracting parties have the legal capacity to enter into the agreement. For instance, a bank's legal capacity to enter into contracts is established and limited by the laws under which it is chartered. Its authority may be further limited by its articles of association, its bylaws, or its board of directors. The individuals who exercise authority by entering into contracts on behalf of the bank are appointed or designated by the board of directors or by executive officers empowered by the board to do so.

The prospective customer need not be concerned with the question of *legal capacity* when he enters established bank premises and deals with an individual located in official or appropriate quarters. Furthermore, when a prospective depositor deals with someone at an officer's desk or at a desk bearing a sign or plate reading "new accounts," he need not *identify* that person or question his *authority* to bind the bank to a routine account contract. The bank is responsible for its banking house and for its personnel, and it would be legally prevented from denying the authority of personnel manning the various desks and stations therein.

On the other hand, it would be unwise for a person to deal with a self-styled bank representative on a street corner or in a local tavern without being completely satisfied as to the identity and authority of the "representative." Nor would it be prudent, even on bank premises, to try to establish an account by leaving an initial cash deposit with an elevator operator.

Capacity, Identity, and Authority—The Banker's View

The banker at his desk finds himself in a somewhat different position. He is on his home ground, but many who approach him to open a bank account are complete strangers. Such a person will present himself as a certain individual, and perhaps also may claim to be a corporation treasurer, the proprietor of a small business, or the executor of an estate. Before entering into any deposit contract, the banker should satisfy himself on three points:

1. *The legal capacity* of the prospective depositor.
2. The *identity* of the negotiating party, and whether the account is to be opened in the individual's name or in some other name.
3. The *authority* of the negotiating party if he/she is acting on behalf of someone else.

All of these points have somewhat more significance for the banker than for the depositor.

Legal Capacity

If the account is to be opened in the negotiating party's individual name, the question of capacity seldom presents a problem. Individuals who are under legal age (minors) and those who have been adjudged mentally incompetent lack the legal power to enter into binding contracts. Although it is not always possible to detect a minor or an incompetent, this is largely a matter of the banker's judgment, based on his evaluation of the person's appearance and manner.

If the account is to be opened in the name of a corporation, an association, a trust, or an estate, it is a relatively simple matter to determine that the banker is dealing with a duly constituted "legal entity," which is a *legal person* as opposed to a *natural person*. Legal entities are created by law or by court action. For example, a corporation is normally chartered by the laws of the state in which it is domiciled. On the other hand, a decedent's estate owes its existence under the law to a court of jurisdiction, which gives it legal life and formally appoints one or more persons to handle the estate's affairs. Thus, a "legal entity" has standing in the eyes of the law. It can sue and be sued in its own name and it has the capacity to enter into contracts, including bank account contracts. Reference to public records or the many available commercial records can quickly establish that the banker is dealing with a duly constituted legal entity.

Identity

Regardless of whether the account is to be opened in an individual name or in the name (title) of a legal entity, the identity of the negotiating party, who makes contact with the bank, must be established beyond reasonable doubt.

Establishing the identity of an individual is by no means an exact science. As banks operate today, there is no *absolutely positive* documentary means of identification, even when a document contains a picture and a signature. Automobile registration cards, operator's licenses, credit cards, voter registration cards, letters of introduction, and passports are helpful, but all of these and other common means of identification have been forged or misused at some time or another. Fingerprinting has been used to some extent by a few banks, but unless the prints can be checked against another authentic file, there is no assurance that the name given by the prospective depositor is his true name. Certain experienced bankers maintain that two separate evidences of identity issued at different times, such as an automobile registration card currently dated and an old draft registration card, offer more reasonable assurances than a single otherwise unsupported piece of evidence, such as a brand new Social Security card. While there is a logical basis for this reasoning, the thief who steals a wallet might have no trouble producing two such pieces of evidence. In the final analysis, establishing the identity of an individual is largely a matter of judgment, experience, and, to some extent, instinct. It is a process of gathering and evaluating sufficient bits of evidence to justify reaching a favorable conclusion.

The objective, of course, is to establish beyond reasonable doubt that the stranger is the person he claims to be, which is extremely important as far as the bank is concerned. But the other side of the coin must be viewed. Perhaps 90 percent of the strangers who enter banks to do business are perfectly honest and offer genuine and valid documents of identity. Moreover, experienced bank personnel in the normal, everyday course of business satisfactorily make judgments about the identity of strangers without embarrassing or offending honest persons, while at the same time frequently weeding out undesirable imposters.

Authority

While establishing identity of the negotiating party is necessary in all cases, the question of authority arises only when a person seeks to act in *other than* his or her individual capacity. For instance, suppose a stranger represents himself to be John Jones, Treasurer of XYZ Corporation. As indicated previously, the first step is for the banker to be satisfied that he is the John Jones he claims to be. The second step is to determine that he is in fact Treasurer of the XYZ Corporation. It safely can be assumed that the treasurer of a corporation has the authority to establish a bank account in the corporate name, but the authority to sign checks and other orders for the withdrawal of corporate funds is another matter that will be covered later. It will be seen, as we discuss the various types of bank accounts, that the nature of acceptable evidence of authority varies in almost every case.

Contractual Obligations

It has been stressed that a bank account is a legally enforceable contract. It would be advisable, therefore, to discuss the obligations of the contracting parties before turning our attention to the various types of bank accounts. Since banks actively and aggressively solicit deposit accounts, it is both logical and equitable that they should assume the lion's share of the contractual obligations, and this is indeed the case.

The Bank's Obligations

Even though the relationship is not supported by a written contract, when a bank opens a demand account it tacitly agrees to do two things for the depositor:

1. Accept deposits consisting of United States coin and currency and financial instruments payable on demand.

2. Honor orders for the withdrawal of deposited sums only in strict accordance with the depositor's instructions.

This seems simple enough, but there is more to these traditional services than meets the eye of a casual observer.

Accepting Deposits

As noted above, deposits may consist of money in the form of coin and currency or in the form of financial instruments which are claims to money.

Aside from the question of counterfeits, the receiving of coin and currency deposits presents no problem. In any event, bank personnel, through their training and experience, should be in a far better position to detect spurious coin and currency than the average depositor.

The acceptance of checks, drafts, notes, or other financial instruments, however, involves a different kind of responsibility. In order to collect a claim to money, a bank must arrange to present the instrument, either directly or through an intermediary bank, to the party primarily liable for payment. But why should the party primarily liable pay a bank that is not named in the instrument as payee when there is no evidence, apart from possession of the instrument, that the bank is in fact acting on behalf of the rightful owner? The answer to this logical question lies in the fact that the depository bank *indorses* the instrument and in so doing guarantees to the party primarily liable that it has good title or is acting on behalf of someone who has good title and that all prior indorsements, including that of the named payee, are genuine and authorized. In simple layman's terms, the collecting bank says to the payor: "Here is a financial intrument issued and made payable to Joe Doakes in which you are named as payor. We ask that you pay the amount of the instrument to us on the strength of our unconditional guarantee that the Joe Doakes named as payee *and no one else,* personally indorsed the instrument or authorized it to be indorsed on his behalf, and that either he has already received the money or its equivalent value or we will see that he does. Further, if at a later date Joe Doakes should successfully press a claim against you to the contrary we will see that you are reimbursed. You may pay us with complete safety because the entire resources of this bank stand behind our commitment."

This is a pretty strong undertaking, and the implications are of considerable interest. Suppose, for instance, the check is mailed to Joe Doakes, the payee, and the mail is intercepted by a thief—not an uncommon occurrence. The thief knows if he attempts to cash the check at the drawee bank, he will be closely questioned as to his identity. Instead, he goes to a bank—any bank—and opens an account in the name of Joe Doakes with an initial deposit of $10 or $20 in cash. Since the opening of an account involves the receipt of funds by the bank, rather than the payment of funds, there might be a tendency to be somewhat less concerned about the matter of identification. If the thief is successful in passing himself off as Joe Doakes, he then can deposit the intercepted check and any other checks rightfully belonging to the real Joe Doakes that he can lay his hands on. After waiting a reasonable time for the bank to collect the check (s) on the strength of its guarantee, the thief can withdraw the money and be well out of town before the forged indorsements are discovered, which could be weeks or even months later! The loss must be borne by the bank that opened the account for the thief.

The above is not a bizarre figment of imagination. Similar incidents have occurred many times—as many banks that have suffered such losses will testify. This story should emphasize the importance of identification when opening accounts for strangers.

But let us consider another possibility. Richard Roe is a professional "paperhanger" who manages to keep one step ahead of the sheriff. His latest jump lands him in a new town where he is not known. He opens an account *in his own name,* using authentic and acceptable documents of identification. One such document is a registration card for a late model Cadillac, generously paid for by banks with which he had dealt. Richard Roe is not a petty thief—but he hires petty thieves to steal checks for him. Roe forges the names of the legitimate payees, adds his own indorsement, and deposits the checks in his new account. The accommodating bank collects the stolen checks for him, again on the strength of its guarantee. As we know, the bank has a back-to-back guarantee from Richard Roe by reason of *his* warranties as an indorser. When the skullduggery is discovered, the bank must make good on its commitment. It cannot escape from its rather permanent location at Broad and Main Streets, and it has the money to make good. But what about Richard Roe? He is now sunning himself on the beach at Acapulco—the guest of his friendly bank. Even if he is located and extradited, in all probability he has spent the money, and the hapless bank is left holding the bag.

Again, this is not a wild excursion into the imaginative world of fiction. And it strongly suggests that when opening an account for a stranger, particularly the out-of-town stranger, it is wise to go beyond the routine of identification. In the matter of collecting deposited items, the bank is obligated by law and custom to stand behind the credit and legal commitments of its depositors. For the protection of the bank, its shareholders, and the community it serves, it should obtain *and check* references. It is clearly justified in satisfying itself that a prospective depositor has a favorable record of honest dealings and a trail of respectability that can be verified. He need not be wealthy, nor socially prominent, nor a Nobel Prize winner—but the bank that fails to check the background of strangers needlessly exposes itself to persistent and costly losses.

Let us look at this topic from another angle. When a bank makes a loan, it advances money to the borrower. Naturally, there is an element of risk involved. In assuming such a risk, the bank relies on *the borrower's ability to honor his commitment* to repay principal and interest at maturity according to the terms of the contract. Bankers call this "extending credit."

When a bank opens an account, it does not advance money; on the contrary, it receives money or claims to money in the form of a deposit. But, as has been demonstrated, the bank agrees to continue to accept checks and other financial instruments, which it collects for its depositor by adding its unqualified indorsement to each instrument, thus making itself liable under the general contract and warranties of an indorser. Naturally, there is an element of risk involved. In assuming this risk, the bank relies on its *depositor's ability to honor his commitment* as a prior indorser. In effect, the bank guarantees its depositor's credit, because it assures the drawee bank or other payor that it need have no concern as to the financial ability of any prior indorser to stand by the contractual obligations and warranties of an indorser.

What is the difference between "extending credit" and "guaranteeing credit"? None at all, really. Exposure to loss exists in both instances, and the only variation, if a loss occurs, is whether the bank parts with its money at the beginning or at the end of the transaction cycle.

On the other hand, there are important traditional differences in the manner in which banks approach these respective credit relationships. When a bank extends credit by making a loan, it first investigates and satisfies itself as to the prospective borrower's financial status and determines whether it can, with reasonable safety, *rely on the borrower's commitment to repay*. For instance, even when applying for a moderate consumer loan, the applicant must furnish specific information: where he lives and how long he has lived there; whether he owns his home and, if so, whether it is mortgaged and for how much; where he is employed and for how long; where he has charge accounts and how much is owed; and, finally, his approximate income. Usually the bank will make a decision in 24 hours, during which time it verifies and considers the data furnished in the application.

But when a bank guarantees credit by opening a deposit account, any effort to obtain information beyond the name, address, and place of employment of the prospective depositor seems to be the exception rather than the rule. Moreover, verification of these few facts, if indeed any investigation is made, tends to be superficial at best. In other words, the acceptance of the account is taken for granted; rarely does a bank make a positive decision that it can, with reasonable safety, rely on the new depositor's *ability to honor his commitment as an indorser.*

This is rather odd in view of the fact that the loss exposure of the bank that *extends credit* is limited to the amount of the loan, while there is no limit to the dollar volume of indorsed checks that a bank will collect for its depositors. Thus, when a bank *guarantees credit,* the loss exposure is indeterminate and could easily be 20 to 30 times the loss exposure in the average consumer loan.

It is natural to ask: Is this disparity in procedure with respect to extending credit as opposed to guaranteeing credit justified? The answer has to be "yes," for banks need deposits to exist, and no bank can afford to view all prospective depositors with apparent suspicion. The person who applies for a loan expects a careful investigation, but the person who opens an account does not and tends to resent what is often considered an invasion of privacy. Unfortunately, unscrupulous "paperhangers" capitalize on this fact of life.

There is yet another point to be considered. From the viewpoint of the depositor, a satisfactory banking relationship often involves more than deposits and the withdrawal of funds. It is a common practice for depositors to turn to their banks when they need signatures guaranteed on a variety of documents and securities, including E Bonds, other registered bonds, and stock certificates. It would be inconsistent for a bank to refuse to accommodate a depositor making such a request, while at the same time cheerfully agreeing on a continuing basis to guarantee his signature (and his credit) on an assorted variety of paper instruments.

The foregoing discussion should convince even the most skeptical that the bank personnel responsible for opening deposit accounts should receive thorough training so that they can fully realize their responsibilities. Bank personnel who fail to establish within reasonable limits that a prospective depositor is reputable and trustworthy not only expose the bank to needless losses but also encourage the unscrupulous. The sage advice of the United States Treasury Department, "Know your indorser," which appears on all Treasury checks, might well be taken seriously by a bank's new account personnel, for every depositor automatically becomes the bank's indorser.

In any event, the depositor frauds previously described are real and cannot be ignored on the basis that 98 percent of the people with whom banks deal are honest. This is true—but the swindles of the 2 percent can be disastrous. Happily, losses can be held to a minimum by the bank that sees to it that personnel to whom it assigns the duty of opening accounts are not only courteous and tactful, but well-trained, well-informed, and fully aware of the responsibility involved in what to the uninformed appears to be a purely routine function of little significance.

Honoring Orders for the Withdrawal of Funds

Turning our attention now to orders for the withdrawal or payment of funds, we again find that the bank assumes some rather serious responsibilities.

In the first place, the bank agrees that it will honor checks and other orders *only* if actually signed by the depositor himself or someone duly authorized to sign on the account. Thus, the bank is fully responsible for forgeries, and if by chance it pays a check or honors an order bearing a forged or unauthorized signature, it must, on receipt of the depositor's statement to that effect, reverse the debit and absorb the loss. Of course the bank has signature card files and authorization files to guide it in this respect—plus the knowledge that no human being ever signs his name in exactly the same way twice. Yet forged signatures can be and have been detected, but this is an art that requires experience and special skills.

In the second place, the bank agrees to honor checks *only as issued* by the depositor. This means that the bank is fully responsible for any material alteration to the instrument after it has been delivered to the payee by the drawer. A material alteration can take the form of an increased amount (in which case the bank can only charge the original amount to the depositor's account), a change in the name of the payee, the striking out of words such as "payment in full," or even a change in the date of the instrument.

A third responsibility concerns the depositor's right to cancel his order to pay. Courts have consistently upheld the right of the drawer of a check to order payment stopped, provided the drawee bank receives the stop order before the item actually has been paid. If a bank fails to comply with a stop payment order received in time, it must reimburse its depositor to the extent of any loss sustained.

There are other responsibilities, too, but the three cited should underscore the penalties for improper payments. On the other hand, an improper refusal to pay can be more serious. A bank that fails to honor a genuine order properly presented and thereby causes financial discredit to its depositor might find itself defending a suit for damages in an amount bearing no relationship to the amount of the dishonored instrument.

Again, it should be emphasized that the objective here is to create an awareness of the nature of the responsibilities assumed by commercial banks under demand deposit account contracts. It should also be stressed that commercial banking has been and is conducted in a very successful manner. The point to be made is that commercial banking is a highly technical field of endeavor, not only in the deposit account contract area but also in all other monetary functions it performs, and a successful commercial banking enterprise depends in large measure on a staff of competent, well-trained, and knowledgeable personnel.

The Depositor's Liabilities

The depositor's responsibilities with respect to a demand deposit contract are a great deal less burdensome than those of the bank because, as has been indicated, commercial banks must continuously and aggressively solicit demand deposits. A commercial bank cannot exist without a steady inflow of deposited funds and, to ensure its natural objective of a steadily expanding deposit base, it must offer high quality services and inspire confidence in its ability to discharge fully its obligations to depositors in a businesslike manner.

The depositor has some obligations, too, although they might be classified under a single heading: "avoidance of negligence." The individual or business that fails to handle its checking account in a responsible and diligent manner may find that carelessness in this respect could be deemed sufficient cause to relieve the bank of certain of its responsibilities. The following list of improprieties indicates how a bank's best efforts to provide efficient service can be frustrated:

1. Carelessness in signing checks to the extent that reasonable comparison with specimen signatures is not feasible.

2. Carelessness in drawing checks so that frequent corrections (alterations) are made before checks are issued.

3. Signing checks in blank without proper control.

4. Signing checks with rubber stamps or facsimile devices without proper control. (Most banks ask for indemnity when mechanical signing devices are used).

5. Failure to examine and reconcile statements promptly.

6. Failure to report irregularities promptly.

In addition, just as a bank is responsible for its personnel, so the businessman depositor must be responsible for breach of trust on the part of his employees. For example, a businessman normally assigns the duty of preparing checks for his signature to a trusted employee and, in some cases, also permits that same employee to reconcile the bank statement. No one can question his right to assign duties as he sees fit. However, it is obvious that a bank would be fully justified in refusing to accept a loss made possible only through substantial negligence or carelessness of a depositor or through misplaced confidence in the integrity of an employee of the depositor. On the other hand, reasonable care and diligence on the part of the depositor logically and rightfully places the main burden of responsibility on the bank.

The Advantages of Making Payments by Check

Since a depositor must assume some responsibilities, one might question why anyone should even bother to open a demand deposit (checking) account with a bank. Aside from the bank's service in presenting and collecting financial instruments, there are many advantages in making payments by means of checks.

1. Money in a bank account is safe. The depositor enjoys the benefits of insurance paid for by the bank. Money carried on the person or kept at home can be lost or stolen, and burglary insurance can be expensive.

2. A check can be drawn for the exact amount due, thus eliminating the need for suitable denominations or change.

3. Making payments by check is quick, convenient, and economical. Checks can be prepared at home and can be mailed to creditors at nominal cost regardless of the distance involved, thus avoiding the inconvenience of purchasing money orders or making cash payments at each creditor's office.

4. Unlike cash, checks can be forwarded with safety by firstclass mail, uninsured. If a check is lost or stolen en route, the depositor is protected. The banking system is responsible for checks paid with the forged indorsement of the payee.

5. The drawer of a check has the assurance that the party designated as payee, that is, the party for whom the payment was intended, actually received the money. A paid and cancelled check is a valid receipt.

Checking accounts are no longer considered a luxury to be enjoyed only by big businesses and wealthy individuals. They are a virtual necessity today, even for the average individual and household.

The establishment of a demand deposit relationship carries responsibilities both for the bank and the depositor. From the bank's viewpoint, the opening of an account is much more than a routine function to be performed by unskilled personnel. It involves the legal capacity and identity of the person negotiating with the bank, and, if the account is to be opened in other than the negotiator's individual name, determining his authority to open the account and to furnish the bank with documentary evidence to support arrangements for the withdrawal of funds. In view of the bank's potential liability to others in connection with the collection of financial instruments, the person representing the bank must be reasonably confident that the depositor is entitled to a routine guarantee of credit.

The depositor also assumes some responsibilities, which for the most part can be discharged by proper and prudent handling of the bank account.

Questions Based on This Chapter

1. What is the legal relationship between a bank and its depositors?

2. How can a bank be absolutely sure of the identity of a stranger who wishes to open an account? Why is the establishment of identity so important?

3. When a bank accepts a deposit, it is receiving money or claims to money from the depositor. How can this involve any possible liability of the bank?

4. Under what circumstances is it necessary for a bank to obtain authority for the withdrawal of funds?

Chapter 5

The Commercial Bank and Its Depositors

Part II: Types of Bank Accounts

The Purposes of This Chapter:
1. To classify and describe the various types of bank accounts.
2. To discuss sources of authority for accounts opened in other than individual names.
3. To emphasize the importance of taking proper action when an account is closed by someone other than the original depositor.
4. To point out the necessity, in certain situations, of obtaining and abiding by instructions of a court of jurisdiction.

In the following pages, which deal with the most frequently encountered types of bank accounts, no attempt will be made to cover detailed procedure in the opening of an account, such as obtaining and filing signature cards, documents of authority, and executing such forms as may be necessary to establish the account on the bank's records. The mechanical steps involved vary with each individual bank. In addition, there are variances in the several state laws which could have a bearing on some of the procedures. In many respects the relationship between a bank and the natural or legal person with whom it enters into deposit account contracts is substantially the same in all states, and the intent here is to deal only with matters of general interest involving principles that apply equally to all banks.

Furthermore, a bank's concern in this area is not confined solely to the process of establishing the account relationship. If every bank account were to be closed by the same natural or legal person who opened it, life would be somewhat easier for the parties involved. But this is not always the case. More frequently, perhaps, an account will be closed by someone other than the original negotiator. For instance, an individual depositor may die, be declared incompetent, be forced into involuntary bankruptcy, or his assets, including his bank balances, may be attached by creditors and seized by court order. Similarly, partnerships may be dissolved, and corporations may be liquidated, merged, acquired, or declared bankrupt. In fact, the process of closing an account is sometimes a more complicated process than its initial establishment. Although it would be impossible to cover every conceivable development that could take place after an account is opened, those more frequently encountered will be discussed.

Since a bank thrives on deposit balances, a new depositor deserves a warm and friendly welcome. Then there is important information to be communicated by both parties. The customer may have questions. If not, the banker should volunteer information concerning its service charge policy, normal banking hours, and any special rules or privileges of which a depositor should be aware. In connection with time and savings accounts, applicable Federal Reserve regulations and state laws should be carefully explained. The opportunity to discuss other bank services unrelated to deposit accounts should not be ignored.

At the same time, the banker must be satisfied as to three important points with respect to the party dealt with, that is, the person's legal capacity to enter into the contract, the identity of the individual, and any necessary authority if the person is not acting in an individual capacity.

Individual Accounts

The single name individual account is probably the least complex of all, since it involves only the bank and a natural person representing and acting solely on behalf of his or her own self.

Capacity

In the absence of actual knowledge or significant evidence to the contrary, the prospective depositor's legal capacity can be safely assumed.

Identity

The identity of the individual must be established beyond reasonable doubt. The unlikelihood of obtaining *positive* proof of identity has already been discussed. It is sufficient here to repeat that while the person representing the bank must rely entirely on perceptive judgment in evaluating the evidence offered, there is no reason to adopt the attitude that danger is lurking behind every bush.

More important is the necessity of *obtaining and checking* references, particularly in the case of persons not previously residing or employed in the community. No only does this sound procedure help to verify identity, but it also provides the only justification for assuming an important obligation under the bank's contract, that is, guaranteeing the credit of the prospective depositor in connection with indorsed and deposited instruments.

Authority

The question of authority is not involved in the case of a single name individual account, for the source of authority is the individual himself, who unquestionably has the legal right to act for himself.

Since an individual has complete control over his personal account, he can, if he so desires, confer on another person or persons the power to handle banking transactions for him. While the depositor is his own source of authority, anyone designated to act on his behalf must be properly authorized. In this case the authority is contained in a document known as a power of attorney, which is signed by the depositor and filed with the bank. If the document is prepared by the depositor or his legal counsel, it should be referred to an officer or the bank's legal counsel for approval. In its broadest form, a power of attorney may give the attorney unlimited authority to do anything that the principal could do for himself. Generally, banks prefer to use their own form (see Exhibit 3), which in many instances is restricted to a specific bank account and limits the power granted to the indorsing of checks for deposit and the signing of checks and other orders for the withdrawal of funds. Other bank forms grant wider powers, but in general these are limited to banking transactions.

A person so authorized is known as an "attorney-in-fact" and should sign checks in the following manner:

John Doe, by Richard Roe, attorney-in-fact

A depositor can terminate the authority granted to an attorney-in-

Exhibit 3: Power of Attorney Form

𝕶𝖓𝖔𝖜 𝖆𝖑𝖑 𝕸𝖊𝖓 𝖇𝖞 𝖙𝖍𝖊𝖘𝖊 𝕻𝖗𝖊𝖘𝖊𝖓𝖙𝖘

	DEMAND ACCOUNT
	SAVINGS ACCOUNT
ACCEPTED BY	OFFICE

THAT _____

do make, constitute and appoint _____

_____true and lawful attorney for_____and in_____

name:

1. To withdraw all or any part of the balance in _____

account number _____in
THE INSTITUTE NATIONAL BANK
by drawing checks, if a demand account; or, by giving the required prior notice and by executing the proper withdrawal order or receipt if a savings account.

2. To endorse notes, checks, drafts or bills of exchange which may require_____endorsement for deposit as cash in, or for collection by said bank.

3. To do all lawful acts requisite for effecting any of the above premises; hereby ratifying and confirming all that the said attorney shall do therein by virtue of these presents.

This power of attorney shall continue in force until due notice of the revocation thereof shall be given in writing.

*In witness whereof*_____ have hereunto set_____ hand and seal this_____day of_____, one thousand nine hundred and _____

SIGNED, SEALED AND DELIVERED
    IN THE PRESENCE OF

(SEAL)

A typical (short-form) power of attorney. Many banks also use a longer form that grants wider powers to the attorney-in-fact. Instead of the signature of a witness (or witnesses), some banks prefer a formal acknowledgment before a notary public or other authorized official.

fact at any time by giving proper notice to the bank in writing. Unless earlier revoked in writing, however, the authority continues to remain effective during the lifetime of the depositor.

Death of a Depositor

There are a number of possible circumstances in which any depositor can lose the legal capacity to control his bank account. In most cases our laws provide a set procedure for the appointment of someone to act for and on behalf of a legally incapacitated depositor. The most frequently encountered circumstance is, of course, the death of a natural person. In this event, our courts will, if required or requested, take charge and assume the responsibility for seeing that the deceased person's worldly goods are properly disposed of, in accordance with the wishes of the decedent or as the laws of the state of domicile provide.

What the courts do, in effect, is to create a new legal entity to take the place of the deceased person. This is known as the decedent's "estate," and someone is appointed by the court with authority to represent the estate legally.

If the deceased person has left a will, the document must be presented for probate and judicially determined to be valid. Often, when writing a will, the testator (a person who leaves a will) names a specific person to handle his estate, and unless the court finds valid reasons for disqualification, it will appoint that person "executor" of the estate. If the will does not name a proposed executor, or if the person named cannot or will not serve, or if there is no will, the court will consider applications from interested parties and appoint the best qualified applicant as "administrator" of the estate.

Since bank balances are part of a deceased person's worldly goods, the bank or banks involved, upon receipt of notice of death, must deal *exclusively* with a duly appointed executor or administrator with respect to funds on deposit. Thus, notice to the bank of the death of a depositor automatically cancels all existing powers of attorney. The Uniform Commercial Code permits a bank to honor outstanding checks signed by the depositor for 10 days after the date of death, unless otherwise instructed by someone having an interest in the account.

Since executors and administrators do not act in their individual capacity, the bank must obtain for its files a document of *authority,* which is an official certificate of appointment issued on behalf of the court by the Office of the Register of Wills, the Prothonotary, or other judicial representative. Usually, this document is an abbreviation of the official certificate and is known as a "short certificate."

As in all cases, the basic principles of self-protection must be applied by the bank in the light of the circumstances surrounding each situation and with due regard for the convenience of its customers. Frequently, a depositor may die leaving little in the way of assets other than personal effects and a modest bank balance of a few hundred dollars. In situations of this kind, for the bank to insist that letters of administration be applied for and an estate be created would be to stretch too far its zeal for technical perfection.

Many banks will pay the balance in a decedent's account to the undertaker to be applied against funeral costs, which represent a preferred claim. Others will pay the balance (not in excess of a certain amount, say, $1,000 or $1,500, depending on bank policy) to a member of the immediate family (such as the widow or widower, a son, daughter, brother, or sister) upon receipt of a written statement to the effect that all debts and taxes owed by the decedent have been provided for, that there are no other substantial assets, and that an estate will not be created. The document should also indemnify the bank against possible claims by other legal heirs. Admittedly, there is an element of risk in this procedure, but the risk is small and should be weighed against the injustice of putting a bereaved family of modest means to unnecessary legal expense. (See Exhibit 4.)

Incompetence

Logically enough, a natural person is deemed to be of sound mind, unless and until he is adjudged by a court of law to be mentally incompetent. Occasionally, such a judicial decision is made on the basis of professional testimony by doctors and psychiatrists. As in the case of death, a bank is not affected until it has knowledge of an adjudication of incompetence.

Again, our courts assume the responsibility for seeing that the business affairs of the incompetent are properly handled by creating a legal entity, known as an incompetent's "estate," and by appointing a guardian or a committee to represent the estate legally and act on behalf of the incompetent.

In connection with a deposit balance, the bank must, in order for it to recognize the orders of the guardian or committee with respect to the withdrawal of funds, obtain for its files a certified copy of the official certificate of appointment issued by authority of the court of jurisdiction.

Bankruptcy—Attachments

Our courts also assume responsibility for settling certain legal disputes

Exhibit 4: Claim for Decedent's Bank Balance

	DEMAND ACCOUNT
CLAIM FOR DECEDENT'S BANK BALANCE	SAVINGS ACCOUNT
ACCEPTED BY	OFFICE

I/WE, the undersigned, hereby make claim to the remaining balance in the account of _____,

#_____, who died on _____.

I/WE hereby declare and aver, to the best of my/our knowledge and belief, that there are no other substantial assets belonging to the decedent, that there are no taxes or debts owing to the State of _____ or the Government of the United States, that the decedent died intestate, and that Letters of Administration have not been applied for, and will not be applied for.

I/WE, further declare that the undersigned is/are rightfully entitled to claim the balance in the account referred to above or to exercise judgment as to the disposition thereof after all expenses of the last illness and funeral of said decedent have been paid.

In consideration for the payment by The Institute National Bank of said remaining balance either to, or by direction of the undersigned, it is agreed that my/our executors, assigns and successors, shall and will at all times hereafter indemnify and save harmless The Institute National Bank, its successors and assigns, from and against all actions, suits, claims, damages and expenses which it or they may be obliged to pay, sustain or bear by reason of its having paid the remaining balance in the decedent's account in accordance with this agreement.

IN WITNESS WHEREOF, and intending to be legally bound hereby, I/We have hereunto set my/our hand(s) and seal(s).

_____

_____

When the nature and size of a deceased depositor's personal assets do not warrant the formation of an estate, banks will honor a claim or application for payment of a bank balance of modest amount on receipt of a death certificate and a document such as that illustrated.

between debtors and creditors, in which banks frequently become involved.

For instance, if a debtor is unable to pay his creditors, three or more creditors can petition a court of jurisdiction to place the debtor in involuntary bankruptcy, or the debtor himself may file for voluntary bankruptcy. In either case, if the petition is granted, the court again creates a legal entity (known in this case as a bankrupt's "estate") and appoints a "receiver in bankruptcy." The receiver is authorized by court order to seize the bankrupt's assets (including the deposit balance and any other assets in the bank's possession), liquidate them, and distribute the proceeds (less costs) among creditors on a pro rata basis. A certified copy of the court order provides the bank with the necessary *authority*.

Sometimes a debtor is completely solvent, but because of a dispute simply refuses to pay a certain creditor. In such circumstances, the creditor may petition a court for a declaratory judgment against the debtor. The court considers the petition, hears the evidence presented by both sides, and, if it determines that the debt is just and payment is properly due to the creditor, it will issue the judgment in favor of the creditor. Upon the strength of the judgment, the creditor can obtain copies of a "writ of attachment," which may be served on banks or anyone else in possession of assets of the debtor.

When a writ of attachment is served on a bank, it must first be sure that the debtor named in the writ is, in fact, its depositor. If there is any doubt as to the identity of its depositor due to a difference in the name as it appears on the bank's records as compared with the name of the defendent inscribed in the writ, it must ask the court for instructions and cite the discrepancy and any other pertinent facts.

On the other hand, if the debtor and the depositor are indeed one and the same person, the bank must impound funds on deposit (as well as any other assets in its possession, such as securities held in custody or safekeeping, or excess collateral pledged to secure a loan) in an amount sufficient to cover the real debt *plus costs and interest*. Then it awaits a specific order from the court as to disposition of the assets impounded.

There are other circumstances where funds in a depositor's account must be paid to or withdrawn by someone other than the person who originally opened the account, but the situations described here cover the most common examples.

Joint Accounts—Individuals

Perhaps the most misunderstood account, as far as the public is concerned, is the joint account. Depositors who share a joint account are generally referred to as "tenants." Although in theory any number of joint tenants might share a single account, many banks are reluctant to accept accounts in the names of more than two tenants. For ease of expression, the following discussion refers specifically to two-party joint accounts, but the principles involved can be applied to multi-party joint accounts.

In substance, a joint account is exactly what the name implies, that is, a joint undertaking. Basically, both parties have equal rights, and neither party has exclusive rights. This means that all transactions, including orders for the withdrawal of funds in deposit, should be authorized or signed jointly *by both tenants*. However, as a matter of convenience, it is customary for joint tenants to sign an agreement providing that either party may make deposits and sign checks for the withdrawal of funds. Some agreements authorize either tenant to indorse and deposit checks drawn to the order of the other tenant. In effect, the agreement represents a mutual exchange of powers of attorney, with each tenant agreeing that the signature of his or her co-tenant shall simultaneously have the same force and effect as his or her own signature. The powers exchanged, however, are strictly limited to the terms of the agreement. Unless otherwise stipulated, for instance, if a third party is to be appointed as attorney-in-fact, joint action would be required, and the power of attorney authorization should be signed by both tenants.

It should be noted that this exchange of powers of attorney is *reciprocal*. While either tenant has the power to withdraw the entire balance at any time, neither tenant can properly cancel the co-tenant's right to sign alone without automatically cancelling his own right to sign alone. Such an instruction would obviously nullify the *reciprocal* exchange of powers of attorney, and the account would revert to its basic status—*a joint undertaking*. A dispute between two tenants sometimes results in a unilateral attempt by one tenant to foreclose the rights of the co-tenant. In these circumstances, a bank would be well advised to insist on the signatures of both tenants for all subsequent transactions.

Capacity

As in the case of a single individual, in the absence of actual knowledge or significant evidence to the contrary, the legal capacity of the tenants can be safely assumed.

Identity

The procedure for establishing identity would be the same as for an individual account, although in many cases (such as a husband and wife joint account) establishing the identity and checking the references of *one* of the tenants should suffice. However, such a judgment by bank personnel should be based on the circumstances in each partic- ular case.

Authority

It could be said that a person who signs a check drawn on a joint account is signing as the authorized representative of a joint tenancy rather than in an individual capacity. This suggests the necessity for some kind of documentary *authority* for the bank, and the joint account agreement described in part above, when signed by both ten- ants and filed with the bank, supplies this need.

Death of a Co-Tenant

Joint account agreements are normally supplied by the bank, some- times as a separate document, but more frequently as a part of the specimen signature card. The wording of these agreements may vary from state to state to conform with local laws, and sometimes may vary among banks located in the same state. In all cases, the agreement should cover the contingency of the death of one of the co-tenants. In this respect, agreements take one of two forms: (1) those that provide for the right of survivorship, and (2) those that do not so provide.

1. *Right of survivorship.* Where the agreement provides for right of survivorship, each tenant authorizes the bank, in the event of his or her death, to deal with the survivor as the *sole and absolute owner* of all funds on deposit. This means that the survivor acquires complete control of the account, and the bank can disregard any claims thereto by the estate of the deceased tenant, except in the most extenuating cir- cumstances, such as definite evidence of or an allegation by an inter- ested party of the presence of deception, fraud, or duress at the time the agreement was signed. If extenuating circumstances are alleged to exist by the estate, counsel should be consulted.

Bank personnel responsible for opening new accounts should be especially familiar with applicable state laws and local customs with regard to joint accounts. The banker, rather than the customer, should be the expert. The banker should first determine what the depositors intend to accomplish by a joint account arrangement, especially so when the right of survivorship is involved. A bank cannot and should not offer legal advice, but it can suggest that legal counsel be consulted when it appears that the intended purpose will not be realized by a survivorship account.

A joint account with the right of survivorship has been referred to as a "poor man's will." Many persons have the mistaken impression that such an account makes it possible to transfer funds to another person (in anticipation of death) without the payment of inheritance taxes. As a matter of fact, most states have laws requiring the depository bank to notify the state revenue department in the event of the death of any party to a joint account, whereupon the state revenue officer proceeds to levy and collect any tax that might be due.

Where an elderly depositor supplies all or most of the funds in a proposed joint account with right of survivorship, the bank has a duty to explain the nature of the arrangement as tactfully as possible. The co-tenant probably will be a younger person, possibly a relative. In all probability, such an arrangement will ultimately result in an outright gift (bequest) upon the death of the elderly tenant. If this is understood and such is the intent, well and good. But in many cases the elderly person has drawn a will and simply wants "someone to take care of my affairs and pay my bills if I should get sick." This objective can be achieved by executing a power of attorney in favor of the younger person. The power of attorney is good for the lifetime of the principal, but upon death, an executor or administrator properly should take over, pay the remaining debts, and settle the estate as the decedent intended that it be settled.

2. *Without right of survivorship.* Where the agreement does not provide for the right of survivorship, the death of a co-tenant severs the joint tenancy. In the absence of specific evidence to the contrary, joint tenants are presumed to have equal interests in funds on deposit. Thus, where there are two tenants, the bank is justified in paying half of the balance to the survivor and half to the estate of the deceased tenant. The presumption can be rebutted by oral testimony, but the burden of proof is on the one seeking to establish different proportions of ownership. Some banks insist that both the executor or administrator of the estate and the survivor jointly sign instructions as to the disposition of funds on deposit.

Bankruptcy—Attachments

It is possible, of course, for a joint tenant *individually* to file a petition in bankruptcy or to be forced into involuntary bankruptcy in proceedings that do not involve his co-tenant. Or, perhaps as the result of a judgment, the assets of one of the tenants may be attached by court order.

If, for instance, the tenants happen to be husband and wife, it is especially important for the bank to be familiar with the state statutes.

In some states, such as Pennsylvania, husband-wife joint tenants are known as "tenants by the entireties," which means that *both* tenants own *all* of the account. The law regards a joint tenancy "by the entireties" as an indivisible whole, not subject to legal proceedings arising from financial difficulties suffered by one of the tenants individually. Normally, in states that have adopted this concept, the joint account is inseverable and immune from such legal proceedings unless both tenants file *jointly* in bankruptcy or both tenants are named as defendants in a court-issued writ of attachment.

If the joint tenants are other than husband and wife or in states that do not recognize the concept of an "indivisible whole," the interests of the two tenants can be separated, and the share belonging to the individual bankrupt or the individual named in a writ of attachment can be impounded.

Legal complications involving joint accounts do not often arise, but they can be troublesome. The bank has an obligation to protect its depositors' interests. Counsel should be consulted and furnished with all pertinent data regarding the account, so that the bank will have legal representation in any court proceedings. Once the court has rendered its decision, the bank, of course, must be guided by the court's orders.

Fictitious or Assumed Names

In the business world, it is frequently advantageous to assume a fictitious name in order to present a more favorable business image. Such assumed names are generally referred to as "trade names" or "trade styles." For example, "Ace Fence Mending Company" might sound a bit more impressive for business purposes than simply "Ebenezer J. Hooha, Fence Mender."

Though this is a longstanding business practice, the improper use of a fictitious name could very well serve the purpose of hiding the identity of an unscrupulous businessman. For this reason, most of our states have laws which regulate the use of fictitious names and require that they be registered with the state government. Thus, the assumed name *and* the names and addresses of those who do business under that name are made a part of public records available for inspection by any interested parties. The purpose, of course, is to fix full responsibility on the *person(s)* who registered the name, with respect to contracts entered into and liabilities incurred in that name. Proper registration not only identifies the registrant(s) but also gives the trade name the status of a legal entity in the sense that the registrant(s) can enter into enforceable contracts, bring suit, and be sued *in the assumed name.* However, the registrant(s) is individually accountable for its obligations and debts.

Banks are frequently requested to open an account in a fictitious trade name. As long as the assumed name is recognized legally under state laws, the bank may properly open an account bearing a fictitious trade-name title. On the other hand, it is considered against public policy for banks to open accounts in "straw" names or any name that has not been legally approved, for this would make it relatively easy for a fraudulent operator to conceal assets by placing them beyond the reach of legitimate creditors, would permit tax evaders to conceal unreported income and even would make it difficult to identify an extortioner with his ill-gotten gains.

Sometimes a question arises as to whether or not a name is fictitious under the state law and, thus, whether registration is required. Although the laws of several states may vary in this area, as a general rule, a name that portrays a true condition in all respects and clearly identifies the individual or individuals behind the enterprise is not considered fictitious. For example, "Bill Smith's Machine Shop" may not be considered fictitious if the name represents a machine shop owned solely by Bill Smith and no one else. Ordinarily, the use of the world "company" or "association," or the omission of the family name (as in "The Bill Smith Machine Shop Company" or "Bill's Machine Shop") would indicate the necessity of registration to identify clearly the true owner or owners. Obviously, the banker must be familiar with the applicable laws with respect to fictitious names.

If a single individual registers a fictitious name, the business is usually called a "proprietorship." If two or more persons register the name, it would be a partnership or perhaps an unincorporated association. Since partnerships and unincorporated associations are covered separately, the remaining portions of this section will deal exclusively with proprietorships.

Capacity

Where registration is required, the applicant usually receives formal certificates of registration, one from the state government and one from the county or other local political unit in which the enterprise is domiciled. The certificates will show the assumed name and the name and address of the person doing business under the trade name. Exhibition of either certificate would be sufficient evidence of legal capacity to enter into a bank account contract. The bank may make a photocopy of the certificate for its files or simply record the date and the identifying number of the certificate and the issuing court or state official.

Identity

It must be remembered that possession of a registration certificate does not in itself identify the registrant. In some cases, certificates of registration or certified copies can be obtained simply by paying a small fee. The bank should identify the person negotiating for the opening of the account as the registrant named in the certificate.

Authority

The authority of an identified individual registrant need not be questioned. But if someone other than the registrant is to sign checks, authority must be established by the filing of a power of attorney or its equivalent, signed by the proprietor. The power conferred should be limited to the signing of checks on behalf of the trade name, unless otherwise intended.

Death of a Proprietor

The death of a proprietor should be handled in the same manner as the death of an individual depositor, except that it would not be wise to avoid the creation of an "estate." However small the business conducted under the trade name, there probably would be assets to be liquidated and debts to be paid, all of which properly should be handled by an executor or an administrator.

Bankruptcy—Attachments

Voluntary or involuntary bankruptcy of a trade-style proprietorship is the equivalent of the bankruptcy of the individual registrant, for he is personally responsible for debts incurred in the trade name. A writ of attachment naming either the proprietorship or the individual registrant as debtor must be applied by the bank to assets in either name.

Partnership Accounts

In many respects a partnership is not unlike a joint account, but in certain other respects the ground rules are quite different. While there are no uniform laws governing joint accounts, practically all states have adopted the Uniform Partnership Act, which is a special body of law dealing with partnership affairs. Banks and others who do business with partnerships should be familiar with the general principles of partnership law.

As we have seen, the usual bank form of joint account agreement contains a mutual exchange of powers of attorney, so that each tenant individually can conduct banking transactions on behalf of the joint tenancy. Partnership law contains similar but somewhat broader provisions in that each partner is automatically deemed to be an authorized agent for the partnership in all routine business transactions, so that an individual partner's actions, taken on behalf of the partnership, are binding on his fellow partners.

A partnership is usually a business venture conducted by two or more persons. It may do business under the family names of the partners, such as "Smith, Jones, and Brown" or it may, as we have seen, adopt an assumed name. In the former instance, depending on applicable state laws, the name may not be considered a fictitious name, provided that the business was actually conducted by three individuals named Smith, Jones, and Brown, and no one else. If Smith should die, however, and Jones and Brown for business reasons wished to continue doing business under the more familiar original name, or if a Mr. Green were to be admitted to the firm as an additional partner, the name would automatically become "fictitious," thus requiring registration according to most state laws.

The above comments are generalizations, of course, and may not necessarily conform with the laws of all states.

Capacity

The registration of the partnership's trade name as required by state laws satisfies the element of capacity. Exhibition to the bank of a formal certificate of registration is sufficient evidence of the partnership's capacity to enter into binding enforceable contracts. If the partnership name is not fictitious, the capacity of the individuals involved need not be questioned.

Identity

Where there are multiple partners, it would be impractical and unreasonable to insist that each partner present himself personally to be identified. Normally, a single partner will personally contact the bank to negotiate the opening of the account, and under the law he has the power to do so. After the identity of this individual has been established to the bank's satisfaction, it is safe and reasonable to accept his verification of the signatures of the other partners. On the other hand, if the account is opened and signatures are furnished by other than a partner (a bookkeeper, messenger, or other person), it would be wise for the person responsible for opening the account to pay a courtesy call at the firm's office, ostensibly to thank the partners for the account, but also to make sure that they are aware of the opening of the account and of the filing of specimen signature cards.

Authority

As a general rule, the specific terms and details of a partnership arrangement are spelled out in a partnership agreement signed by the individual partners. Some banks require the filing of a copy of the partnership agreement in order to insure that each partner, under the terms of the agreement, has full authority to deal with the bank on behalf of the partnership. Most banks, however, relying on the general provisions of partnership law, prefer to obtain, on a bank form, a shorter form of agreement between the partnership and the bank, which deals exclusively with transactions related to the bank account. The document should be signed by all the partners, if practical, but at least by a majority of the partners, and it should specifically provide authority for those who can sign checks, make loans, or otherwise deal with the bank. Such a special agreement is accepted by most banks in lieu of the actual partnership agreement and, in fact, is more suitable for the bank's purposes. The form also serves in lieu of a power of attorney when one or more of those authorized to sign checks are not actual partners.

Death of a Partner

Unlike the situation with respect to certain joint accounts, there is *ordinarily* no provision for rights of survivorship in a partnership agreement. However, while it would be unusual, there is nothing in the law that would prevent partners from agreeing that surviving partners shall become sole and absolute owners of a deceased partner's interest in the firm.

Under the law, the death of a partner automatically terminates the partnership, which then technically ceases to exist and must be dissolved and liquidated. However, the surviving partners have the right to continue the business during liquidation so that the affairs of the defunct partnership can be terminated in an orderly manner, and this right carries with it the power to handle and control all assets including bank balances. The purpose of this provision of the law is to prevent the estate of the deceased partner from stepping in and claiming or seizing bank balances or other partnership assets, thus crippling efforts to conduct an orderly liquidation. The surviving partners are required to render an accounting to the estate, to disclose fully financial data incident to the liquidation, and in reasonable time to pay over to the estate the deceased partner's share of the liquidation proceeds.

In many cases, the surviving partners will wish to continue the business under the same trade name. Thus the liquidation may proceed only as far as may be necessary to provide sufficient cash or acceptable value to satisfy the deceased partner's estate. A new successor partnership is formed, or, if there is only one surviving partner, the business is continued as a proprietorship. In either case, the registration of the original name must be amended to delete the name of the decedent, and the new registration certificate should be exhibited and identified on the bank's records.

Bankruptcy—Attachments

A partnership, like any other business or an individual, can file for bankruptcy voluntarily or be placed in involuntary bankruptcy. Upon receiving notice of the bankruptcy proceedings, the bank must freeze the balance and await orders from the court, which invariably directs the bank to turn over the balance and any other assets in its possession to the control of a referee or receiver in bankruptcy.

Although individual partners are jointly and severally responsible for debts incurred in the partnership name, it is possible for a partner to limit his personal responsibility; however, this fact must be publicized or otherwise made known to those who extend credit to the firm. In general, however, all the personal assets of all partners must be made available to satisfy the debts and costs of a partnership bankruptcy.

A writ of attachment is not applicable unless the document names the partnership itself as judgment debtor. A writ naming one of the partners *individually* as judgment debtor has no effect with respect to the partnership bank account. The debtor partner's interest in the partnership may be attached, but in this case the writ should be served on the partnership and not on the bank.

Corporation Accounts

A corporation always conducts its business under a fictitious name, simply because the word "corporation," or "company" or "inc." (incorporated), or some designation similar thereto, must be included in the corporate name. But corporations are in a class by themselves. They are subject to a separate body of laws and statutes and do not register under the usual laws governing the use of trade styles by individuals. The most significant difference between corporations and individual proprietorships or partnership trade styles is that the owners of a corporation (its shareholders) are not personally liable for debts of the corporation, except in the relatively infrequent cases where shares of stock are assessable.

As previously stated, a corporation is a legal person as opposed to a natural person, but as such, under the law, it has all the legal rights and standing of a natural person. It can transact business, enter into enforceable contracts, and sue and be sued in its corporate name. In fact, a corporation has one decided advantage over a human being—its life is not mortal and presumably it can continue its existence forever. On the other hand, its charter can be revoked or rescinded by the state or it can be dissolved and liquidated, either voluntarily or through involuntary bankruptcy.

The shareholders or stockholders are actually the legal owners of a corporation, and, while ultimate control rests in their hands, as a group they are not particularly fitted to become engaged in or even to supervise normal business activities. (An exception would be a closed family business, where all or a majority of shares are held by family members or intimate friends.) However, stockholders can and do exercise some measure of control by adopting bylaws which may specify the purposes of the corporation and place broad limitations on its activities. As a general rule, stockholder approval is required for certain unusual types of contracts or undertakings, such as mergers or acquisitions, the bulk sale of plants and equipment, and changes in the capital structure, such as the issuance of new stock or the incurring of long-term corporate debt. Normal corporate activities are entrusted to a board of directors who are elected by the shareholders and whose duty it is to assume active direction of the corporation's affairs. The managing board, in turn, elects or appoints active executive officers to whom specific authority is granted to conduct day-by-day corporate business. Any business contracts not covered by powers so conferred require action or ratification and confirmation by the board.

The question confronting a bank and anyone else doing business with a corporation is the proper level of authority that must be sought to ensure binding contractual relations. Although the stockholders are the actual owners, it would be impossible to conduct business with what may be a large and scattered group. Thus it is well established by law and by custom that the board of directors is the active governing body of a corporation; therefore, authority stemming from the board of directors may be considered sufficient evidence of the validity of normal business negotiations carried out in the corporate name.

Capacity

The legal capacity of a corporation is established merely by determining that it has been properly chartered, generally by the state of domicile. In many cases the existence and activities of the corporation may be so well-known to the bank that inquiry on this point would be unnecessary. If the name of the corporation is unknown, its legal status can readily be confirmed by reference to an agency report or any available commercial manual. As a last resort, to resolve any lingering doubt, inquiry can be made of the proper department or an appropriate official of the state of incorporation. It should be obvious that a bank that deals with an illegal corporation could be exposed to sizable losses.

Identity

As in the case of multiple partners, it would be unreasonable to expect each person authorized to sign corporate checks to present himself personally for purposes of identification. The officer of the corporation who negotiates the deposit account contract with the bank should be identified; following this identification, that officer's verification of other authorized signatures should be sufficient. In a situation in which completed signature cards are not personally delivered to the bank by the negotiating officer, they should be received in a sealed envelope accompanied by a letter of transmittal signed by the negotiating officer. Depending on circumstances, the person responsible for opening the account might deem it wise as well as courteous to make a friendly call on a senior officer at his office.

Authority

When a bank opens an account in the name of a corporation, the basis for all banking transactions is a certified copy of a resolution adopted by the board of directors authorizing the opening of the account and empowering certain corporate officers or representatives to act for the corporation in the handling of ordinary banking transactions. Banks supply corporate depositors with a special form for the purpose of obtaining the required proof of authority and instructions for the handling of the account. The wording of this prepared document contains an appropriate resolution, which is adopted by the corporation's board of directors at a regular or duly called special meeting. After quoting the resolution, the document usually continues with a certification prepared for the signature of the corporation's secretary, which states that the resolution was duly adopted by proper action of the board of direc-

Exhibit 5: Corporate Resolution with Certificate of Election

CORPORATE RESOLUTION	ACCOUNT NUMBER
	OFFICE
	ACCEPTED BY
(account title)	DATE

"RESOLVED, that an account in the name of this Corporation be established or maintained with the INSTITUTE NATIONAL BANK and that all checks, drafts, notes, or other orders for the payment of money drawn on or payable against said account shall be signed by any _____ (indicate number) person or persons from time to time holding the following offices of this Corporation.

_____   _____   _____

_____   _____   _____

(Indicate title only; not individual's name.

FURTHER RESOLVED, that said INSTITUTE NATIONAL BANK is hereby authorized and directed to pay all checks, drafts, notes and orders so signed whether payable to bearer, or to the order of any person, firm or corporation, or to the order of any person signing the same.

The undersigned, Secretary of _____ _____ (name of corporation) hereby certifies that the above is a true and correct copy of a resolution regularly adopted by the Board of Directors of the Corporation at a duly called meeting of the Board held on _____ (date), at which a quorum was present and voting throughout; and that said resolution is presently in full force and effect.

I further certify that the persons named below are those duly elected or appointed to the Corporate Office or capacity set forth opposite their respective names.

NAME	TITLE

In Witness Whereof, I have hereunto set my hand and affixed hereto the Corporate Seal of this Corporation

(Corporate Seal)

Dated: _____   Secretary

A typical form of corporate resolution to establish or maintain (continue) a corporation demand deposit account. The wording of such documents is not standard. Each individual bank, with the advice of legal counsel, prepares its own form to conform with state laws and to serve its own individual requirements.

tors. In addition to inscribing his signature, the secretary normally affixes or applies an impression of the official corporate seal.

Bylaws adopted by the shareholders represent a higher level of authority than action by the board of directors, and, in some cases, the corporate bylaws go into great detail, even to the extent of conferring on certain officers the power to handle bank accounts. When officers are so empowered, the bank should obtain a certified copy of the section of the bylaws that contains this specific authorization, in lieu of a resolution of the board of directors.

Because of their more permanent nature, bylaws invariably confer powers on position titles (president, treasurer, and so on) rather than on incumbents by name. Indeed, some board resolutions adopt the same style. Whenever powers are conferred on titles, the corporate secretary must furnish the bank with a certification of the proper election or appointment of named individuals to the offices indicated, as official changes take place. Such a document, to which the secretary also affixes the corporate seal, is known as a certificate of election.

It is important for a bank to examine carefully all corporate resolutions submitted on other than the bank's form to make certain that they are adequate and that they contain the necessary authority to cover specifically the action of the corporation officers or designated representatives in depositing and withdrawing funds and in the performance of other acts necessary to conduct business pertaining to the corporation's account. The corporate resolution, together with related papers, if any, must be carefully filed by the bank, for collectively these documents represent the basic authority for the payment of many billions of dollars annually in corporate funds.

"Death" of a Corporation

While a corporation does not die in the ordinary sense, its life as a "legal being" can cease for a number of reasons.

A corporation's charter can be revoked or rescinded by the state that gave it legal life. In this case it must cease to do business, but if it is solvent, its officers or one or more trustees appointed by its board of directors would be charged with the responsibility of liquidating its assets, paying its debts, and distributing the residue equitably among its shareholders. The appointment of the liquidating officers or trustees should be supported by a certified copy of the pertinent resolution.

A corporation may be absorbed by merger into or acquisition by another corporation, in which case it loses its separate existence and identity. Although the bank may be furnished with evidence of the merger or acquisition, it should not assume for itself the responsibility of transferring funds on deposit or other assets to the acquiring corporation. This should be done on the effective date of the merger or acquisition as one of the final acts of the board of directors of the expiring corporation, pursuant to shareholder approval. The bank should be furnished with a certified copy of an appropriate resolution of the board, which may instruct its officers to make the transfer or specifically authorize the bank to do so.

A corporation may absorb by merger or acquisition one or more other corporations, in which case it would not lose its identity, as would the absorbed units. However, it may wish to change its corporate name to reflect expanded activities. This must be accomplished by applying for a new charter or amending its existing charter. In the latter case, the bank should be furnished with documentary evidence of the change, certified by an appropriate official of the state of incorporation.

Bankruptcy—Attachment

Bankruptcy can, but does not necessarily signify, the legal "death" of a corporation. Under certain circumstances, with the approval of a court of jurisdiction, a corporation may seek an "arrangement" with its creditors, reorganize, and continue to do business under its original name and charter.

When a bank is notified that one of its corporate depositors has been declared bankrupt or placed in a temporary bankruptcy status, it will be instructed by the court to deliver control of all assets in its possession, including the deposit balance, to a receiver in bankruptcy or (in the latter case) to a trustee or trustees who will control the business until a final decision is made.

When a bank is served with a writ of attachment naming one of its corporate depositors as judgment debtor, it must impound all or as much of the deposit balance and other assets as may be required to cover the real debt *plus court costs, interest, and other such expenses.* It then awaits a court order directing the disposition of the impounded funds or assets.

Fiduciary Accounts

Generally speaking, a fiduciary is a legal person (an individual or a corporation) authorized to take title to and administer property for the benefit of others. Normally, fiduciaries are appointed in order to obtain professional or business expertise in the handling of the property where the beneficiaries are not considered qualified, for one reason or another, to assume this responsibility. As the name indicates, those who appoint fiduciaries place in them a considerable degree of confidence and trust, and the law takes a rather dim view of any breach of that trust, particularly those that work to the disadvantage of beneficiaries.

Fiduciaries invariably find it necessary to open a bank account. The banker must be familiar with the laws of his state applicable to fiduciary relationships. Many states have adopted the Uniform Fiduciaries Act, which is of special interest to banks. Among other things, this legislation accepts the principle that it is the fiduciary and not a depository bank on whom the primary responsibility has been placed; hence, a depository bank is not expected to police the actions of the fiduciary by minutely examining all transactions to ensure that the fiduciary is, in each case, properly acting in the interests of and for the benefit of the beneficiaries. On the other hand, the bank cannot ignore what would be considered overt evidence of wrongdoing.

To illustrate this point, if a fiduciary should withdraw cash from his fiduciary account, the bank is not expected to inquire as to the reason for the cash withdrawal or to determine that such funds will be used solely for the benefit of the beneficiaries. But if the fiduciary should attempt to pay a *personal loan* made by the depository bank by offering a check drawn on the fiduciary account, the bank would certainly be on notice of possible wrongdoing and would have to satisfy itself that a breach of trust was not involved.

A fiduciary is usually given a more descriptive title depending on the nature of the relationship. For instance, fiduciaries who are appointed by an agreement or deed of trust are known as *trustees*; those appointed to administer the property of minors or incompetents are generally known as *guardians*; and, as indicated earlier, those appointed to administer and settle a decedent's estate are known as *executors* or *administrators,* depending on whether the fiduciary is named in the will.

Before discussing the normal steps to be taken in opening a fiduciary account, it should be mentioned that there are two distinct types of "trust accounts." For want of better designations, they will be called "formal trusts" and "informal trusts"; since they differ in material respects, they will be discussed separately.

Formal Trusts

A formal trust may be described as one supported by formal documentary evidence, which in many cases is filed as a matter of public record. Included in this category would be decedents' estates created by a will or by the granting of letters testamentary; trust estates created under the terms of a will or by a recorded agreement or deed of trust; trusts created by court appointment of fiduciaries for incompetents, bankrupts, minors, and others; and other trusts created by unrecorded but identifiable written deeds or agreements of trust.

Capacity

If the fiduciary is an individual, the question of capacity can be taken for granted. In the case of corporate fiduciaries, there may be a question of whether the corporate charter permits it to function as a fiduciary in a matter not related to its corporate purpose. Most corporate fiduciaries are banks, and the authority of a bank to exercise fiduciary powers can easily be determined if need be. Where there is any doubt, counsel should be consulted.

Identity

The identity of an individual fiduciary or of an individual representing a corporate fiduciary is established in the usual way. However, it would be wise to repeat that the identity of an individual fiduciary should not be taken for granted solely on the basis of possession of a document of authority. In many cases, short certificates or certified copies of certificates of appointment or other court documents can be obtained by an aggressive knowledgeable person simply by the payment of a nominal fee.

Authority

The question of the extent to which a fiduciary's authority should be probed seems to be a matter of individual bank policy, and, in this respect, there are wide differences of opinion. Some banks insist on obtaining a certified copy of the will, agreement, deed, or other recorded supporting document so that it can examine the specific authority vested in the fiduciary and determine whether there are any important limitations of authority that would affect the fiduciary's relationship with the bank. It is reasoned that since the document is a matter of public record, the bank could be charged with knowledge of its content. Other banks would rather not, as a depository bank, have in their possession a document to which it is not a party. Particularly in states that have adopted the Uniform Fiduciaries Act, many banks prefer to rely on the principle that a depository bank is not required to share the fiduciary's responsibility by policing his actions. When the bank's role is limited to the servicing of deposit accounts, this position appears to be tenable. Of course, when the bank itself is the fiduciary or co-fiduciary, certified copies of all relevant documents are necessary. It is obvious that a bank would be well-advised to establish a definite policy in this area and to communicate that policy to all personnel charged with the responsibility of opening new accounts.

Death of a Fiduciary

Where one of two or more fiduciaries dies, it may be necessary to appoint a substitute. Sometimes the authorizing document (will, agreement, deed, or others) provides for this contingency. If the trust is under the control of a court of jurisdiction, the appointment would be made by the court. In the case of an unrecorded document, the surviving fiduciary or fiduciaries might be required to appoint a substitute or might be permitted to function without the appointment of a substitute, depending on its terms. The bank must obtain satisfactory evidence of the appointment of a substituted fiduciary, either in the form of a certified copy of the court appointment or a certificate executed by *all* of the surviving fiduciaries.

The death of a single individual fiduciary can present problems. If court action is necessary, the procedure takes time, and there could be matters that require periodic and timely attention, such as the distribution of income to beneficiaries. It is generally conceded that the executor or administrator of the deceased fiduciary's estate has a responsibility in this respect as part of his duty to wind up the decedent's affairs, pending the appointment of a substitute. Some banks will honor checks drawn by the executor or administrator on the trust account, if they appear to represent administrative obligations of the deceased fiduciary. If there is doubt as to the propriety of such action, counsel should be consulted.

Bankruptcy—Attachments

The probability of bankruptcy proceedings against a trust estate or the service of a writ intended to attach trust property is rather remote but not inconceivable. In either case, the position of a depository bank is clear. Notice of such a condition would be received by direction of a court, following which the court's instructions must be obeyed to the letter.

Obviously, any legal proceedings against a person or corporation individually, that happens at the time to be acting also as a fiduciary, would have no bearing whatsoever on trust property.

Informal Trusts

As indicated above, a "formal" trust is described for our purposes as one that is established, conducted, and terminated under the aegis of our courts of law or governed by a formal identifiable document. It follows then that an "informal" trust is one that is not court supervised or so governed. An informal trust is established when one or more individuals deposit a sum of money in a bank account and the bank is simply notified by the suggested title of the account that the money is being held in trust for one or more *named beneficiaries*. Such an account is usually captioned "A (the depositor) in trust for B (the beneficiary)." Thus the depositor not only provides the trust funds but also appoints himself as fiduciary.

The striking difference between the two kinds of trust is immediately apparent. In a formal trust, a property owner (trustor) formally transfers title to certain property to a fiduciary (trustee), and the fiduciary is legally and morally bound to obey the trustor's instructions as set forth in the supporting document, whether it is a will, a deed, or an agreement. Ordinarily in an informal trust there is no such document, but since the trustor and the trustee are most often one and the same person, the fiduciary is neither legally nor morally bound to anyone but himself. Such a "trust" (sometimes called a *Totten Trust*) is established voluntarily simply by opening the account entitled as indicated above or in a similar manner. Moreover, if the trust were established by the unilateral action of a single party acting as both trustor and fiduciary, there seems to be no reason why it cannot be terminated at any time by the same party. For this reason, informal trusts are regarded as completely revocable during the life of the self-appointed fiduciary.

Most (but not all) informal trust accounts are opened by parents or other relatives "in trust for" minor children. In connection with this particular type of account, there is an important exception to the above comments with respect to revocation.

Many states have adopted what is called the Uniform Gifts to Minors Act, which provides tax relief for those who make gifts of money or other property to minor children, in that income derived from the "gift" is taxable to the minor and not to the donor. But one cannot have his cake and eat it too, and gifts made under this act are definitely *irrevocable*. In order to qualify for the tax relief, the donor must make clear his intention to surrender his right to reclaim or retrieve the gift at a later date. The legislation specifies that the account must be entitled, "A as custodian for B," under the " (state) Uniform Gifts to Minors Act."

Capacity—Identity—Authority

The considerations for establishing the capacity and identity of fiduciaries are the same for both formal and informal trusts. However, the question of authority does not arise in the case of an informal trust, since the bank is dealing with one or more individuals acting on their own authority, as is their right. If the donor selects someone else to act as custodian (under the Uniform Gifts to Minors Act) the depositor's instruction to open the account in the custodian's name is sufficient authority.

Death of a Fiduciary

The death of a fiduciary of an informal trust does not normally present a problem for the bank. Again, familiarity with the laws of the state of domicile is important. The laws of most states permit the depository bank to pay the balance in such an account to the beneficiary or beneficiaries upon the death of the fiduciary. If the beneficiary is a minor, the law may require the payment to be withheld until the minor reaches legal age. Ordinarily, the estate of the deceased fiduciary has no claim on funds placed in trust. If the balance is unusually large, the bank may wish to contact the executor or administrator to assure itself that the decedent's estate is solvent and that no claim to the balance will be made. Whether the estate could successfully claim the "trust funds" in the event of the estate's insolvency is a matter for a court of law to decide.

Bankruptcy—Attachment

In an informal trust where, as in most cases, the fiduciary is also the trustor or donor, bankruptcy of the fiduciary could pose problems. If it can be shown that the motive in placing the property in trust was plainly to keep certain assets "in the family," so to speak, by removing them from the claims of creditors, it is quite possible that the "voluntary" trust would be set aside by the court. The bank, in the event of a claim by a receiver in bankruptcy, would look to the court for instructions. However, if the fiduciary were not also the trustor (the original owner of the trust property), bankruptcy of the fiduciary as an individual should not affect the voluntary trust.

The same considerations would apply if the bank were served with a writ naming the fiduciary (as an individual) as judgment debtor. In order to persuade the court that the voluntary trust arrangement should be voided, it would have to be shown that the motive in creating the trust was an intent to defraud creditors.

Unincorporated Associations, Clubs, Social Groups, Others

Many unincorporated associations, social clubs, athletic clubs, and church groups, formed for social or charitable purposes and not for profit, have very informal organizations. Income is usually derived from nominal dues or donations. Officers may or may not be elected or re-elected annually.

Such associations or groups often require banking services, and banks should be more than willing to provide adequate services. However, a bank's approach to such accounts should be flexible enough to fit the circumstances confronting it, for they can range from a Tuesday Morning Sunshine Club with balances in the $25 to $50 area to a rather substantial fund-raising unit with balances that may at times run well over six or seven figures.

It goes without saying that a bank should exercise reasonable care in handling the funds of all depositors not only because that is the essence of good banking service, but also because it could be held liable if an unlawful diversion of funds resulted from its negligence. It would not only be frustrating, but almost unconscionable to talk to the treasurer of a Sunshine Club in terms of "legal capacity" and "legal entities." On the other hand, those who conduct substantial fund-raising efforts owe it to their benefactors to handle such funds in a businesslike manner with proper controls, and a bank owes it to itself and the public to see that the account is neither established nor handled with complete indifference to the nature of such funds.

Capacity

Except in the case of larger organizations, a bank need not concern itself with legal capacity, for most of these associations will not be listed in the official records of the state of domicile or in the usual commercial services. The bank must depend, to a considerable extent, on the person or persons contacting and dealing with the bank.

Identity

The identity of the person representing the organization should be established in the usual manner. In many cases, the person will be known to the bank, perhaps as an existing depositor. If he or she is a complete stranger, however, it is especially important to obtain and check references (which, of course, should be done regardless of the type of account).

Authority

Many banks feel that signature cards alone constitute sufficient authority for those who withdraw funds from "club" accounts. While this is probably so, rarely does even the smallest group fail to elect a secretary with the responsibility of writing minutes of meetings. However informal such minutes might be, they would be of some value in the bank's file, for the secretary would likely record the election of new officers, and action, if any, taken by the membership of the group with respect to bank accounts.

For larger groups, the bank should inquire as to whether bylaws have been adopted, and if so, whether they deal with the organization's funds or define the duties of the officers. Where applicable, a certified copy of relevant sections of the bylaws should be obtained, and if there is an active board of directors or an executive committee, appropriate resolutions should be obtained. In connection with the election of officers, a more formal "certificate of election" should be furnished by the secretary for the bank's files. To express this as a principle, a bank should make an effort to seek such proper authority as may be readily available, but the *degree* of effort would be determined by the particular circumstances before it.

Death—Incompetence

The death or incompetence of an individual member of the type of association under discussion presents no problem as far as the bank account is concerned, but if the individual had authority to sign checks, the vacancy would have to be filled by election or appointment.

Bankruptcy—Attachment

In the case of larger organizations that in the course of normal operations must assume obligations or seek credit for the rental and furnishing of quarters, for the purchase of office equipment and supplies, and for certain operating costs including salaries, bankruptcy of the association as such or legal action resulting in a declaratory judgment is a distinct possibility, but an exceedingly rare event for the typical social club. In either case, however, the bank would obey the instructions of the court of jurisdiction.

Public Funds

Public funds may be defined, in general terms, as monies legally obtained from the citizens of a community for the purpose of providing public services for the comfort, safety, convenience, and general well-being of the community, Public funds are derived from many sources including taxes of all kinds, fees, licenses, fines, loans, and public borrowings. They are deposited in banks by the federal government or state governments and political subdivisions thereof, such as cities, towns, boroughs, villages, school districts, irrigation districts, and the like. In most cases, banks selected as depositories must be approved by the ruling body and are required to pledge specified types of assets to secure the safety of these deposits.

Because of the sensitive nature of such funds and the fact that in a very real sense they belong to the community at large, it is not uncommon to find specific statutes, laws, or local ordinances prescribing the procedure for the handling and deposit of such funds and for their withdrawal by check or other means. Needless to say, the bank is charged with knowledge of such statutes, laws, and ordinances, and it would find itself in a very vulnerable position if it contributed even innocently to the misuse of public funds.

Capacity

The existence and the legal capacity of political units or their subdivisions are self-evident by their taxing powers.

Identity

While officers of political units are sometimes well-known in the communities they serve, if this is not the case, the establishing of identity is even more important than where other than public funds are involved. The outside chance of being approached by an imposter is so remote as to be practically nonexistent, but considering the penalty in loss of prestige as well as in financial terms, it is certainly better to be safe than belatedly sorry. If several persons are authorized to sign checks, it is advisable to have signatures verified by a recognized official, either directly on the signature card or in a letter of transmittal.

Authority

As indicated earlier, it is rare that provisions for the withdrawal of public funds are not incorporated in laws or ordinances. Since a depository bank is charged with knowledge of all applicable legal directives, it must be absolutely certain, consulting counsel where necessary, that it has obtained proper authority according to the law in permitting the withdrawal of funds. Proper documentary evidence is frequently furnished to the bank, but where the law is specific and the bank has knowledge of its provisions, no further authority is necessary.

Joint Venture Accounts

At times, two or more business firms may wish to open a special account in connection with a specific joint undertaking. These are what might be called *true* joint accounts and they differ in important respects from the type of personal joint account previously discussed.

In the first place, rarely is there a "mutual exchange of powers of attorney" permitting a single party to sign alone. Both or all participants must join in delegating authority to those authorized to sign checks and otherwise handle the joint venture account. If two corporations are involved, the bank should be furnished with a special resolution from each of the boards of directors specifically authorizing the opening of the account and stating (in identical manner) the individuals whose signatures are to be recognized in connection with the withdrawal of funds. If there are subsequent deletions, additions, or substitutions of signatories, *both* boards of directors must join in the amendment to the original instructions. If other than corporations are involved, the normal type of authority for each participant should be obtained. The important thing is that *all* participants must act in concert in giving instructions to the depository bank.

Obviously, it has not been possible to cover every conceivable type of account and every imaginable contingency that could arise. Nevertheless, what has been said concerning the elements of capacity, identity, and authority, both in opening and closing accounts, can be logically applied to almost any situation.

The question of legal capacity probably is of the least concern and is often simply taken for granted, perhaps justifiably so. Nevertheless, it is important to know that the bank is not dealing with a legal phantom.

From the bank's viewpoint, the greatest exposure to loss in the opening of a deposit account lies in the area of establishing the identity of the person with whom it deals. It will be recalled that this involves more than merely determining that the person is who he says he is. Considering the nature of a bank account and the fact that every depositor inevitably becomes the bank's prior indorser, it is of the utmost importance to learn something about the prospective depositor's character and reputation. Fortunately, in most cases, such diligence on the part of the bank will be rewarded with favorable information. But in those few cases where the bank finds it prudent, on the basis of the information received, to refuse to accept the account, there could be serious problems. Under the Fair Credit Reporting laws, the bank might be forced to explain its decision and even be compelled to reveal the source of unfavorable reports. Unfortunately, laws designed to protect honest people often make it easier for the dishonest to prey on society. This is a problem that banks have to face.

The determination of authority requires little more than an understanding of the legal structure of corporations, partnerships, unincorporated associations, and various joint relationships and seeing to it that the bank's authority, particularly for the payment of funds, stems from the normal logical source and is joined in, where indicated, by *all* participants in the account relationship.

Bank personnel assigned to the new account desk have definite responsibilities, and their training must go beyond instructions as to the use of signature cards and authorization forms. A clear understanding of the nature of the relationship between the bank and its depositor is essential, particularly with respect to the bank's obligations and its potential liabilities. With this knowledge and awareness the responsibilities are not difficult to discharge, but lack of adequate training in this area can be costly.

Questions Based on This Chapter

1. In your own words, explain why it is necessary for a bank to be satisfied as to a depositor's legal capacity and identity and as to his authority where a person acts in other than an individual capacity.

2. Is it proper for a bank to open an account in an assumed name?

3. How does a bank establish authority for withdrawals from a corporate account?

4. What is:
   a) A power of attorney
   b) The right of survivorship
   c) A writ of attachment?

Chapter 6

The Deposit Function

Part I: Acceptance and Proof

Purposes of This Chapter:

1. *To explain how financial instruments are collected.*
2. *To distinguish between cash items and collection items.*
3. *To discuss the responsibility of a teller in accepting a deposit.*
4. *To describe the proof operation.*

The Collection of Financial Instruments

As an important adjunct of our monetary system, one of the most significant services rendered by commercial banks to the public at large is that of converting the tremendous volume of paper financial instruments issued and received daily by individuals, business organizations, and governments, into usable money, that is, coin, currency, or demand deposits. This is, in essence, the deposit function.

Paper financial instruments, generally classified as *orders* to pay money or *promises* to pay money do not constitute actual money. They are more accurately described as *claims* to money. When a check is deposited in a checking account, the depositor receives a provisional credit; strictly speaking, the depositor should not be permitted to draw checks against that credit until the item or items it represents have been presented and paid. A deposited financial instrument must be properly presented to the party liable thereon at the right time and in the right place, and, if it is honored, the funds it represents will then be made available to the depositor and be recognized as "usable money." In other words, a depositor is free to issue checks against his collected balance or withdraw the amount of the collected balance in coin and/or currency.

In a normal day the volume of paper financial instruments handled by our banking institutions runs into many millions of items, and annually to about 26 *billion* items. It is the responsibility of commercial banks to convert these instruments into usable money by redeeming the claims they represent. There is more to this process than meets the eye of the uninitiated.

Suppose, for instance, a check drawn on a Boston bank is received and deposited in a local bank by someone residing in Phoenix, Arizona. It should be obvious that the check must be transported *physically* to Boston to be presented for payment. There are two logical reasons for this. First, the drawee bank has an indisputable right to inspect the item itself in order to determine that it is valid and genuine and in all other respects eligible for payment. Second, if the drawee bank finds the check in order for payment, it has an equally clear right to take immediate physical possession of the item so that this claim to money on deposit in the Boston bank can be removed from circulation by cancellation. Subsequently, the cancelled check will be made available to the issuing depositor as evidence that the payment called for has been made.

Furthermore, money, like most things that are tangible in nature, has a definite location. If the check is paid, it is paid *in Boston*. It is then necessary to have the payment transferred to the local bank in Phoenix where the item was originally deposited, so that the money is *available in Phoenix* to the rightful owner.

On the other hand, suppose that the Boston bank finds after visual inspection that it cannot properly pay the check, and dishonors it. In this case the dishonored check must then be returned physically to the possession of the Phoenix depositor, who is not only entitled to evidence of the dishonor but may need the returned check to substantiate a possible claim against a party secondarily liable for payment, such as a prior indorser.

The value of this banking service should be readily apparent. Were it not for the collection services of our banking system, those who receive checks would face a serious problem in successfully redeeming these "claims" to money. It would be necessary for the payee of a check to present the item in person to the drawee bank, which might be located in the same city or town, but could just as easily be located thousands of miles away. It would further be necessary for the presenter, upon arriving at the drawee bank, to prove beyond any reasonable doubt that he is indeed *the payee* named in the check. No bank could afford to make payment of a check to an unknown second indorser. If the payee elected to send a representative in his place, or if the payee happened to be a partnership, a corporation, or an estate, the problem would be compounded. But those who daily receive checks or other financial instruments—from the average wage earner to the largest corporation—do not need to give these problems a second thought. The instruments are all handled easily, safely, and efficiently through our banking system. In addition, as opposed to the inconvenience, time, and expense of personal presentation by the payee, the cost of handling the vast bulk of such instruments through the banking system is reckoned in terms of pennies per item, with practically no cost in time or inconvenience to the depositor.

Cash Items and Collection Items

To facilitate the herculean task of processing and collecting approximately 26 billion pieces of paper annually, the banking system separates financial instruments into two broad classifications: *cash items* and *collection items*. A vast majority of financial instruments are eligible to be handled as *cash items*. *Collection items,* while far less numerous, are much more difficult to handle. It is important for the student of banking to understand the basic philosophy underlying the distinctly different methods of processing these two groups of financial instruments.

In simple terms, a cash item may be defined as coin, currency, or a financial instrument that a bank will accept for *immediate credit* to the depositor's account, before it has been presented for payment.

A collection item, on the other hand, is a financial instrument that is accepted by a bank against receipt only, and the bank *withholds credit* to the depositor's account until it has evidence that the item has been presented for payment, and that it definitely has been paid.

For those readers who may be experiencing their initial introduction to the language of banking, a brief word of explanation is in order. Every sphere of activity develops its own particular language or jargon, and banking is no exception. For instance, the term *cash item* is not limited to that which the general public normally regards as *cash,* that is, coin and currency, and *collection items* are not the only items that are *collected.*

Banking terminology, unfortunately, is not standard throughout the country, and banking terms and their uses sometimes vary in different areas and even in different banks. Some banks, particularly Federal Reserve banks, refer to collection items as *noncash items,* and there is considerable logic behind this distinction. Cash items are for the most part claims to money, and these claims to money have to be redeemed or collected; thus reference is made in banking circles to "cash items in process of collection." The point to remember is that the words *deposit* and *collection* as normally used are applied to both cash items and collection items. Cash item "deposits" are received for immediate credit and subsequent "collection" in terms of money. Collection item "deposits" are received against receipt, and are generally "collected" in terms of money, although in this case there could be other forms of consideration.

However, it should be made clear, before proceeding further, that the classification of any particular item as a cash item or a collection item is not dictated by the requirements of law. The two classes were developed by banking institutions over many years for the purpose of facilitating the collection of a wide variety of financial instruments. In the course of development, certain criteria surfaced that have been generally accepted by practically all banks. Nevertheless, any depository bank is free to handle any item as either a cash item or a collection item, as it may see fit. Whether immediate provisional credit is granted or whether credit is withheld until final payment is in hand is strictly a matter between the depository bank and its depositor.

Cash Items

There are a number of different kinds of items that qualify as cash items, including coin and currency, but the vast majority consists of demand drafts drawn on banks—ordinary checks.

The rather ingenious method by which millions of paper cash items are handled daily is based on an amazing optimistic faith in people. Banks accept these pieces of paper for deposit with complete confidence that an overwhelming majority will be promptly paid on presentation and will ultimately result in a valid transfer of funds from a debtor to a creditor. So great is this confidence that banks are more than willing to credit depositors' accounts as of the day of deposit with the face value of all cash items. This practice greatly simplifies accounting procedures, principally for the bank because of the volume handled, but obviously for the depositor as well. However, it is clearly understood between both parties that the immediate credit given for cash items is *provisional,* and that the exceptional items that are returned unpaid will result necessarily in a reversal of the original credit.

When a cash item reaches its ultimate destination and is presented for payment to the drawee bank or other payor, it must, within strict time limits, either be promptly paid or promptly dishonored and returned. If the item is paid, those involved in the processing cycle (payee, indorsers and collecting banks) are never informed of that fact. They are informed only of dishonor by the return of the unpaid item. Thus the entire process of redeeming cash items is based on the premise that no news is good news.

One might reasonably ask, "Why such a loose system? Why not inform all parties as to the fate of each specific item, instead of making them *assume* that an item has been paid?" The answer is that such a procedure would *double* the already mountainous volume of paper handled. Every check forwarded to its destination would have to be matched by another piece of paper tediously retracing the collection route with the required information. If it were not for the universal banking practice of accepting the majority of financial instruments on pure faith that most will be paid promptly, the handling of ordinary financial instruments would be infinitely more complicated and expensive, and the process of collection would be greatly impeded. Actual experience over a number of years has completely justified the decision of bankers to rely on the general honesty of people who issue checks and other financial instruments.

Characteristics of Cash Items

What characteristics must an item possess to qualify for handling as a cash item? The principal qualifying requirement for all cash items is *uniformity.* More specifically, a cash item must have the following characteristics:

1. It *must* be payable on demand or upon presentation.
2. It *may not* have any papers, documents, or other articles attached.
3. It *may not* be accompanied by special instructions.

There is a very good reason for these rather inflexible characteristics. Items that meet these specifications do not require close individual inspection and can be handled in bulk. They can be processed by experienced bank personnel with little more than a casual glance at each item.

Cash items can be dispatched for presentation without delay, for they are due and payable on the day of presentation. There are no documents or papers to be inspected, recorded, or otherwise handled, and there are no *special* instructions to be relayed to those who may subsequently handle the instruments. This is not to say that cash items are processed without *any* instructions. Actually, there are standing instructions with respect to cash items, but they are simple and uniform and are so well understood in banking circles that they are rarely even mentioned. In essence, a collecting bank is instructed to present all cash items as promptly as possible, to demand payment thereof, and, if payment is refused, to return the item without delay. For this reason, cash items are never outstanding for lengthy periods of time and the fate of each item can be determined in a matter of days. Therefore, except for bare essentials—the amount of an item, its source, and the point to which it was dispatched—elaborate descriptive records need not be kept.

Collection Items

The advantages of the cash-item processing system become more apparent as we examine the somewhat more complicated manner in which collection items are handled.

It will be recalled that a collection item is an item for which a bank will *not* extend immediate credit. The bank issues a receipt, but withholds the credit until it receives positive evidence that the item has been paid. It cannot be assumed, however, that the practice of withholding credit for collection items is based entirely on a lack of faith, for a substantial number of collection items are also paid promptly on presentation. It is rather, in many cases, because the complex nature of collection items makes it impossible to predict with any degree of certainty precisely when a particular item may be paid.

Characteristics of Collection Items

Although the characteristics of cash items are restrictive, by contrast those of collection items are completely flexible.

The characteristics of collection items, when expressed in the same format, may be stated as follows:

1. A collection item *may* be payable on demand or presentation or it *may* be payable on a future date.

2. A collection item *may or may not* have documents, papers, or other articles attached.

3. A collection item *may or may not* be accompanied by special instructions.

Despite the apparent flexibility, a collection item will be found to fail to conform with *at least one* of the standard requirements of a cash item and, indeed, it may fail to conform with all three.

For instance, a collection item may be payable on a specific future date and require presentation precisely on that date. If there is any considerable distance between the point of deposit and the place of payment, ordinary prudence would suggest forwarding the item well in advance of the maturity date to ensure proper presentation on that date. It would be unreasonable to expect a bank to grant immediate credit for an item that legally cannot be presented for payment for several days or even weeks. If a document such as a bill of lading is attached, presentation may depend on a coincident event, perhaps the arrival of a shipment of goods. Furthermore, if the shipment consists of perishable goods, there undoubtedly would be special instructions in the event of dishonor, to provide for proper storage and insurance. Obviously, simply returning the draft and bill of lading promptly to the depositor could result in spoilage of the entire shipment.

Another example of a collection item would occur if a depositor, for reasons important to him, would simply insist that he receive a formal *written advice* of payment of an item that otherwise would be acceptable as a cash item. This request would be a "special instruction" as opposed to the uniform practice of giving notice only of the *nonpayment* of a dishonored cash item.

These are but a few of the reasons why collection items require individual attention by well-trained personnel; why they cannot be handled in bulk with the speed and efficiency that the more uniform characteristics of cash items make possible; and why it would be impractical for banks to extend immediate credit for such items.

The magnitude of the additional detail made necessary by the special nonstandard handling of collection items is readily apparent. Each item must be handled individually. Instructions must be studied and relayed clearly and precisely. Attached papers or documents must be identified and examined by bank personnel to ensure that they are in proper form. To facilitate tracing and identification, each processing bank normally assigns its own collection number to each collection item that it handles. For these reasons, it is not surprising that the cost of handling a single collection item is something like *one hundred times* as much as the cost of handling a cash item.

Receiving and Accepting Cash Item Deposits

There are several different kinds of cash items, each of which requires its own special processing techniques. In this respect cash items may be grouped as follows:

1. U.S. coin and currency;

2. Clearing items (checks drawn on banks within the vicinity of the depository bank) ;

3. Transit items (checks drawn on out-of-town banks located beyond the reasonable vicinity of the depository bank) ;

4. On-us items (checks drawn on the depository bank) ;

5. Miscellaneous items (ordinary demand drafts drawn on other than banks, *matured* notes, certificates of deposit, and bonds and coupons eligible for immediate credit, such as obligations of the U.S Treasury, government agencies, other banks, and well-known corporations).

Given the fact that most financial transactions are settled by check, it is not surprising that these familiar instruments constitute the vast majority of all cash items deposited in banks. By volume, the greatest number of checks are concentrated in the second and third categories. Checks drawn on the depository bank, as well as coin, currency, and miscellaneous items, are received in relatively smaller quantities.

Receipt of Deposits

There are several ways in which bank customers may make deposits other than through a receiving teller's window during banking hours. When cash is not involved, deposits may safely be made by mail. Many banks offer other facilities, such as lobby depositories (so that customers may avoid long lines during rush hours) , night depository facilities (so that customers, particularly retailers, may make deposits on weekends or at any hour of the day or night), and other automatic devices where personal contact with a teller is not involved.

Whenever bank deposits are *not* received personally by a bank representative, however, special precautions must be taken. Since the depositor does not receive immediately a receipted copy of his deposit slip, he has no evidence that he made the deposit until an acknowledgment is received later in the mail. Disputes as to whether or not a deposit was made can be very embarrassing, and many banks institute some form of dual control for the protection of both the depositors and the bank. For instance, the procedure may require that at least two bank representatives be present when the deposits are removed from a vault, safe, or other depository equipment and that they prepare and sign a log carefully recording the number and identity of the deposits found.

Depositors are frequently required to sign a contract, particularly in the case of night depository facilities, in which they agree, in consideration for the free use of the special facility, that the debtor-creditor relationship between the bank and the depositor will not exist until deposits so made have been located and verified.

Acceptance of Deposits

Regardless of how deposits are received, they must be *carefully examined and accepted by an experienced teller* at an early stage. The unwary banker who believes that accepting deposits involves nothing more than counting coin and currency and stamping the depositor's receipt may be in for a rude shock. Failure to examine with reasonable care the nature of cash items offered for deposit and the account to which they are to be credited can expose the bank to very sizable losses.

Before the bank's responsibilities in accepting deposits are discussed, it should be pointed out that whether a deposit is received at a teller's window or in the mail room or by someone assigned to the task of removing deposits from a receptable, the person who accepts the deposit and signs the receipts assumes all of the responsibilities of a receiving teller. Although personal contact with the customer may be missing, it cannot be assumed that a clerk in the mail room requires any less training in the responsibilities of accepting a deposit than the authorized teller at a window.

The Responsibilities of a Receiving Teller

Anyone who accepts deposits on behalf of a bank performs the duty of a receiving teller and is responsible for—
1. Verifying the amount of cash (if any) by actual count;
2. Detecting any counterfeit coin and currency received;
3. Determining that all items are eligible for receipt as cash items;
4. Checking to see that all items have been indorsed by the depositor;
5. Being alert for any irregularities in connection with the deposit;
6. Issuing a receipt to the depositor.

Considering the volume of daily deposits received by even our smaller banks, it is evident that these duties must be handled quickly but not carelessly. Moreover, it is impractical as well as unnecessary to subject each item to a minute inspection. Nevertheless, the seemingly casual inspection by a well-trained teller usually reveals conditions that require closer inspection.

1. *Verifying the amount of cash by actual count.*

At the outset a common exception to this rule should be mentioned. Quite frequently deposits of what is called "bulk cash" are received in the form of rolled or bagged coin or banded currency, in each case identified as to the amount and the name of the depositor. Whether or not these are received at a teller's window, most banks use special equipment to verify bulk cash deposits. Thus it is customary to accept such deposits subject to later verification, and customers who make such deposits agree to this procedure.

For security reasons, coin and currency are not processed in the same manner as other cash items. Loose coin and currency are immediately counted and either retained in the teller's department or promptly sent to a "money" department. A memorandum called a "cash ticket," which indicates the amount of the coin and currency part of the deposit, is substituted for settlement purposes. Loose cash should be counted by a teller in the presence of the depositor or, if received through one of the special depository facilities, the amount should be verified as promptly as possible, preferably by two tellers.

As previously indicated, it is not wise to include cash in deposits by mail. When this is done, many banks return with the deposit receipt a note cautioning against the practice and disclaiming responsibility for cash sent through the mail.

2. *Detecting any counterfeit coin and currency received.*

Despite the tremendous improvements made over the years in the minting of coin and in the printing of paper currency of uniform design by the U.S. Bureau of Engraving and Printing, counterfeit money still appears with annoying regularity. The public rarely is able to detect reasonably good counterfeits. Bank tellers must be thoroughly trained in this area. They are the experts in the public eye and are also the bank's only line of defense. Once a teller accepts bogus money in a deposit and places it in the cash drawer, there is practically no chance of proving from whom it was received. Thus the bank stands the loss. The amount of counterfeit money accepted by bank tellers and charged to profit and loss each year is a good indication of the effectiveness of the bank's training program in this area.

3. *Determining that all items are eligible for receipt as cash items.*

It would be unnecessary as well as impractical for a teller to inspect each item individually to check the standard characteristics of cash items. Furthermore, the risk involved is probably not any greater than the risk in accepting any paper "claim to money" for immediate credit, with the understanding that it will be presented for payment as soon as possible and *promptly* returned if dishonored. Nevertheless, the experienced eye of a well-trained teller will detect quickly any bulky items that perhaps indicate a draft with some documents, securities, or a special letter of instructions attached, or an item of nonstandard size which might bear a closer look. On the other hand, to expect a teller to detect a check-size promissory note payable six months in the future in the middle of a deposit containing a dozen or more "claims to money" would be asking too much.

4. *Checking to see that all items have been indorsed by the depositor.*

Everyone who indorses and thus transfers title to a cash item in the collection process, from the party who received the item from the named payee to the last bank in the collection chain, *warrants the sufficiency of all prior indorsements* to all subsequent holders as well as to a drawee bank or other payor (U.C.C.Sec. 3-417). Each party who accepts a cash item, including a depository bank, relies on this firm legal commitment of *its* indorser that all prior indorsements (if any) are genuine, authorized, and otherwise in order. Obviously, any warranty is no better than the financial ability of the warrantor to honor the commitment, and those who accept financial instruments must satisfy themselves on this point.

Unquestionably, a bank relies heavily on the warranties of its depositor-indorsers and reaches its decision to do so in each case when the account is opened. It would be pointless to spend time carefully examining all indorsements on deposited cash items and searching for technical irregularities, all of which are fully covered by the warranties. The teller is not expected to see that each item is indorsed by the payee precisely as drawn or that a special indorsement is followed by the indorsement of the designated transferee. It is sufficient at this point merely to see that the deposited items have been endorsed by the depositor. This can be done rather quickly by flipping through the reverse side of the instruments.

The presence of the depositor's indorsement has a practical significance apart from the warranties. A dishonored cash item requires immediate attention, for the provisional credit to the account must be reversed and prompt notice of dishonor given to the depositor, all of which is normally accomplished by physically returning the unpaid item. The depositor's indorsement quickly identifies the number of the account to be charged and the name of the person who should receive notice. If the depositor's indorsement is missing, the bank should be able to trace the item through its processing journals back to the original deposit slip; however, this takes time, and an unreasonable delay might result in a justified presumption by the depositor that the item had been paid on presentation.

5. *Being on the alert for irregularities in connection with the deposit.*

This is perhaps the most important responsibility and the most difficult to discharge. There is no simple checklist for the teller to follow, because "irregularities" that might expose the bank to potential loss can take an almost infinite variety of forms. This is not surprising, since most of them are designed to deceive the unwary. Well-trained tellers, who have been taught that accepting deposits is not a dull, routine, and completely innocuous function and who have been made aware of some of the more common tricks of check thieves and con artists, are frequently able to spot telltale danger signals.

The most frequently encountered fraud perpetrated at the receiving teller's window involves the unlawful *conversion of funds*. This is simply a case in which a dishonest person takes a legitimate check payable to someone else and succeeds in depositing it in his account, with or without a forged indorsement of the payee. An unlawful conversion of funds usually involves a relatively new account rather than that of a regular customer of long-standing, and a good teller knows instinctively if this possibility is fairly remote. Nevertheless, it is wise in accepting any deposit, to flip through the face side of checks and other financial instruments to see if the name of the depositor corresponds with that of the payee named in the instruments. If the names do not agree, it does not automatically follow that an unlawful conversion is involved, but the teller should be satisfied that the deposit is normal and regular.

For instance, wage earners quite frequently cash their paychecks and other checks at check-cashing agencies, local supermarkets, grocery stores, drugstores, or taverns. It is quite normal for check-cashing agencies and local retailers to deposit regularly checks that are not drawn payable to the order of the depositor. The bank relies on the retailer's warranty that the prior indorsement of the named payee is genuine, and any question on that score should have been settled when the account was opened. But the average individual depositor is not in the habit of cashing paychecks, social security checks, tax refund checks, and others for his friends and neighbors in the community. On occasion this may happen, but regular deposits of such checks payable to persons other than the depositor certainly warrant investigation and possibly referral to an officer. Any unusually large check, say in a four- or five-figure amount, made payable to other than the depositor, deserves more than a casual glance.

Many unlawful conversions involve checks payable to legal entities, such as corporations, trade-styles, partnerships, decedents' estates, rather than to natural persons. Checks payable to corporations are normally deposited to an account in the payee corporation's name and should never be accepted for deposit to an account in any other name without proper investigation. Although most unusual, such a transaction could be perfectly proper, but the bank is entitled to demand and obtain satisfactory authorization. Similarly, checks payable to any other kind of legal entity should not be accepted for deposit to an account in any other name and certainly not to an account in an individual name without careful investigation.

It is not possible, nor would it be particularly productive, to attempt to describe in detail all of the potential hazards and pitfalls associated with the acceptance of deposits. Banks have made considerable progress in recent years, not only in technology but also in their efforts to stem the sizable annual losses to those who habitually prey on bank tellers, but it must not be forgotten that the so-called "paperhanger" has made considerable progress too. He is smart, resourceful, well-acquainted with banking practice and he knows that it is much easier and safer to deposit stolen or fraudulent checks than to attempt to cash them.

Currently banks lose more money through the acceptance of fraudulent deposits than through other forms of teller activity. In addition to stolen checks, a professional crook, through contacts with unscrupulous printers, can easily obtain spurious checks of nationally known corporations and even spurious pre-encoded deposit slips. In many cases even an experienced teller will find no obvious cause for suspicion. Nevertheless, the receiving teller is the only line of defense, for once a fraudulent deposit is accepted, the success of the paperhanger's scheme is practically assured.

An experienced teller, well-acquainted with the bank's regular customers, knows that the great majority of deposits offered can be accepted safely with hardly more than a casual glance at the deposited items. Detecting the irregular fraudulent deposits, like recognizing counterfeit currency, requires a certain feel for the unusual. Banks owe it to their tellers to provide adequate, carefully developed training programs, so that the teller can be a reasonable match for the professional crooks who sometimes confront them.

6. *Issuing a receipt for the deposit.*

Depositors sometimes make notations or changes on multiform deposit slips. To avoid later unpleasantries, a teller should make sure that the total on the depositor's receipt agrees with the total on the copies retained by the bank, which will be posted as a credit to the account.

The foregoing is a rather full description of the responsibilities of those who accept deposits of cash items on behalf of a bank. Experience, particularly in recent years, has amply demonstrated the high degree of exposure *at this point* in the handling of deposits. If an irregular and fraudulent transaction is accepted by a receiving teller, whether that person is a window teller, a mailroom teller, or a proof clerk performing the duties of a receiving teller, there is no reasonable chance of detecting the fraud in subsequent stages of processing. Education and adequate training are the only effective protection against the schemes of those who have been led to believe that they can make a comfortable living at the expense of the banking community.

Receipt and Acceptance of Collection Item Deposits

The acceptance of a collection item deposit is a considerably less critical stage of the processing cycle than the acceptance of cash-item deposits, for once cash items are entered in the collection process, those who handle them are concerned with little else than the amount of the item. There is no time for examination or close inspection; indeed, much of the handling is done automatically by sophisticated electronic equipment, for cash items must be presented for payment as quickly and economically as possible. By contrast, collection items are subjected to the most careful scrutiny *after* acceptance at every stage of the processing cycle.

The responsibilities of bank personnel who accept collection items for deposit are therefore considerably less specific. They are:

1. *To make sure that adequate instructions have been received.*

What might be considered adequate depends on the nature of the item. Collection items are not necessarily accompanied by special instructions. However, when an item is associated with a shipment of a marketable and perhaps perishable commodity, instructions should provide for the control and protection of the merchandise in the event of non-payment.

2. *To make sure that attached papers and documents are in proper form for subsequent handling.*

Whether such documents are negotiable or non-negotiable, it is important to see that they are properly indorsed or assigned at the outset. Failure to discover such an omission until presentation of the item could result in an embarrassing and perhaps costly delay.

3. *To issue a receipt to the depositor.*

The form of the receipt for collection items may vary depending on the kind of item deposited. In some cases the receipt may contain only the date, the amount, and the depositor's name. Generally, however, receipts given for collection items contain much more detail, as they should. In addition to the item itself, attached valuable documents should be briefly described in the acknowledgment.

The Proof Operation

Regardless of how cash item deposits are received by the bank, the next processing step is generally known as the *proof operation,* which has two specific objectives:

1. To verify the total of the deposit; and
2. To establish control totals for the several departments responsible for handling specific kinds of items.

The need for the first objective is rather obvious. Except in the case of certain special types of credits, the deposit ticket is prepared by the depositor. The bank initially accepts the depositor's calculation of the total amount of the deposit and gives him a receipt for that amount. It is necessary at an early stage, therefore, to verify the accuracy of the depositor's figures.

The second objective is to prepare control totals for the various processing departments. The importance of this objective, not only in the initial proof operation but also in every stage of the processing procedure, cannot be overemphasized. A good-sized bank might receive cash item deposits in a single day totaling $500,000,000, which is immediately credited to depositors' accounts. The pieces of paper that make up most of that sum may range in amounts as low as one dollar or less to items of one million dollars or more. There may be as high as 50 or 100 different channels through which many thousands of items are collected.

Every bank, of course, aims to account for every penny of the amounts credited to depositors' accounts. This is by no means a simple task, and perfect settlements are frustratingly elusive. Nevertheless, for any bank to lose control of the dollar value of cash items that it handles daily, as they are shuffled and reshuffled in the course of preparing them for presentation and payment, would be a disaster with potentially serious consequences.

In earlier bank operating systems, the two objectives of the proof operation were viewed as entirely unrelated, and each one was achieved by a separate process. In modern systems, sophisticated equipment has been designed especially to accomplish both purposes in a single operation.

Individual Deposit Proof

Verification of the total amount of a deposit requires determining that the amount of each item is listed correctly on the customer's deposit slip and that the depositor's addition of the listed amounts is correct. Originally this was done by visual comparison and mental verification of the addition. When adding machines became available, it was found more effective for a teller or a proof clerk to prepare a separate listing and total of the deposited items. Since the listed amounts were usually in the same order, comparing the bank's listing with the depositor's list and locating any discrepancy was a relatively simple matter. This method became known as "individual deposit proof," since each deposit was proved and settled individually before considering the next objective, the establishment of control totals.

The next step was to commingle the deposits by grouping all the deposit slips and *sorting* the deposited items into as many groups as desired to facilitate further processing. Following the sorting operation, each group of items (including the deposit slips) had to be listed and totaled to provide control figures for the processing departments.

The use of the individual deposit proof method, which is rather infrequent if not nonexistent in these days, requires three steps to accomplish the two objectives:

1. A listing to prove the deposit total;
2. A sort to separate the items according to destination;
3. A listing of the sorted items to provide control totals.

The Group or Batch Proof System

At some point in time, an ingenious bank operations specialist decided that the two objectives could be handled in a single operation. Why list the same items twice, in different order, as in steps one and three? He argued convincingly that a given group of cash items had to add up to the same total no matter how they are arranged and no matter how many times they are resorted and rearranged. Such irrefutable logic could not be denied, and the group or batch proof system came into being.

As the system developed, groups of deposits (called batches) of manageable size (perhaps two or three hundred items) were handled as a unit. Instead of proving the depositor's total of each deposit as a separate initial step, the items were commingled and immediately sorted into groups according to their destination. Then each group was listed on a columnar journal sheet, which also included a recap of the totals of the several deposit slips. To settle the batch, a recap of the group totals was compared with the recap of the deposit slip totals. If these two figures agreed, it was assumed (allowing for a possible counter-error) that both the listing and addition of each individual deposit slip were correct. If the recap figures did not settle, it was somewhat more difficult to compare amounts listed on the several deposit slips with corresponding amounts in the various group listings on the journal sheet in order to locate and adjust the difference, but this problem was minor compared with the benefits derived in speed and efficiency.

Thus the *three steps* required by individual deposit proof in order to achieve the objectives were reduced to *two steps* by the batch proof method.

1. A sort to separate items according to destination; and
2. A listing to prove the deposit totals and establish control totals simultaneously.

It is doubtful that any bank in the country uses the individual deposit proof method today, as the practice of realizing the *two* objectives of the proof operation in a single operating step has been adopted universally. Moreover, the batch proof system is seldom performed today in precisely the manner described. Nevertheless, the two systems have been described in some detail intentionally for illustrative purposes. It is interesting to note that this particular innovation, developed more than a half century ago, achieved a savings in handling time of at least 30 percent without sacrificing or jeopardizing either of the basic objectives of the proof operation.

In any high volume operation the saving of a single small step in the processing cycle can produce handsome rewards, and bank operating personnel, methods experts, and other technicians constantly search for new ways to improve processing techniques. In the search, however, it is imperative to keep in mind not only *what* is done, which is a means to an end, but also *why* it is done, which is the end itself—the objective. In the quest for better tools and better methods, basic objectives are sometimes de-emphasized or forgotten entirely. When this occurs there is the danger of changing a system, a method, or a program in order to gain a relatively trivial advantage at the cost of reaching a less than satisfactory end result.

Since collection items do not receive immediate provisional credit and must be handled individually rather than in bulk, there is no need for a proof operation to verify the depositor's total. As soon as collection items are received they are sent to a collection department and are dispatched for presentation directly from that department. Therefore, since no other department is involved, there is obviously no need for a preliminary sort and the establishment of numerous control totals.

By assuming the task of collecting millions of financial instruments daily, our nation's commercial banks make a major contribution to the effectiveness of our monetary system.

All financial instruments must be physically presented to the party primarily responsible for payment. In the interests of speed, efficiency, and economy, financial instruments are classified as either cash items or collection items. Cash items are handled in bulk. They are presented for payment as promptly as possible and, unless they are dishonored and returned within certain time limits, they may be assumed to have been paid. By contrast, a collection item cannot be assumed to have been paid until a written advice of payment has been received.

Because of the speed with which cash items are processed, special care must be exercised when deposits are accepted to guard against unlawful conversion of funds, for which the depository bank may be held responsible.

Questions Based on This Chapter

1. The chapter describes the different method of handling cash items as contrasted with collection items. What justifies the obvious inconvenience of the two classifications with different handling procedures?

2. Why is physical presentation of a financial instrument a necessary prerequisite for payment?

3. Why is it necessary for a receiving teller to verify the amount of cash in a deposit by actual count at the window, when it is not necessary to verify the total amount of the deposit at the same time?

4. What are the objectives of a proof operation?

Chapter 7

The Deposit Function

Part II: The Collection of Financial Instruments

The Purposes of This Chapter:

1. To emphasize the necessity of harmonizing the elements of speed and cost in collecting financial instruments.

2. To point out the desirability, where volume is sufficient, of presenting and collecting local items through a voluntary clearing arrangement.

3. To describe the three principal methods of collecting transit (out-of-town) items.

4. To explain how settlement is made for items collected through the Federal Reserve System.

Once a deposit is received and accepted by a bank, it is of the utmost importance that it be processed as quickly as possible. This is true whether the deposit is a cash-item deposit eligible for immediate credit or a deposit of one or more collection items where the actual credit is withheld until specific advices of payment have been received.

Particularly in the case of cash items, the speediest possible collection of these claims to money assumes considerable importance. Cash items *in process of collection* are, in bank terminology "float" or "uncollected funds." There is an inevitable time lag between the instant a check is credited to the depositor's account and the moment when it is paid and debited (charged) against the drawer's account in the drawee bank. Obviously during this time period there is an inflation of the level of *total demand deposits* in the banking system, since the funds represented by the same check appear in both the account of the depositor and in the account of the issuer of the check. Thus the dollar volume of "float" or "uncollected funds" does not constitute money or even claims to money but is more accurately described as a temporary illusion.

Among the many practical incentives for prompt collection of cash items are the following:

1. The very theory of the cash item system and its acceptance by the business world depends on the *prompt* presentation of such items and the equally prompt return of unpaid items. Remember, no one is ever advised that a specific cash item has been paid. Failure on the part of the banking system to recognize the necessity for reasonably fast and efficient check processing would create for both banks and their customers an intolerable situation, for neither could ever determine with any degree of certainty the amount of usable funds in demand deposit accounts. The Uniform Commercial Code recognizes this need, with respect to both the presentation of items and the return of dishonored items, and also by prescribing penalties for those who fail to exercise ordinary care.

2. The depositor is very much interested in limiting the time required to redeem his claims to money. Since the credit extended for cash items is provisional, the depositor is subject to a charge-back for any item that is not paid on presentation; the sooner this contingent liability is removed the better for all parties concerned. Furthermore, depositors know or should know that the bank does not expect them to draw against uncollected funds. On the other hand, it would be unreasonable to expect depositors to wait an inordinate length of time before drawing checks to pay their bills.

3. Finally, from the bank's viewpoint, "float" or uncollected funds are idle and useless since they cannot be used for loans and investments or any other purpose. On the other hand, available (collected) funds are of considerable value to bankers since they can be utilized profitably in many ways. From an earnings standpoint, every bank is interested in controlling and minimizing its "float" by limiting the period during which cash items are in process of collection.

For these reasons, as soon as the objectives of the proof operation have been achieved, cash items must be distributed promptly to the several departments or units that are responsible for converting these claims to money into usable funds. Thus, for example, transit items are routed to the department responsible for collecting out-of-town checks, either as a single group under one control total or in several groups according to the geographic location of the drawee banks, each under a separate control total. Clearing items are routed to a department or unit responsible for preparing packages of checks for presentation through a clearinghouse or, if such facilities are not available, for hand presentation by messenger or by courier service. "On-us" items and deposit slips are routed to the bookkeeping department for posting as debits and credits respectively to the various accounts. And miscellaneous items, such as coupons and matured bonds, are routed to the units that handle such items. In every case the department receiving the various items is furnished with listings and control totals to facilitate the respective department or unit settlements.

The actual number and the names of these departments and units vary considerably among banks and depend on the volume and nature of the items handled. In some banks a single department may handle all cash items, with units or specialized personnel within the department assigned to certain types of items. In other banks the departmental structure could be quite complex. For instance, a transit department may be responsible only for the collection of out-of-town checks and independent departments may be established for other items, such as the messengers' department for items collected by hand presentation, an out-clearings department for items drawn on participating clearinghouse banks, a coupon department, and a securities clearance department for matured bonds.

For the purposes of this text, discussion will concentrate on the types of items to be collected, rather than on the names and organization of the departments involved. From time to time, the more common departmental names will be used, but the reader should have no difficulty in identifying the function with the operating system employed in his or her bank.

Collection of Cash Items

For reasons already discussed, cash items payable on demand should be presented for payment as quickly as possible. Yet other factors also must be considered, and "quickly as possible" must be brought within the realm of practicality. For instance, the fastest way for a New York City bank to collect a check drawn on a Los Angeles bank might be to have a bank representative take the next direct flight to Los Angeles to present the check personally to the drawee bank. To collect a $100 check in this manner would be ridiculous, but if the check were for $100,000,000, it could very well be worthwhile. The positive advantages of speedy collection must be weighed against the possible negative effects of the *cost* involved. Further, the volume and dollar amount of the item or items involved can either magnify or minimize the advantages and disadvantages of the other two factors.

Obviously, each bank must carefully analyze the volume, amount, and mix of the cash items it normally receives to determine its most practical collection channels.

Local Items

Clearing items have been defined as checks drawn on banks within the vicinity of the depository bank. A broader term, *local items,* would also include ordinary drafts, matured notes, and other items payable by other than banks.

There are three ways in which local items can be presented for payment:

1. Direct presentation by messenger;
2. Presentation through the services of another bank;
3. Presentation through the facilities of a clearinghouse association.

While there are practically no limitations on the kinds of items that may be collected by messenger or through a correspondent bank, the rules of a clearinghouse association are more restrictive. In general, only checks drawn on participating member banks may be collected through the clearing, although special provisions may be made for certain items collectible through participating banks.

Presentation by Messenger

On the surface, direct presentation by messenger appears to be the speediest and most convenient method of presentation but again there are other factors to be considered. For one thing, the average number of collection points to be covered each day determines the number of messengers required and thus affects the salary expense. Another factor is the volume of items presented to the respective drawees or payors, for presentations in bulk invariably require two trips by the messenger, one to present the items and then, after reasonable time for inspection of the items to determine their eligibility for payment, a return trip to collect the payment and any dishonored items.

Collection of local items by messenger is more suited for light volume and special situations than for bulk presentations. Where a single item may involve a large dollar amount or where there is special concern about final payment, direct presentation by messenger often provides the most practical means of presentation.

Presentation Through Correspondent Banks

When the services of a correspondent bank are used, the local bank becomes simply a depositor, and the correspondent assumes the responsibility of presenting the checks for payment. The local bank like any other depositor receives immediate provisional credit for the amount of the deposit but, because of the volume involved, the correspondent bank probably keeps more closely posted as to the amount of the local bank's balance that represents "uncollected funds."

Under certain circumstances it could be advantageous to present local items through a correspondent bank, particularly where there is no clearinghouse association or where the local bank, for one reason or another, is not a member of such an association. In arriving at a decision, all relevant factors must be considered, including the proximity of the correspondent bank. If the bulk of local items received each day can be delivered to the correspondent on the same day by messenger or courier service, any delay in presentation will be minimized as most large correspondents process items steadily during evening and night hours. On the other hand, if the local bank's deposit must be dispatched by mail and cannot possibly be received until the next business day, there will be a loss of *at least* one day in the availability of funds. The impact of this loss can be measured approximately by determining the average daily dollar volume of local items received and calculating the resulting loss in income, which can then be weighed against the additional cost of the alternative of sorting local items by drawee banks and other payors for presentation and collection by messenger.

Presentation Through a Clearinghouse

A clearinghouse is a voluntary association of a group of local banks organized primarily for the purpose of facilitating the exchange (presentation) of checks drawn on or payable by members of the group and the settlement of balances resulting from the exchange.

A clearinghouse arrangement unquestionably offers the most practical, economical, and efficient method of collecting local checks (clearing items) and other acceptable cash items, especially in view of the fact that clearing items invariably represent the bulk of all local items received.

A simple illustration should quickly reveal the advantages of a clearinghouse arrangement. Consider a medium-sized city in which there are six banks. In the normal course of business each bank will receive daily from its depositors a substantial number of checks drawn on the other five banks. In the absence of some better arrangement, Bank A would have to send checks drawn on the other five drawee banks by messenger for presentation and payment. In view of the volume, it is quite likely that the messenger would have to make two stops at each drawee bank to allow time for examination of the checks between the time of presentation and actual payment. This would mean a *minimum* of 10 messenger trips per bank or 60 messenger trips for the group. Moreover, since such checks are received continuously throughout each banking day, and since all banks strive to limit the volume of uncollected checks in hand, there would be a strong temptation for each bank to make as many daily presentations as the dollar amount warranted. The result would be a steady stream of messengers going to and from each bank, and dozens of clerical personnel in the several banks would be constantly engaged in either preparing checks for presentation to other banks or examining checks presented by other banks, to say nothing of issuing innumerable bank drafts to pay for checks presented and processing those bank drafts received in settlement from drawee banks.

By contrast, a typical local clearinghouse operates in the following manner: A common meeting place for representatives of the participating banks is provided, substituting a single point of presentation for numerous separate points. The clearing or exchange takes place at a single predetermined hour each day instead of at random unpredictable hours. Bulk presentation of checks other than at the regular clearing hour is prohibited, but by mutual agreement the member banks may present special single items at any time.

At the latest practical hour before the clearing, each member of the group prepares five packages, containing checks drawn on each of the other participating banks. When the volume of clearing items is particularly heavy, packages of checks are frequently delivered by presenting banks to the drawee banks via courier service at certain hours during the night preceding the day of settlement. The total dollar amounts of such checks are carried forward on the package presented at the clearing settlement. At the appointed hour, the packages are exchanged by delivery to representatives of the respective drawee banks. Thus the representatives of each bank arrive at the clearinghouse with five packages of checks drawn on the other banks and depart with five packages of checks drawn on itself. Actually, the exchange of packages, regardless of the number of banks in the group, takes place in a matter of minutes.

So much for the physical advantages. The benefits derived from the settlement procedures are even more spectacular. A clearinghouse settlement is based on the principle of offsetting counterclaims and liquidating only the *net* balances. Furthermore, participating banks do not settle with each other individually. Each bank settles with the clearinghouse, thus substituting a single settlement for each bank in place of many individual interbank settlements.

In general, the settlement procedure is handled in the following manner. Each bank is represented at the clearing by a settlement clerk and, where warranted by the clearing volume, by one or more messengers. Normally the settlement clerk sits at a desk assigned to his bank, while the messenger delivers his bank's prepared packages to the settlement clerks of the respective drawee banks. As soon as the exchange of packages has been completed, the messengers are free to return to their respective banks to permit as early a start as possible on the considerable task of proving and then examining the often substantial volume of checks received. The settlement clerk remains at the clearinghouse until the settlement has been completed.

The settlement clerk arrives at the clearinghouse with a partially completed settlement sheet, which shows in one column the names of the other participating banks; in a second column is the dollar amount of checks delivered (presented) to each of the listed banks and the column total, which of course, is the amount of his bank's clearing credit; in a third column is the dollar amount of checks presented to his bank by each of the other banks.

The figures in the second column are available and are filled in and totalled *before* the clearing. As the packages are exchanged, the settlement clerk transcribes the total dollar amount of each package received to its appropriate place in the third column. He then totals the column to determine the amount of his bank's total clearing debit. (See Exhibit 6.)

Exhibit 6: Individual Bank Clearinghouse Settlement Sheet
INSTITUTE NATIONAL BANK
Clearinghouse Settlement Sheet

(Column 1) Bank	*(Column 2)* C.H. Debit*	*(Column 3)* C.H. Credit*
First National Bank	$153,498.72	$140,321.55
First State Bank	92,200.65	116,902.84
Erehwon Trust Co.	85,116.07	90,787.21
Farmers State Bank	120,648.93	103,165.30
Mechanics National Bank	101,009.23	98,545.29
	$552,473.60	$549,722.19

* Column 2 (clearinghouse debit) represents the dollar value of checks presented to the banks named for payment and the total of this column is Institute National Bank's *gross credit* in the settlement. Column 3 (clearinghouse credit) represents the checks presented by the other banks drawn on Institute National Bank, and the column total is that bank's *gross debit* in the settlement.

An individual bank's clearinghouse settlement sheet. Each participating bank prepares a similar record.

The clearinghouse manager (or whoever is responsible for the overall settlement) then receives from each settlement clerk a memorandum with the following information:

1. His bank's clearing credit—the total amount of checks presented *by* his bank drawn on the other participating banks;

2. His bank's clearing debit—the total amount of checks presented *to* his bank by the other participating banks; and

3. The settlement clerk's calculation of the net balance due *to* or *from* his bank as a result of the exchange. (See Exhibit 7.)

Exhibit 7: Individual Bank Clearing Summary

INSTITUTE NATIONAL BANK

Total Debits	Total Credits
$549,722.19	$552,473.60
	2,751.41
	Net Credit

An individual bank's clearing summary. From such summaries received from each settlement clerk, the clearinghouse proof is prepared.

The clearinghouse then prepares a summary of the entire exchange; if the total of column 3 (due to clearinghouse) equals the total of column 4 (due from clearinghouse), the settlement is completed. If the totals of these two columns do not agree, an error has probably been made by one of the settlement clerks in listing or adding the amounts of packages received. In any event, the error or errors must be located and corrected before the settlement clerks are dismissed.

Obviously, if a bank's clearing debit exceeds its clearing credit, it owes the difference to the settlement. If the opposite is true, it receives the difference from the settlement. (See Exhibit 8).

Exhibit 8: Clearinghouse Proof

Bank	Balance Due C.H.	Bank Debit	Bank Credit	Balance Due Bank
Institute National Bank	—	549,722.19	552,473.60	2,751.41
First National Bank	6,522.39	541,632.55	535,110.16	—
First State Bank	—	441,852.29	447,724.15	5,871.86
Erehwon Trust Co.	—	382,296.79	398,155.70	15,858.91
Farmers State Bank	5,623.43	477,481.45	471,858.02	—
Mechanics National Bank	12,336.36	446,859.97	434,523.61	—
TOTALS	24,482.18	2,839,845.24	2,839,845.24	24,482.18

The Clearinghouse Proof. The two outer columns and the two inner columns must be in balance. Note that while checks valued at more than $2,800,000 have cleared in this hypothetical settlement, the actual payments by Debit Balance Banks (distributed among Credit Balance Banks) are less than 1 percent of the total amount involved.

The actual liquidation or settlement of the net balances can be handled in various ways. The most common and convenient method of settlement is through accounts carried by the participating banks in a nearby correspondent bank or on the books of the Federal Reserve bank or branch serving the territory. In the latter case, if a participating bank is not a member of the Federal Reserve System, arrangements can be made to settle its balances through the account of a member bank. To accomplish the settlement, the clearinghouse manager simply forwards a summary of each day's clearings to the common depository, and the net debit and credit balances are posted to the participating banks' accounts.

The superiority of a well-organized and efficient clearinghouse arrangement over the more haphazard method of collecting local checks by messenger should be obvious. A few bookkeeping entries each day can serve to settle the clearing of many thousands of checks in a simple operation, and as a glance at the clearinghouse summary vividly illustrates, the single *net* debit or credit balance paid or received by each bank represents only a small fraction of the total dollar volume of items cleared.

This rather detailed explanation should reveal the basics of a clearinghouse settlement. In many areas the operation has been further simplified, although the fundamentals are essentially the same. In some cities a Federal Reserve bank or branch provides the meeting place, sorts and delivers the packages, completes the settlement, and debits or credits, as required, member banks' reserve accounts. In other areas the settlement is computerized. Instead of completing its own settlement sheet, each bank provides input data for the computer (the dollar amount of checks delivered to other participating banks), which completes the settlement and gives each participant a printout detailing the settlement data.

Organization of a Clearinghouse Association

Since a clearinghouse association is a voluntary organization, local area banks may join the association or not as they see fit. Despite the obvious advantages, there are situations in which a bank, after careful consideration, perceives offsetting disadvantages in its particular case and elects not to join the group.

When such an organization is formed, the usual practice is to adopt a set of bylaws and to elect officers of the association from among the officers of the member banks. The clearinghouse officers serve without compensation; however, a clearinghouse manager may be appointed, in which case the manager, together with any other necessary staff employees, would be salaried.

A source of income is necessary to pay any salaries and to furnish and maintain quarters for the clearing operation. Such funds are usually provided by—

1. Membership fees;
2. Current assessments on members;
3. Fines imposed for violation of rules.

Membership fees are usually nominal, and the major source of income is current assessments based on a projected budget. After the budget has been adopted the amount required is prorated among the members on some equitable basis, such as the dollar volume of items cleared for a preceding period.

Few associations can operate efficiently without adopting certain rules and regulations to govern the conduct of their members, and clearinghouse groups are no exception. Fines are levied for such incidents as late arrivals for scheduled clearings, delays in clearings caused by errors in settlement sheet calculation, or other unseemly conduct on the part of messengers or settlement clerks that tends to obstruct or impair the efficiency of the clearing operation. In addition, rules must be established to govern the handling and adjustment of dishonored items.

Return Items

Since items cleared through a clearinghouse arrangement are cash items (mostly checks), it is not surprising that the "cash item principle" prevails. Each bank takes at face value the total amount appearing on packages presented to it by other participating banks and grants immediate, provisional credit to each presenting bank in the settlement. In the normal course of events, however, the packages will contain some items that cannot be paid by the drawee bank for one reason or another. Some may be "missorts" (items drawn on banks other than the receiving bank), while others may be dishonored for such reasons as insufficient funds, payment stopped, and so forth. Obviously, the provisional credit must be adjusted, and clearinghouse rules generally provide for the manner of handling return items and set time limits within which they must be received by the presenting bank or notice of intention to return an item given to the presenting bank. In some cases they are returned by messenger directly to the presenting bank and reimbursement received in the form of cash, bank draft, cashier's check, or provision for credit in the next day's clearing settlement. In larger cities, where volume is heavy, a special "reclamation clearing" (return item) may be held on the day following presentation, in which case a settlement similar to the regular clearing settlement provides the means of adjustment. With respect to time limits, a clearinghouse rule must conform to any state statutes dealing with the subject, such as the Uniform Commercial Code. The local rule may impose shorter time limits but may not extend the limit prescribed by law.

Potential Expansion of the Clearinghouse Principle

The original idea of clearinghouse exchanges and settlements was conceived many years ago. At first it was adopted by large metropolitan cities where the relatively high volume of local clearing items made its obvious advantages especially attractive. The ever increasing volume of checks soon led to the establishment of clearinghouses in more moderate sized cities, followed by the formation in rural areas of county-wide clearing facilities. In recent years the Federal Reserve System has been very active in sponsoring regional clearinghouses that embrace banks in two or more counties.

It is quite possible that the full potential of this simple but efficient arrangement has not yet been fully realized. Given improved transportation facilities, special communication networks, and the advantage of fully computerized settlements, even state-wide clearing possibilities are not unlikely. Certainly this or any other method that holds promise of eliminating or substantially reducing the volume of float in the banking system fully warrants serious consideration and experimentation.

Collection of Transit Items

Checks and other cash items drawn on banks or otherwise payable outside a depository bank's local area are called *transit items*. In most banks the department or unit responsible for presentation and collection of these out-of-town items is known as the *transit department,* although other names, such as country check department or remittance department, are frequently used. There is probably no other department in modern banks that varies so widely in organization, numbers of personnel, equipment, and operating methods.

In a small bank that handles a relatively small volume of out-of-town items the transit function is really a by-product of the proof function, and at the end of the day a single clerk may take all transit items, recap the control totals, drop them in an envelope, and mail them unsorted to a correspondent bank or a Federal Reserve bank.

In a large bank, particularly a correspondent bank, the transit department is a complex, highly organized operating unit. Transit checks, particularly those deposited by large corporations, must be sent directly or indirectly to innumerable cities, towns, and even isolated villages throughout the length and breadth of the continental United States, as well as to off-shore states, territories, and dependencies. The dollar volume handled daily by a moderately large bank runs into many millions. Therefore, it becomes extremely important to employ sophisticated, efficient methods designed to maximize the speed of the collection process (thus making funds more quickly available) while at the same time controlling the considerable costs involved in a complex operation.

An efficient transit manager keeps himself well posted as to current mail schedules and plane and train timetables, and he periodically checks on the reliability of the various modes of transportation. Unlike the smaller bank, the larger bank does not dispatch all items at one time at the end of the day. Depending on volume and destination, checks are dispatched at all hours of the day or night, with the objective of ensuring, as far as is practical, that each check will be presented at the earliest possible moment. Again, unlike the smaller bank, a large bank cannot limit its sendings to one or even a half dozen points. Depending on volume and destination, a large bank may develop sorting patterns covering 40, 50, or more separate sending points. Correspondent banks usually have account relationships with banks in all major cities, and the number of sending points depends to some extent on the number of such relationships. Furthermore, the sorting pattern used on Mondays through Thursdays may not be the same as the pattern used on Fridays, when the next presentation date is a weekend away. Not only that, but a sorting pattern used up to 2 p.m. on a given day might be replaced with an entirely different pattern after 2 p.m., because a deadline has been missed.

Since the available channels, time schedules, and sending points are almost infinite, the effective operation of a transit department requires considerable expertise. But this is a practical world and banking is a practical business. Complex sorting patterns and variable time schedules are not virtues in themselves. They must produce tangible values in improved efficiency, in better service, or in dollars.

Clearing Channels

In general, there are three principal channels through which transit items are collected:

1. By direct sending to the banks on which they are drawn or by which they are payable;

2. By depositing them in a correspondent bank;

3. By depositing them in a Federal Reserve bank or branch.

The third method is available only to members of the Federal Reserve System.

Direct Sending

The disadvantages of direct sending of transit items are somewhat similar to those of direct presentation of local items. Presentation of transit items is usually made by mail instead of by messenger. Obviously, direct sending results in the fastest possible presentation of an item, but the lack of an effective method of payment or remittance can partially or entirely nullify the benefit. For instance, where there is no interbank relationship, the drawee bank normally remits in the form of a bank draft payable to the sending bank. (A bank draft is a check drawn by a bank on one of its correspondent banks.) In certain circumstances, direct presentation is futile. Suppose a bank in Virginia sends items directly to a non-correspondent drawee bank in northern Illinois. The drawee bank might pay the items by mailing a draft drawn on its Chicago correspondent. Upon receipt of the remittance, the Virginia bank now knows that the individual cash items were honored but, as far as availability of funds is concerned, it now has an item that must travel almost the identical route to be presented for payment to the Chicago bank.

In addition to possible remittance problems, each non-correspondent direct sending point involves a separate mailing and the preparation of a separate cash letter. (A cash letter is an interbank transmittal letter which accompanies cash items sent from one bank to another. Where a correspondent relationship exists, involving regular daily sendings, the cash letter can be quite informal, often consisting merely of a tape listing of the amounts of the items enclosed, identified by the sending bank's indorsement stamp.) Obviously, where the daily dollar volume is small, the cost of many direct sendings in postage as well as clerical time would be prohibitive.

For these reasons direct sendings are useful and practical only in special circumstances, such as:

1. Where an account relationship exists between the two banks and the dollar volume warrants a separate cash letter.

2. Where either the depositor or the collecting bank has a definite interest in an unusually large dollar amount or special items of some kind.

3. Where a check, although handled as a cash item, may be accompanied by instructions to "wire advice of payment or nonpayment." (This is a courtesy that banks render one another in *single* isolated instances, although drawee banks do not normally advise payment of a cash item.)

Collecting Items Through Correspondent Banks

A correspondent bank relationship exists when one bank maintains an account with another bank. Large metropolitan banks customarily establish account relationships with other large banks in principal cities throughout the United States so that they can serve their larger customers by making payments and transferring funds with relative ease to any point in the nation. Usually, however, the term is applied to a large bank located in a major financial center that numbers among its depositors many smaller country banks to which it offers a wide variety of financial services. In this respect, a correspondent bank serves as a "bank for banks" by collecting transit items and collection items, offering investment analysis and advice, furnishing credit information, participating in large loans, assisting in international transactions, and rendering computerized data processing and other specialized banking and financial services that the smaller banks cannot provide for themselves.

Prior to the formation of the Federal Reserve System in 1913, correspondent banks provided the only practical facilities for collecting out-of-town items, although admittedly in a rather haphazard and inefficient manner. As further evidence of the benefits of healthy competition, the well-planned and effiicent Federal Reserve check collection system compelled correspondent banks to improve considerably the speed and efficiency of their own check collection services in order to retain the balances of their bank customers.

The correspondent bank system continues to handle a substantial volume of transit items and these banks take pride in the speed and flexibility with which they can handle items payable anywhere in the country. In many cases, due to the number of direct sending points to which they regularly dispatch cash letters, correspondent banks effectively can reduce the time required to collect items payable in specific areas. Furthermore, most correspondent banks will accept all of a smaller bank's transit items unsorted in a single package.

Settlement for transit items collected through a correspondent is facilitated by the account relationship. The smaller bank normally maintains an account with the larger bank, although in some cases the relationship is reciprocal, that is, each bank carries an account with the other. In general, the flow of checks goes from the smaller bank to the larger bank but, again, when warranted by volume, a return flow of checks to the smaller bank can be arranged. Thus, settlement can be effected by crediting the sending bank's account with the receiving bank or debiting the receiving bank's account at the sending bank. In the latter case, the debit entry usually is delayed to allow for the time the items are in transit. Although less frequently used, settlement can also be made by a remittance from the receiving bank, either in the form of bank draft or wire transfer.

For many years, correspondent bank relationships have been mutually beneficial. The balances maintained by the smaller banks are frequently more than sufficient to compensate for services rendered, while the correspondent is always available, at a moment's notice, to offer special services or to assist in solving a banking problem.

Routing Transit Items Through the Federal Reserve System

In the banking system as a whole, the largest percentage of transit items is handled by the Federal Reserve banks. As indicated previously, the earlier check collection methods employed by correspondent banks were far from satisfactory, and the constantly increasing use of checks as a means of settling business and personal transactions toward the end of the nineteenth century served to bring these shortcomings into sharper focus. Among other important considerations that pressed for banking and monetary reform and led to the passage of the Federal Reserve Act in 1913 was the very definite need for improved check collection facilities.

The Par Collection System

When the Federal Reserve System was established, there were two separate groups of banks in the nation—par banks and nonpar banks. A par bank is a bank that honors checks drawn on it at full face (par) value, no matter by whom presented. A nonpar bank deducts an *exchange charge* when remitting for checks drawn on it and presented by collecting banks. Over the years the number of nonpar banks has been dwindling, and there are very few still in existence.

An exchange charge should not be confused with a service charge, which is a charge collected by a bank from its depositors for banking services rendered. An exchange charge is not levied against customers, but against collecting banks that present items by mail.

Since checks drawn against demand deposits represent claims to our most common form of money and in fact form the bulk of our circulating medium of exchange, the Federal Reserve System has long held to the belief that checks should be accepted freely at face value. The System has always vigorously opposed the practice of levying exchange charges. Whatever reasons may be offered to justify such charges, it is difficult to escape the conclusion that the practice represents a discriminatory depreciation of some dollar claims.

In 1916 the Federal Reserve System established its par collection system, which is an extensive network composed of both member and nonmember banks. All member banks of the System *must* remit at par for checks payable in United States dollars, and those nonmember banks that voluntarily agree to do so are included in the par collection system. The 12 Federal Reserve banks, their 24 branches, member banks, and participating nonmember banks together form the most extensive check collection system in the world. It is strictly a par collection system; consistent with its objection in principle to the levying of exchange charges, the System does not permit Federal Reserve banks or branches to accept nonpar items for collection, either as cash items or as noncash (collection) items.

Settlement for Items Collected Through the Federal Reserve System

Member banks that avail themselves of the check collection services of the System deposit checks in a Federal Reserve bank or branch in much the same manner as any bank's own customers deposit cash items for immediate credit. Because a member bank's balances with the Federal Reserve bank of its district involves its legal reserves, however, the deposit credits are handled in a somewhat more complicated manner.

All banks are required by law to maintain reserves against their deposit liabilities. Banks that are not members of the Federal Reserve System must observe the laws of the state in which they are domiciled and by which they were chartered. Banks that are members of the System must keep the bulk of their reserves in the form of noninterest-bearing balances (available funds) with the Federal Reserve bank or branch that serves the area in which they are located. In calculating their legal reserves member banks are permitted to include coin and currency in their vaults.

Availability Schedules

Each Federal Reserve bank publishes a "Schedule of Availability of Credits" for the member banks of its district. These schedules define the time limits or closing hours for the receipt of deposits of various types of cash items, according to where they are payable, and the period of time required before specific items deposited are considered to be available funds. There are three classes of availability:

1. Immediately available items;
2. One-day deferred availability items;
3. Two-day deferred availability items.

Checks classified as immediately available are credited on the day deposited to the *reserve account* of the depositing member bank and qualify as available funds in calculating the bank's legal reserve requirement. The one-day and two-day items are credited to a deferred availability account and thus do not qualify as available legal reserves. However, the deferred availability balances are automatically transferred to the depositing bank's *reserve account* at the expiration of the deferred period.

It should be noted that the maximum time of deferred availability by any Federal Reserve bank is two days. To facilitate settlements and the calculation of legal reserves, the Federal Reserve System absorbs all float (uncollected funds) beyond two days, even though in many cases it could take three or four days for actual presentation and collection of a particular item, depending on the respective geographic location of the depository member bank and the drawee bank.

A small or medium-sized bank might deal exclusively with the Federal Reserve bank or branch in which it maintains its reserve account. A larger bank handling a sizable volume of transit items might find it worthwhile to make as many as 36 sorts and send a separate cash letter to each Federal Reserve bank or branch of the system. When cash letters are sent directly to Federal Reserve banks or branches in other districts, a copy of the cash letter is sent to the local Federal Reserve bank or branch, which credits the sending member bank's reserve or deferred account according to the applicable availability schedule.

Obviously, direct sending to all 36 Federal Reserve banks and branches as opposed to sending all items to a single bank could result in a considerable increase in the dollar amount of available funds, but there are many other factors to be considered by the transit manager.

For one thing, the daily average volume handled, both in item count and dollar amount, are important considerations, and the cost in clerical time in making so many additional sorts and in preparing the necessary cash letters must be weighed against the probable value of increased availability. The proximity to the local Federal Reserve bank must be considered. Deposits hand-delivered to the local Reserve bank within the prescribed time limits would be processed the same day, and the items deposited might be received by the other Federal Reserve banks and branches at the same time as direct sendings.

Another consideration is the sorting requirements of the local Federal Reserve bank. Where the daily average number of items does not exceed 300, Federal Reserve banks as a rule will accept them unsorted in a single cash letter. For larger volumes, sorting in the various availability groups is encouraged, with a separate cash letter for each group. In the case of unusually large volume, Federal Reserve banks reserve the right to require further sorting within the availability groups.

Processing of Collection Items

In most banks the responsibility for handling collection items is delegated to a special department or at least to specially trained personnel. As a rule, departments or units that customarily handle cash items (proof, clearings, transit, and so forth) are not equipped to handle the more complex and individualized collection items. There are several good reasons for the complete separation of cash item and collection item processing.

In the first place, the operating procedures are quite different. Cash items are handled in bulk, in large groups or packages under total dollar control, while collection items must be handled individually. Only in rare cases can a number of similar items be handled as a group. In the second place, the accounting procedures are different. As soon as cash items are received, accounting entries are generated. Deposit credits increase the bank's liabilities (demand deposits) and the coin, currency, and other items deposited become bank assets (cash and due from banks). By contrast, the receipt of collection items does not ordinarily generate any entries. In due time, entries will be made if the item is paid, but the accounting process is initiated by the payment received rather than by the deposit itself. For these reasons a separate department or unit to handle collection items is almost a practical necessity.

Types of Collection Items

While there is an infinite variety of collection items, in general they may be divided into three broad classifications:
1. Drafts, with or without valuable documents attached;
2. Promissory notes and acceptances;
3. Miscellaneous items.

Drafts

A *draft* is an order to pay that involves three principal parties:
1. The drawer, who is the party issuing the order;
2. The drawee, the party to whom the order is addressed; and
3. The payee, the party to whom payment is to be made.

A check is an order to pay and thus falls within the broad definition of a draft. But a check is a special kind of draft, in that the drawee must be a bank and the instrument must be payable on demand.

Ordinary drafts, like checks, are most commonly used in connection with the sale of goods or merchandise, but the roles played by the drawer and payee are reversed. For instance, when a person buys something it is common practice to give the seller a check in payment. In this case, the drawer of the check is the *purchaser,* the drawee is the bank on which the check is drawn, and the bank is instructed (ordered) to pay the *seller.* When an ordinary draft is used, the drawer is the *seller,* and the drawee is the *purchaser.* In other words, the drawer (seller) orders the drawee (buyer) to pay the party presenting the draft. The drawer (seller) may name anyone he chooses as payee (someone to whom he may be indebted), or he may name himself as payee, for obviously the seller is entitled to control payment of the proceeds of his sale. In the latter case the drawer-payee simply indorses the draft for deposit to his account, thus transferring to his bank his title to the instrument.

The ordinary draft can be quite useful in commercial transactions since it provides a means of protecting both the seller and the buyer. To illustrate this point, it will be helpful to describe a few of the more common types of commercial transactions.

Manufacturers of durable goods, such as refrigerators, washing machines, sewing machines, lawn mowers, sell their products to distributors and retailers all over the country. A familiar problem arises: Should the manufacturer ship his merchandise to a buyer located 1500 miles away on a promise that a check will be mailed when the merchandise has been received? Or should the buyer forward his check on the promise that when it has been received and collected the merchandise will be delivered?

The versatile draft solves the problem for both parties. The manufacturer delivers the merchandise to a railroad, trucking company, or other carrier for transportation to the city or town in which the buyer is located and receives a special kind of receipt called a *bill of lading.* A bill of lading is more than an ordinary receipt; it is a *title document*— that is, it gives the holder, to whom it has been duly negotiated or assigned, the right to present the document to the transportation company and claim the merchandise as the legal owner. The manufacturer draws a draft on the buyer and, after attaching the bill of lading to the draft, deposits it in his bank with instructions to surrender the bill of lading to the drawee (buyer) *only* upon certain conditions, usually upon receipt of payment in full of the draft. Thus the manufacturer is assured that the buyer cannot obtain the merchandise until his conditions are met, while the buyer knows that as soon as he complies with the terms of the sale agreement he will receive legal evidence of ownership of the merchandise and the ability to demand delivery from the carrier.

The terms of the draft may vary depending on the agreement between the buyer and seller. The draft may be drawn payable "at sight," that is, payable on presentation and demand; or it may be made payable a certain number of days after presentation or after the issue date of the draft. Where credit terms are extended, it is customary for the drawer (seller) to authorize the presenting bank to surrender the bill of lading upon *acceptance* of the draft.

Acceptance is a legal term. When a time draft (one not payable on demand) is presented to the drawee, he is not immediately obligated to make payment. But under the law, the drawer may instruct the presenting bank to insist on the drawee's "acceptance," by which the drawee acknowledges the right of the drawer to issue the order to pay and promises to pay the instrument when it falls due. Legally, a draft is "accepted" when the drawee simply signs his name on the instrument. As a rule, however, the drawee inscribes the word "accepted" vertically across the face of the instrument, indicates the date of payment (and perhaps the place of payment), and then signs his name. Refusal by a drawee to "accept" a properly presented time draft is the equivalent of dishonor.

It should be noted that by "acceptance" the drawee, in legal effect, converts the drawer's *order to pay* into the drawee's *promise to pay*. If the draft had its origin in the sale of goods, the accepted document is known as a *trade acceptance.*

Another example of this type of collection item is found in commercial transactions involving staple commodities, such as cotton, coffee, grain, soybeans, frozen foods. Because of their bulk and sometimes perishable nature, many commodities are stored in warehouses as soon as they are produced, and sales by farmers, processors, brokers and dealers are rarely accompanied by physical bulk delivery of the actual commodity. Instead, delivery is accomplished by negotiation or assignment of *warehouse receipts,* which, like bills of lading, are title documents. In essence, a warehouse receipt evidences an agreement between the warehouseman and the person storing the goods whereby the former acknowledges receipt of the merchandise, agrees to furnish proper safe storage (depending on its nature) and to release all or part of the merchandise to the holder of properly negotiated or assigned warehouse receipts and payment of storage charges. Thus, dealers in many commodities also find the draft a useful instrument, in this case by attaching warehouse receipts to a draft drawn by the seller and naming the buyer as the drawee.

The draft can be used in a great variety of commercial transactions, wherever it is advantageous to have *delivery* and *payment* for merchandise sold take place simultaneously. Brokers, dealers, and investors frequently use *security drafts* (drafts to which stock certificates or bonds are attached) as a means of protecting two parties dealing at arm's length. Mortgages, deeds, and savings account passbooks are frequently delivered "draft attached." Jewelry, precious gems, rare books, and art objects have been delivered and payment assured through the use of drafts.

Sometimes, even "reverse" transactions are handled by the collection department. That is, instead of a delivery of something being made upon receipt of a payment in money, a payment will be made in exchange upon delivery of the item. The most common example of this type of transaction is probably the distribution of legacies under the will of a deceased person. There are releases to be signed, and if the beneficiaries are located in several different states the executors frequently deliver to a local bank prepared releases with checks payable to the legatees, with instructions to deliver the checks only after identification of the respective payees and the signing of the releases.

Promissory Notes and Acceptances

A promissory note is a promise to pay as opposed to an order to pay and, as previously indicated, an acceptance by the drawee of a draft has the legal effect of converting an order to pay to a promise to pay. Most promises to pay are entirely unconditional, although not necessarily so in the case of a non-negotiable instrument. When a promise to pay is signed and issued, presumably the promissor has already received whatever consideration is involved; and when a draft is accepted, delivery of title documents attached to the draft in all probability motivated the execution of the acceptance. Thus, notes and acceptances are for the most part clean documents, that is, with no documents attached. Generally, the instructions that accompany this type of collection item are very similar to those that accompany cash items. They are to be presented for payment when due and returned promptly if dishonored. For these reasons, notes and acceptances are relatively easy to handle and seldom involve serious problems other than to see that they are properly presented at maturity.

Miscellaneous Items

The wide range of miscellaneous collection items is so diverse that it would be futile to attempt to categorize them or discuss their individual problems. Some are quite uncomplicated, such as matured bonds and coupons of lesser known corporations and purely local municipalities. Suffice it to say that these, like the other more familiar types, require careful individual attention by experienced personnel.

City and Country Collections

Depending on volume, a collection department may provide separate units to handle city (local) collections and country (out-of-town) collections.

It must be remembered that all collection items are not received from local depositors. City collections are most frequently received from out-of-town banks because the drawee, payor, or other party involved is a local company or business. In many cases, the local bank simply notifies the person to whom the item is to be presented that it has been received and requests that payment be made and the item picked up at a collection teller's window. Or city collections may be presented by messenger at the office of the party obligated.

Most country collection items, however, are received from local depositors and are payable or collectible at out-of-town points. These items may be dispatched by first class mail, airmail, or special delivery depending on the urgency required, either to a correspondent located in the general vicinity of the party to whom it is to be presented, or to a non-correspondent with the request to remit by bank draft or wire transfer. If the local bank is a member of the Federal Reserve System, it may also use the facilities of the System's noncash collection service.

Settlement for Collection Items

The precise manner of settlement or payment for collection items is of considerable importance. Cash items receive immediate but *provisional credit*. The credit will be reversed by the depository bank and all other banks in the collection chain if the item is dishonored, provided only that such action and notice thereof is timely. But since credit is not extended for collection items until actual payment has been received, the depositor and any intermediate collecting bank have the right to assume that notification of payment, by credit or otherwise, is *final* and *irrevocable*. This places a special burden on all who handle collection items and particularly on the presenting bank.

It is characteristic of collection items that when they are paid a written advice of payment is sent by the presenting bank to its indorser, and each indorser in turn notifies the immediate prior indorser. Any party receiving such an advice of payment can regard it as conclusive.

The presenting bank faces a problem when a payment is received from a non-depositor. It is customary to require payment in cash, certified check, or official bank check. If the presenting bank accepts a plain check, sends its advice of payment, and later finds that the check is uncollectible, it must stand the loss. If the party making payment is a depositor and the balance in the account is sufficient to cover the amount involved, the presenting bank can safely accept an uncertified check, even if drawn on another bank. If it chooses, it can place a hold on the depositor's account to protect itself.

For banks other than the presenting bank the problem is practically nonexistent. Where the services of another bank are used, whether it is a correspondent or a non-correspondent, there is always the remote possibility that the bank may be declared insolvent and close its doors, *after* an advice of payment has been sent but *before* the corresponding credit has been processed or a remittance draft has been paid. This would be serious *only* if the bank knew or had reason to know of the unsound condition of the collecting bank agent. The Uniform Commercial Code (Sec. 4-202) requires only that a bank use "ordinary care" in the selection of qualified agents. Nevertheless, negligence in this respect might compel the bank to accept such a loss.

Collection Department Records

Collection department records are necessarily much more detailed and complicated than the records of a department handling cash items. In many cases, the letter of transmittal that accompanies cash items (cash letter) may be no more elaborate than a tape listing with an identifying stamp. A collection item may be outstanding for a longer period of time and, when an advice as to its fate is not received in reasonable time, it is often necessary to inquire as to its status. For this reason, it is necessary for each bank to keep a detailed description of each item together with a complete record of the instructions that accompanied it. Very often the instructions are so detailed that a separate letter is warranted.

The handling of a collection item internally may require most if not all of the following writings:

1. A receipt for the depositor;
2. A forwarding letter of transmittal;
3. A debit entry (where payment is received in the form of a credit to an account in another bank or a debit to an account in the handling bank) ;
4. A credit entry (to credit the depositor's account) ;
5. A credit advice (to notify the depositor) ;
6. An audit copy (for control purposes) ;
7. One or more file copies (for the department's files) ;
8. A tracer (where necessary to check on the status of a collection item).

Years ago, banks learned that all of these writings could be produced in one effort by the use of multicopy forms. These forms are especially designed to meet the needs of individual banks. They can provide space for the destination of the item, the name of the depositor, name of the drawee or payor, due date, date sent for collection, amount, place payable, description of any documents attached, special instructions, and the sending bank's collection number.

It is customary for banks to assign a special collection number to each collection item they handle. Thus a single collection item may have as many as *three* different collection numbers, assuming that there is an intermediate collecting bank as well as a presenting bank in addition to the depository bank. All correspondence with reference to a collection item should refer to the appropriate bank collection number.

The several copies of the completed multicopy forms are used as required for each step of the procedure. For instance, when the item is dispatched the letter of transmittal goes with the item; file copies are placed in the appropriate file; the audit copy goes to the audit department; and the debit and credit entries together with the advice of credit are kept in a pending file until payment or notice of non-payment is received. In the latter case, of course, unneeded copies are destroyed.

Exhibit 9. Typical Collection Department Multicopy Form

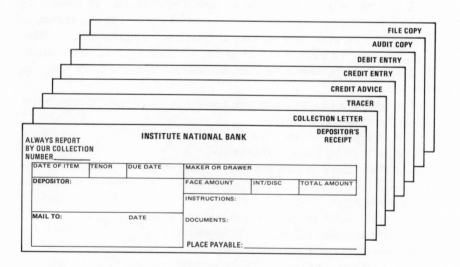

This form is for illustrative purposes only, to show how a single typing can produce all essential records. Whether a bank uses a 6-copy, an 8-copy, or a 10-copy form and the purpose of each copy depends on its own particular needs. For instance, many banks include an audit copy; others have different methods of audit control.

Instructions

Mention has been made of the necessity of obtaining adequate instructions at the outset. This point warrants further emphasis. Obviously, the extent and complexity of the instructions depend on the nature of the items, and they can cover so many possible events and contingencies that it is impractical to attempt to provide a meaningful list. In the case of documentary drafts, it is absolutely essential to obtain clear instructions as to delivery of the documents. Are documents to be delivered against receipt, or upon acceptance of the draft, or only upon payment? In the event of non-payment, should the item and the attached documents be returned promptly or held for further instructions? Is telegraphic advice of payment or non-payment required? If documents represent title to merchandise or commodities, and payment is refused, should the shipment remain in the carrier's possession subject to demurrage charges, returned to the drawer of the draft, sold at the best local market price, or properly stored pending further instructions? Whatever the instructions are, they must be faithfully carried out. Banks in the collecting chain are agents or sub-agents of the depositor. Should failure to exercise ordinary care in following instructions result in a loss, the depository bank could become liable for the loss.

Collection Charges

Service charges for handling collection items vary with the type and complexity of the transaction, but they are reckoned in dollars per item rather than in pennies, as in the case of cash items. In addition, charges are made to compensate for out-of-pocket expenses, such as postage, insurance, demurrage.

Banks render a very valuable service to the business and commercial communities through the competent performance of well-trained personnel in the collection department. Handling the many varieties of collection items involves responsibility, careful attention to detail, and strict compliance with the depositor's instructions. It is not surprising that the cost of handling a collection item greatly exceeds the cost of handling a cash item.

Considering the huge amount of money involved, an efficient system of collecting cash items is of the utmost importance to the depository bank.

There are a number of channels available for dispatching items to their respective places of payment, but sometimes the most direct channel may prove to be the most costly. In reconciling the elements of speed and cost, the volume handled is often the deciding factor, since the number of items varies inversely with the cost per item.

Prompt presentation of collection items is also important. However, the necessity for individual handling and closer scrutiny of items and any attached documents, together with the more detailed records that must be kept, tends to slow the presentation process somewhat.

Questions Based on This Chapter

1. What three factors must be considered in selecting a channel for collecting transit items?

2. Briefly describe the advantages of a clearinghouse arrangement for the collection of local items?

3. What is a nonpar item? Why do Federal Reserve banks refuse to handle nonpar items?

4. Among the documents sometimes attached to drafts are bills of lading and warehouse receipts. Briefly describe the nature of these documents.

Chapter 8

The Deposit Function

Part III: Savings Accounts and Other Time Deposits

Purposes of This Chapter:

1. To describe the nature of savings accounts and other interest-bearing time deposits.

2. To distinguish between savings-type and investment-type deposits.

3. To discuss briefly the terms of a time deposit contract, particularly with reference to the payment of such deposits before maturity.

Contrasted with demand deposits, time deposits actually represent temporarily stored or deferred purchasing power—money not needed for current expenses that the depositor intends to leave with the bank for a certain period of time. On the other hand, demand deposits represent money in motion—the principal means of payment immediately available to cover current operating expenditures of governments, businesses, and individuals. In short, demand deposits are a very substantial part of the nation's working capital.

Because of the nature of time deposits, banks are permitted to pay interest on such funds, but only if the depositor makes a binding commitment that limits or could limit the right to make withdrawals on demand. There are many different types of time deposits, ranging from the familiar savings account to the sophisticated negotiable time certificate of deposit, but all types require a definite agreement between the bank and the depositor, the terms of which must conform to applicable laws and regulations.

Savings-Type Deposits vs. Investment-Type Deposits

Perhaps the most important segment of the time-deposit category that involves the greatest number of depositors, although not necessarily the greatest number of dollars, is the savings account. For the most part the balances carried in savings accounts represent the gradual accumulation of personal income over a period of time—that portion of the income produced by the depositor's own investment of capital or labor (or both) set aside for future use. Savings deposits, particularly those of individuals, traditionally have exhibited a decided tendency toward gradual expansion over long periods of time and a considerably greater degree of stability than demand deposits. These characteristics are a natural consequence of the fact that individuals' savings accounts generally represent longer-range thrift objectives of the depositors, such as purchasing a car, or a major appliance, or providing college education for children.

In sharp contrast, at the other end of the scale, many time deposits represent temporarily idle funds of wealthy individuals, commercial organizations, or other large investors. This type of time deposit frequently represents much larger sums of money for temporary investment rather than the gradual accumulation of small sums with a long-range purpose in mind. The large investor-depositor has many more channels available for the profitable employment of idle funds and is not particularly interested in whatever convenience a local bank might offer. Such funds therefore seek the highest rate of return wherever it is available. From the bank's viewpoint, investment-type deposits are much more fluid. They can flow into banks or be drained out of banks in sizable amounts, depending on how competitive bank rates are with other available money market rates at any given time.

Between these two extremes there are other types of time deposits which, in varying degrees, have the characteristics of both savings accounts and short-term investments.

Legal Background

The banking industry is subject to a considerable degree of control by both state and federal governments, and there are many regulations at both levels specifically directed toward the savings and time-deposit areas of banking. With respect to demand deposits, the laws and regulations are relatively clear in that they simply prohibit the payment of interest on this class of bank deposits, but those affecting the payment of interest on savings and other time deposits are more complicated.

At the federal level, the Congress has placed much of the responsibility for the regulation of interest-bearing accounts in the hands of the Board of Governors of the Federal Reserve System. But other federal authorities also are involved as their areas of regulation overlap. Thus the Board of Governors supervises primarily banks that are members of the Federal Reserve System and the Comptroller of the Currency also has jurisdiction over national banks, while the Federal Deposit Insurance Corporation has the power to regulate insured banks. Although there are specific areas of control where the regulations of these three federal bodies are not precisely identical, in most respects there is a substantial degree of uniformity. In fact, any other condition would be rather incongruous, since a federally-chartered national bank, for instance, is under the direct supervision of the Comptroller of the Currency, but must be an insured member of the Federal Reserve System and thus subject to the regulations of all three authorities. Presumably, if regulatory provisions differ, a national bank would be bound by the most restrictive.

Without question, the most far-reaching regulation governing time deposit accounts is the Board of Governor's Regulation Q. Its provisions apply to virtually all the nation's banks since the comparable rules of the Federal Deposit Insurance Corporation are practically identical.

At the state level also there is some overlapping of laws and regulations. A state-chartered bank is governed primarily by the laws of the state from which it received its charter. Yet if it is a member of the Federal Reserve System and thus necessarily an insured bank, it is subject also to the control of the applicable federal bodies. Only a non-member, noninsured bank is governed solely by state laws and regulations. Fortunately state member banks seem to have little difficulty with this situation, although the general rule is that state laws and regulations can be more restrictive but not more liberal than the corresponding federal regulation. For instance, state member banks are not permitted to pay higher rates of interest on time and savings deposits than the maximum rates allowed by the laws of the state in which they are located, even if such rates are lower than those permitted by Regulation Q.

Regulation Q

It should be noted that Regulation Q is not the fountainhead of all restrictions with respect to savings and time deposits. The basic restrictions are found in Section 19 of the Federal Reserve Act in which the Congress authorized the Board of Governors of the Federal Reserve System "to prescribe such regulations as it may deem necessary to effectuate the purposes of this section and to prevent the evasion thereof." The Act itself provides that—

1. "No member bank shall, directly or indirectly, by any device whatsoever, pay any interest on any deposit which is payable on demand";

2. "No member bank shall pay any time deposit before its maturity except under such conditions and in accordance with such rules and regulations as may be prescribed by the said Board" [of Governors]; and

3. No member bank shall "waive any requirement of notice before payment of any savings deposit except as to all savings deposits having the same requirement."

Any change in these basic restrictions would require action by the Congress in the form of recision of or amendment to Section 19 of the Federal Reserve Act. It is the duty of the Board of Governors to *administer* these broad mandates, and in this connection the Board is specifically authorized and directed, among other things, to define the terms used in the legislation, to determine what constitutes the payment of interest, to prescribe maximum rates of interest for time and savings deposits having different maturities, and even to regulate the manner in which rates of interest may be advertised and accounts solicited.

Thus, Regulation Q is not in itself the cause of its restrictions, but rather the effect of legislative directives. An examination of its provisions reveals two basic legislative objectives:

1. To recognize, as did the Congress, the difference between savings-type deposits and investment-type deposits and to encourage, by means of less burdensome restrictions, the depositors of smaller sums whose principal motivation is thrift.

2. To preserve the sanctity of time-deposit contracts by imposing more stringent restrictions on depositors of larger sums whose primary purpose is to secure a more profitable short-term investment and to prevent any depositor from repudiating with impunity the obligations of a legal contract while at the same time seeking to retain the benefits offered in exchange for those obligations.

Savings Accounts

Regulation Q not only distinguishes savings accounts from other time accounts but it specifically lists the types of depositors for whom member banks may open savings accounts. Stated simply, savings accounts may not be opened for any profit-making organization. Eligible depositors include one or more individuals, as well as organizations that have identifiable individual participants or beneficiaries and corporations, associations, and other organizations operated primarily for religious, philanthropic, charitable, educational, fraternal, or other smilar purposes, but not operated for profit.

For example, savings accounts may be maintained by a charitable or religious order, a trade association, a club, a labor union, a charitable fund such as a Community Chest, a university, or a college. On the other hand, funds of municipalities and other public bodies may not be deposited in a savings account, except those of school districts, which qualify under the "educational" provision.

Regulation Q also provides that member banks *must reserve the right to require at least 30 days' notice* for the withdrawal of all or any part of a savings account. However, member banks are not obliged to enforce this right to require notice and may permit unlimited withdrawals on demand, providing that the privilege is offered on a nondiscriminatory basis and is made available to *all* of the banks' savings account depositors. Similarly, a member bank may partially enforce its right, by requiring 30 days' notice for the withdrawal of amounts over a certain figure (say, $1,000, $5,000), but such restrictions cannot be imposed on a selective basis and must apply equally to all savings depositors.

Like any other time deposit, a savings account must be supported by a contract or agreement binding on both the bank and the depositor. The terms need not be contained in a formal document signed by the two parties, but they must be expressed in writing and the writing must be delivered to the depositor by the bank when the account is opened. For instance, where the normal savings passbook is used, the terms of the contract (specifically including the fact that the bank reserves the right to require notice for the withdrawal of all or any part of the deposit) are printed in the passbook.

Acceptance of Savings Accounts and Savings Account Deposits

The basic procedures applicable to the establishment of demand-deposit accounts apply with equal force to the opening of savings accounts.

With few exceptions, most savings-account deposits are cash-item deposits; thus the same bank-depositor relationship is involved as in the case of demand-deposit accounts. The savings-account depositor also receives immediate (provisional) credit for items deposited, and the deposit credit will be reversed if a deposited item is dishonored. Obviously, it is no less important to identify savings-account depositors and to establish the authority of persons who intend to sign for withdrawals in other than their individual capacity. Also, in any case where periodic deposits of checks are received the bank relies heavily on the warranties of its depositor-indorser regardless of the type of account involved, and it must be satisfied, at the time the account is opened, that it is justified in assuming this exposure.

After the account has been opened, those who accept savings deposits have responsibilities identical to those who accept demand deposits. The teller is responsible for the amount of cash deposited and for the genuineness of coin and currency. Financial instruments must be eligible for handling as cash items and must be indorsed by the depositor. Finally, there is the ever-present need for alertness with respect to *potentially* dangerous irregularities, particularly where items are payable to a name other than the title of the account to which they are to be credited.

A classification of savings accounts by type does not greatly differ from a similar classification of demand accounts, viz:

1. Individual

2. Joint, in the names of two or more persons with or without the right of survivorship

3. Fiduciary accounts (where beneficiaries can be identified and are themselves eligible as savings account depositors)

4. Organization accounts (corporations, clubs, associations, school districts, and others) not operated for profit.

Closing of Savings Accounts

Any concern a bank may have with respect to the closing of a savings account by other than the depositor would be the same as in the case of a demand deposit account and should be handled in much the same manner, with perhaps one exception. In the eyes of the law, physical possession of the savings account passbook of a deceased depositor may have considerable significance and raises the question of whether the delivery of the passbook by the depositor creates a presumption that the depositor intended to bequeath the balance in the account to the possessor in the event of the depositor's death. In such circumstances, if a passbook is presented to a bank by someone claiming the balance in the account of a deceased depositor as a bequest evidenced by delivery of the passbook, legal counsel should be consulted and any applicable state laws or court decisions should be reviewed. It would seem that the presumption of an intended bequest could be rebutted by evidence to the contrary in most jurisdictions. In any event, such a claim should not be honored without the approval of counsel.

No-Passbook Savings Accounts

At one time, the passbook was a standard feature of all bank accounts, both demand and time accounts. In the days of hand-posting operations, it was not economically feasible for a bank to render periodic statements of account to their depositors. Therefore, the passbook was essential since it constituted the depositor's only record of the condition of his account.

The introduction in the early part of the century of mechanical posting machines and looseleaf ledgers changed the situation materially. Banks discovered that duplicate copies of a depositor's ledger record could be produced as a byproduct of the normal posting operation and that it actually would be cheaper to send depositors copies of the ledger record than to expend tellers' time at the window by posting and balancing passbooks.

Oddly enough, it is extremely difficult at times to persuade customers to change habits of long standing even when the change obviously benefits the depositor. Long after checking-account depositors were accustomed to receiving detailed monthly statements showing all debits, credits, and the resulting balances, a substantial number insisted on retaining their passbooks and presented them regularly for balancing. It took years to phase out the checking-account passbook.

Similarly, banks for some time have been in a position to render periodic statements covering savings accounts with considerable saving of expense. In attempting to phase out the savings passbook, many banks now offer "no-passbook" accounts or "statement" savings accounts. Because savings acounts are considerably less active with respect to deposits and withdrawals, statements can be rendered on a quarterly basis, but many banks combine both checking-account and savings-account activity on a single statement form that is furnished to the depositor each month.

If anything, the public shows more reluctance in giving up the savings-account passbook than they did the checking-account passbook. Even where banks pay a lower rate of interest on passbooks accounts, it is surprising how many depositors cannot be persuaded to switch to a no-passbook account. The change will eventually take place, but again it will take time.

As far as Regulation Q is concerned, a no-passbook account is no different from a passbook account, as long as both qualify as savings deposits as defined by the regulation, that is, the bank merely *reserves* the right to require notice for the withdrawal of funds, and the rate of interest paid does not exceed the maximum rate allowable for "savings deposits."

Other "Savings" Deposits

Banks offer a number of other so-called savings devices designed to meet the needs of regular savings department customers who want to receive a higher rate of return and are willing to commit their deposits definitely to a period of from 90 days to as long as six years. These depositors may have longer-range thrift objectives in mind and, in reaching for the higher rates, they assume some of the characteristics of investor-type depositors.

Regardless of the name a bank applies to an interest-bearing account, it is Regulation Q and not the bank that determines the true nature of the account. Thus, any deposit accepted by a bank under a contract that specifies a maturity or that definitely requires notice for the withdrawal of funds is a "time deposit-open account" and not a "savings deposit" as defined by the regulation. This is so whether it is a passbook or a no-passbook account. Such accounts have higher maximum rates of interest that normally increase as the commitment period lengthens.

Savings Certificates of Deposit

In addition to regular savings accounts, many banks offer "savings certificates" to those with longer-range objectives .This type of deposit is not recorded on the bank's books as a ledger account in the depositor's name but is evidenced by the certificate itself, which is a special kind of receipt. The bank keeps a copy of the receipt so that it has a record of the certificate number and the depositor's name.

The terms of the contract usually are printed on the face of the certificate and as a rule provide for a definite commitment by the depositor for a period of not less than 90 days in order to qualify for the higher rates. In this case too, despite the fact that they may be called "savings certificates," they are classified by Regulation Q as "time certificates of deposit" and not as "savings deposits."

Since savings certificates are designed for the regular savings-department customers, they are issued in small denominations, in some cases as low as $25. They can be issued in either negotiable or non-negotiable form, although the advantages of a negotiable savings certificate are somewhat obscure. Besides the danger of theft or loss of the certificate, opportunities for negotiation and sale at a fair price are rather limited in the absence of a competitive organized market for such certificates. Regulation Q requires the presentation and surrender of all time certificates of deposit in order to obtain payment.

Discount Savings Bonds

Another type of savings facility offered by some banks is the discount savings bond, which is not unlike a savings certificate of deposit. The discount bond differs mainly in the fact that the maturity value (principal and accumulated interest) is printed on the face of the instrument, rather than the actual purchase price as in the case of savings certificates. Thus a $50 bond maturing in five years might be sold at a discount price of $40, or whatever amount which with compound interest at a specified rate would equal $50 at maturity. This kind of savings instrument might appeal especially to those who with some long-term objective in mind might prefer to think in terms of the full value at maturity, rather than amounts currently set aside.

In many respects discount savings bonds resemble Series E United States Savings Bonds and like the more familiar E Bonds, they often may be redeemed before maturity according to a pre-stated schedule of increasing valuation, subject to the requirements of Regulation Q.

Other Time Accounts

Banks are permitted to accept, in addition to the savings-type accounts described above, other kinds of interest-bearing deposits on which they may pay higher rates of interest. In at least one respect the regulations governing other time deposits are less restrictive than those applicable to savings accounts but in most respects they are more restrictive. For instance, there are no restrictions as to the class of depositors eligible to open time-deposit accounts. Anyone and anybody, including corporations operating for profit, may utilize this banking service. While a profit-making association may not open a savings account, the average savings-account customer may place a portion of his long-term savings in the investment-type time deposit.

Time Deposits—Open Account

Although modern banks today are considerably more aggressive in soliciting investment-type funds, this kind of account is by no means new. For many years large banks have offered interest-bearing time accounts to profit-making organizations, other associations, and individuals having large sums to invest for a limited period of time. In fact, there has always been a definite need for this service, for at one time, savings banks and commercial banks with savings departments actually limited the amount that they would accept from a savings-account depositor in any calendar year. As strange as this may seem, bankers supported this policy with reasonable logic. They preferred the stability inherent in the level of savings deposits of thousands of small savers and were reluctant to accept large sums that could move out as quickly as they were received, thus producing potentially embarrassing changes in the level of the traditionally stable savings deposits.

These accounts were and still are commonly referred to as "time deposits-open account" and are more or less conventional deposit accounts carried on the bank's book as a ledger record in the depositor's name.

The regulations require that each such account must be supported by a written contract signed by the depositor. The contract may specify a definite maturity date or it may provide for the withdrawal of all or any part of the deposit subsequent to the receipt of notice of the depositor's intention. The period of notice may not be less than 30 days, but the contract may stipulate 60, 90, 180, or more days of notice. Thus a fixed maturity date can be established at the time the account is opened or a determinable maturity can be established at a later date by the depositor's action in giving the required *written* notice of intention to withdraw all or any part of the deposit.

Time Certificates of Deposit

In recent years, the time certificate of deposit has assumed a new and important role in our country's money markets. Certificates of deposit themselves are not new since banks have issued both time and demand certificates of deposit for many years, whenever it was desired to have the deposit obligation represented by a financial instrument instead of in the form of a ledger record. In some cases, this could be very helpful, for the depositor could place official evidence of his deposit with an escrow agent as a good faith gesture in connection with obligations assumed in a business contract. Obviously, it would be difficult to accomplish this purpose if the deposit existed in the form of a credit balance on a bank's ledgers.

In former years such certificates were issued in non-negotiable form; the depositor could assign his rights in the deposit to another, but, of course, the assignment would be subject to any defense or counterclaim the issuing bank might have against the original depositor.

The change in the importance of time certificates came about in 1961 when New York City bankers conceived the idea of issuing negotiable certificates in bearer form. This meant that under the Uniform Commercial Code, the depositor could at any time before maturity "negotiate" the certificate by simply selling it to another party, who in most cases would qualify as a holder in due course. The Code provides that a holder in due course takes a negotiable instrument free from any claims to it and immune from practically all defenses available to the issuing bank, so that the bank would be obliged to honor the certificate on presentation and surrender it at maturity.

The negotiable certificate of deposit became an important money market instrument. Necessarily, it has some limitations. Sellers and purchasers of money market instruments are accustomed to dealing in large, round amounts. There is a secondary market for such certificates, but to be readily salable the instruments normally must be in amounts of $1,000,000 and larger in multiples of $100,000, and made payable to bearer.

Thus the holder of a negotiable certificate of deposit need not have his money tied up until the maturity date: he can convert it into cash before maturity at anytime, without incurring the penalties imposed by Regulation Q, simply by offering it for sale. There may, however, be a market penalty. Money market instruments sell at current money market rates and, if the general level of interest rates should rise sharply after the certificate is purchased, the depositor may have to sell it at a substantial discount from face value. Sales transactions are handled in the same manner as bond market transactions, that is, time certificates are sold at a price per $100 unit (99, 100, 101, and so forth) plus accrued interest at the certificate rate to the date of settlement.

Time certificates of deposit can be exceedingly flexible instruments and various terms and conditions are possible. They can be issued in negotiable or non-negotiable form. As indicated earlier, savings-type certificates are usually issued in non-negotiable form, while the large round-amount certificates are normally negotiable. Some may be renewable at the option of the holder; others may be considered automatically renewed at maturity if not surrendered. The renewal privilege may be subject to a rate adjustment to the bank's then current rate for like certificates and would definitely be subject to any changes in the maximum rates established by Regulation Q.

Ordinarily, certificates are payable at a specified maturity date stated in the certificate, but they may be made payable at the expiration of a specified number of days after the date of the certificate or at the expiration of a specified number of days following the giving of written notice to the bank of the depositor's intention to withdraw the deposit,

135

in which case the date on which the required written notice is given establishes the maturity date. If variable maximum rates are in effect, the length of the required notice (which must be at least 30 days) controls the highest amount of interest that may be paid. Needless to say, all terms and conditions must conform with Regulation Q or other applicable regulations.

Withdrawal of Time Deposits Before Maturity

The general rule of Regulation Q and most other federal and state regulations is that *no time deposit may be paid before maturity,* and the rule applies whether a specific maturity date is fixed in the contract, fixed by the expiration of a specified number of days after the date of a certificate of deposit, established by the giving of written notice by the depositor as required by the terms of the contract, or established by a bank which exercises its right to require notice for the withdrawal of all or any part of a savings deposit.

As indicated earlier, one of the objectives of Regulation Q is to ensure that the contracts supporting interest-bearing time accounts will not be treated lightly either by the banks or by depositors, particularly since the terms of the contract could affect the allowable rate of interest paid. Any officer or employee of a member bank who acts in bad faith and willfully disregards Federal Reserve regulations would be subject to severe censure. The matter would be referred to the bank's board of directors, and that board would be required to state what punitive action was taken or to justify its decision not to take such action.

As far as the depositor is concerned, the Regulation recognizes that unpredictable events do occur and that absolutely rigid adherence to the contract terms could inflict disproportionate harm and damage on a person who executed the contract in good faith and then suddenly found himself confronted with a serious emergency. Thus the regulation provides an "escape door" for those who find their contractual obligation excessively burdensome, but it imposes certain penalties on those who choose this means of exit.

Understandably, attempts to press for the fullest possible compliance with contract obligations while providing relief for those who really need it have posed a difficult and vexing problem for the Board of Governors. Prior to July 5, 1973, Regulation Q provided for withdrawals *before maturity* in the event of an emergency where inability to withdraw a time deposit would work an "undue hardship" on the depositor. The Regulation required the depositor to file with the bank a written, signed description of the emergency condition (which the bank only could accept "in good faith") and also required a penalty of the forfeiture of three months *accrued and unpaid* interest. Unfortunately, the word *emergency* means different things to different people, and banks and their depositors rarely agreed on what did and what did not constitute a bonafide emergency. The regulatory authorities could do no more than lay down broad guidelines; the individual banks had to make the decisions. One thing was certain: the application of the emergency rule by thousands of different banks, affecting many more thousands of disappointed depositors in varying stages of irritation, anger, and frustration, hardly produced equitable results.

Regulation Q was amended effective July 5, 1973, and the hard-to-administer emergency clause was abandoned. The amended regulation shifts from the bank to the depositor the responsibility of deciding whether or not the seriousness of the need for withdrawal before maturity warrants the violation of his contractual obligation. Thus Regulation Q now takes the position that any depositor who entered into a time-deposit contract to obtain a higher rate of interest may, *at his sole option,* withdraw the deposit before maturity. But if the depositor elects to withdraw before maturity the rate of interest for the entire length of the contract must be reduced to the lower savings-account rate and three months' interest, whether or not already paid, must be forfeited. The forfeited interest is calculated at the lower savings account rate, but if excess interest has already been paid at the contract rate, such excess is deductible from the amount withdrawn. If the amount withdrawn has been on deposit for three months or less, *all* interest is forfeited.

The Regulation requires banks, when accepting deposits subject to the terms of a time-deposit contract, to furnish the depositor with a written statement describing fully and clearly the penalty provisions that apply should the deposit, contrary to the contract provisions, be withdrawn before maturity.

Payment of Interest on Time Deposits

Regulation Q sets the maximum rates a bank may pay on savings and time deposits. These vary with the amount deposited and the length of the depositor's commitment with respect to maturity. Generally, a time deposit must be committed for at least 90 days to earn more interest than savings deposits. No point would be served in quoting actual rates, because the rates and the deposited amounts to which they apply change from time to time. Such changes are published by the Board of Governors in the form of amendments to the applicable section of Regulation Q.

After the final date of maturity, a time deposit immediately converts into a demand deposit, and no interest may be paid on such deposit subsequent to the maturity date. When, as required by a time-deposit contract, written notice of the depositor's intention to withdraw has been given, at the expiration of the notice period such deposit becomes a demand deposit. No interest may be paid on it unless the depositor has meanwhile advised the bank in writing that the deposit will not be withdrawn pursuant to such notice.

Loans Secured by Savings and Other Time Deposits

Regulation Q provides that banks may make loans on the security of savings and other time accounts provided that the rate of interest on the loan is not less than 2 percent per annum more than the rate of interest paid on the deposit securing the loan. This restriction does not apply to savings accounts unless the bank has exercised its right to require notice for the withdrawal of savings deposits.

Tax Reporting

All banks, like other payers of interest, are required to report annually to the Internal Revenue Service all interest payments of $10 or more and to identify the recipient in each case by a taxpayer identification number. A copy of the report must be furnished to the taxpayer. As a rule, an individual's social security number serves as the taxpayer identification number. Those who do not have a social security number and others such as businesses, trusts, and estates are assigned a special identifying number upon application.

Penalties are provided both for banks which do not comply with these regulations and for depositors who fail to furnish their taxpayer identification number on request.

NOW Accounts

This text deals primarily with the operation of commercial banks, which are not permitted to honor checks (demand drafts) drawn against savings accounts except in isolated instances where, for example, an account is being closed. Yet, in this chapter dealing with savings deposits it would be remiss to fail to mention a comparatively new development that began with certain mutual savings banks and savings and loan associations.

Recent federal and state laws permit depositors in two states (New Hampshire and Massachusetts) to transfer funds from savings accounts by means of negotiable orders of withdrawal (NOWs). It would be surprising if the precedent thus set does not spread rapidly to other states.

Regulation Q has been amended to permit member banks in those states to accept NOWs. However, the use of NOWs is limited to depositors who generally qualify as savings depositors under the Regulation, and the rate of interest paid on such accounts is limited to the maximum allowable on savings deposits. The Regulation also limits the number of NOWs that can be accepted from a customer per year and restricts advertising and solicitation of such accounts to residents of the two states mentioned.

Savings accounts and other time deposits generally represent temporarily stored or deferred purchasing power, while demand deposits represent money immediately available for current operating expenses. For this reason, banks are permitted to pay interest on savings and time deposits but may not pay interest on demand deposits.

There are two distinct types of interest-bearing deposits—savings-type deposits and investment-type deposits, and the objectives of the depositors in each case are usually quite different.

The saver regularly accumulates small portions of current income over a long period of time, either with longer-term objectives in mind or perhaps to provide a fund to be used only in extreme emergencies. On the other hand, the objective of the investor is usually short-range— to obtain the highest rate of interest on temporarily idle, larger sums of money while awaiting opportunities for more permanent utilization.

Savings and other time deposits represent an important source of funds to commercial banks as well as to other types of financial institutions. It is not surprising that banks offer a wide variety of deposit contracts designed to appeal to both savers and temporary investors.

Questions Based on This Chapter

1. Distinguish between "savings-type" and "investment-type" deposits.

2. What are the basic objectives of Regulation Q?

3. Do the procedures involved in the opening of and the acceptance of deposits in a savings account differ materially from the procedures applied to demand deposit accounts?

4. What advantage accrues to the holder of a large, round amount negotiable certificate of deposit payable to bearer?

Chapter 9

The Deposit Function

Part IV: Devices and Systems—
Some Developments

Purposes of This Chapter:

1. To describe some older developments that have significantly contributed to the smooth processing of checks and other paper documents by depository banks.

2. To illustrate the tremendous breakthrough in paper handling made possible by Magnetic Ink Character Recognition (MICR).

3. To demonstrate the potential of electronic data processing as applied to proof operations and the check collection function.

This chapter, despite its title, is not intended to serve as a technological handbook for bank operating personnel. The development of devices and systems will be discussed in general terms, with primary emphasis on the objectives they were designed to achieve, and no attempt will be made to explore in comprehensive detail the many different methods used by banks in proving deposits or collecting cash items. There is no uniform system nor should there be, for the characteristics and needs of thousands of independent banks of assorted sizes and structures necessarily vary considerably. Much depends on the location and size of any particular bank and the volume and mix pattern of the items it customarily handles. Moreover, bankers, banking associations, and equipment manufacturers are constantly seeking new and improved methods, so that precise descriptions of how things are done at any point in time quickly tend to become obsolete.

On the other hand, certain developments in the areas of both equipment and techniques have proved to be of such significance in the process of collecting cash items that they are used by virtually all banks. It is on such devices and systems that attention will be concentrated.

Proof Machines

The acceptance of bank deposits is still a function of human expertise and experience. No machine or automatic mechanical procedure has yet been developed that can ring bells or flash red lights when an unlawful misappropriation or conversion of funds is concealed in an innocent-looking deposit.

After the acceptance of the deposit, there is the dual objective of proving the accuracy of the listing and addition of the deposited items (as submitted by the depositor) and establishing controls for the processing department.

Earlier manual methods of achieving these objectives have already been discussed and need not be repeated here, except to recall that three separate operations once considered necessary to accomplish the objectives were reduced by the "batch system" to only two operations. But the batch system was at best a semi-manual system. While wide-carriage adding machines facilitated the listing and totaling of sorted checks on batch journal sheets, the checks still had to be manually sorted as a separate preliminary step.

In due time the combined efforts of bank operating specialists and equipment manufacturers developed specially adapted proof machines designed to achieve all the purposes of the proof function in a single operation with very little additional effort. There are competing manufacturers, and the several sophisticated proof machines available may have somewhat different features, but all perform substantially in the following manner.

The operator works with an unsorted group of deposits, arranged in the same manner in which they were received, that is, each deposit intact (deposit slip with its deposited items). The amount of each deposited item is indexed in a standard keyboard, but after each indexing a special maneuver takes place. The operator depresses one of a number of selector keys and drops the item into a slot or pocket. In some models, the pocket is in a fixed location, and the selector key activates a signal which identifies the pocket. In others, the pockets are located in the perimeter of a circular drum, and the selector key revolves the drum until the designated pocket is positioned under a fixed slot located to the left of the keyboard. In the latest models, checks and deposit slips are automatically conveyed to the selected pocket via a transport system.

Following the indexing of the deposited items (debits), the total amount appearing on the deposit slip is indexed (the offsetting credit), and the selector key for credits is depressed. Each indexed amount appears on *two tapes:* (1) on a master tape where all amounts are listed in the order in which they are processed; and (2) on a tape assigned to the pocket to which the item was sorted as determined by the selector key. Each pocket tape lists and totals only items routed to that pocket.

Thus proof machines with selector mechanisms really accomplish three purposes, including the basic objectives.

1. Elimination of Preliminary Sorting. The additional step of depressing a selector key after indexing each item completely eliminates sorting as a separate preliminary operation, since sorting becomes a byproduct of the listing operation.

2. Proof of Deposit. The accuracy of the customer's listing and addition on the deposit ticket is verified by what is known as a "zero-out proof." It will be recalled that the deposit-ticket total (credit) is indexed immediately following the listing of the deposited items (debits). The machine automaticaly subtracts the credit from the total of the debits, and if the result is anything but zero, the machine locks or otherwise signals to the operator the presence of an error. Location and adjustment of the difference is simplified because the master tape normally lists all debits in the same order in which they appear on the deposit slips—the one virtue of the primitive "individual deposit proof."

3. Establishment of Control Totals. Control totals are automatically established because the selector key causes each indexed amount to be listed on the tape assigned to the pocket selected.

The number of selector pockets can vary from a single pocket to as many as 40 pockets in some models. Many banks can efficiently utilize 40-pocket machines. On the other hand, a small bank that sends most or all of its items unsorted to a nearby correspondent bank might find as few as two pockets entirely sufficient for its purposes, using one pocket for on-us items and the other pocket for everything else. Proof machines are expensive and, generally, the more complex, the more expensive they are. Even a large bank that cannot effectively use a multi-pocket machine in its proof operation should consider less expensive, more suitable equipment to fit its particular needs.

Expediting Check Collection Processes

Following the proof operation, the process of converting checks and other claims to money into actual usable funds begins. Considering the fact that even a moderate-sized bank handles a volume exceeding 100,000 items a day, it is obvious that devices and systems tending to expedite the process are much sought after. At the same time, it is equally obvious that effective controls must be maintained during all stages of the collection procedure.

The major objectives of the department or departments responsible for collecting cash items may be stated as follows:

1. To make sure that, whatever processing system is used, records are produced that will permit, *after* items have been processed, the identification and tracing of any particular item from its source to its destination.

2. To utilize the most effective method of sorting items according to the collection channel selected.

3. To furnish listings and totals, both to accompany groups of items dispatched (cash letters) and for department records to facilitate balancing with the control totals.

4. To indorse all items processed to permit direct presentation to and demand for payment from the drawee bank or to transfer to an intermediate collecting bank the legal right to present the item for payment. (It should be noted that the Uniform Commercial Code permits abbreviated, less formal indorsements between banks in the collection chain, but this does not affect the standard warranties and engagement to honor of an indorser, which apply as well to indorsing banks.)

Recordkeeping

The advantages, both to the bank and its depositors, of collecting cash items as quickly as possible have already been emphasized, as well as the need for relating maximum speed with acceptable cost. But if cash items must be handled in bulk as speedily and as economically as possible, it is evident that there is little time for painstaking, meticulous recordkeeping. It would be unduly optimistic not to expect, considering the billions of items handled by the banking system, that single checks and groups of checks will occasionally be lost in the shuffle. The ability of a depository bank to identify and, if necessary, to reproduce copies of lost items is an invaluable asset, particularly from the standpoint of customer relations, but it must be achieved at reasonable cost.

Years ago, when adding machines and typewriters were still considered frivolous luxuries, all deposited checks handled by banks were carefully described on bank records in pen and ink before they were permitted to leave the premises on their way to presentment and payment. Handwritten transmittal letters (cash letters) contained the name of the depositor as well as the amount of the check and the full name of the bank on which it was drawn. In those days handwriting, with appropriate flourishes, was an art; bound ledgers, tall stools, and green eyeshades represented the bank's most valuable pieces of equipment; and checks were rare enough to warrant what would be considered, by today's standards, tender loving care. The speed of modern business permits no such fastidiousness; yet those Spencerian exercises had a purpose—that of identifying items no longer in the bank's possession. A way had to be found to achieve the purpose without the painstaking flourishes.

National Numerical System

As early as 1910 the American Bankers Association recognized the need for an easier, more uniform method of identifying checks, and particularly those payable by out-of-town banks. A shorthand numerical code was developed that assigned a specific number to each bank in the country, indicating its name and location. The code is a hyphenated system composed of a prefix number, a hyphen, and a suffix number, and is known as the *national numerical system* or the *numerical transit system.*

The Association assigned prefix numbers 1 to 49 to large cities according to their size at that time. For instance, New York City received prefix number 1; Chicago 2; Philadelphia 3; and so forth. The several states were assigned prefix numbers 50-99, and territories and dependencies were assigned prefix number 101.

The suffix number provides individual bank identification and, when combined with the prefix number, accurately identifies the drawee bank. For instance, if the ABA transit number (as an individual bank code is called) is 1-8, the prefix (1) indicates that the bank is located in New York City, and the suffix (8) identifies the bank as the First National City Bank; if the ABA transit number is 8-9, the prefix (8) indicates that the bank is located in Pittsburgh, Pennsylvania, and the suffix (9) identifies the bank as the Pittsburgh National Bank; while if the ABA transit number is 88-94, the prefix (88) indicates that the bank is domiciled in the state of Texas, and the suffix (94) identifies it as the First National Bank of Amarillo, Texas.

The numbers of all banks are listed in a book called the *Key to the*

Numerical System, commonly known as the Key Book. The American Bankers Association assumes the responsibility for assigning code numbers to newly organized banks, maintaining records, and publishing annually an updated Key Book, with interim supplements as needed.

This simple, effective system is still in use, having served banking well for over half a century. It should be noted that the system was originally designed solely for recordkeeping purposes. Banks instruct and encourage depositors to use the ABA transit number to identify checks on deposit slips, which are important basic records. In the early days of manual sorting the numerical code was not considered a sorting aid, as the information it contained (the name and location of the drawee bank) was printed plainly on the face of the check. However, as later developments are discussed, it will be noted that automatic check-handling techniques have expanded the usefulness of the ABA transit number beyond its original limited role of identifying items on bank records.

Use of Microfilm

Another valuable aid in identifying items that have been processed is the growing practice of photographing them on microfilm. The merits of photographing *all* items are still debated by operating specialists. For example, a bank processing 500,000 transit items a day may have occasion later to refer to only 50 photographs for identification and tracing purposes. Thus, 499,950 photographs serve no purpose—yet they do involve expense. On the other hand, a photograph of just one of the 50 trouble cases conceivably could save the bank as much or even more than the cost of photographing 500,000 items. Photographs can be duplicated in hard-copy form, and in many states are legally presentable for payment, with appropriate guarantees by the presenting bank, in lieu of a lost item.

Some banks microfilm *all* transit items; others, only certain items, such as those cashed at a teller's window. If the photographing process must be performed as a *separate operation,* the loss of valuable time must be added to the cost. But if a photographing unit is attached to another piece of equipment so that the process becomes a byproduct of a necessary operation, only the additional cost of the more sophisticated equipment need be considered.

The Check Routing Symbol—A Sorting Aid

A relatively recent innovation was the development of the *check routing symbol* by the combined efforts of the Committee on Check Collections of the Federal Reserve System and the Bank Management Committee of the American Bankers Association. The check routing symbol is also a type of numerical code but, unlike the ABA transit number, the developers had an entirely different purpose in mind. Designed primarily as a sorting aid, the routing symbol provides a fast and efficient means of sorting checks collected through the Federal Reserve System by segregating items according to the Federal Reserve bank or branch serving the area in which the drawee bank is located. Thus the check routing symbol identifies geographic areas rather than individual drawee banks. Because the boundaries of Federal Reserve districts do not follow state lines and in some cases cover all or parts of several states, the routing symbol has proved to be of considerable value in manual sorting systems. However, since it does not identify a particular bank (all banks in a given geographic area have the same routing symbol), it has little if any value for recordkeeping purposes.

The routing symbol is composed of either three or four digits. If it has three digits, these indicate the following:

1. The first digit designates one of the Federal Reserve districts that are numbered 1 to 9.

2. The second digit indicates which Federal Reserve bank or branch serves the territory in which the drawee bank is located. The Federal Reserve head office of the district is identified by the digit 1 and branches (if any) are identified by digits 2 to 5. Numbers 6 to 9 indicate special collection arrangements.

3. The third digit serves two purposes:

   a) It assists in the separation of items that are received for immediately available credit from those that are received for deferred availability. The figure "O" identifies items that are immediately available if received in time (according to the availability schedule of the district) on the day of deposit. All other numbers in the third position indicate that the item is received for deferred availability.

   b) The third digit also facilitates the sorting of items by states when necessary as when other than "O," it indicates the state in which the drawee bank is located.

If the routing symbol has four digits, the first two digits designate one of the Federal Reserve districts that are numbered 10 to 12. The last two digits have the same meaning as the second and third digits in a three-digit number.

Only banks that participate in the Federal Reserve par collection system are eligible to receive a routing symbol. However, financial institutions other than commercial banks have been assigned district codes where it is felt that such identification will aid in processing their items.

Like the ABA transit number, the check routing symbol was developed during the era of manual sorting of checks. It was extremely useful because the name and location of the drawee bank, prominently displayed on the face of the check, did not necessarily indicate the Federal Reserve bank or branch to which the item could be sent for maximum speed in presentation. As with the ABA transit number, later developments of automated check handling greatly enhanced the potential value of the routing symbol.

Magnetic Ink Character Recognition

Completely automatic check handling for routine operations became a realizable possibility during the 1950s when the Bank Management Committee of the American Bankers Association developed a machine-readable numerical language. Specially designed numerals printed on checks in magnetic ink can be read electronically by sophisticated equipment. Called MICR (Magnetic Ink Character Recognition) this technological discovery opened the door to a new era of paper-instrument handling.

A special design for each of the numerals from 0 to 9 was created with two objectives in mind: first, so that the arrangement and density of magnetized particles in the ink would so individualize each character as to virtually eliminate the possibility of misreading the characters when passed rapidly before electronic reading heads and, second, so that the newly designed characters would not be so distorted as to be unrecognizable by the human eye.

Exhibit 10: Magnetic Ink Character Recognition

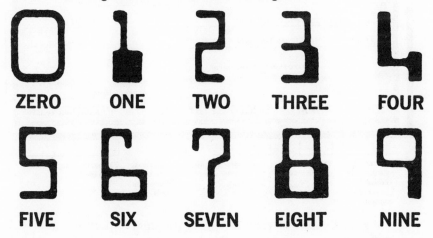

ZERO   ONE   TWO   THREE   FOUR

FIVE   SIX   SEVEN   EIGHT   NINE

It was also necessary to provide a precise location for the magnetic ink characters so that paper instruments could be fed into special equipment in a manner that would cause the inscribed numerals to pass directly within the limited range of a reading head. This problem was solved by making the right-hand edge and the lower edge of the paper documents the reference points; that is, the magnetic ink characters, depending on the type of information represented, must be inscribed within a predetermined space as measured from the right-hand edge and contained within a 5/8-inch band measured upward from the bottom edge.

The enticing prospects of MICR compelled bankers to abandon older concepts with respect to the handling of paper instruments, but it is not surprising that several years were required to develop the system to its present effectiveness. It is not only possible but quite likely that we have not yet realized the full potential of this innovation.

Because of space limitations, the system had to be based on numeric character recognition rather than on alphabetic characters. Therefore, the first step for banks eager to take full advantage of the tremendous potential was to assign numbers to all demand-deposit accounts—a sizable task in itself.

Exhibit 11: A Modern Check

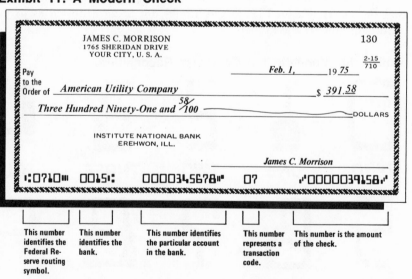

| This number identifies the Federal Reserve routing symbol. | This number identifies the bank. | This number identifies the particular account in the bank. | This number represents a transaction code | This number is the amount of the check. |

A study of Exhibit 11 reveals that, of the information that is MICR encoded, only the amount of a check or a deposit is variable. Therefore, all other information can be pre-encoded before delivery to depositors. On checks this would be the transit routing symbol (a combination of the routing symbol and the ABA transit number), the account number, and a transaction code (which distinguishes debits from credits) ; while for deposit slips, just the account number and the transaction code suffice.

Customers had to be weaned away from the habit of using blank unencoded checks and deposit slips, for substantial use of uncoded documents could seriously impede the inherent efficiency of the system. As it is, the general practice is for the depository bank (the first bank in the collection chain) to encode the dollar amount of checks, thus permitting all other automated banks in the collection process to take full advantage of automatic handling.

At this point, it might be well to point out that changes in processing systems often result in a shift of important responsibilities which are sometimes overlooked. For instance, at one time it was difficult for a proof clerk to make an error that would not be corrected during further processing steps. But if a proof clerk happens to be operating a modern machine that automatically MICR-encodes the amount of checks, an undetected error could have a rather long life. If other intermediate collecting banks and the drawee bank happen to be fully automated, it is not only possible but quite likely that the error will persist until a confused depositor attempts to reconcile his statement. Without question, automation has shifted an important responsibility to the proof clerk.

Electronic Sorting

The sophisticated pieces of equipment specially designed to handle MICR-encoded documents are called *document-handlers* or *sorter-readers*. Checks and other encoded documents are fed into this equipment, one at a time, but at incredible speeds, and pass before the reading heads. This equipment can be adjusted to read MICR data in any particular location. That is, the machine will read the amount of the instrument or the account number, or any other encoded data.

Document-handlers or sorter-readers by themselves can do little more than sort documents, but they can do it at incredible speeds and with extraordinary accuracy. For instance, if the reading heads are adjusted to scan the transit routing field, checks can be sorted by Federal Reserve districts or by Federal Reserve head offices and branches or by individual drawee banks. If the reading head scans the account-number field, on-us checks can be sorted in account-number order. In a sorting operation the equipment can read only one digit at a time, thus a fine sort in any field requires a number of passes of the items through the equipment, depending on the number of digits in the encoded group.

If desired, the equipment can be set to read the amount field, and checks can be sorted in ascending or descending order of amounts, though it is difficult to conceive of a useful objective of such an operation.

After passing by the reading head the documents are directed to a series of gates, one of which is opened to receive each item, depending on the magnetic character recognized by the reading head. Each gate leads to a specific pocket in which will be found, after processing, all items bearing an identical number in a certain position in one of the encoded fields.

But fast, accurate sorting is by no means the limit of MICR potential. This is only the beginning. When the document handlers or sorter readers are electronically connected to (interfaced with) a computer, the possibilities become almost unlimited.

The Computer—Electronic Data Processing

An electronic computer is one of the marvelous wonders of the modern world. A digital computer, such as is used in banking, has amazing capabilities. It can store a fantastic amount of data in its electronic memory, but what is more, it doesn't forget where it puts things as humans do. When asked to, it can retrieve any particular bit of information or change it or even erase it. It has a built-in electronic calculator that can add, substract, divide, or multiply, and it can do these things at speeds that are measured in *nanoseconds* (billionths of seconds).

The computer sits like a king on a throne, surrounded by peripheral equipment, which can read data from such things as paper tape, magnetic tape, or punch-cards, and feed this information into the computer. The computer can digest, rearrange, compute, store, or otherwise manipulate these data, and on command can disgorge all or any part of its stored information by typing or printing the information, or by reproducing it in the form of paper tape, magnetic tape, or punch-cards.

A completely automated computer operation is sure to awe the uninitiated. The casual observer of a computer complex in action stands in open-mouthed wonder at the dazzling spectacle of checks streaking through a sorter reader at speeds that his human eye can only reflect as a confused continuous blur. But his feeling of abject inferiority is complete as he views the huge, silent, ominous-looking computer frames while being told that within that faceless hulk, in the last *five seconds,* the equivalent of something like 25 manhours of sustained effort was accomplished easily and accurately. The imposing statistics may vary, depending on the circumstances and the narrator, but the awesome part is that they are generally accurate.

It must be remembered that all the inanimate things we use in banking (or any other activity)—from such commonplace items as pencils, paper clips, and filing cabinets to such technical marvels as cathode-ray tubes, computers, and other electronic devices—are simply tools created, designed, motivated, and operated by man for the purpose of fulfilling specific functions. All functions have a purpose or objective, and the objective is achieved by a course of action. The inanimate tools, including the computer, do what they are made to do or told to do. If objectives are to be changed or if the means by which the objective is achieved are changed, the human brain must devise and install the change, and the tool or tools must then be redesigned or restructured by man to conform.

Electronic data processing has very properly invaded every phase of banking but, at this point, our discussion will be confined to the impact of EDP on the deposit function.

EDP and the Proof Operation

Electronic data-processing techniques have probably had fewer salutary effects on the proof operation than on the check collection process. For one reason, the depository bank is expected to MICR-encode the amount of the item, and encoding units are more easily installed in the manually operated proof machines. Actually, such functions as encoding, indorsing, and photographing are often handled as separate operations but, if they can be obtained as byproducts of another essential function, so much the better. Generally speaking, all items should be fully MICR-encoded before they reach the EDP complex. For this reason, many large banks with sophisticated computerized systems continue to use proof machines with encoding capabilities for the proof operation.

However, when a large correspondent bank receives fully encoded deposits from a bank customer, it is possible to bypass the proof operation altogether. As had been pointed out, a document-handler (sorter-reader) can read dollar amounts, but by itself can do little else than sort documents in some manner according to amounts. However, when a document-handler is teamed up (interfaced) with a computer, deposit totals can be verified, items sorted and control totals established, all of which are essentially what a proof machine accomplishes. But there is a big difference. A computer document-handler team

151

can easily outperform the best manually operated proof machine, with much more accuracy and at considerably faster speeds. The only thing it cannot do is locate and adjust a depositor error—but neither can a proof machine. This requires the skill and experience of bank personnel.

EDP and the Check Collection Function

Electronic data-processing techniques have a much more dramatic effect when applied to the check collection function.

The process is basically one of sorting checks according to predetermined channels through which they will be dispatched for ultimate presentation and payment, whether they be local checks, out-of-town checks, nonpar checks, or whatever. They may be sorted for direct presentation to the drawee banks, either through a clearing facility or otherwise, or they may be sorted according to the geographic location of the drawee bank and sent to a Federal Reserve bank or branch or to some other intermediate collecting bank such as a correspondent.

In all cases, the handling bank will have established a suitable sorting pattern or patterns. For a small bank with a very simple constant sorting pattern, the cost of a sophisticated EDP system might well be questioned. But for the larger bank, handling daily a substantial volume both in terms of units and dollars, with a series of sort patterns attuned to available transportation schedules at any given time, a computerized system can mean substantial benefits in time, efficiency, and availability of funds.

To the computer/document-handler team, a printer is added. The sorting patterns are programmed into the computer's memory. The computer can control one or more document handlers and printers. It tells the document handler what sorting pattern to use and, upon direction, it can order the document handler to change the program on any day of the week or at any time of the day. Using the MICR data captured by the sorter-reader, the computer settles with preestablished control figures and instructs the printer to prepare for each group of sorted items a detailed list of individual amounts and the total dollar amount, either in the form of a cash letter or in whatever form may be desired. Each list can be identified with a batch or settlement number and may contain other pertinent data, such as the transit number of the bank to which the group of items will be dispatched.

All observers of the banking scene agree that electronic data-processing techniques have produced radical and highly beneficial changes in the area of bank operations. So far, however, we have discussed only the area of the deposit function. There is much more to come.

Attempts to describe at any given time the great variety of sophisticated methods by which banks seek to realize their operating objectives would be as futile as chasing a rainbow. Any approach to the subject must necessarily be rather broad-brushed.

The purpose of this chapter is simply to describe some of the newer systems, equipment, and techniques, while at the same time trying to keep in mind the basic and important objectives. The basic principles of bank operations should never be unintentionally obscured by the brilliant and dazzling spotlight of technological phenomena. Technology gives us improved tools and techniques for reaching our goals, but does not necessarily change those goals.

Questions Based on This Chapter

1. What was the original purpose of the National Numerical System? Why was it not considered a sorting aid?

2. What is the *check-routing symbol* and what is its primary purpose?

3. Name the specific equipment that was especially designed to handle MICR-encoded documents.

4. Banks pre-encode MICR data on checks and deposit slips *before* delivery to their customers. What data cannot be pre-encoded?

Chapter 10

The Payments Function

Part I: The Bookkeeping Department

Purposes of This Chapter:

  1. To discuss the duties of a bank bookkeeping department.
  2. To explain the validity tests applied to items presented for payment.
  3. To describe the role of the bookkeeping department as a communications center.

It is not surprising that bank terminology lacks uniformity throughout the country and even in different banks in the same general area. Therefore it would be helpful to explain what is usually meant by the term *bookkeeping department* in banking.

   In many commercial organizations, the *bookkeeping* or *accounting department* refers to the unit that maintains the basic financial records of the organization. In banking, the comparable unit is generally referred to as the *general ledger department* or the *general books,* while *bookkeeping department* has traditionally meant the function of recording the activity in depositor's checking accounts. Over the years this department has been variously referred to as the *bookkeeping de-*

partment, individual ledgers, or more recently *demand deposit accounting.* For the purposes of this chapter, the older term *bookkeeping department* will be used.

The bookkeeping department maintains a *subsidiary ledger,* that is, it records the account detail (name, address, account number, debits, credits, and current balance) of each checking account customer of the bank. The *general ledger* account (demand deposits) is a control account that reflects only the summary totals of daily debits and credits and the total amount of the bank's demand deposit liability.

Actually, demand deposit liability is sometimes subdivided into other subsidiary ledgers, such as *public funds* or *correpondent banks.*

The payment function and the deposit function of commercial banks certainly go hand in hand, and together they contribute significantly to the smooth performance of our monetary system. It was noted that an essential element in the processing of deposits is the collection of checks and other claims to money by speedy presentation to the drawee bank or other obligated party. The payment function finds the bank in an entirely different position, and it must decide rather quickly whether it will pay (honor) or refuse to pay (dishonor) items presented to it as drawee bank or as paying agent.

To avoid needless repetition of words, the following discussion will refer mostly to the payment of checks, but the principles apply with equal force to all cash items chargeable against demand deposit accounts.

From the viewpoint of the payor bank, checks and other items presented to it are received through various channels. Most on-us items are checks, and most checks are presented by other banks, such as Federal Reserve banks, correspondent banks, or local clearinghouse banks. A much smaller number are presented at a teller's window (either personally by the holder or in the deposit of a regular customer) or by other departments, such as the loan, collection, trust, or investment departments. Regardless of the channel through which on-us checks are presented or received, *all* such checks must ultimately find their way to the bookkeeping department for posting to the drawer's account.

One thing should be made clear. The bookkeeping department *pays checks*—not in the more spectacular manner of passing out cold hard cash to the presenter, but every bit as effectively by posting the check and thus reducing the depositor's balance.

Just as the posting of a cash-item deposit is a provisional credit, so the posting of a check or other eligible instrument is a provisional debit. However, unless the bookkeeping department takes action to reverse the debit prior to the expiration of the applicable time limit for dishonor and return of the item, the payment is final, and subsequent recovery is possible only in the event of a breach of one of the warranties of the presenting indorser.

Thus the *primary function* of the bookkeeping department is to maintain complete, accurate, and current records of the accounts of all demand depositors. And its most *important and essential duty* in connection with the performance of that function is to examine carefully all checks and other orders for the payment of funds to determine their validity and eligibility for payment. It should be pointed out, however, that while the bookkeeping department examines *all* checks during the posting process, in the case of checks paid *in cash* at a teller's window, the teller assumes full responsibility for determining validity and eligibility for payment.

To visualize the magnitude of this responsibility, consider the fact that the average bank bookkeeping department pays out many millions of dollars of depositors' funds annually on the sole authority of innocent-looking pieces of paper bearing little more than a date, a name, an amount, and a signature. There is no doubt that a major share of the responsibility for the smooth performance of the payment function rests on bank bookkeeping personnel.

Duties of the Bookkeeping Department

The following discussion will emphasize *what* the bookkeeping department must do to discharge its many duties and responsibilities properly. Specific references to *how* the objectives are sometimes achieved are for illustrative purposes only.

In carrying out its primary function, the bookkeeping department performs the following collateral duties, which will be discussed in some detail, since each is related to a specific objective.

A. *Posting* all debit and credit items to the respective depositor's accounts, and *settling* the results of the posting operation with control totals and the general ledger control account.

B. *Examining* all posted items to determine their validity.

C. *Furnishing periodic detailed statements* to all depositors as instructed.

D. *Communicating vital information.*

E. *Miscellaneous* duties.

A. Posting and Settling

Because of the heavy volume and extremely rapid pace of modern business activity, it is important that all entries affecting the balances in depositors' accounts be posted as promptly as possible so that demand-deposit balances are reasonably up to date and currently available to depositors and authorized banking personnel. Yet this is one area where accuracy must also be a prime objective.

In discussing proof operations mention was made of the importance of controlling the huge daily dollar volume, as items are sorted and re-sorted to prepare them for the various processing departments. Errors made in the proof operation are serious, but at least there is a chance of other bank processing departments detecting and adjusting them. But undetected errors made in the bookkeeping department invariably are caught by depositors and can do much to damage irreparably the reputation and image of the bank in the eyes of the depositor—to say nothing of the potential damage that could be inflicted on the bank's profit and loss account.

There was a time when settlements accurate to the last penny was an inviolable rule of all banks, to be achieved at all costs. But the steadily increasing volume of transactions finally reached a point where the rule had to be tempered with some reason. Many banks have adopted a policy of ignoring differences of less than one dollar and of limiting the time spent in locating differences of even larger amounts. Why spend $25 of clerical time (or overtime) in trying to locate a $5 difference? Such logic is persuasive, especially when it is considered that another department, another bank, or a depositor will probably discover and report the discrepancy. But there is another view, particularly where depositors are concerned. There is nothing more irritating to the conscientious depositor—whether an individual, trustee, treasurer, or comptroller—than having to spend *his* valuable time in locating and correcting a minor error made and ignored by the bank.

If there is any operating department of a bank that must place a high premium on accuracy, it is the bookkeeping department, not only because it often provides the sole area of contact with depositors but also because all depositors have a special concern in the accuracy with which their bank balances are handled. Furthermore, balance errors can produce serious consequences should the bank wrongfully dishonor a customer's check.

For the most part, control figures covering credits (deposit slips) and debits (checks and other items chargeable to depositors' accounts) are received from the proof department. But this may not be the only source of posting entries delivered to the bookkeeping department. In some banks miscellaneous items, both debits and credits, are regularly received directly from other departments rather than from a proof center; or they may be generated in the bookkeeping department itself. Examples of such entries are debits covering service charges, interest on loans, charges and fees for securities purchased, return items, and so forth, while miscellaneous credits result from such transactions as paid collection items, proceeds of securities sold, or interest on time deposits. Whatever the source of posting entries, accurate settlements with proof department controls or interdepartmental settlement sheets must be a constant objective.

B. Examining All Items

The careful examination of all posted items is perhaps the heaviest responsibility of bookkeeping personnel. All debit postings to individual ledger accounts represent the transfer of ownership of depositor's money to someone else—a function that cannot be treated lightly. On the other hand, the posting of credits increases depositors' balances *and* the bank's liabilities.

Internally prepared debits and credits do not require an extensive examination routine. It is sufficient to see that they have been prepared on regular bank forms and bear the initials of responsible personnel in the originating department. Items that do not meet these relatively simple requirements should be investigated.

On the other hand, all checks and other forms of depositors' orders to pay, as well as normal deposit credits, are prepared externally by the depositor. These must be examined carefully. Ordinarily, deposit credits present no problem for the bookkeeping department, for they have already been scrutinized by a teller and have passed through the proof (of deposit) operation. Unless there is some obvious reason for investigation, the bookkeepers can accept externally originated credits as valid.

Externally prepared debits, however, present an entirely different problem. The vast bulk of such debit items consists of ordinary checks, although other types of financial instruments may be involved, such as non-negotiable transfer drafts, trade acceptances, or promissory notes made payable at the bank. In all cases, the bookkeeping department must be sure that any debit instrument that serves to reduce a depositor's balance is duly authorized and eligible in all respects for payment.

A check is a compact and tersely written instruction ordering the payment of a specified amount of a depositor's funds to someone. It must be remembered that this piece of paper is the only authority the bank has to justify the reduction of a depositor's balance. If, for any one of a number of possible reasons, the payment is not made in accordance with the depositor's instructions, and a loss occurs, it is the bank, not the depositor, that must suffer the loss. In view of the astronomical dollar volume of depositors' funds disbursed daily on the basis of such brief orders, it is obvious that checks must be examined with great care in order to determine their validity and eligibility for payment. Fortunately for the banking industry, an extremely high percentage of the checks processed are valid and genuine. Nevertheless, the failure to subject checks to a strict examination routine involves exposure to potential losses of considerable proportions.

The Validity Tests

The examination of checks requires the application of a number of tests to determine the validity of each item. The failure of a check to pass any one of these tests constitutes sufficient grounds for refusal to pay the item. There are nine such validity tests to which all checks must be subjected, some of which can be applied merely by inspection of the check itself, while others require reference to other bank records.

1. The check must name the bank to which it is presented for payment as drawee.

2. The account to which the check is to be charged must be subject to withdrawal by check.

3. The check must bear a genuine and authorized signature or signatures.

4. It must not have been altered in any way.

5. It must not be postdated or bear a stale date.

6. It must be satisfactorily indorsed.

7. There must not be an effective stop-payment order on file.

8. There must be no "hold" against the account.

9. The account to which the check is to be charged must have a sufficient collected balance.

All of the above conditions must be met or where circumstances warrant, deliberately waived.

Although the reasons for these validity tests should be fairly obvious, a brief explanation of each of the tests is in order.

1. A bank has no authority to charge a check against a depositor's account unless the instrument specifically names that bank as drawee. It must be an order addressed to the bank that pays it.

2. The account to which the charge is to be made must be subject to withdrawal by check. Savings accounts in commercial banks are not subject to withdrawal by check, even where notice for the withdrawal of funds has been waived.

3. A genuine signature is the signature of the specific person purported to have signed the check. An authorized signature is the signature of a person who has been duly empowered to sign checks for the withdrawal of funds from an account bearing a title other than his individual name. A person so empowered signs in a specific capacity, such as treasurer, trustee, agent, executor. In some cases an order for the withdrawal of funds may require two or more authorized signatures. It should be noted that a signature can be genuine but not authorized, and, conversely, the name of a properly authorized person inscribed on a check may not be his genuine signature.

4. A bank is authorized to pay checks *only as drawn by the depositor.* If a check has been materially altered after it has been issued and delivered by the depositor, the bank must assume full responsibility for the alteration. Thus if the amount of the check is raised or the name of the payee, or the date, or the name of the drawee bank has been changed, the depositor can hold the bank accountable for any resultant loss. There is one possible exception to this general rule. Depositors at times are extremely careless in drawing and issuing checks and make it relatively easy for an unscrupulous person to alter a check in such a manner as to defy detection. Where a bank has acted in accordance with reasonable standards of examination and the depositor is guilty of gross contributory negligence, the burden of a resulting loss *may* be shifted from the bank to the depositor.

Minor alterations often appear in checks, but even the most innocent looking must be examined carefully to weigh the possible effect. On the other hand, bank personnel must exercise reasonable judgment. For instance, a check payable to the local telephone company that appears to have been raised from $13.85 to $15.85 probably should not be questioned. It would be more reasonable to assume that the drawer had corrected an error in writing the check than to conclude that the telephone company had deliberately raised the amount of the check after it had been received. Whenever the integrity and responsibility of the payee need not be questioned, it would be foolhardy to dishonor checks bearing minor alterations and strike-overs involving relatively small amounts.

5. A postdated check is a check bearing a future date, and a bank has no authority to charge a postdated check against a depositor's account. A stale date is an old date or one not considered current, that is, reasonably close in point of time to the date the check is presented for payment. Whether or not a date is considered stale depends on governing statutes or individual bank policy consistent with such statutes. Under the standard version of the Uniform Commercial Code, a bank is *under no obligation* to honor a check presented more than six months

after its date. It should be noted that the Code does not *prohibit* the payment of such a check and a bank in good faith may pay and charge an item older than six months to the depositor's account. In many cases, the bank may feel reasonably certain that the depositor would prefer to have the check honored, as, for instance, in the case of a dividend check. Where any doubt exists or where the amount of the check is fairly large, most banks will contact the depositor for specific instructions.

6. The indorsement of the party presenting a check to the drawee bank is extremely important. When a depositor issues a check payable to a specific legal person, as is most frequently the case, the drawee bank, if it pays the check, is required by law and custom to assure the depositor that the designated payee received the payment or equivalent credit therefor. If any person other than the named payee unlawfully received the funds represented by the check, by forging the payee's indorsement or indorsing it on behalf of the payee without proper authority, the depositor's right to demand that the drawee bank restore the amount of the check to his account is well established. Actually, the law allows a depositor *three years* following receipt of a statement to claim reimbursement for checks found to bear a forged indorsement.

The degree of responsibility assumed by a drawee bank with respect to indorsements depends on the manner of presentation. If a check is presented personally by the designated payee at a teller's window, the drawee bank is fully responsible for the identity and the indorsement of the payee. But the bookkeeping department does not deal directly with the payees. Nearly all checks paid by the bookkeeping department are received from collecting banks or depositors. Therefore, a "satisfactory" indorsement to the bookkeeping department is simply the indorsement of a presenting bank or the presenting depositor. If, as could be the case, the collecting bank or the depositor is also the named payee there should be no problem, because the record would show that the payee did receive the money. Where the payee is another party (usually unknown to the drawee bank), then the collecting bank or the presenting depositor assumes responsibility for the payee's indorsement.

To review briefly why this is so, it must be recalled that under the laws affecting negotiable instruments every indorser warrants that *all* signatures on the instrument are genuine or authorized, and the full warranty protects all subsequent transferees. When a check is presented to the drawee bank for payment, however, the warranty applies to all prior indorsements but excludes the drawer's signature, since a drawee bank is expected to know and recognize the signature of its depositor. The logic of this well-established principle of the law of negotiable instruments becomes apparent when it is recognized that the drawee bank in most cases has no knowledge of how, by whom, or under what circumstances the payee's indorsement was inscribed.

In the relatively few cases where on-us checks are routed to the bookkeeping department by other departments or units of the bank, those accepting such checks are responsible for the validity of prior indorsements, if any.

7. Since a check is a written instruction directing a bank to pay funds from the drawer's account, it has long been recognized that the issuer has a clear right to countermand his instruction. A drawer may order his bank to stop payment on any item payable against his account, but the law provides that such orders must be received "at such time and in such manner as to afford the bank reasonable opportunity to act on it" before payment of the item. If, for instance, a stop-payment order is received in the bookkeeping department at 10:00 a.m. and the check in question is presented and paid at the teller's window at 10:02 a.m., clearly the bank did not have "reasonable opportunity to act" on the countermanding order and would not be held responsible.

It would be logical to assume that a stop-payment order, like the check to which it refers, should be in writing and officially signed by the depositor. However, the circumstances that give rise to stop-payment orders frequently come about very suddenly, and from the drawer's viewpoint time is of the essence, for in all probability the check may already be in the process of collection. The fastest way to communicate with the bank is by telephone. When an oral stop-payment order is received, the bank should request that it be officially confirmed in writing as promptly as possible. Until the confirmation is received, however, the bank is *on notice* and has a duty to take reasonable steps to protect its depositor's interests. The standard version of the Uniform Commercial Code provides that an oral stop-payment order is good and binding upon the drawee bank for 14 days.

A stop-payment order is usually based on a dispute between the drawer and the payee or some other party, and the bank that inadvertently pays a check over a stop-payment order often finds itself facing a loss in connection with a transaction in which it was not directly involved. To prevent unjust enrichment at the bank's expense, the Uniform Commercial Code provides that the drawer demanding reimbursement must prove the fact and extent of the loss. The Code further provides that, having honored the check, the bank acquires whatever legal rights other parties to the instrument (drawer, payee, holder in due course, or other party) may have against the party deemed to be unjustly enriched to the extent necessary to protect it from loss. On the other hand, a bank that fails to obey a stop-payment order properly given shall certainly be held accountable for any unrecoverable loss directly attributable to its error. The law merely provides that it may recover from anyone wrongfully profiting by the mistake.

8. At times it becomes necessary to place a restriction on an account. Instructions to that effect are handled by the bookkeeping department and are known as "holds." The instruction may order the entire balance frozen or a specific part thereof, or it may in some other manner restrict payments from the account.

There can be a number of reasons for holds, including receipt of notice of the death of an individual depositor, notice of the bankruptcy of an individual or commercial depositor, service of a court order such as a writ of attachment, or some situation involving exposure in another department of the bank. For instance, a teller who pays a large on-us check at the window may place a hold against the account for the amount of the check, as protection during the several hours of processing time before the item reaches the bookkeeping department. Also, depositors are urged to report promptly to the bank the loss or theft of blank checks; when this occurs it is wise to place a hold against the account requiring that all checks be referred to a designated person for referral to the depositor, to guard against forgeries.

9. The final validity test has to do with the balance against which the check has been drawn. Under practically all systems, an *insufficient balance* will be revealed as a result of the posting operation, for the account will show a negative balance.

The determination of whether there are sufficient *collected funds* to cover the check(s) posted presents a more difficult problem. In this respect, *collected* funds should not be confused with *available* funds. To illustrate, suppose a check is deposited in a bank on the *first* day of the month and is drawn on another local bank. Assume further that both banks are members of a clearinghouse association. The check would be presented through the clearinghouse on the *second* day of the month, and on that day the funds represented by the check would be *available* to the presenting bank in the clearinghouse settlement. For instance, if settlement is made on the books of the local Federal Reserve bank, the amount of the check would either reduce the net debit or increase the net credit to the bank's reserve account.

But this *availability* is conditional; it does not mean that the item in question has been finally *paid* and thus *collected*. Under our delayed posting procedure, the drawee bank would post the item on the *third* day of the month, and on the *third* day, the drawee bank could return the item or give notice of its intention to dishonor in the manner and within the time limits set by the rules of the clearinghouse. Thus, while the money represented by the check would be (provisionally) *available* on the second day of the month, the presenting bank could not consider the item as finally collected until the close of business on the *third* day of the month or whenever the time limit for the return of the check had expired.

This illustration refers to a local item. It should be apparent that in the case of transit items collected through the Federal Reserve System, the period between the time the depositing bank receives available funds in its reserve account and the time when dishonored items can be properly returned is much longer.

Strictly speaking, a depositor should not draw against funds represented by cash items until, following presentation, the time has expired for the return of dishonored items. However, because most cash items are paid on presentation, and because of the difficulty of maintaining accurate and precise records of the amount of uncollected funds for every account, bookkeeping personnel must use considerable judgment. As a matter of policy, most banks establish guidelines to simplify the procedure by taking a reasonable calculated risk. For instance, bookkeeping personnel may be held responsible only for determining that the closing balance in an account, after posting all of the day's transactions, is greater than the amount of deposits made on that day. This policy anticipates few if any dishonored items, but may be entirely justified by the bank's experience.

Regardless of the guidelines established, an alert bookkeeping staff will give careful consideration to new accounts, special situations, and especially large deposits (in relation to the average balance) made within the last several days.

Where the depositor has overdrawn his account or has apparently drawn against uncollected funds, such instances are referred to designated personnel or an officer, who may approve or disapprove payment of the check or checks involved. If payment is disapproved, the bookkeeper reverses the debit posting by a credit entry for the corresponding amount, and the check is returned to the source from which it was received (the presenter), with the notation "insufficient funds" or "uncollected funds" to explain the reason for dishonor. If an overdraft is approved, the customer is notified and requested to make a covering deposit. Incidentally, banks are required to show overdrafts among bank assets, since they actually represent unauthorized loans or extensions of credit.

C. Forwarding Detailed Statements

As an adjunct to its responsibility for maintaining current and accurate records of the bank's demand depositors, the bookkeeping department must keep each depositor advised as to the status of his account. This is most frequently accomplished by forwarding, periodically as instructed, detailed statements showing the opening balance for the period, all debit and credit transactions, and the closing balance.

The careful preparation of customers' statements is an especially important duty, for in many cases the statement is the only regular contact a customer may have with the bank. The neatness and accuracy of the statement or the lack of these qualities form a vivid picture of the bank's effectiveness in the customer's mind. It goes without saying that efforts must be made to check the contents of the statement envelope before it is sealed and dispatched to the customer.

Actually, the rendering of statements is a measure of protection for the bank, for otherwise it would have no way of telling whether it has been handling debit and credit items properly and accurately. The depositor has an obligation to exercise reasonable care and promptness in examining the statement and its contents. The Uniform Commercial Code requires a depositor to detect his own unauthorized signature on or any alteration of an item he has issued, within a reasonable period not exceeding 14 days after a statement has been made available to him, and to notify the bank promptly in order to prevent the same forger or other wrongdoer from continuing his fraudulent activities indefinitely. The Code wisely recognizes that there can be extenuating circumstances. For instance, a bank may establish that the depositor failed to act with reasonable care and promptness, in which case the depositor may not assert a claim against the bank. But such a claim is not precluded if the depositor can establish that the bank failed to exercise ordinary care. The burden of proof is on the party seeking to establish the negligence of the other party.

In any event, the Code establishes a maximum time limit regardless of care or lack of care on the part of either the bank or the depositor, and no claim may be made against a bank with respect to an unauthorized signature or alteration of an item unless such claim is made within one year from the time the statement and the item or items have been made available to the depositor; and a claim with respect to an unauthorized indorsement must be made within three years from that time. These provisions of the Code simply recognize the fact that there should be an automatic termination *at some time* of the liability of a drawee bank.

Cancelled Checks

As a rule cancelled checks are enclosed with the statements, while deposit slips and other credits are retained in the bank files. There are exceptions to these general practices. In some cases banks have agreed to keep and file cancelled checks and produce specific items for customers on request. Obviously, in such a case the depositor should by agreement waive his right to examine paid items. In other cases, some banks have adopted the practice of returning deposit slips with the statement, particularly in the case of "bobtail" statements which show, in addition to the opening and closing balance, only the total amount of debits posted and the total amount of credits posted. "Bobtail" statements are, of course, less acceptable for active accounts because of possible reconcilement difficulties.

Incidentally, the term *cancelled checks* as used above is appropriate, because it is customary for banks to mark clearly on the face of checks after they have been *posted* and *paid,* a stamp or other clear indication of this fact, to prevent their reuse.

Cycle Statements

Corporations and business concerns generally insist on receiving statements and cancelled checks as of the end of each month so that these will coincide with their own accounting procedures, thus facilitating reconcilements. Most individuals and many non-commercial depositors do not particularly care at what time of the month the statement is dated, provided that it is regularly received.

In order to minimize the crushing effect of an enormous end-of-the month peak load, many banks forward statements (other than those for commercial and heavy-volume accounts) on a cycle basis. Under a cycle system a group of accounts (roughly $\frac{1}{20}$ of the total number) is closed off each business day, and the statements are processed and mailed. Thus every account receives a statement at some time during each month, but statement preparation is spread over as many working days as possible, thereby relieving to some extent the month-end peak load.

Undelivered Statements

The regular receipt of statements and cancelled checks affords protection both to the bank and to the depositor. Therefore, when this vital channel of communication is disrupted for one reason or another, "ordinary care" might require some action on the part of the bank.

For instance, if statements are returned undelivered by the post office, an investigation is indicated, particularly if the account remains active. Sometimes customers prefer to pick up their statements at the bank rather than have them forwarded by mail or other delivery service. In such cases, the statements should be delivered *only* to the depositor or to a definitely authorized representative. Further, if statements are not called for over a period of time, inquiries should be made, particularly if the account is active. At times a depositor, contemplating an extended trip, will ask that statements be held undelivered for several months. This is not an unusual or unnatural request, but it would be wise to have such withheld statements examined carefully by supervisory personnel, who should be especially alert for unusual activity or the possibility of forged signatures. Where accounts are classified as inactive or dormant, it is common practice to discontinue forwarding statements. In the interests of good customer relations, however, efforts should be made to contact the depositor, as there is always the possibility of persuading the customer to reactivate his account.

D. Communicating Vital Information

Few people outside of banking operations realize the important role played by the bookkeeping department as a communications center. In the course of a normal day the bookkeeping department receives more inquiries for account information, both from inside and outside sources, than does any other department of a bank. In view of the volume of transactions affecting the many thousands of accounts handled by the average bookkeeping department, it is clear that a great mass of data must be so arranged and filed as to be available on short notice and that facilities for communicating such information must be adequate.

Deposit tickets and miscellaneous credits must be accurately filed and promptly retrievable. Cancelled checks, prior to the scheduled statement date, must be carefully filed. Personnel constantly refer to these records. For instance, when a stop-payment order is received, the first duty of the person responsible is to refer to the cancelled check file to see if the item has already been paid. If it has, the customer is notified and the stop-payment order may then be ignored. Of course, balance information should be as current as possible and readily available to those entitled to receive such information.

A system that places these vital data at the fingertips of bookkeeping personnel is essential, but equally necessary is the experience and training required to know how and under what circumstances such information is to be divulged.

Confidentiality

Every bank customer feels, and rightly so, that his balance and the details of his banking transactions are strictly confidential. Information regarding any account should be given only under unquestionably proper circumstances.

167

Many requests for information come from top management or from other departments of the bank, and these should be promptly and accurately answered to ensure the smooth functioning of the bank as a whole. But such information should never be revealed to an unknown voice by telephone. Bookkeeping personnel should be well-trained in this respect, or it would be too easy for an unscrupulous imposter, familiar with bank procedure, to pry information from an unwary bookkeeper.

Bank credit officers, through the Robert Morris Associates,* have developed a strict code of ethics governing the long-established practice of sharing information among banks. As long as the code of ethics is observed by all bankers, this practice can be beneficial to the banking industry, to businessmen, and to bank depositors as well. From the viewpoint of the public, this is a very sensitive area, and recent legislation may compel some modification of bank practices. Where information is given to other banks, the request should be handled either by designated bookkeeping personnel or by someone to whom the voice of the inquirer is recognizable, to ensure that the person receiving such information is authorized to do so.

A number of inquiries are received from sources other than banks, and these are probably the most difficult to handle. Many people do not realize that whenever they offer a personal check they are (unwittingly perhaps) giving the name of their bank as a reference. Businessmen and merchants, naturally enough, are reluctant to deliver valuable merchandise for a stranger's check. They frequently ask the drawee bank, directly or through their own bank, whether a certain check is likely to be paid on presentation. The drawee bank can, without divulging confidential information, indicate that the check is or is not "good at the moment." (For obvious reasons, a bank cannot certify or guarantee payment of a check by telephone. The item must be formally presented for payment.) Actually, information of this kind, passed on to reputable merchants and businessmen, can be very helpful to the drawee bank's customers in their business transactions. But the right of the inquirer to receive such information must be firmly established by the banks involved, for information improperly divulged can result in serious consequences. It is evident that considerable judgment must be used in this area. While such information may originate in the bookkeeping department, in many banks such matters are handled by credit department personnel dealing with their known counterparts in other banks or in reputable commercial establishments.

The role of the bookkeeping department as a communications center is not limited to supplying information on request. It must also take

---

* A trade association of bank credit department personnel.

the initiative in supplying information to other areas of the bank. Since the success of any bank depends to a considerable extent on its ability to attract and retain deposit liabilities, management of the bank must necessarily keep in close touch with the constant and sometimes sharp changes in the deposit liability level. This is especially important to those responsible for handling the bank's money position and maintaining the level of required legal reserves. While the daily aggregate level of deposits can be obtained from the general ledger as well as from the bookkeeping department, only the latter can supply the details that occasionally shed light on the reason for sharp changes. In many cases, a list of the larger depositors that shows daily, weekly, or monthly changes in their respective deposit balance is maintained and made available to management. In addition, a report of unusually large deposits or withdrawals in excess of a predetermined amount may be furnished on a daily basis. The bank-depositor relationship is a very sensitive one, and in any individual case that relationship can improve or deteriorate, which in either case will be revealed by changes in the size of the balances maintained. The change can take place suddenly or over a period of time. An alert management will insist on being kept well-informed in this respect so as to take prompt and appropriate steps as may be necessary.

A great deal of special information important to other areas of the bank is normally directed to the bookkeeping department. Special instructions such as stop-payment orders or holds resulting from deaths, court orders, attachments, or internal situations not only require action by bookkeeping personnel, but also frequently must be relayed promptly to tellers and other interested personnel or departments, such as the credit department or the loan department. The failure to perform this communication function promptly and accurately can result in considerable embarrassment and possible financial loss.

E. Miscellaneous Duties

The number and extent of other duties assigned to the bookkeeping department depend to a considerable degree on the internal organization of any particular bank. It will suffice here to review three such duties that concern bookkeeping personnel, although responsibility may be assumed by other departments.

Return Items

During the normal processing of daily check transactions, there will inevitably be some items that fail to pass one or more of the various validity tests. Such checks are known as "return items" or "go-backs," and they must be returned to the bank, business concern, or individual who presented the item to the drawee bank for payment. If a provisional credit was extended at the time of presentation, as in the case of presentation by means of a deposit or through a clearinghouse exchange, reimbursement must be obtained. In some banks, a special return item department, which may or may not be an organizational unit of the bookkeeping department, assumes this responsibility. In any event, bookkeeping personnel must see that dishonored on-us items are delivered to the responsible person in ample time for proper handling.

The drawee bank has a limited time in which to make a decision regarding payment or non-payment of an item. The time limit is set by the Uniform Commercial Code and by local rules and regulations. For instance, members of a local clearinghouse association may by mutual agreement require a return of unpaid items earlier than stipulated in the statutory regulations. Under ordinary circumstances, the presenter of an item, whether a collecting bank or a depositor, may consider a provisional credit irreversible after the expiration of the applicable time limit. The standard version of the Uniform Commercial Code excuses delays beyond the prescribed time limits only if caused by circumstances beyond the control of the bank, such as war or emergency conditions, provided the bank exercised such diligence as the particular circumstances may have required. Obviously, the prompt and efficient handling of return items is of the utmost importance.

Bookkeeping personnel may be authorized under broad guidelines to make the decision to pay or return items but, in many sensitive cases, an officer must be consulted. In such cases, especially prompt action is necessary to allow time for possible delay in communication.

Inactive and Dormant Accounts

Over a period of time, it is inevitable that a number of accounts will become inactive. An inactive or dormant account is one in which there has been no depositor-generated activity for a consecutive number of months. The period of inactivity before such accounts are so classified may vary from three to six months or even a year, depending on individual bank policy. There are a number of reasons why dormant accounts should be segregated from active accounts and receive special attention; among these are the following:

1. The constant handling of such accounts during normal operations wastes clerical time or machine time or both, unnecessarily clutters the ledger files, and tends to make trial-balances and other settlements more difficult.

2. Under the laws of most states, the balances in these accounts must

be escheated to the state, after a specified period of time, and the record-keeping necessary to comply with the law is facilitated by segregation.

3. If unprotected, such accounts sometimes become a target for dishonest bank personnel. To guard against this possibility, many banks not only segregate dormant accounts but also place them under strict audit or dual control.

Maintaining and Preserving Records

Banks are required by law to keep for a period of five years, a record of all checks, drafts, notes, or money orders drawn on or paid by the bank as drawee or paying agent. Since debit items are invariably returned to the drawer or maker, it is customary to microfilm all on-us items paid and charged to depositors' accounts.

Banks are also required by law to maintain for two years all records necessary to reconstruct a demand deposit account. Therefore, in addition to debit items, all credit items (deposit slips and credit memoranda) must be retained, either in original form or copies.

It is the responsibility of the bookeeping department to be sure that it can, if requested, reconstruct any demand deposit account including the ability to identify the source and disposition of all debt and credit items.

The bookkeeping department is one of the most sensitive of operating areas in a commercial bank. Many billions of dollars are paid out annually on the strength of the brief and concise instructions often hastily inscribed on checks. Because depositor's funds are involved, a high premium must be placed on the accuracy of the duties performed by the bookkeeping department. All checks and other orders for the payment of depositors' funds must be subjected to a series of validity tests, and the bank must assume full responsibility for items improperly charged against a customer's account.

171

Questions Based on This Chapter:

1. What is the primary function of a bank's bookkeeping department?

2. Why is the goal of accurate settlements of such special importance to the bookkeeping department?

3. Is an oral stop-payment order an effective instruction to the drawee bank?

4. What is the difference between *available* funds and *collected* funds?

Chapter 11

The Payments Function

Part II: Tellers' Operations

Purposes of This Chapter:

1. To discuss the teller's role in the "payment function" of a commercial bank.

2. To distinguish between "paying" and "cashing" a check.

3. To emphasize the importance of controlling the amount of cash held at tellers' stations.

4. To describe some of the tricks employed to defraud bank tellers.

The teller in a modern bank is a person who wears many hats. Years ago the teller's present duties were considerably fragmented. There were receiving tellers who did nothing but accept deposits; paying tellers whose sole duty was to pay or cash checks; collection tellers who handled only collection items; and "special" tellers who handled certifications, statement deliveries, issued cashier's checks, and performed other miscellaneous duties.

The modern teller (or *unit teller* as the person is sometimes called) may handle all of the above duties and more. While all banks do not operate in the same manner, in many cases tellers are expected not only to pay *and* receive, but also to certify checks; receive instalment loan payments, "club" payments, mortgage payments, and utility bill payments; sell traveler's checks, money orders, and official checks; and in some cases even open accounts for individuals.

All of these services are often combined and entrusted to the unit teller for two very good reasons: (1) to save valuable lobby space, particularly since the sharp increase in the number of branch offices; and (2) to provide better service to customers by making it unnecessary for them to go to perhaps three separate windows for routine banking transactions.

Undoubtedly it would take several chapters to describe and explain what transpires during a busy day in the life of a bank teller. But the *format of this text is based on principal banking functions,* and a teller's duties spread over a number of functions. For instance, the duties of a teller in connection with the receiving of a deposit are quite different from those associated with the paying of a check, and for this reason they are discussed separately. This chapter is concerned solely with the teller's role in the payments function.

"Paying" and "Cashing" Checks

Although the terms *pay* and *cash* are used somewhat loosely in discussing teller operations, there is a logical difference between the two. A check is an *order to pay* addressed to the drawee bank, and it can be paid only by the bank on which it is drawn. Strictly speaking then, a check is *paid* when the drawee bank uses the drawer's funds in obeying the order to pay, following which the instrument is removed from circulation and becomes a "paid and cancelled" check. A check is *cashed* when a bank advances money to the holder of an instrument that must be presented for *payment* to another bank, the drawee. A bank is under legal obligation to pay checks presented to it as drawee if they meet the requirements of being good, and the payee offers satisfactory evidence of his identity. On the other hand, the cashing of checks drawn on other banks is a courtesy or an accommodation, rather than an obligation.

Payment of Checks by Tellers

As previously indicated, the vast majority of on-us checks are presented for payment by collecting banks. A much smaller percentage are received from depositors or from other departments of the bank. All of these checks are routed to the bookkeeping department, where they are examined, posted, and paid if found to be in proper order. The bookkeeping department, relying on the warranties of indorsers, assumes full responsibility for the payment or dishonor of such checks.

Another relatively small but important number of checks may be presented at a teller's window, either by the payee in person or by a holder who acquired the instrument by negotiation. These checks are also routed to the bookkeeping department for further processing (posting, cancelling, and so on), but in this case *the teller assumes full responsibility for payment.*

The payment of checks at a teller's window involves a very important and delicate contact with depositors and the public. If a mistake is made in paying a check at a teller's window, it is most difficult to correct the error. Obviously, there is no record of such a transaction except the teller's recollection of the amount of money he paid and the statement of the person receiving the money as to the amount the teller gave him. It is virtually impossible to reenact the scene. In many cases the person receiving payment of a check at the teller's window walks away with his cash and may never be seen again.

An unjustified refusal to pay a check can produce very embarrassing and sometimes very costly results. A dishonored check (one not paid upon proper presentment) is a serious reflection on the drawer's credit and possibly on his integrity as well. If a bank should refuse payment of a check without proper cause, even though through an innocent mistake, the depositor could bring suit and might be awarded sizable damages by a court. And the amount of damages would not necessarily relate to the amount of the check that had been wrongfully dishonored.

The Teller's Responsibility in Paying Checks

When a check is paid in cash at a teller's window, not only is it *legally* paid (Uniform Commercial Code), but it also is paid in a very practical sense, since the possibility of recovering the cash paid out by "returning" the item later is questionable in most cases.

Thus, checks paid at a teller's window must be subjected to all the validity tests *at that point.* However, the tests are applied under vastly different circumstances. The following comparison is not intended to downgrade the payment responsibilities of bookkeeping personnel, for volume alone adds to the weight of those responsibilities; rather, the purpose is to emphasize a sharp difference in the environment in which a teller works—a difference that tends to make identical duties more difficult to discharge.

It must be remembered that the teller is always confronted with a live customer, who naturally wants to be served as quickly and as conveniently as possible. Several other customers may be waiting in line who also wish to be served as promptly as possible. Both bookkeepers and tellers are subject to pressure. With the bookkeeper it is volume pressure—a time schedule to be maintained and a deadline to be met. With the teller, however, it is mostly "people pressure," and at times this can be most disconcerting.

The nature of the problems faced by tellers in applying the validity tests can vary considerably, depending on the bank's system of operations. All tellers know *what* must be done in each case, but the system dictates *how* it is done. For instance, in some sophisticated systems, each teller has ready, direct access to important account information in the electronic memory of a computer, and an inquiry will evoke an accurate automatic response in a matter of seconds. Where this means of communication is available and the validity test can be satisfied by this type of information, the teller is not at a tremendous disadvantage. But in the more conventional systems, such information must be obtained by reference to bank records or upon inquiry, relayed by bookkeeping personnel, either of which may take considerably more time. On a busy day, time is a relatively scarce commodity for the teller dealing with people in a hurry.

The following paragraphs deal with *what* must be done by a teller in applying validity tests to items presented for payment.*

1 and 2. *The teller must be sure that his/her bank is named as drawee bank, and that the item is drawn against a checking account balance.* In addition to the obvious need to be aware of whether a check is presented *for payment* or simply to be *cashed,* a teller must either make inquiry or rely on memory for assurance that the checking account indicated does exist. The fact that the name of the bank is imprinted on the check or the presence of an MICR-encoded account number are not *conclusive* evidence of this fact.

For the bookkeeper, the problems associated with these tests are almost negligible. First, checks are already sorted and determined to be on-us items before they reach the bookkeepers; second, the posting operation in practically all systems should quickly reveal the existence or nonexistence of the demand deposit account in question.

3. *Signatures.* Both tellers and bookkeepers must have a good memory for the general appearance of authorized signatures of customers of the bank. Obviously, it would be impossible for anyone to have an accurate

---

* The numbers in the following paragraphs refer to the numbers assigned to the validity tests in Chapter 10.

mental image of the many thousands of signatures involved. On the other hand, it is surprising how consistently experienced bank personnel are able to approve genuine signatures with hardly more than a casual glance, and at the same time be instinctively alerted by some obscure sign suggesting that a closer inspection is necessary. To attempt to identify such "signs" would be futile. This is one of the occupational skills that all human beings can develop over a period of time. A "sign" could be something in the general appearance of the check—its size, color, the manner in which it is written, the circumstances in which it is presented, or simply just an intuitive feeling that something is wrong. Both bookkeepers and tellers are usually quite sensitive to situations where a careful inspection and comparison of the signature on a check with the specimen signature on file is warranted.

But this is where the difference starts. For the teller, the comparison often means stepping away from the window to the signature card file and leaving customers standing in line. The bookkeeper can make the examination while filing the check and can refer perhaps to specimen signatures in the check drawer file-guides or to previously paid checks in the file. In any event, the bookkeeper can always more thoroughly examine a suspicious signature without the distracting knowledge that someone is standing by patiently (or impatiently) waiting for action.

4 and 5. *Dates and Alterations.* Both bookkeepers and tellers are responsible for post-dated checks, stale dates, and altered checks. The teller, however, must consider these points in conjunction with the simultaneous application of all other validity tests. By contrast, a bookkeeper's work can be arranged so as to focus attention on certain features while for the moment ignoring others. For instance, by inspecting the face side of all checks at the same time, the bookkeeper can concentrate solely on dates and possible alterations by limiting the examination to these two tests.

6. *Satisfactory Indorsement.* As had already been pointed out, the bookkeeping department does not come in direct contact with the named payees of on-us checks. Therefore, to bookkeeping personnel a "satisfactory" indorsement is simply the indorsement of a depositor or that of a collecting bank. Furthermore, the examination procedure is relatively simple because most of these indorsements are rubber-stamped "for deposit only" indorsements or the familiar "bank stamps." Exceptions to this general rule, where the bank may be required to see that checks bear the personal indorsement of the payee, as in the case of annuity checks, are relatively few and present no serious problems.

The teller's problem with respect to indorsements can be quite different. In some cases, the payee of a check might be well-known to the teller, such as an employee of a corporate depositor who regularly presents a paycheck drawn on the bank. But, in many cases, the payee presenting the check is a complete stranger, and the teller is faced with the matter of identification, which is certainly not the least of a teller's problems.

While a bank has an obligation to honor properly drawn and signed on-us checks issued by its depositors, it also has the right to demand reasonable evidence of the identity of an unknown payee. But what is "reasonable evidence"? There are two extremes to be avoided. The first is a "play-it-safe" attitude that rejects automatically any type of documentary evidence that has ever been forged. For instance, it is known that automobile drivers' licenses, even those with photographs, have been counterfeited. The "play-it-safe" teller therefore rejects *all* drivers' licenses, completely ignoring the fact that there are many thousands of genuine drivers' licenses carried in the wallets of honest citizens. On the other hand, the teller who accepts anything with a name on it and resolves every doubt in favor of a stranger is likely to incur a sizable string of losses. Neither approach to the problem is justified.

Establishing identity, as has been said, is a matter of gathering bits of evidence, putting them all together, and arriving at a considered judgment. There is hardly any single unsupported bit of evidence that is completely acceptable; yet no evidence, favorable or unfavorable, can be ignored. To the credit of the many thousands of bank tellers, it must be said that "strangers" are satisfactorily identified every day in the normal course of business. While there have been losses, in view of the volume of traffic in bank lobbies, these have been surprisingly minimal. Better and more intelligent training methods could make losses even less frequent.

7 and 8. *Stop-Payment Orders and Holds.* Most banks have found it impractical to attempt to maintain current hard-copy lists of stop-payment orders and holds at *each* teller station. Normally such information is reported directly to the bookkeeping department and relayed to teller departments to the extent deemed necessary.

In any bookkeeping system, conventional or computerized, there are a number of devices that can alert bookkeepers automatically to the existence of stop-payment orders or holds as checks are posted. But the teller has no such automatic backstops. The existence of a stop-payment order or a hold can be determined only by checking the records, and the initiative must come from the teller. On a busy day with long lines of customers waiting to be served, any delay, however slight, can be disconcerting to both the teller and the customer: A decision must be made. In many cases, because of the account in question, the amount of the check, and other factors, the teller may feel completely justified in not taking the time to check the records or make inquiry. Nevertheless, all such decisions carry a degree of responsibility and, to some extent, add to the pressure of the teller's duties.

9. *Sufficient Collected Balance.* Overdrafts are readily isolated in all bank bookkeeping systems, either by printing the deficit balance in red, or by the automatic locking of a posting machine in conventional systems, or by the automatic printout of a list of overdrawn accounts in computerized systems.

Determining whether a check has been drawn against uncollected funds is more difficult, but at least the bookkeeper has helpful data readily available, such as the date of receipt and size of recent deposits. Even computerized systems at best produce educated guesses, for the time within which a dishonored check can be returned to the depository bank depends on the collection channel selected and the possibility that one or more intermediate collecting banks may be involved in the collection process.

In this area, too, the teller is at a distinct disadvantage and must come to a decision. Information regarding the sufficiency of balance and the probable extent of uncollected funds is almost as quickly available to the teller as it is to bookkeeping personnel, but the teller must take the initiative and seek the information. There is no automatic reminder that an unfavorable situation exists. In many cases inquiry is not necessary, but the decision rests on the teller's judgment and evaluation of the situation at hand.

The Teller's Responsibility in Cashing Checks

In many respects, cashing a check drawn on another bank presents a less complicated situation to a teller than paying a check drawn on his own bank.

A moment's thought should make this clear. When *cashing* a check, a teller is not concerned with the genuineness of the drawer's signature, or whether there are sufficient collected funds, or the existence of a stop-payment order or a hold, for only the bank on which the check is drawn would have knowledge of and bear the responsibility for these conditions. In fact, the only so-called validity tests of interest to a teller cashing a check drawn on another bank would be those evidenced by obvious irregularities, such as unmistakable alterations or a stale-dated or post-dated check. Hence, the most important consideration for which the teller is responsible in the *cashing* of an apparently properly drawn check is his evaluation of the ability of the person cashing the check to reimburse the bank promptly *if* the check is dishonored on presentation. This is not to say that *cashing* checks involves less *exposure* than *paying* checks. The point is that this single consideration is the basket that holds all of the eggs.

Since the cashing of a check drawn on another bank is a courtesy or an accommodation rather than an obligation, tellers ordinarily cash checks only for depositors or persons well-known to the bank. But this in itself is not enough when a relatively large amount is concerned, because, in either case, the person could be "well-known" to have limited financial means. If the check is subsequently dishonored, in all probability the money will have already been spent, and the person who cashed the check, however willing, may simply be financially unable to refund the money, except in small instalments over a protracted period of time. In these circumstances, it would be unfair to both the bank and the "casher" to advance funds simply on the assumption that the check will be paid.

But there are other things to be considered, one of which is the reputation and standing of the drawer of the check. Where the financial responsibility of the drawer need not be questioned, the probability that the item may be dishonored is remote; even in that unlikely event, the bank, acting in good faith, would enjoy the favorable status of a holder in due course.

Certified Checks

In certain types of business transactions, it is common practice to request that settlement be made in the form of a certified check. This is especially true in the case of real estate settlements where the seller receives the certified check in exchange for the deed that represents legal title to the property. Or bids on substantial contracts are often required to be accompanied by a good faith deposit in the form of a certified check in an amount equal to a percentage of the total contract price.

Although acceptances and certified checks have been briefly described elsewhere in this text and in the glossary, it would be appropriate at this time to review the nature and effect of certification of a check, which should also explain why such requests are made.

It will be recalled that a draft, which is an order to pay, may be made payable on demand or at a definite time. The Uniform Commercial Code provides that the payee or other holder of a *time draft* is not required to wait until the maturity date to discover the intention of the drawee. Thus the law gives such holder the right to present a time draft *for acceptance* before its due date. The holder of a *demand draft* has no such right, since the instrument entitles him to presentation for immediate payment, but not for acceptance.

Certification of a check is the legal equivalent of acceptance of an ordinary draft. Since a check by definition is a demand draft, the Code specifically states that a bank is under no obligation to certify a check, *unless otherwise agreed*. Therefore, while a bank is under no obligation to do so, it may certify or agree to certify a check if it so desires. Ordinarily, a bank will not certify a check except on the request of its customer, the drawer. Under certain clearinghouse rules, a drawee bank may certify a check before returning it to the presenting bank for improper indorsement.

When a bank does certify a check, however, it becomes primarily liable on the instrument. The check is no longer the drawer's *order to pay*—it is now the bank's *promise to pay*.

In many banks, the certification of checks is considered a function of paying teller operations, and this is logical, for certification is simply deferred payment rather than immediate payment. For this reason, before a check is certified, it must be subjected to all of the validity tests for payment, with the exception of the matter of indorsement. A typical bank certification stamp might read as follows:

Exhibit 12. Bank Certification Stamp

CERTIFIED

PAYABLE ONLY AS ORIGINALLY DRAWN
AND WHEN PROPERLY INDORSED

(DATE)
_____

INSTITUTE NATIONAL BANK
EREHWON, ILL.

_____
(AUTHORIZED SIGNATURE)

DO NOT DESTROY

A typical bank certification stamp. Many banks use rubber stamps for this purpose. But rubber stamps are easily obtained, and fraudulent "certifications" are not without precedent. There is a growing tendency among banks to use machine stamps that include the amount of the check (perforated) on the stamp to prevent raising the check *after* certification and to assign a number to each certification for control purposes.

After certification, the instrument is delivered to the drawer (or in exceptional cases to such other party as the bank may have agreed to accommodate) to be used for the purpose intended. However, since the bank is now obligated to honor the certified check when ultimately presented for payment, it must provide funds to meet the newly created liability. To accomplish this, a debit memorandum is prepared and the amount of the check is charged against the drawer's account and transferred to "certified checks outstanding" or some similarly worded liability account on the bank's general ledger.

The importance of subjecting the check to all applicable validity tests is apparent, for as far as the drawer is concerned, certification is the equivalent of actual payment. The bank appropriates the drawer's funds to meet its future obligation.

It should also be clear why certified checks are required in certain types of transactions. A certified check is no different from an uncertified check in that both are claims to money rather than money itself. But a claim against a bank is considered far superior to a claim against a depositor's balance, and with good reason. *Bank funds* (as direct bank obligations are called in financial circles) are required in many transactions that involve the delivery of securities, documents of title, or other items of considerable value for monetary consideration, where it would be unwise to introduce the uncertainty of subsequent presentation and possible dishonor of a plain check. The ultimate payment of bank funds can be endangered only by rather remote and unlikely possibilities, such as insolvency of the obligated bank or impoundment of the funds by court order.

It is not surprising, therefore, that *bank funds,* including certified checks, are generally accepted by everyone as representing a final and irrevocable payment of money. The Uniform Commercial Code adds substance to the practice by taking the position that the drawer of a check has no right to stop payment on a check after it has been certified. This position is eminently fair and necessary to protect those who readily accept certified checks in good faith and give value therefor.

However, practical problems sometimes arise for which banks must provide a solution. Certified checks are sometimes lost, stolen, or inadvertently destroyed. The drawer's account has been charged for the amount of the check. Assuming that the item may never be presented for payment, how can the bank reverse the certification debit and restore the funds to the drawer's account? Moreover, is the bank justified in making that assumption? As far as it knows, the certified check is outstanding and it could be presented at any time by a legitimate holder for value. On the other hand, should the assumption be borne out, the drawer would be unjustly penalized if the bank simply cited the Code as a reason for impounding the drawer's funds indefinitely. Obviously, a practical solution to a practical problem had to be found.

Despite the fact that the drawer of a certified check has no *legal* right to order payment stopped, most banks will accept the equivalent of a stop order supported by:

1. An affidavit (a sworn written statement) of the drawer stating the circumstances. Many banks have developed a standard form for this

purpose. If the certified check was lost or stolen, the affidavit should state whether the loss or theft occurred while the item was in the drawer's possession or after delivery of the item to the payee. If the check was inadvertently destroyed, the statement should indicate by whom and how the destruction took place.

2. A request that the amount of the certified check be restored to the drawer's account (thus reversing the certification debit) and that payment be refused should the item be presented for payment.

3. Suitable indemnity to protect and hold the bank harmless from any loss, damage, or injury resulting from its action in crediting the drawer's account and refusing to honor the certified check should it, by chance, be presented. The nature of the indemnity may vary, depending on circumstances and the bank's appraisal of the degree of exposure. If the amount of the certified check is sizable and the financial status of the drawer is limited or cannot be determined, the bank should insist on a formal bond of indemnity of a recognized bonding company, for which the drawer must pay a fee. On the other hand, the bank might feel justified in accepting the drawer's unsecured promise to hold the bank harmless and protect it from loss.

To illustrate, suppose an individual depositor obtains a certified check for $36 to reserve World Series baseball tickets that are never issued because his team collapsed in the home stretch, or suppose a corporation to which the bank extends an unsecured line of credit of $5,000,000 loses a certified check for $1,000. In either case, it would be unreasonable for the bank to insist on a formal bond of indemnity.

In most cases of this kind, the missing certified check is never presented for payment, and neither the bank nor its depositor suffers a loss. If the certified check had been stolen from the drawer and subsequently had been negotiated by means of a forged payee's indorsement, the certifying bank could refuse payment on such grounds, by furnishing an affidavit by the payee that he did not indorse or authorize the indorsement of the instrument. In the event that the check disappeared after delivery by the drawer to the payee but before the payee supplied his indorsement, the same would hold true. In this case, however, the indemnity given by the drawer to his bank should be supported by a similar agreement of indemnity running from the payee to the drawer.

Control of Cash

Bank tellers must have on hand at all times an adequate supply of both coin and currency in proper denominations in order to meet the needs of its customers. In fact, the services that banks furnish in this respect are indispensable to the smooth functioning of our monetary system. Coin, currency, and the ability to make change are still required for a great variety of miscellaneous commercial transactions. It is extremely embarrassing for a bank to run out of cash denominations of any kind, even when an acknowledged shortage of certain coins exists. The public expects, and with some justification, that banks should always be able to supply its cash needs.

To be able to meet the demands of the community it serves requires considerable judgment and skill on the part of those responsible for the management of a banking office. There is a tendency to play safe by overestimating reasonable needs, but control of the amount of cash, particularly in branch offices, is very important. For obvious reasons, excessive cash holdings unnecessarily tempt fate.

The control of cash is a problem for the managing officer or branch manager and the head teller, and decisions should be based on a careful study of the daily ebb and flow of cash in each particular banking office. There are a number of other factors to be considered. One would be the proximity and accessibility of sources of replenishment, such as a local Federal Reserve bank, or in the case of a branch, the bulk cash department of the main office. Another would be the frequency of scheduled deliveries: can they be made daily or only once or twice a week?

With this information, the office manager should first set an overall limit of cash for the office. It must be remembered that cash-flow patterns change as do other factors, and the manager and head teller should review periodically the maximum figure to determine whether the limit is excessive or unduly restrictive in the light of experience. Then the maximum amount to be held at each of the several tellers' stations should be considered, keeping in mind that this is the most accessible supply available to the lone bandit. The next step is to determine the amount and denominations of a reasonable supply of reserve cash for the office. Whenever facilities permit, reserve cash should always be held under time-delayed combination locks in the office vault and *not* in the bottom drawer of tellers' stations.

Every teller has a personal interest in the cash-handling procedures and should see that office rules are meticulously obeyed. For instance, large bulk-cash deposits should be removed from the teller's station as soon as possible and placed with reserve cash pending proper disposal. Similarly, prepared payrolls should not be kept at tellers' stations until they are ready for delivery.

Holdups

Obviously the most compelling reason for effective cash control is to make holdups as unprofitable as possible. Because of the nature of the business, banking offices will always be subject to attacks by armed bandits, but the frequency and probable success of such attacks depend in large measure on the defensive ingenuity of bankers.

The main reason why the public turned to the earliest banks centuries ago was *protection*. Despite the great variety of banking services offered today, protection is still the most valuable service. No bank can afford to abdicate its responsibility to protect its assets, which for the most part are owed to its depositors. However, adequate protection is the responsibility of bank management and not that of employees. Therefore, the first rule is: *All bank tellers should be instructed and ordered to show no resistance to holdup bandits.*

This rule should not be interpreted as abject surrender, for there is much that banks and bank tellers can do to assist in the prompt identification and capture of holdup men. Tellers should be carefully trained as to how they should act *if* they should be confronted by a bandit, and this training should not be limited to an off-the-cuff two-minute lecture by a head teller. Instructions should be clear and precise and, after discussion, should be made available in writing. While the nature of the instructions may vary depending on the banking office and its physical facilities, the following essential points for employees to follow are invariably included:

1. Obey the bandit's instructions to the letter, but no more or no less.

2. Remain as calm as possible; do not do anything that would excite your adversary.

3. Be sure that decoy or marked money is included in any cash taken.

4. Try to make mental notes concerning the physical appearance of the bandit confronting you (height, approximate weight, color of hair and eyes, scars, and other descriptive information) as well as his voice or any characteristic action.

5. Sound whatever alarm may be available *as soon as you are certain that your action will not be detected.*

6. After the ordeal is over, do not discuss the incident, particularly your mental image of the bandit, until you have been questioned by a law enforcement officer.

There is no way of telling how any individual will react during the traumatic experience of a holdup. Some tellers have fainted on the spot; others have displayed remarkable coolness and have frustrated hardened bandits in the most incredible ways. There was one teller who returned a holdup note with a disarming smile as she purred, "I'm sorry, sir, but these transactions have to be approved and initialed by our manager." The bandit fled in utter confusion. *Nevertheless, personal heroics must be strongly discouraged.* When they are unsuccessful, the results can be tragic.

Protective Devices

While there are many protective devices available, bank management must consider carefully what may be required for any particular office. No attempt will be made here to recommend what is best for all banks.

Silent alarm systems that alert local police are especially effective, but there is always the question of how soon they can be safely activated. In this connection, bill-traps that activate an alarm as soon as marked bait money is removed from the teller's drawer are worthy of consideration.

Surveillance cameras can be very helpful, but again there is the question of activation. If they are set to take a picture frame every 15 seconds, day in and day out, the cost of operation and maintenance can be quite expensive in terms of the benefit derived. If the cameras must be activated by the victimized teller, they might produce nothing more than a photo of the bandit's coattails as he scoots out the front door. On the other hand, surveillance cameras have produced excellent pictures that have helped to identify and convict bank robbers.

Armed guards are still used effectively, but their use requires thought, for a single armed guard in an isolated office could be a sitting duck for a murderous bandit.

Devices that should be most carefully considered, and possibly avoided, are those that are potentially dangerous to employees as well as customers, such as *timed explosive devices* that produce tear gas or malodorous or staining substances. One thing banks have learned from experience is that mechanical devices can be and sometimes are activated accidentally. If such a device goes off in the hands of a thief and aids in his capture, well and good. But if by chance such a device harms or even embarrasses an innocent customer, the consequences could be serious.

Branches in isolated rural areas with wide-open escape routes or offices in high crime areas need maximum protection. Yet mid-city offices, where an escaping bandit can easily be lost in a crowd, cannot be considered safe either. While it is bank management's responsibility to provide the most effective protection devices available, there is no cut-and-dried answer. To purchase and install everything available regardless of cost or suitability could be self-defeating in the long run.

Fraudulent Schemes and Practices

Bank tellers are the constant target of thieves, swindlers, and confidence men. This is true of almost all phases of teller activity including the seemingly harmless function of receiving deposits. A teller's training goes far beyond teaching the basic skills of counting money and making settlements, although such fundamental training cannot be ignored. An essential part of the teller's training is exposure to the operating methods of the swindlers who prey on bank tellers. Furthermore, this must be somewhat of a continuous course of instruction, for professional crooks are clever and resourceful, they are well-acquainted with banking procedures, and they are constantly inventing new deceptive tactics. It is especially important for the training director to recognize that when his bright young charges take over a teller's station they are in the major leagues as far as fraud is concerned.

Each bank will naturally devise its own training programs, but inclusion of the following points is well worth considering:

1. *Unnecessary exposure.* Tellers must be taught the danger of leaving large sums of money exposed to view on or near the deal-plate. Modern bank architecture, particularly some of the low, exposed teller's counters, may be planned by the interior designer to be warm and friendly, but it tends to make the operations of sneak thieves much easier. Tellers must learn never to turn away from the station with cash drawers open or a sum of money on the counter within reach of a person at the window. It is surprising how far the average person can reach through the service opening or even over an unprotected counter.

This "housekeeping" rule applies to the department as well as to the individual tellers. It is tempting fate to use exposed tables or counters behind the teller stations as temporary storage space for large sums of money such as payrolls or bulk cash deposits.

2. *Distractions.* No teller can avoid distractions, but there should be an awareness that distractions can be natural or contrived. It is the most natural thing in the world for customers to chat with tellers as money is counted or a check is examined. But garrulous strangers while not necessarily crooks should suggest a little extra caution. A teller must concentrate on the transaction at hand, and when normal concentration is broken, it is wise to re-check the transaction to make sure that a "contrived" distraction has not accomplished its purpose.

3. *Unusual transactions or circumstances.* There are so many tricks and devices especially designed to victimize bank tellers that it is possible to mention only a few in this text.

One of the favorite ruses involves a simple request for "change." An affable stranger approaches a teller and offers several $50 or $100 bills, which is disarming in itself. He usually carries his "distraction" with him—often a winsome child of five or six years. The stranger simply requests smaller denominations for his large bills, but when the obliging teller hands him the money, he may suddenly change his mind about the denominations or decide that he would like to keep one of the large bills. Money and conversation are freely exchanged. Then at the proper time the "distraction" engages the teller in some childish conversation or asks "daddy" a cute question, which naturally produces broad smiles from both parent and teller. Finally, the proud daddy is satisfied and leaves, and through clever sleight-of-hand manipulations, he has managed to swindle the confused teller out of several hundred dollars. This may sound incredible, but it is surprising how often this trick has worked.

Another swindle involves the so-called split-deposit or cash-back deposit. The crook approaches a teller with a deposit slip accompanied by a sizable check, say $600, usually drawn on an out-of-town bank. The customer needs $350 for current expenses and only wishes to deposit $250 in his account, which is the amount listed on the deposit slip. What the teller is actually confronted with is a request to "cash" a $350 check. The purely incidental deposit aspect of the transaction is the "distraction." An inexperienced teller often concludes that if a person holding a $600 claim to money is willing to leave $250 with the bank, the transaction must be legitimate and there can be no doubt but that the check will be paid. The fallacy of this reasoning has been demonstrated thousands of times. But there is another side to the coin. A split deposit transaction can be entirely acceptable if the teller views it in the proper light. Many wage-earners need some cash on payday, and where a paycheck is concerned, this type of transaction can be convenient both for the employee and for the bank. However, as mentioned earlier, a check should be cashed *only* if the teller is sure that the payee will be able to refund the money if the check is dishonored or if the financial responsibility of the drawer is unquestioned. If either alternative can be answered in the affirmative, the split-deposit need not be feared. But the teller must be aware of the fact such a transaction involves *the cashing of a check;* the subsequent deposit of a portion of the cash is incidental.

Swindlers often play on human emotion or use psychological approaches to delude the unwary. Many bankers recall a "happy father" character with something less than enthusiasm. The crook first opens an account with the bank. He is affable and friendly and, in the course of making routine deposits and withdrawals, quickly ingratiates himself with as many of the bank's personnel as possible. When the stage is set, a consummate actor, he suddenly bursts into the bank laden with boxes of cigars and boxes of expensive candy. He is delirious with joy. His wife has just presented him with a son! He lavishly distributes cigars to the men, candy to the women, and shows pictures of his newborn son taken through the window of the hospital nursery. His ecstasy is contagious, and soon the whole office is sharing his exuberance. Before he leaves, he remembers that he has a check to cash—no doubt something to do with the happy event, perhaps a substantial check from proud grandparents to start the young lad's college fund. Could any teller be so inhuman as to apply normal standards in such circumstances? The answer to this question lies in the fact that our "human" tellers have already contributed enough money to the "happy father" to put a dozen sons through medical school!

Mimicry

One of the most successful frauds that has plagued bankers recently has been the "fake payroll." This ruse relies primarily on the swindler's ability to impersonate certain corporate officers in telephone conversations by almost perfect renditions of the voice and speech habits of people well-known to bank personnel. It is part of a scheme in which the clever crook does not personally enter into his fraudulent transaction until he is sure that his plan has been successful.

This swindle is well-planned and perfectly executed. It begins with the crook, on some pretext or another, gaining several interviews with the financial officer, usually the treasurer, of a local corporation. During his visits, he also becomes acquainted with the receptionist and with the messenger who makes deposits and picks up payrolls at the bank. He learns all he can about how banking transactions are handled. When he is set, he telephones a teller at the bank and orders a special "bonus" payroll, posing as the corporate financial officer. His mimicry is perfect. In one case, he talked to a girl who knew the treasurer in high school, and he completely convinced her that he was indeed her old classmate. Of course, since a bonus payroll is highly confidential, at his request she promised not to mention it to anyone, so as not to eclipse an announcement the corporate president was expected to make when the bonus was distributed. He asked her to wrap the payroll in plain brown paper and deliver it to the regular company messenger when he called. He then called the messenger, again representing himself to be the treasurer and asked him to go to the bank, pick up a package, and deliver it to the receptionist. Meanwhile, the receptionist did not think it unnatural when a frequent visitor to the treasurer's office told her that a package would be delivered to her office for him, and politely requested that she please hold it until he called. Neither the messenger nor the receptionist had any idea of what the package contained. Subsequently, he arranged for the package to be picked up by a cab driver and delivered to him far from the company's office or the bank.

As unbelievable as it may seem, this intricate hoax has been successfully perpetrated innumerable times, on each occasion netting the imaginative swindler amounts in the area of $8,000 to $14,000.

189

Shorts and Overs

Unexplained tellers' differences have been an increasingly vexing problem for many banks. In one respect, this is not too surprising, since the rapid proliferation of bank offices enlarged the area of exposure by greatly increasing the number of bank tellers and tellers' stations. For reasons already discussed, when a teller's cash drawer does not settle at the end of a busy day, it is extremely difficult to locate and to reconcile the difference satisfactorily. Shortages invariably must be charged against profit and loss, and for the bank with several hundred full-time and part-time tellers, the accumulated shortages over a period of time can reach embarrassing proportions.

Management and supervisors cannot adopt the philosophy that unexplained differences are simply an unavoidable cost of doing business. To do so is not only shortsighted but exceedingly dangerous. Furthermore, while shortages represent a direct loss, overages cannot be ignored. An overage usually means that a customer has been shortchanged, which is not a pleasant thought for the bank striving to enhance its public image. Or, as is sometimes the case, a belated but necessary settlement adjustment of, say, $100 could quickly convert a $10 overage into a $90 shortage.

In some banking offices, there is a too-eager tendency to throw overages into a "kitty box" without investigation, in the hope that this will partially offset shortages. This practice leads to manipulated settlements and cannot be defended on any grounds. Management, particularly the auditing staff of the bank, should not only prohibit the use of "kitty boxes," but take steps to see that none exist.

Each bank tends to develop its own teller training program, and the teaching of approved teller procedures and effective settlement techniques should be an important part of a teller's training. Absolute perfection is probably unattainable. The sensitive nature of the tellers' contact with customers and the public is well-known, and careless or shoddy performance at this point can be disastrous. The least that management can do is to let it be known that it views tellers' differences, both overages and shortages, with considerable concern. Furthermore, there should be visible evidence of that concern, for *unconcern* is contagious. Most tellers are naturally interested in the accuracy of their performance as a matter of personal pride. But this innate desire for personal proficiency can quickly be smothered if management consistently demonstrates a lack of interest in quality achievement.

In summary, a teller's life can be an exciting one. A teller must be fast, efficient, and competent—well versed in money, monetary transactions and financial instruments. In addition, the teller must be sufficiently worldly-wise to cope with the professional "paperhanger" who makes a comfortable living by defrauding banks and merchants out of hundreds of millions of dollars annually. There is no substitute for experience in the teller's arsenal of defense weapons, but until that experience has been acquired, carefully devised and intelligent training methods must fill the gap.

Questions Based on This Chapter:

1. What is meant by the term *unit teller?*

2. In what respects do the responsibilities of a teller in paying checks differ from those of the bookkeeper?

3. Describe the nature of a certified check.

4. In the event of a holdup, what can a teller do to aid in the identification and apprehension of the bandits?

Chapter 12

The Payments Function

Part III: Devices and Systems

The Purposes of This Chapter:

1. *To describe briefly the evolution of bank bookkeeping methods from hand-posting to modern sophisticated systems.*

2. *To show how the illusive goal of accuracy has been a strong influence in the selection of newer systems.*

3. *To outline briefly the application of electronic data processing to the bookkeeping process.*

If the impact of modern technological systems on the process of collecting cash items can be described as sensational, as it well might be, then the impact of modern methods and particularly electronic data processing systems on the payments function must be described as *revolutionary.*

As has been noted, the greatest volume of actual payment transactions handled by drawee banks is processed in the bookkeeping department. In this area, electronic data processing has tremendous potential, as it does in any area where a great mass of data must be handled with the highest possible degree of accuracy.

The true value of modern data processing techniques can be best appreciated by reviewing briefly the evolution of bank bookkeeping methods from the days when technology had not progressed beyond quill pens, inkwells, green eyeshades, and high stools.

The primary function of the bookkeeping department is to keep and maintain complete, accurate, and current records of the accounts of demand depositors. The importance of complete and up-to-date records is self-evident, but in such a sensitive area the accuracy of depositors' accounts records is the foremost consideration. Recognition of this fact by bankers is clearly evidenced by one of the most popular bookkeeping systems for many years, appropriately called the "dual posting system."

Conventional Bookkeeping Systems

Following the era of hand-posting, mechanical methods were introduced to bank operations in the early part of the century in an effort to keep pace with the mounting volume of demand deposit activity.

At that time, the introduction of adding machines and posting machines marked a great step forward and enabled fewer people to handle more work in less time. But the objective of accuracy remained as elusive as ever. Indeed, the early adding and posting machines, like other mechanical devices, were known to malfunction at times. In addition, no mechanical device, not even the computer, can rise above the skills of the people who operate it. Compared with hand-posting, posting machines for all their positive advantages seemed to increase rather than decrease the number and variety of possible errors.

Thus, for many years a dual posting system seemed to be the only way to achieve the objective of accuracy. This system required one operator to post debits and credits to an account ledger card, while another operator, using the same posting media (checks, deposit slips, and debit or credit memoranda) would duplicate the posting process to another set of records. Since it was highly unlikely that two *separate* operators would make the same error, a high degree of accuracy was achieved, but at considerable cost. Every item had to be posted twice, and this *literally* doubled the cost of the posting operation. One advantage of the system, however, was the fact that the second posting provided an identical detailed record of account activity, which served as the customer's statement. Although everyone knew that dual posting was wasteful and expensive, its persistent popularity illustrates the dominance of basic objectives (in this case, accuracy) over the methods we employ.

193

Bankers and equipment manufacturers struggled for years with the obvious objection to dual posting. *Single* posting systems with an assortment of special features designed to capture at least some of the accuracy of dual posting were devised.

Account Numbering Systems

One of the major disadvantages of most single posting systems was the fact that there was no way to guard against a bookkeeper inadvertently pulling the wrong ledger card and posting entries to the wrong account, which, of course, could produce serious consequences. The dual posting system provided a very effective check on this type of error through a comparison of the updated account balances.

Efforts to guard against this particular disadvantage of a single posting operation eventually led to the "tronic" systems. Posting machines with limited electronic capabilities were designed which required special ledger sheets with multiple rows of magnetic-ink stripes on the reverse side. The magnetic ink stripes have the ability to accept encoded impulses representing digital information, which can be read by the machine in subsequent operations.

However, the effective use of the "tronic" equipment requires that account numbers be assigned to all accounts, and, of course, customers' checks and other posting media also have to be identified by the proper account number. The account number is permanently recorded on the magnetic stripes on the ledger sheet. After each posting, the new balance not only appears in conventional characters on the face side of the ledger sheet, but also in magnetized encoding on the reverse side. Each posting operation erases the previous encoding and automatically substitutes encoding representing the new balance.

The "tronic" systems have two advantages. The first involves a partial comparison. Before posting, the operator indexes the last three numbers of the account number, which the machine compares with the number encoded in the magnetic stripes. If the three digits do not compare favorably, the machine locks. This partial comparison, while not eliminating all possibilities, greatly reduces the chance of posting to the wrong account. The second advantage of such modified single posting systems lies in the fact that the opening balance is automatically entered in the machine as the sheet is inserted, thus eliminating balance pick-up errors—a common failing where manual indexing is required.

Many banks began to number accounts years ago—some in anticipation of computerized bookkeeping systems and others to take advantage of the newly available machines.

Account numbering in itself presents unique problems. Depending on the system used or contemplated, a choice must be made between alpha-numeric systems (to preserve alphabetic filing sequence) or straight numeric systems. The system must be flexible enough to allow for expansion, and provision must be made for methods of numbering new accounts as well as for the reuse of numbers released by account closings. An adequate system can provide for classification of groups of accounts, which has significant advantages in sorting, controlling, and reporting by groups of accounts. In addition, the use of a self-checking digit provides an effective way to guard against transpositions and other human errors in encoding account numbers on documents. A check digit is a suffix digit that a computer, by means of a programmed mathematical formula, can use to test the validity of the account number.

Automated Bookkeeping

MICR (magnetic ink character recognition) made it possible to encode checks, deposit slips, and other posting documents in a machine-readable language. Sorter-readers or document-handlers made incredibly fast and accurate sorting of paper documents an attainable reality, but it took the electronic memory and the mass storage capability of a computer to supply the final touch.

A computer can be programmed to handle the bookkeeping process flawlessly—as long as the input data is accurate and reliable. The balance and related account numbers of many thousands of accounts can be fed into and retained in its prodigious electronic memory, together with an almost unlimited assortment of vital statistics applicable to each individual account. The nature and extent of such statistics may vary with the needs of each particular bank and the capacity of the equipment used, but Table 1 illustrates the range of useful data that can be recorded. All such information is recorded on a master record, which can be in the form of magnetic tape, disks, punch cards, or any other media acceptable by the computer. In the following discussion, it shall be assumed that magnetic tape is used as the input medium.

The following passages very briefly describe the manner in which the bookkeeping process is performed by a computerized data processing system.

First, let it be assumed that the data contained in the master record has been assimilated by the computer through magnetic tape input. The next step is to prepare another magnetic tape to serve as the posting run or, as it is called, the *entry run*, which must contain such vital data as the amount of each transaction, the number of the account affected, and a transcode to distinguish debits from credits.

All items to be posted in the day's work are passed through sorter-readers, which capture and record the MICR data on magnetic tape

Table 1. Example of information contained in master record

Account Number
Abbreviated Account Name
Alphabetic Sequence Number
Current Ledger Balance
Current Available Balance
Accumulated Monthly Balance (00.00 omitted)
Accumulated Uncollected Funds (00.00 omitted)
Previous Month's Average Balance (00.00 omitted)
Date of Last Transaction
Number of Debits—Current Day
Total Amount of Debits—Current Day
Number of Credits—Current Day
Total Amount of Credits—Current Day
Number of Debits—Current Month
Number of Credits—Current Month
Number of Checks Deposited—Current Month
Accumulated Service Charge—Current Month
Date of Last Statement
Balance as of Previous Statement
Number of Debits since Last Statement
Total Amount of Debits since Last Statement
Number of Credits since Last Statement
Total Amount of Credits since Last Statement
Scheduled Dates for Special Statements
Amount of 3 Day Deferred Credit (00.00 omitted)
Amount of 2 Day Deferred Credit (00.00 omitted)
Amount of 1 Day Deferred Credit (00.00 omitted)
Group Assignment Code
Industry Classification Code
Restricted Account Code (Dormant, Deceased, etc.)
Miscellaneous Codes

to serve as input media to the computer. The sorter-readers also sort the physical documents in account number order.

Since it would be impractical to wait until all transactions have been assembled before starting the operation, checks presented in cash letters or through the clearinghouse might be processed fairly early in the day in several "package" runs, without waiting for teller transactions and interdepartmental debits and credits that are normally received much later. This makes settlements much easier by isolating possible errors, as each package contains a "package control ticket," and the computer automatically balances the dollar amount of items recorded on the input tape with the total on the control ticket, thus accomplishing the objective of settling to previously established control figures.

After all the day's entries have been processed, the several transaction tapes produced by the package runs are merged by the computer to form the final entry-run tape. During the merging operation, the computer sorts all data into account number order and the desired posting order, such as credits before debits, interdepartment debits before check debits, and so forth. The final entry-run tape is then processed against the master control data as the computer subtracts debits from and adds credits to the opening balance of the activated accounts. A new updated master control tape is then produced containing a new balance for each account, together with updated statistical data, to serve as the basis for the next day's activity.

Statements

In order to have the necessary details for preparing statements at the end of the month or at the end of a cycle, as the case might be, it is necessary to create a tape record containing an accumulation of all transactions posted to each account since the date of the last statement. The computer accomplishes this with relative ease simply by merging each day's transaction (entry-run) tape with the previous day's accumulated transaction tape. Following this operation, the computer assembles the data required to prepare statements for those accounts scheduled to receive them at the close of that day and delivers the detailed activity to a high-speed printing device. After the data have served their purpose they are not carried forward to the new accumulated transaction tape.

Rejected Items

It sometimes happens that a sorter-reader is unable to read correctly the magnetic ink characters on checks or other documents. This condition can occur through mutilation of a document, faulty printing, or possibly malfunction of the feeding mechanism of the document handler. Or, as mentioned earlier, the computer may be unable to verify the accuracy of the account number through the check digit calculation. All such items are sorted into a reject pocket and must be handled and disposed of manually. Items otherwise eligible for posting must be reentered into the system by means of substitute documents or some other acceptable input device. Ineligible items must be adjusted through contact with the source from which they were received.

Informational Reports

From the foregoing discussion, it is evident that an automated bookkeeping system, utilizing the capabilities of a computer, relieves the bookkeeper of the tedium of sorting paper documents, posting debits and credits, and the often difficult task of settling to control totals. But this is not the entire story. Providing vital information to supervisory and top management under the more conventional systems was often a crude, laborious, pick-and-shovel job. With the aid of sophisticated instruction programs and depending on the needs and requirements of each individual bank, the computer can produce an almost unlimited variety of statistical reports.

The following is an example of some of the reports that the computer can produce by creating an output tape to supply data to a high-speed printer.

1. *Daily journal and balance report.* This report lists for each account all of the day's transaction activity coded to indicate the type of entry (checks, deposits, miscellaneous debits, and credits), together with balance information. Used primarily for reference purposes, the daily journal is most useful in connection with inquiries commonly received concerning individual accounts.

2. *Overdraft report.* All accounts that become overdrawn as a result of posting the day's transactions as well as accounts with negative balances carried forward from the previous day are listed. Where items are returned to correct the overdraft condition, reversal entries are put through on the following day.

3. *Accounts drawing against uncollected funds.* The accounts listed on this report would depend on the specific formula adopted by individual banks. The formula might include a generous "calculated risk" factor, or it could be based on fairly precise information. For instance, some banks might decide to list only those accounts with closing balances *less* than the amount of deposits in the current day's work. Although such a formula ignores the possibility that a substantial amount of uncollected funds might remain from previous deposits,

the experience of a given bank over a period of time could well demonstrate that the risk taken had been reasonable. At the other end of the scale, it is possible to program a formula that would include as uncollected funds all items that could still be returned under the legal time limits, and list on the report all accounts with balances that do not at least equal the total of uncollected funds so calculated.

4. *Restricted accounts report.* Restricted accounts are those against which "holds" have been placed, and all such accounts affected during the day's activity, together with a code indicating the nature of the restriction, are listed on this report.

5. *Closed accounts and zero balance accounts.* This information can be contained in two separate reports or in a single report. Accounts officially designated as closed by management or by the depositor are removed from the records. Accounts not so designated that show a zero balance as a result of the day's posting would naturally prompt an inquiry to determine the depositor's intentions. Certain accounts, such as dividend, salary, and payroll accounts might normally be reduced to a zero balance between distribution or payment periods and by suitable coding can be omitted from this type of report.

6. *Accounts with substantial increases or decreases in balances.* Listings on this report would be determined by a management-approved formula applied to balance changes as a result of the day's postings. The formula might be based on dollar amounts (increases or decreases of $10,000, $50,000, $100,000 or whatever amount management considered significant) or on percentage changes (say, an increase or decrease of 50 percent or more of the previous month's average balance). In this type of report, it may be necessary to eliminate by coding a large number of accounts where such changes are not particularly significant.

7. *Posting-run exceptions.* All debit and credit transactions for which a corresponding account number was not found on the master record are listed on this report. Normally, such items would be posted to a suspense account (for settlement purposes) pending disposition on the following day.

8. *Stop-payment suspects.* A listing is made by accounts showing the number and dollar amount of check transactions in the current day's work that correspond with the dollar amount of a stop-payment order on file for the account on which such checks are drawn. A substantial majority of checks in use at the present time do not have magnetically encoded check numbers, and in these cases it is not possible for the computer to detect specific checks on which payment has been stopped. Manual inspection of stop-payment suspects by bookkeeping personnel is necessary to determine whether any items for a corresponding amount

represent the specific check covered by a stop-payment order. It should be mentioned that it is possible to include check numbers on the MICR-encoded data, and the practice is growing in popularity.

Automation and Other Bookkeeping Department Duties

In addition to the elimination of much of the routine manual operations by bookkeeping personnel, a computerized system also has a beneficial effect, though to a lesser degree, on certain other of the department's duties.

For instance, the application of certain validity tests has been made much easier. No longer is it necessary for bookkeeping personnel to examine each account separately to determine the existence of stop-payment orders, holds, or an insufficient balance condition. Standard computer reports pinpoint those accounts where active consideration of these particular tests is indicated, and all other accounts, in these respects at least, can be ignored. The computer also verifies the fact that it is an on-us check and that the indicated demand account does in fact exist. Nevertheless, pending further dramatic technological developments, it is still necessary to examine each individual check to see that it has a genuine and authorized signature, that it has not been materially altered, that it is not post-dated or stale-dated, and that it bears a satisfactory indorsement.

Even in its function as a communications center, the burden of the bookkeeping department has been lightened to some extent in those banks where other departments have direct access to computer information. This is a relative benefit, though, as many inquiries require the personal attention of qualified bookkeeping personnel.

In other areas, the computer offers little help. Paid checks must be carefully filed for ready reference, and at statement time they must be counted and verified and carefully combined with the proper statement before being finally prepared for delivery.

Automation has truly revolutionized the bookkeeping process, but this has not lessened in any way the need for competent and experienced personnel and supervisors to operate and manage this very critical phase of bank operations.

Devices That Aid the Paying Teller

While there are many devices that have eased somewhat the heavy responsibilities of tellers in their performance of the payments function, it cannot be said that anything has really revolutionized the paying teller's life.

Tellers must still take the initiative in applying the validity tests.

There are no reminders or back stops to jog the teller's memory. Yet some modern devices have eliminated some of the agonizing moments spent on the telephone or at a central file seeking information. Touch-tone pads conveniently located give the teller direct access to the computer's store of information, with a complete accurate response in a matter of seconds. Microfilm signature files quickly provide specimen signatures for comparison almost instantaneously.

In the savings account area, on-line tellers' machines have eliminated the hazards of the hand-posting of passbooks at the window. An *on-line device* is one that provides input and receives output directly to and from the computer. For instance, the teller indexes the account number, a code indicating the type of transaction, the amount of the transaction, and the balance shown in the passbook. Using this input, the computer first compares the balance shown in the passbook with the balance in the computer's memory. If the two balances agree, the computer uses the input data to post the transaction and instructs the machine to make a similar entry in the passbook so that the two figures remain in balance. If these two amounts do not agree, due to a prior transaction processed by the computer but not entered in the passbook, the computer instructs the machine to supply the missing entry to bring the passbook into balance. The most common example would be an interest credit made automatically at the end of an interest period but not yet entered in the passbook.

All such devices, especially those involving direct access to a computer, are extremely helpful and do much to lighten the teller's burden. The search for additional refinements is never-ending, and no attempt has been made here to cover the complete scope of strategies that have been used or the many projects even now being planned and tested.

Some bankers and scientists believe that eventually the computer and sophisticated peripheral equipment will succeed in completely eliminating any need for experience and judgment on the part of bank bookkeepers and tellers. Perhaps so. Automatic teller machines that can both accept deposits and paychecks are now in use as are "tellerless" lobbies where customer contact is made via closed-circuit television and pneumatic tubes. It is now at least technologically possible for depositors to "talk" to their bank's computers and receive quick answers to inquiries in a pleasant recorded voice.

For years, banks have spent much time, effort, and money in constructing the image of warm, friendly, and human institutions concerned about customers' needs, which certainly seemed to be a worthwhile objective. Completely automated banking will require some means of making inanimate machines, pneumatic tubes and recorded voices as warm and friendly as direct human contact.

In any event, trained and experienced tellers and bookkeepers seem destined to remain for some time as important elements in the performance of the payment function of banks. No matter how rapidly vital information can be made available by technological devices, signatures must still be compared, improper dates must be considered, and alterations must be detected; while for the teller, the problem of paying the right amount of money to the *right party* still exists. If and when *checks* as a means of making payments are eliminated, these problems may disappear, but for the moment, at least, they are real and practical and cannot be ignored.

Electronic Funds Transfer Systems

For some time now, bankers and others involved in the nation's payment system have been exploring the feasibility of converting our existing paper-based payment system to electronic funds transfer. Although the acceptance of this concept and large volume use is still in the future, considerable effort has been expended in establishing the standards, networks, and specific services that will be required to support an EFTS environment.

Government agencies and large corporations are constantly faced with the necessity of creating huge quantities of paper checks covering periodic payments to individual recipients. One such example of periodic mass payments provides a striking comparison of our present paper procedures to an electronic approach to the problem.

For instance, every month the Social Security Administration makes payments to millions of our citizens. First the checks have to be prepared, and the paper is subsequently handled by the Postal Service, by the individual payee, a depository bank, one or more intermediate collecting banks, and by the drawee. Then the checks must be cancelled, microfilmed, and the records filed for reference purposes. One handling can be eliminated by sending the check directly to the payee's bank, which is being done in many cases.

The electronic equivalent of this system would be for the Social Security Administration to furnish the Federal Reserve bank with magnetic tape or punched cards acceptable to its computer, which would give details, such as the name of each designated payee, the amount to be paid, the transit routing symbol of the payee's bank and the payee's account number. It would be a relatively easy matter for the Reserve bank computer to sort the data according to Federal Reserve banks and branches. Each bank and branch in turn could use its computer to sort the data according to the intended depository bank. The Social Security Administration would make a single payment to the Federal Reserve System, which would be distributed to the district banks and branches, and each depository would receive the total amount to be credited to accounts on its books. It is not difficult to visualize the application of this technique to other mass payment operations and the tremendous potential savings in time, energy, and paper handling.

Over the years there have been many significant developments and improvements in bank bookkeeping techniques, many of which were made necessary by the gradual but persistent increase in the use of checks drawn on demand deposits as a means of making payments. Within the last two decades the introduction of electronic data processing to banking has virtually revolutionized bookkeeping methods.

It is quite evident that the full potential of computerized bookkeeping has not as yet been realized. The dream of a completely checkless and cashless society through electronic funds transfer systems is certainly within the realm of possibility and may be with us sooner than we realize. Nevertheless, the "paper tiger" will not disappear overnight, and for several years to come, competent training methods designed to enable banking personnel to handle our present payments systems will be necessary, even as we move closer and closer to the better world of the future.

Questions Based on This Chapter:

1. What is the primary function of a bank bookkeeping department, and what is considered the foremost objective in performing this function?

2. Describe some of the management reports that can be generated automatically by a computerized bookkeeping system.

3. Give some of the reasons why skilled banking personnel are still an important element in effective bookkeeping operations.

4. What is meant by the term *on-line devices?*

Chapter 13

Loans
and
Investments

Part I: The Money Function

The Purposes of This Chapter:

1. *To distinguish between bank loans and bank investments.*

2. *To explain how commercial banks create money and add to the total of money supply by making loans and investments.*

3. *To point out the shortcomings of the narrow but useful definition of money supply known as* M_1.

The loan function of commercial banks is divided into two distinctly different activities. A bank can either negotiate a loan with a borrower or purchase certain types of investment securities.

What is the difference between a loan and investment? A *loan* may be simply defined as money lent at interest, while an *investment* is more broadly defined as the outlay of money for either income or profit, or both. A loan is the exchange of money for a promise to repay at a later date. An investment is the exchange of money *either* for a promise to repay at a later date, or for a share in a venture that carries the right to share profits, if there are any, but with no obligation to repay the amount invested. Thus, an investment can be the purchase of evidence of indebtedness, such as the bonds or notes of an obligor, which are promises to repay the amount invested with interest, *or* the purchase of certificates of ownership, such as common or preferred stock, which do not involve a legal obligation to pay back the amount invested. In the event of liquidation, however, owners of shares of stock have a claim against the liquidated assets of the issuing company after all creditors have been paid in full.

Generally, commercial banks are prohibited from purchasing stock certificates (or equities as they are called) for investment purposes. However, there are a few instances where the purchase of equities is required or permitted by banking laws, such as the (required) purchase of stock of the Federal Reserve banks by member banks, and the (permitted) investment in the shares of certain banking affiliates and subsidiaries. Therefore, the term *investments* in this part of the text will refer to the purchase by banks of debt obligations rather than to equity investments.

From the banker's outlook, there are two significant differences between loans and investments. One difference concerns the nature of the transaction, and the other relates to the purpose of the transaction.

A bank loan is the result of direct negotiations between the bank (the lender) and the customer (the borrower) and involves a rather close and intimate relationship. Ordinarily, no other party is involved, and the terms of the loan (maturity, interest rate, security, and so forth) are determined privately by agreement between the two parties.

On the other hand, bank investments rarely bring the two principal parties (lender and borrower) together. A securities dealer (or in the case of new issues, an underwriter) acts as an intermediary between the lender and the borrower. Thus, the lender deals with a *market,* rather than directly with a borrower. While the bank (lender) is certainly aware of the identity of the "borrower," the borrower may have no idea of the identity of its lenders except where bonds or notes are registered in the owner's name.

In addition, the very purpose of a bank's loans differs considerably from the purpose of its investments. Making loans is a very definite part of a bank's obligation to the community it serves, because the community is the principal source of the bank's funds (deposit liability). A bank makes loans for the purpose of performing a normal and expected service, notwithstanding the fact that interest earned on loans normally constitutes its greatest single source of income. Investments are not influenced by external considerations but are made for the purpose of achieving the objectives of an asset management program, which, simply stated, are liquidity and the gainful utilization of all funds with minimal risk exposure.

The Money Function

Both commercial bank loans and investments do have one thing in common, in that both activities have the power to *create* money by adding to the nation's money supply. Thus the term *money function* used as a heading for this section is not really a separate function. Actually, it is a natural economic consequence of the extension of credit by the bank's loan and investment function.

The Creation of Money by Commercial Banks

According to the narrow but generally accepted M_1 definition, money supply has two components:

1. Demand deposits *adjusted* (which means all accounts subject to withdrawal by check, except domestic interbank deposits, U.S. government deposits, and cash items in process of collection), and

2. Coin and currency *in circulation* (which means outside of the Treasury, Federal Reserve banks, and the vaults of commercial banks).

The *total* of these two components represents the nation's money supply, or funds in private hands immediately available for spending purposes by the public. Any monetary transaction that increases either of these two components, without simultaneously producing an offsetting or counterbalancing effect, creates new money by adding to the total of money supply.

A few examples of routine monetary transactions should illustrate this point.

1. A person stops at a newsstand and purchases a newspaper or magazine using loose change in his pocket for the purpose. A certain amount of coin and currency in circulation changes ownership, but the total of coin/currency in circulation does not change and the transaction does not affect any demand deposit account. Therefore, the total of money supply is unchanged.

2. Later in the day, the newsdealer deposits accumulated excess coin and currency in his bank. The coin/currency component of money supply *decreases* by the amount of the deposit as coin/currency moves *out* of circulation and *into* the bank's vault. However, the demand deposit component of money supply *increases* by the same amount as the deposit is added to the newsdealer's checking account balance. In effect, one form of money is simply exchanged for another form of money, but the total of money supply is unchanged as an increase in one of its components is counterbalanced and offset by a decrease in the other component.

3. A department store customer pays his monthly bill by mailing a check to his creditor. Demand deposits at the department store's bank

206

will rise when the check is deposited, but demand deposits at its customer's bank will decline by the same amount as the check is charged against the drawer's account. Thus, in the vast majority of instances the issuance and collection of a check represents only a *change in ownership* of a certain amount of demand deposits, but does not change the total level of demand deposits or the total amount of money supply. Exceptions to this statement would occur where either the drawer or the payee of a check is a domestic bank or the U. S. Treasury. Since the M_1 definition excludes demand deposits of banks and the U. S. government, increases or decreases in such funds affect total money supply only to the extent that the increases come from or the decreases are added to money supply in private hands.

4. A commercial bank makes a loan and credits the proceeds to the borrower's account. Demand deposits at the lending bank increase, *but in this case there is no offsetting effect.* The loan transaction does not affect the pre-existing level of demand deposits elsewhere, nor does it affect the pre-existing amount of coin and currency in circulation. Thus, since the demand deposit level at the lending bank rises, and the transaction does not otherwise affect existing components of money supply, *new money is created* and added to the total of money supply.

If the borrower requested and received the proceeds of his loan in currency, the effect would be the same. In this case, the coin/currency component of money supply would increase as cash moved *out* of the bank's vault and *into* circulation; no other form of money would be affected; and again, new money would be created in the form of an addition to total money supply.

5. When a bank makes an investment, the ultimate result is the same, for instance, if the bank purchases bonds on the open market, it may pay the dealer by using funds in demand deposits carried with a correspondent or, if it is a member bank, with the Federal Reserve bank. Since domestic interbank demand deposits are not included in the M_1 definition, the *payment* by the bank does not affect total money supply. But when the bank's funds are deposited in the dealer's checking account, the level of the demand deposit component increases and the net effect is an increase in total money supply. Note, however, that if a bank buys bonds from another commercial bank, there would be *no change* in total money supply, as neither the payment nor the receipt of funds would affect the components of money supply.

If a bank subscribes to a new issue of bonds offered by an underwriter on behalf of a private obligor, the effect would be the same. The *payment* by the bank would not affect money supply, but the deposit of the bank's funds in the borrowing issuer's demand deposit account would increase the demand deposit component of money supply.

On the other hand, the effect would be the same but somewhat delayed if a bank subscribes to a new issue of U.S. Treasury securities. The Federal Reserve handles subscriptions for Treasury securities, and the bank's subscription payment would be credited to the U.S. Treasury account with the Federal Reserve bank. Where permitted, the funds might temporarily be credited to the subscribing bank's Treasury Tax Loan Account. However, neither domestic interbank deposits nor U.S. government demand deposits are included in the M_1 definition of money supply. Therefore, when commercial banks subscribe to new Treasury issues, there is no *immediate* effect on total money supply. Ultimately, when the U.S. Treasury spends the money raised by the sale of the securities, the potential created by the bank's purchase is realized as the several payees of the Treasury checks deposit them in private checking accounts.

Effect of Commercial Bank Loan Payments

Of course, no one borrows money from a bank with the intention of leaving it indefinitely in a demand deposit account. Most borrowers use the proceeds of loans to issue checks to their creditors or to make new purchases of things they want and need or to buy raw materials or perhaps to withdraw cash to meet payrolls or personal expenses. But in the private sector all of these transactions involve only a change in ownership of money and do not affect the newly increased level of money supply. In other words, the new money created by a commercial bank loan will remain somewhere in our monetary system, either in the form of demand deposits or coin and currency in circulation, no matter how or when the proceeds of the loan are spent.

The payment of a commercial bank loan, however, has the opposite effect on total money supply. Whether the borrower uses his demand deposit balance or hands the bank a bundle of cash to repay his loan, in either case, one of the components of existing money supply is reduced, there is no counterbalancing increase elsewhere, and the total money supply declines. In short, when commercial bank loans are *made*, money supply increases; when commercial bank loans are *paid* the total of money supply decreases.

Limited Scope of M_1 as Definition of Money Supply

The M_1 definition of money supply has been termed a "narrow" definition, and this is true. In addition to interbank deposits and U. S. government deposits, it will be noted that savings accounts and time deposits are also excluded from the M_1 components of money supply.

Therefore, the foregoing descriptions of the effect of certain monetary transactions on money supply must be qualified somewhat. For instance, to the extent that people withdraw savings or time deposits to pay bills or make purchases, total money supply, as thus defined, increases; conversely, to the extent that checks drawn on demand deposits (adjusted) are deposited in savings or time accounts, money supply decreases. Naturally, there is a constant movement of funds between the demand and time deposit categories. To the extent that the *net* swing increases demand deposits, money supply increases; to the extent that the *net* movement decreases demand deposits, money supply decreases.

In the rather complex world of finance, it would be extremely difficult to find a simple definition of the entire volume of money available for spending that would serve all statistical purposes. Certainly M_1 has its shortcomings; nevertheless, economists and others find it a rather effective way of relating the amount of available purchasing power to the value of things offered for sale in the marketplace.

Traditionally, commercial banks have been the chief source of the nation's supply of money, our circulating medium of exchange. Originally banks supplied money by paying the proceeds of bank loans in banknotes (paper currency). Over a period of years, demand deposits have replaced coin and currency as the principal means of making payments. Nevertheless, whether a borrower receives the proceeds of a commercial bank loan in currency or as a credit to a demand deposit account, money supply, as defined by M_1, increases. Thus, as the volume of commercial bank loans and investments increases, money supply tends to increase. Conversely, a decrease in the volume of commercial bank loans and investments tends to decrease the circulating amount of money supply.

Questions Based on This Chapter:

1. With respect to the relationship between the lender and the borrower, what is the difference between a bank loan and a bank investment?

2. A commercial bank borrower requests and receives in currency the proceeds of a loan. What is the effect on total money supply?

3. Describe the two components of money supply that are included in the M_1 definition.

4. When a depositor cashes a check at his bank, how does the transaction affect the total of money supply?

Chapter 14

Loans
and
Investments

Part II: Commercial Bank Loans

The Purposes of This Chapter:

1. *To explain the difference between commercial banks and other lenders.*

2. *To describe in general terms the structural organization of the loan function.*

3. *To discuss the necessity for each individual bank to establish its own unique loan policy.*

4. *To describe the responsibilities of the credit department and the loan operating and accounting department(s).*

Although banks extend credit both by making loans and by purchasing investments, the loan portfolio should and generally does dominate this traditional banking function. There are many external factors, including general economic and business conditions, that affect the relative size of a commercial bank's loan portfolio as compared with its investment portfolio. Actually, the size and even the composition of a bank's loan portfolio are influenced considerably by the needs and demands of its depositors and the community it serves. And these are factors over which a bank has very little control.

The purchase of investments, by contrast, is a deliberate action on the part of bank management, motivated more by internal considerations than by external pressures. The nature of such internal considerations and the role played by the investment portfolio in the management of bank funds will be discussed later. At this point, it will suffice to point out that bank loans are originally generated by a *borrower's* decision, while investments are the result of a *bank management* decision.

Although banks have other ways of acquiring funds, the predominant solid base of its normal deposit liabilities provides the bulk of the wherewithal for banking activities. Banks are organized and chartered to provide financial services to a community. Some banks serve only a single town and its environs; others serve counties or trade areas; while larger banks serve one or more or all of the 50 states. Many large banks have branches or banking interests abroad and serve segments of the international community. Regardless of its size, a bank draws its deposit base from the residents of the community it serves, whether that community be local, national, or international in character. And every bank has a very real and primary obligation to satisfy the loan demands of its depositors to the extent that it reasonably can. While there are nonbank lenders that offer specific types of loans, most business depositors rely entirely on their commercial banker to supply working capital, seasonal loans, and, to some extent, capital loans. Only the large corporate borrowers with established reputations and credit standing have the financial muscle to bypass commercial banks and tap other market sources of long- or short-term loans.

Differences Between Banks and Other Lenders

Commercial banks differ from other lenders in at least two important respects. The first is the variety and flexibility of credit extended. Other financial institutions tend to specialize in one or more specific areas of lending, such as instalment credit, mortgage loans, long-term business loans, various types of collateral loans, and so on. Banks, on the other hand, are often referred to as department stores of finance because of the wide range of financial services offered. In the field of credit extension no other type of lender engages in as many varied forms of financing as the modern commercial bank. Generally speaking, the larger the bank, the wider the variety of specialized loans available.

Most banks, large and small, make loans to individuals, to businesses of every size and description, to hospitals, churches, municipalities—in short, to almost every conceivable kind of borrower including, in some cases, other banks. Banks make demand loans and short- and intermediate-term time loans; unsecured loans and a wide variety of collateralized loans; instalment loans and mortgage loans; and to a *limited extent*, other types of long-term loans.

The flexibility of borrowing arrangements is another characteristic of the bank loan portfolio. Because banks can offer a wide variety of loan terms and conditions, and arrangements for many kinds of collateral security, a good banker can tailor a loan package to suit the special needs of individual customers. No other type of lender can match the flexibility of the commercial bank if the banker is intelligent and imaginative in his approach to loans.

The second major difference between banks and other lenders arises from the nature of the bank/depositor relationship. A mere "money broker" with some credit standing can buy and sell funds dispassionately by dealing with markets where a wide variety of financial obligations are regularly traded, without having any direct contact with or caring too much about the sources of funds bought or the users of funds sold. But commercial bankers, if they are to fulfill their role in our financial society, must be much more than "money brokers." The fact is that commercial banking normally involves a close and intimate relationship between the bank and its customers, particularly its borrowing customers. There is much more to it than the offering and utilization of routine banking service. The contact is between *people* rather than with impersonalized markets; and mutually beneficial relationships between people depend to a considerable extent on mutual trust and respect. The borrower who reveals personal and confidential data to a lending officer must have complete faith in the belief that such information will be handled discreetly and properly. Similarly, the banker's faith in the integrity of the borrower is more important to him than cold financial data or even collateral security. The nature of commercial banking is not particularly suited to transient contacts, and the best relationships are those of long duration. Many customers regard their banker as a constant source of dependable financial advice and counsel. The banker, on the other hand, knows that the success of his institution depends on his ability to attract and retain a substantial and growing volume of deposits.

Given this type of relationship, it is obvious that no bank can long afford to be unresponsive to the legitimate credit needs of its depositors and the community it serves. Most other lenders have no comparable obligation to prospective borrowers and hence can take a more impersonal approach to applications for credit. Thus, nonbank lenders and investors are free to seek outlets for their funds yielding the greatest return with minimum consideration given to other aspects of their relationship to the borrowers.

Organization of the Loan Function

In order to operate effectively, the lending activity of a commercial bank must be a well-organized process, coordinating the significant contributions of several units, each of which has a special area of responsibility. These units are:

1. The board of directors
2. The lending officers
3. The credit department
4. One or more loan operations departments

The four units that form a bank's lending organization must work closely together for maximum effectiveness. Each unit must be fully aware of the role it plays in loan processing and equally conscious of the responsibilities and the contributions of the other units.

For instance, the board of directors sets broad objectives and establishes the overall loan policy for the bank. But to do this, the general knowledge and business acumen of the directors must be supplemented by the banking experience and know-how of the professional experts, the bank's top lending officers.

Decisions with respect to most loans are made by lending officers within the authority delegated to them. For the most part such decisions are matters of human judgment, following a careful evaluation of the circumstances. Lending officers who fail to utilize fully the skills of seasoned credit personnel may be closing the door to a valuable impartial source of useful input to the evaluation process.

Finally, after a loan is approved, the expertise of loan operating personnel becomes extremely important. The very flexibility and wide variety of commercial bank lending and the many types of acceptable collateral naturally expand the range of technical skills required. Furthermore, if and when the quality of a loan starts to deteriorate, not infrequently those who handle routine transactions are the first to observe signs of distress.

Not only a cooperative spirit, but mutual confidence and respect of each unit for the skills and responsibilities of the other units is most desirable. Such an atmosphere is best fostered by frequent contact and completely open lines of communication, particularly between the lending officers, credit department staff, and operating departments.

The Board of Directors

The directors of a bank are elected by its shareholders and charged with overall responsibility for the bank's activities. Since the full board of a bank may meet only once a week at most, and in many cases even less frequently, it is obvious that it must delegate considerable authority to executive officers and key bank personnel to handle the day-to-day banking transactions. Nevertheless, the board cannot escape its accountability for the proper functioning of the bank, and it must exercise reasonable control over all banking functions, and particularly over an activity as important as the lending function.

The board of directors can exercise a very satisfactory degree of control by taking positive action in the following respects:

1. Establishing broad, basic objectives of lending activities to serve as a guide for those who approve loans;

2. Formulating, with the active cooperation of top management, a definite loan policy for the bank;

3. Providing for frequent periodic reviews of the loan portfolio to ensure that objectives are being achieved and that approved policy is being followed.

Despite close identification with the public interest, American banks are privately owned institutions organized to return profits to their shareholders. Therefore, a prime objective in the development of the loan portfolio is to maximize income for the bank. But the profit objective cannot be pursued with such zeal as to exclude other important objectives such as:

1. Adherence to sound lending and credit practices;

2. Provision for the legitimate credit needs of its depositors and the community it serves;

3. Avoidance, by diversification or otherwise, of an excessive or undue concentration of risk, for the protection of depositors and shareholders.

Although basic objectives such as those stated above apply with equal force to all banks, this is not the case when it comes to specific loan policy. No two banks are exactly alike, and a practical, workable loan policy for one bank might be entirely ill-suited for almost any other bank. In short, a bank's loan policy must be hand-tailored to fit its particular circumstances.

Practical Considerations in Establishing Loan Policy

The formulation of a loan policy for an individual bank requires a sincere and honest introspective analysis of the bank's characteristics, its professional capabilities, the type of depositor and the community it serves, and the environment in which it operates.

The first consideration is the character of its deposit base. What is the makeup of its deposits, time and demand? What proportions of its deposits come from individuals, businesses, and other sources? Does the bank have a broad deposit base, or do relatively few depositors account for a large percentage of total deposits? What are the growth trends of various classes of deposits? Are deposits subject to marked upward and downward seasonal swings? What proportion of the bank's capital is invested in fixed assets? How adequate is the bank's capital structure in relation to its deposit liabilities and risk assets? These and similar factors must be carefully analyzed to make intelligent decisions with respect to the employment of deposits and capital funds.

Present and projected economic conditions, both local and general, are usually reflected in a bank's loan policy. Trends within industries in which a bank has borrowing customers must be taken into consideration. Changes in business practices, consumer buying habits, and the like, all have pronounced effects on the structure of bank loan portfolios. It was not until after World War II that commercial banks aggressively sought instalment loans; today, consumer credit is one of the most competitive areas of bank lending.

Bank lending practices in this era are changing rapidly as is virtually everything else. Banks are constantly seeking new ways to put money to work profitably: revolving credit plans for both individuals and businesses are becoming commonplace; direct leasing arrangements are providing another avenue of extending credit; accounts receivable purchase arrangements are increasing; these and other relatively new forms of bank lending have greatly altered the makeup of the traditional bank loan portfolio.

The present and potential demand for various types of loans and the extent to which the other lenders compete for them has a decided influence on a bank's loan policy. A bank must also consider whether the nature and volume of certain types of loans, requiring specialized know-how to service properly, justify training or hiring the necessary staff to handle them. Accounts receivable loans and various kinds of secured inventory loans are examples of highly technical fields that should be avoided if a bank does not have personnel thoroughly familiar with the specialized techniques involved. Naturally, this problem arises more frequently in a small bank with a limited staff than in a larger institution whose loan volume is sizable enough to enable it to have specialists in various types of credit extension.

The shaping of loan policy requires decisions based on periodic analyses of the loan portfolio. Is the portfolio reasonably well balanced with respect to types of loans and borrowers? Is there an undesirable concentration of loans in any particular area? Should the bank adopt a passive attitude with respect to certain types of loans and aggressively solicit other types? Is the ratio of total loans to deposit liabilities considered satisfactory? If an analysis reveals undesirable features in the portfolio, what steps can be taken to correct them?

It would be unrealistic to think that a bank can simply select at will those borrowers to whom it would like to make loans. Even if a bank could select its borrowers, the demand for various types of loans would limit the market for them; there is a practical limit to how far the demand for, say, automobile loans, can be stimulated even by aggressive solicitation and advertising. Without question, the loan needs of a bank's regular customers have a pronounced effect on the types of loans that make up its portfolio.

The influence of these factors varies from bank to bank and cannot always be precisely controlled. A poorly run institution may drift with the tide and in effect permit the loan portfolio to shape itself; but, a primary objective of a well managed bank is to exercise conscious policy direction over the makeup and aggregate of its loan portfolio.

It should now be clear that the formulation of loan policy is not a simple task. Serious thought is required by at least a committee of the board, if not the full board, working closely with top lending officers of the bank. Members of the board must remember that active lending officers are experienced professionals. Except for officer-directors, board members are not directly engaged in banking, but in other occupations. When loan policy is reviewed, lending officers should be encouraged to express their opinions and to make suggestions as to possible changes in policy. Directors must make or approve the final decisions since they, so to speak, are responsible for the general condition of the forest. On the other hand, lending officers are responsible for the individual trees. They are in a better position to witness the application of loan policy to practical cases and therefore have very valuable input as to its effectiveness.

Should Loan Policy Be Expressed In Writing?

This question frequently arises, and bankers and bank directors do not always agree as to the correct answer. Some feel that formal written documents often cause an implacable rigidity that tends to stifle the initiative and maneuverability of lending officers. Others maintain that orally expressed policies are too quickly forgotten and, if remembered, are rarely recalled with consistent accuracy. It is also claimed that since oral policy must be passed on by word of mouth, each restatement tends to reflect the background of the relater as well as his personal interpretation of the policy.

A good loan policy should consist of operating guidelines aimed at specific objectives but allowing some room for discretion. Loan policy must be flexible, but excessive flexibility causes the guidelines to become so fuzzy as to constitute no meaningful policy at all. A written loan policy need not be rigid; in fact, it offers a better chance of clearly defining the degree of flexibility desired. Also, it does much to minimize the possibility of later misunderstanding and misinterpretation.

Too often, the reluctance to express loan policy in writing stems from a desire to avoid the mental exercise required to express thoughts in specific words. In most cases, however, the benefits are well worth the effort, not only because of the effectiveness of written communica-. tion, but also because the process is bound to crystalize the thinking of all concerned.

Lending Authority

Despite its overall responsibility, the board of directors must necessarily delegate a considerable amount of authority in connection with the loan function. For a great many banks, the first step in this direction is the appointment of a special committee of board members whose duty is to exercise direct supervision over the bank's lending activities. Except in the very smallest banks, it is neither practical nor necessary for a committee of directors to approve all loans. Further delegation is desirable. Depending upon the size of the bank and the diversification (by type of loan) of its portfolio, the delegation of authority can be very simple or rather complex.

For instance, in a bank with a legal lending limit of $3,000,000, the loan committee of the board may insist on approving all loans in excess of $1,000,000; senior lending officers might be given authority individually to approve loans up to $1,000,000; and other lending officers or qualified personnel may be given individual authority on loans ranging anywhere from, say, $10,000 to $250,000. Or in larger banks, committees of lending officers may be established with authority to approve certain types of loans in substantial amounts. Whatever pattern of lending authority is established, it is the responsibility of the board or its loan committee to see that there is a pattern, whether simple or complex, and that sufficient authority is delegated to permit, in the interest of good banking service, reasonably prompt handling of loan applications.

The Loan Portfolio: Legal Restrictions

Although banking is generally considered to be a highly regulated industry, at the present time there are surprisingly few legal or regulatory restrictions on bank lending. The extension of credit to the borrowing public, from the average consumer to the giant industrial corporation, is largely left to the judgment of experienced bank lending officers. Most of the legal restrictions now in effect are either designed to protect banks from excesses that could endanger the solvency of the institution or are based on broad public policy.

For instance, all banks are subject to a limitation on the maximum amount they can lend to any one borrower. The basic limitation is 10 percent of the bank's Capital and Surplus accounts; but there are variations of the so-called legal lending limit between regulations of the Comptroller of the Currency (national banks), the Federal Reserve System (member banks), and the statutes or regulations of the several states. For instance, the Comptroller allows a broader base by adding Undivided Profits and certain capital obligations to Capital and Surplus. Other regulatory bodies limit the base to Capital and Surplus, but some allow a higher figure than 10 percent as the percentage limitation. The purpose of this legal restriction obviously is to prevent a bank from exposure to an undue concentration of risk by placing too many of its eggs in one basket.

Both state and national banks are also restricted as to the size and maturity of real estate loans, and in some cases, to the total volume of such loans in relation to the dollar volume of savings accounts. Such regulations are designed to ensure that banks are protected by a sufficient equity margin in individual loans, while the volume of long-term less liquid mortgage loans is related to the bank's most stable class of deposits (savings accounts).

In the public policy area, there are restrictions such as Regulation U of the Board of Governors of the Federal Reserve System. This regulation prescribes the amount a bank can loan against stock market collateral when the proceeds of the loan are to be used to purchase or carry securities listed on a national securities exchange and, in some cases, securities traded in over-the-counter markets. While this rule affords a measure of protection for the lending banks, its main purpose is to prevent a dangerous degree of speculation in securities by the public on the basis of borrowed money with inadequate margin.

There are other types of restrictions, and no attempt will be made to cover all or even the precise nature of existing legal restraints. Laws and regulations are seldom static, and the future may well see new legal restrictions, particularly in the "public policy" area. In periods of tight credit, when interest rates are abnormally high, there is always talk of the desirability of federal regulations designed to channel bank credit into useful productive areas and, conversely, to restrict the use of borrowed funds for non-productive or speculative purposes. In general, however, it must be said that commercial banks have considerable freedom in deciding to whom, how much, how long, and under what terms they will lend money.

Classification of Bank Loans

To control its loan portfolio effectively a bank must have a good loan classification system. There are a number of ways to classify loans: by purpose, type of borrower, maturity, type of security, risk, and so on. Certain classifications are necessary for accounting and audit control purposes; others are required for reports to various supervisory authorities; and still others may be needed for management information and planning.

Bank loan portfolios are often broken down into four broad groupings: (1) commercial loans, (2) consumer credit loans, (3) real estate loans, and (4) interbank loans. The groupings selected by any individual bank depend on the nature of the portfolio and the type of information desired by management.

Commercial Loans

The term *commercial loan* is often used as a catchall for all types of loans not separately categorized. Larger banks often have special departments to handle various types of commercial loans; in very large banks commercial loans may be broken down by industry groups.

Short-term commercial loans are usually evidenced by notes payable in 30, 60, or 90 days, or they may be payable on demand. Intermediate and long-term loans are generally payable in instalments ranging from monthly to annually, and are usually subject to formal written agreements setting forth the terms of the credit.

Most bank loans to businesses are unsecured, although it is common practice for the principals in smaller businesses to indorse or guarantee bank borrowings. Loans to individuals are frequently collateralized or indorsed or both. Almost any form of business or personal asset can be used as collateral for a bank loan. Unsecured loans are based on the general financial responsibility of the borrower as evidenced by financial statements submitted to the bank.

Consumer Credit Loans

Since the interest charge on an instalment loan is normally based on the original amount of the loan, and the average balance outstanding over the life of the loan is usually only about half of the amount advanced, the gross yield on this type of paper is relatively attractive. Compared to other bank loans, however, the average size of consumer credit transactions is small, the risk is generally greater, and the handling costs per loan are higher. For these reasons, the net dollar profit per loan is relatively small, and a bank must have a good volume of such paper for the instalment credit operation to be really profitable. Consumer credit is a specialized field that differs considerably in philosophy and practice from traditional commercial bank lending. In fact the differences are so fundamental that personnel trained in commercial lending are normally ill-suited for consumer lending, and vice versa.

Consumer credit paper is obtained either through direct loans or indirectly through the purchase from the seller or dealer of paper arising from the sale of goods and services. Some banks derive substantial portions of their consumer credit outstandings from dealer sources; others deal exclusively with direct lending.

Banks with dealer customers also usually engage in what is commonly referred to as the wholesale end of consumer lending, which also involves financing dealer inventories. *Inventory financing*, also known as flooring, floor planning, and wholesale floor plan, is that form of credit extended by a lender to a dealer to enable the dealer to carry an adequate supply of goods for display and sale. Where the volume of inventory financing is significant, it would be desirable to classify such loans separately. Although normally much less profitable than the retail end of the business, wholesale floor-plan loans are generally necessary to get the dealers' retail paper.

Real Estate Loans

The extent to which a bank engages in real estate lending normally depends upon the makeup of its deposits and the availability of and demand for other types of loans. In recent years the increase in the proportion of savings and other time deposits in the banking system has heightened the interest of commercial banks in real estate loans. Normally banks concentrate primarily on mortgage loans on residential properties rather than on business properties, because the latter consume relatively larger portions of loanable resources and provide less risk diversification.

Some banks originate mortgage loans for sale to other investors. Under these arrangements the bank usually continues to service the loan on a fee basis and thus is able to provide mortgage financing for its customers without tying up its own funds.

Another facet of mortgage lending in which many banks engage is construction and real estate development financing. This type of lending is essentially short-term, although in some cases the bank may make the permanent mortgage loan after the construction has been completed.

Banks with mortgage banker or broker customers ordinarily are called upon to warehouse mortgages originated for sale to permanent investors. This type of loan is, in effect, a specialized form of short-term inventory financing.

Interbank Loans and Participations

Larger city banks engaging in correspondent banking frequently make short-term loans to their correspondents. In many cases the borrowing bank is not a member of the Federal Reserve System and hence is unable to utilize this source for its temporary loan requirements. Very often, member banks find it more convenient to borrow from their city correspondents. Interbank loans are normally secured by U. S. government securities or other high-grade, readily marketable bonds. Where the city correspondent holds investment securities under a custodial agreement for the smaller bank, a satisfactorily secured interbank loan can be quickly arranged with a minimum of inconvenience.

It is not uncommon for two or more banks to share or participate with each other in loan transactions. For instance, smaller banks sometimes receive loan applications in amounts that exceed their legal lending limit, and they ask their correspondent bank to "participate" in the loan by handling whatever portion is beyond the capacity of the smaller bank. This is accomplished by a participation agreement between the two banks, and the arrangement enables the smaller bank to take care of its customer's borrowing needs locally. Loan participations are generally regarded as one of the principal advantages of a correspondent relationship.

At the other end of the scale, large industrial corporations frequently have need for commercial bank loans in amounts ranging as high as several hundred million dollars. It is customary for a group of banks to handle credits of this size. One of the banks in the group acts as "lead bank," accepting and holding the corporation's note, distributing the proceeds, and subsequently receiving payments of principal and interest, which are distributed to members of the group in proportion to each bank's relative share in the loan.

Loan Commitments

The most common form of bank loan commitment is known as a *line of credit*. A line of credit is a confirmed indication by a bank of the maximum amount of credit it is willing to extend to a borrower over a given period, usually one year. Lines of credit are usually extended only to substantial businesses with definite seasonal or otherwise short-term borrowing requirements. The continuation of the line depends on the borrower's maintaining a financial condition satisfactory to the bank.

Sometimes banks will set internal lines of credit for certain borrowers. The purpose of such a line is to serve as a guide to lending personnel, and its existence is not revealed to the borrower.

Loan commitments in various forms may be extended to any type of borrower in connection with specific transactions. In some cases a bank may charge a fee in consideration for reserving a given amount of credit for a borrower under a loan commitment.

Interest Rates

Although state laws and federal regulations may impose ceilings on rates of interest banks may charge for certain types of loans, the dominant factor controlling rates is the immutable law of supply and demand. When economic activity is at a high level, loan demand and interest rates are normally also high, and the reverse is generally true of lows in the business cycle.

Interest is, in effect, simply the rental cost of money, and like all other costs, the rental price of money tends to vary widely from time to time. In addition to the demand for loans and the ability of lenders to satisfy that demand, other factors influence the interest rate in individual cases, for example, the financial stability of the borrower, the type of credit requested, and the degree of risk involved.

While commercial banks have the power to create money and add to money supply by making loans, it must not be assumed that this is a completely free and unrestrained power. The availability of bank credit is not determined by banks, but by the current policy, at any given time, of the Board of Governors of the Federal Reserve System. When the Board decides, in the interest of the nation at large, that it must reduce money supply, it has the power to restrict the ability of banks to make loans. Inevitably, the demand for loans will then exceed the supply available, and interest rates will rise. When the Board decides that money supply should be expanded, the opposite is true and interest rates fall.

Competition also affects interest rates. The more a bank has to vie with other banks and other lenders for loans, the lower its interest rates are likely to be, which accounts in part for the fact that bank rates in larger cities, where there are more competing sources of credit, are normally lower than rates in small communities.

Special considerations affect every lender and every borrower to some degree, however, and the rate of interest charged in any particular case will reflect such considerations. To ensure a reasonable return to the bank on its loans and equal treatment of comparable borrowers, every bank should establish policy guidelines on interest rates for various types of loans.

The Prime Rate

The lowest rate charged by banks to their most creditworthy customers is known as the *prime rate*. The prime rate is actually a bench-mark—the "wholesale" rate charged for loans in relatively substantial amounts, with low handling costs and the barest minimum of risk. Rates charged other borrowers are scaled upward from the prime rate, depending on the size of the loan, the handling costs, and the financial strength and stability of the borrower.

The prime rate established by the larger banks in the principal money centers has usually been adopted by other banks around the country with respect to their sizable customers, many of whom deal with a number of banks. Some large banks fix their prime rate simply by appraising current conditions and the strength of their customers' demand for loans. Other banks base their prime rate on a fixed formula that takes into consideration the current rate for other high-grade, short-term money market instruments. Regardless of the method used, the setting of a prime rate represents an independent action by each bank, although no bank can completely ignore the element of competition. Actually, the prime rate often varies in different sections of the country and even, at times, with respect to different banks in the same city. Such variations normally exist for relatively brief periods.

Risk Assumption

There is a degree of risk associated with every loan. Unfortunately, the extent of risk on a given loan cannot be precisely determined; whether or not a loan has a higher element of risk than the bank is warranted in taking is a matter of human judgment. A bank that consistently shows abnormally low loan losses may well be failing to take enough risks and hence may not be serving its community and its stockholders as it should. Maintaining the proper balance between too great and too little risk assumption is one of the constant challenges of banking.

It is reasonable and proper to expect that the interest rate charged on loans will vary with the apparent degree of risk involved. The greater the risk, the higher the rate of interest and vice versa.

The Credit Department

The credit department of a commercial bank is normally the chief source of staff support for lending officers. Depending on the size of the bank, its personnel complement may range from a single part-time employee to a highly organized group of a hundred or more well-trained specialists. A basic responsibility of this department is the maintenance of individual credit files on the bank's borrowing customers, but this is by no means the full extent of its responsibilities.

Processing Loan Applications

Applications for loans are received as a rule by lending officers. If the applicant is a regular borrowing customer, the officer may approve the loan on the spot and merely advise the credit department of this fact. If the customer has not previously borrowed or is a more sporadic borrower and less well-known to the lending officer, the credit file will be reviewed, and the credit department may be asked to conduct an investigation to update the file information.

Invariably, loan applications are accompanied by the latest available financial data, which will be considered, analyzed, and added to any existing historical financial record of the borrower. Financial data are usually condensed and transferred to special credit department forms. (See Exhibit 13, Balance Sheet, and Exhibit 14, Profit and Loss Spread Sheet.)

If the prospective borrower is a new customer, the credit department will be requested to conduct an investigation to obtain all available information concerning the applicant. Such information may be obtained directly from the applicant, from previous or existing bank connections, from credit agency reports, from trade creditors, and so forth. In simple terms, the credit department assembles, organizes, and analyzes credit information, including financial data, and submits a condensed report to the lending officer, who has the responsibility of making the decision to approve or decline the application. In many cases, the credit department report is accompanied by specific comments, such as a suggestion to obtain certain additional information from the prospective borrower, suggestions as to possible changes in the proposed terms of the loan with respect to the pledge of security, maturity, rate of interest, or, in some cases, the desirability of obtaining guarantors or indorsers. Naturally, it is the lending officer's prerogative to accept, decline, or defer action on the comments or suggestions.

Exhibit 13. Balance Sheet

INSTITUTE NATIONAL BANK
EREHWON, ILL.

CRE-5 REVISED 3-75   NAME_____

	BALANCE SHEET	DATE				DA
1	Cash on Hand and in Banks					
2	Accounts Receivable					
3	Notes Receivable					
4	Inventory					
5						
6						
7						
8	TOTAL CURRENT ASSETS					
9	Land and Buildings					
10	Machinery, Equipment and Fixtures					
11						
12	Other Receivables					
13	Investments					
14						
15	Deferred Charges					
16						
17						
18						
19						
20						
21	TOTAL ASSETS					
22	Notes Payable to Banks					
23						
24	Notes Payable					
25	Accounts Payable					
26	Taxes (Income and Other)					
27	Other Accruals and Misc. Accounts					
28						
29						
30						
31						
32						
33	TOTAL CURRENT LIABILITIES					
34	Mortgage Debt					
35						
36						
37						
38	TOTAL DEBT					
39						
40						
41						
42	Capital Stock–Preferred					
43	Capital Stock–Common					
44	Surplus					
45						
46	TOTAL LIABILITIES AND NET WORTH					
47	Net Worth					
48	Working Capital					
49	*Net Sales					
50	*Net Profit					
51	*Dividends Paid (Withdrawals)					
52	Contingent Liabilities					
53	Reserve for Depreciation					
54	Reserve for Bad Debts					
55	Current Ratio					
56	Debt to Worth					
57	Sales to Receivables (Line 49 ÷ 2 + 3)	DAYS				
58	Sales to Inventory	DAYS				
59						
60						
61						

Exhibit 14. Profit and Loss Spread Sheet

INSTITUTE NATIONAL BANK
EREHWON, ILL.

CRE-6 REVISED 6-73   NAME _____

	PERIOD ENDING		%	
1	GROSS SALES			
2	Less Ret. and Allow.			
3				
4	NET SALES			
5	Beginning Inventory			
6	Purchases (or Materials used)			
7	Direct Labor			
8				
9	Other Manufacturing Expense			
10				
11				
12	TOTAL			
13	Less Ending Inventory			
14	COST OF SALES			
15	GROSS PROFIT ON SALES			
16	Other Operating Income			
17				
18	GROSS PROFIT ON OPERATIONS			
19	Salesmen's Salaries and Commissions			
20	Advertising			
21	Other Selling Expense			
22				
23				
24				
25	TOTAL SELLING EXPENSE			
26	Officers' Salaries			
27	Other Salaries and Wages			
28	Bad Debts			
29	Depreciation			
30	Rent			
31	Other Administrative Expense			
32				
33				
34				
35				
36	TOTAL ADMINISTRATIVE EXPENSE			
37	TOTAL EXPENSES			
38	NET OPERATING PROFIT			
39	Discounts Earned			
40	Recoveries			
41	Miscellaneous			
42				
43				
44	OTHER INCOME			
45	TOTAL			
46	Discounts Allowed			
47	Interest Paid			
48	Miscellaneous			
49				
50				
51	OTHER DEDUCTIONS			
52	NET PROFIT BEFORE INCOME TAXES			
53	INCOME TAXES			
54	NET PROFIT			
55	Other Surplus Credits			
56				
57				
58	TOTAL SURPLUS CREDITS			
59	Dividends, Pfd.			
60	Dividends, Com. (Withdrawals)			
61	Other Surplus Charges			
62				
63				
64	TOTAL SURPLUS CHARGES			
65	BEGINNING SURPLUS			
66	NET CHANGE IN SURPLUS			
67	ENDING SURPLUS			

An active credit department has need for and must have the means to train specialists in certain areas. As indicated, most borrowers are required to furnish financial statements with loan applications. To the uninitiated, a balance sheet is a neat arrangement of figures revealing that total assets and total liabilities balance nicely to the last penny, while a profit and loss statement might reveal an impressive net profit for a specific period. However, to the trained analyst, financial statements can disclose a wealth of information or lack of information that prompts pertinent and probing questions. Although lending officers are usually quite competent in this area, capable financial statement analysts render invaluable staff support to a bank's lending officers through their ability to analyze critically and interpret financial statements.

Conducting a credit investigation is by no means a dull rule-of-thumb procedure. A well-trained investigator must be imaginative and resourceful. From the data given, an investigator must know what further information is needed and, more important, where such information can be obtained. Invariably, each additional bit of data will suggest additional leads that might be profitably explored.

In addition to the skills required in the competent gathering of information, there is the necessity of presenting that information to the lending officer in a manner that places all pertinent data at his fingertips without making it necessary to wade through a mass of uncoordinated information. A credit file cannot be simply a chronological arrangement of unsorted data if it is to be useful. A well-organized credit file consists of a number of files within a file, with identifying tabs that enable a reviewer to locate readily the particular type of information required. There may be sections for financial data (spread sheets), correspondence between the bank and the subject, correspondence with others concerning the subject, memoranda detailing visits to the borrower's office or plant, memoranda of telephone conversations with or concerning the subject, as well as a section for newspaper or trade publication clippings containing current items of interest directly or indirectly related to the subject. If agency reports have been obtained, these would be placed in a separate section.

The skills to be found among experienced personnel of a well-developed credit department are many and varied. For this reason, the credit department has long been regarded by larger banks as the primary vehicle for training prospective commercial loan officers. These banks usually have formal credit department training programs designed to provide junior credit personnel with the necessary technical background in the art of investigation and the exchange of credit information with banks and other sources, financial statement analysis, as well as lending techniques and procedures. Trainees are often given the opportunity to participate with loan officers in meetings with borrowers and in plant visitations, all of which serve as an excellent foundation for the potential commercial loan officer or credit executive.

The unique skills of credit department personnel are not devoted exclusively to the lending activities of the bank. On the contrary, credit investigations are frequently conducted for customers of the bank, who find this a most useful banking service. In the normal course of business, all banks receive many inquiries by mail and by telephone from other banks and from known credit managers of established business houses. Such inquiries may concern customers of the bank or individuals or businesses located in the community who are not customers. In the latter case the inquiry is answered largely on the basis of information received from other banks. When answering credit inquiries, of course, credit department personnel must observe the provisions of the Fair Credit Reporting Act.

Credit department personnel of various banks are usually well-acquainted with each other through their frequent contacts. They are aware of the confidential nature of the information they exchange and of the necessity of using such information properly and with discretion. As a matter of fact, the Robert Morris Associates, an association of bank lending officers and credit department personnel, has devised a rather strict code of ethics which, in general, is meticulously observed. Any bank that violates the "code" may soon find that its bank sources of information have been cut off. The existence of the code of ethics and the assurance that information divulged will be circumspectly handled has done much to keep open communication channels between bank credit departments, to the considerable benefit not only of the banks themselves but also of the many customers they collectively serve.

Loan Operations and Accounting

After a loan application has been approved by the lending officer, the borrower is requested to sign a note and any necessary related documents and arrange for the delivery of collateral, if any, to the bank. At this point, another department (or departments) assumes responsibility for handling the mechanics of the loan transaction during its existence. In smaller banks, all details may be handled by a single "loan department." In larger banks, responsibilities may be distributed over several departments, such as a "note department," a "collateral department," a "loan accounting department," or even separate departments to handle the different types of loans, particularly mortgage loans and consumer credit loans. Regardless of how the loan operations and accounting function are organized, the duties and responsibilities include the following:

1. *Examination and care of notes.* The notes representing the borrower's liability to the bank are valuable assets and must be properly safeguarded. They must be carefully inspected for technical correctness, and note custodians are usually responsible for seeing that notes have been approved and that the size and type of the loan is within the authority granted to the approving officer.

2. *Distribution of Proceeds.* The proceeds of the loan must be made available to the borrower, either by preparing and processing an entry crediting an account in the bank, by transfer to another bank, or in whatever manner requested.

3. *Calculation and Collection of Interest.* Interest must be calculated and collected, together with any other loan charges or fees. In this area, most banks are on an accrual basis, and interest must be accrued and the necessary entries prepared and processed. On short-term loans interest is frequently deducted from the face amount of the note at the time it is handled. This traditional bank practice of collecting interest in advance is known as discounting (hence the use of the term *discount* rather than *interest* in such transactions). In other cases, interest is billed periodically after it has been earned, usually on a monthly or quarterly basis.

4. *Care and Maintenance of Collateral.* Collateral, although pledged to ensure ultimate payment of the loan, is the property of the borrower and must be carefully safeguarded, preferably under dual control. All collateral must be carefully examined by trained personnel to determine that it is in good form and that the bank has or can readily obtain good legal title to it in the event that liquidation to satisfy the indebtedness becomes necessary. Marketable collateral such as bonds, stocks, or commodities, must be priced periodically to ensure that proper margins are maintained. In many cases, it is necessary to file papers publicly to perfect a security interest in collateral not in the bank's sole possession. There are many different types of collateral including, in addition to those mentioned, life insurance policies having cash surrender value, chattels such as automobiles, major household appliances, machinery and heavy equipment, as well as business inventories, accounts receivable, and assigned contracts. Regardless of the type, qualified personnel must be well aware in every case of the steps necessary to preserve the value of the collateral so as to protect the bank's interests at all times.

5. *Accounting Records.* There are important records to be kept in connection with lending activities; the most important of these are generally known as the discount register, the liability ledger, and the maturity tickler.

The discount register is really a journal, a book of original entry which provides a daily record of all departmental transactions for settlement and control purposes. The term *discount register* is a holdover from the days when banks discounted practically all of their customers' notes, but it is still used in many banks today. The details of each borrower's indebtedness to the bank are recorded in the *liability ledger,* which often includes a description of the collateral and indorsements, if any. In order to ensure that notes are properly presented for payment as they fall due, a *maturity tickler* file is maintained by due dates. A duplicate of the form prepared for this purpose or a special notice is generally mailed to the borrower as a reminder several days in advance of the maturity date of the note.

EDP and Note Department Accounting

An increasing trend in recent years has been toward the use of electronic data processing equipment in note department accounting. Although the form of the records produced by such equipment may be quite different from those produced by conventional methods, basic records such as those described above are essential for effective operations. However, automated loan accounting systems can greatly simplify the task of preparing special reports required by regulatory authorities as well as classification reports, analyses, and other data useful to management in supervising and controlling the nature and quality of the bank's loan portfolio, which is normally the bank's largest and most productive asset.

One of the most important functions of a commercial bank is that of accommodating the credit needs of the community it serves. The responsibility for lending activity is shared by the board of directors, the lending officers, a credit department, and one or more loan operating departments. Open lines of communication and close cooperation between these units are essential for maximum performance in this vital area.

While there are certain broad, basic objectives that apply with equal force to all banks, each bank must formulate for itself a specific loan policy based on its own unique characteristics and the total environment in which it operates. Serious consideration should be given to the advisability of expressing the policy in writing, to ensure effective communication.

In the interest of good banking service, lending authority must be delegated. The full board of directors, for instance, might delegate authority to a committee of board members. That committee in turn might fix definite limits of authority for committees of lending officers and for individual lending officers. However, a loan once made cannot be dismissed from the mind. The loan portfolio must be constantly reviewed, and in this respect the staff units, such as the credit and the operating departments, can be of material assistance.

Questions Based on This Chapter:

1. How do commercial banks differ from other types of lenders?

2. What roles does the board of directors play in a commercial bank's lending function?

3. In what ways does the credit department assist in the processing of loan applications?

4. Name and describe some of the duties of the loan operations and accounting units.

Chapter 15

Loans and Investments

Part III: Investments—Management of Bank Funds

The Purposes of This Chapter:

1. To describe the basic objectives of bank asset management.

2. To distinguish between the liquidity and income sections of a bank's investment portfolio.

3. To discuss the potentials of bank liability management.

The prudent and sagacious management of commercial bank funds is by far the most important responsibility of top management of our nation's banks, principally because an overwhelming percentage of the funds a bank manages is subject at all times to the claims of depositors. A sizable proportion of the total deposits of a typical bank are demand deposits, which are subject to withdrawal without notice. Most time deposits, while theoretically more stable, are subject to withdrawal on fairly short notice. Unlike other debtors, the bank that can no longer meet its deposit liabilities promptly as they become payable simply cannot default or call a meeting of creditors or otherwise stall for time.

It has no choice other than to surrender control of its affairs immediately to supervisory authorities. Such an unpleasant event in the past has often contained the seeds of financial disaster for the community served and the public at large.

The art of managing bank funds concerns both the asset and the liability side of a bank's balance sheet. A bank is a privately owned, free-enterprise organization; in a sense, the asset side supplies the reason for the bank's existence, that is, assets are a means of providing income, net profits, and dividends for shareholders who have invested capital in the bank. Bank assets are highly concentrated in loans and investments. On the other hand, the liability side, which largely consists of deposit liabilities, represents the sources of funds that make the asset structure possible.

In the previous chapter it was pointed out that loans are made in response to external initiatives (the needs and demands of borrowers), while investments are acquired as the result of internal initiative (management decisions). A bank can and should exercise conscious control over its loan portfolio to the extent possible. However, the investment portfolio which can be more completely controlled affords the most effective opportunities for the employment of management skills.

Bank Asset Management

The successful management of a commercial bank's funds requires careful consideration of three important objectives: (1) safety, (2) liquidity, and (3) income.

The problems of asset management become more complicated when it is realized that the three objectives, when viewed individually, are not inherently compatible. For instance, *absolute* safety, found only in cash, rejects all thought of risk, eliminates liquidity as a meaningful consideration, and leaves the bank with no income. The pursuit of maximum income necessarily involves risk, but this imperils safety and rarely provides the degree of liquidity required for a bank. Liquidity that involves elements of both risk and income steers a course between maximum safety and maximum income.

Bank asset management must be constantly directed toward the skillful balancing of the bank's need to achieve, in adequate degree, each of these three important and diverse objectives.

Safety

It should not be necessary to stress the extreme importance of safeguarding depositors' funds. Those who entrust their money to a bank in the form of deposits certainly do so with no intention of incurring any risk. In a sense, depositors are neither lenders nor investors, even if they receive interest on their deposits, for they place their money in a bank primarily because they feel that a bank is a perfectly safe depository. They expect and have every right to expect that their bank will at all times honor its deposit liabilities promptly and without delay. If those who have the responsibility of managing commercial bank funds fail to live up to such natural depositor expectations to the extent that a widespread loss of confidence in the banking system ensues, the nation will surely be in serious trouble.

Despite the importance of safety, however, commercial banking necessarily involves both the acceptance of deposits and the assumption of risk through the extension of credit in the form of loans and investments. These two basic banking functions are inextricably related, and no bank can successfully perform one function without the other.

Liquidity

Anyone engaged in the business of lending money must face the possibility that for some reason or another the borrower may be unable to meet his obligation and repay the debt. There is an element of risk in all loans and investments, however creditworthy the borrower may seem to be. Mention has been made of the fact that the asset side of a bank's balance sheet is concentrated in loans and investments, while deposit liabilities dominate the liability side. How then is it possible for a bank to deal with the contingency that a number of its borrowing debtors may not be able to honor their obligations promptly, while at the same time guaranteeing to its depositing creditors *instant payment* on demand or when due? The answer lies in the word *liquidity,* which in this context may be simply defined as the ability of a bank to convert a sufficient amount of assets into cash readily and at favorable prices, so that it can at all times satisfy both normal and abnormally high withdrawal demands of its depositors.

Despite the assurances from some quarters that modern economics has completely conquered the business cycle (alternating periods of prosperity and depression), it is reasonable to suggest that more concrete evidence of this "triumph" is needed. It is generally agreed that a stronger banking system combined with deposit insurance have made wholesale deposit withdrawals less likely in the future than in the past. Yet no bank can afford to operate on the theory that "it can't happen again." Bankers, perhaps to a greater degree than anyone else, must be acutely aware of the basic need for a high degree of liquidity in their asset structures.

Liquidity in the Loan Portfolio

In prosperous times, which are normally accompanied by stimulated lending activity, both deposit liabilities and loan assets tend to expand rapidly and easily in harmonious proportions. On the other hand, in periods of adverse economic conditions, the contraction that takes place is neither easy nor harmonious. As sales at both wholesale and retail levels decline and unsold inventories mount, production is curtailed, unemployment rises, and both business and individual depositors are forced to draw heavily on their demand deposit balances. Liquidating or contracting a loan portfolio in pace with shrinking deposit liabilities is a painful and often an impossible task, even if the bank resorts to the drastic strategy of calling demand loans and refusing to renew maturing time loans. If the borrower is unable or simply refuses to pay his loan, there is little the bank can do. Bringing suit on the basis of the borrower's note or starting bankruptcy proceedings would involve months of legal maneuvering.

This is not to suggest that during an economic recession all bank loans go into default. On the contrary, many loans are paid off as a coincident result of curtailed activity and the liquidation of excessive inventories. There is a degree of liquidity in the loan portfolio, but, as in the case of loan applications, loan payments are generated by the borrowers' decisions, and it is difficult for the banker to gauge with any degree of accuracy the extent of such liquidity.

Years of practical experience have taught bank managers that the loan portfolio is neither a reliable nor a satisfactory source of the degree of liquidity required to meet the occasional sharp contractions in deposit liabilities. In the first place, attempts to squeeze liquidity out of loans can involve serious customer-relations problems. In the second place, bankers have discovered that in times of adversity, even short-term, so-called self-liquidating seasonal loans tend to become anything but self-liquidating, as borrowers also find themselves in a liquidity bind. Therefore, it is necessary for banks to provide some other source of liquidity, and of all other assets, the investment portfolio is the only logical candidate. The sale of investment assets does not involve customer relations. Since such assets are acquired impersonally by means of open-market purchases, they can be disposed of impersonally, with no thought given to the possibility of the debtor's adverse reaction. Furthermore, both the ability of the debtor to meet his obligation *at maturity,* or alternatively, the possibility of finding (via the market) a buyer willing to pay an acceptable price *before maturity* can practically be assured by confining assets purchased solely for liquidity purposes to high quality, short-term obligations that are actively traded.

Income

The third objective management must consider is the need for income. The bank that *consistently* fails to produce enough income to cover operating costs, pay reasonable dividends to its shareholders, and regularly strengthen its capital position through retained earnings is a potential menace to the community. The banker must never forget that he is a businessman, and as such he is necessarily interested in seeing that the corporation that pays his salary is a profitable undertaking. Under our competitive, free enterprise banking system, the interests of the nation and the community, as well as those of the individual stockholders, are best served by a vigorous and sustained search for profits. But income cannot be the sole objective. Neither the bank nor the community will be best served if the banker unreasonably sacrifices the safety of his funds or the liquidity of his bank in an effort to increase income.

A Schedule of Priorities

Despite the basic importance of the three objectives (safety, liquidity, and income), those who manage bank assets cannot pursue these goals in a complete vacuum, irrespective of other considerations. There are certain priorities with respect to bank funds that simply cannot be ignored. Although these priorities are intimately associated with the basic objectives, they are of such importance in their own right that they require as much attention from bank management as the objectives themselves.

The order of priorities may be stated as follows:

1. The need to provide *primary reserves,* that is, legal reserves, working capital, and an adequate cash inventory.

2. The need to provide for a reservoir of highly liquid investment assets sufficient to cope with unexpectedly sharp deposit withdrawals.

3. The need to provide enough additional liquidity in asset structure to enable the bank to perform its main function of satisfying the legitimate credit demands of the community, including reasonable provision for an unanticipated expansion of such demands.

4. Finally, the need to provide a *minimum* nucleus of intermediate and long-term investment assets to serve as security for public deposits as required, as collateral for emergency temporary loans and as a source of additional income.

Primary Reserves

Because of statutory requirements, the first thing a bank must do is to supply funds for legal reserves, which are based on deposit liabilities. Needless to say, legal reserves *must* be maintained at required levels. Although there are provisions for temporary shortages, which are sometimes unavoidable, such deficiencies must be promptly corrected, and the bank must have the ability to do so.

The next thing a bank must do, as in the case of any other business, is to provide for adequate working capital. All businesses must keep cash on hand or in checking accounts to make purchases, pay expenses, meet payrolls, and so forth, and in addition keep an inventory of its "stock in trade" in order to fill orders promptly. Although banks usually issue their own checks (cashier's check or treasurer's check) for most routine expenses, nevertheless such checks must be honored promptly on presentation like any other checks. In addition, all banks must maintain demand deposit balances with other banks to compensate for services rendered in the collection of transit items, for other banking services, and for the purpose of providing immediately available funds in principal money centers in connection with money transfers. The number and the aggregate dollar amount involved in such correspondent bank relationships vary, depending on the size of the bank. While a small bank may need only one correspondent account, a large bank may find it necessary to maintain dozens of such demand deposit accounts in principal money centers both at home and abroad in order to serve its multi-national corporate depositors. Moreover, since banks service the coin/currency element of our monetary system, it is apparent that a bank's cash needs must not only cover correspondent bank balances, but also its "inventory," for in a sense, coin and currency comprise a necessary part of its stock-in-trade. Banks must be ready at all times to convert demand deposits into coin and currency (and vice versa), when and as required by the community it serves. To do this requires not only an adequate inventory in total amount, but also in whatever denominations of coin or currency that may be reasonably requested. Tellers must have "till money" to perform their services, and there must be ample reserves of coin and currency in a bank's vaults for replenishment purposes as needed and to meet seasonal and occasional unusual public demands.

Money set aside for these purposes is nonproductive and (with one possible exception) earns no interest. An exception may exist where state law permits nonmember banks to keep a portion of their legal reserves in a restricted list of interest-bearing securities. Banks that are members of the Federal Reserve System must keep legal reserves primarily in non-interest-bearing deposits with Federal Reserve banks, although they are permitted to include vault cash as a part of required reserves.

Traditionally, all such funds have been called *primary reserves,* but they are not reserves in the sense of money set aside *exclusively* for emergency situations, since they are absolutely essential if the bank intends to stay in business. Thus, "primary reserves" must be adequate for the several purposes served, but since they produce no income (except as noted above) they must be kept at the lowest practical minimum.

Primary reserves meet the objective of safety but must necessarily ignore the objective of income, and while they may provide monetary liquidity in an emergency, they must promptly be restored to that lowest practical level.

Liquidity Needs

As pointed out earlier, there is a special risk inherent in the commercial banking business that does not exist in the case of nonbank lenders. This risk stems from the fact that banks *must* meet the withdrawal demands of its depositors on demand or when due. It is of the utmost importance therefore, that the managers of a commercial bank provide for a cushion of liquidity to enable it to withstand the special pressures to which banks are subjected should deposits fall sharply in periods of economic difficulties.

As the schedule of priorities indicates, however, a bank must have enough liquidity to cover another kind of contingency. When the demand for commercial bank loans increases, the nation's money supply increases, principally in the form of demand deposits. But the newly created demand deposits move rapidly from bank to bank and are not necessarily evenly distributed over the banking system. It is not uncommon for an individual bank to experience sharply expanded loan demands at a time when its deposits are barely holding a stable level or even may be declining somewhat. Not only does a bank have an obligation to satisfy legitimate loan demands to the fullest extent possible, but also every bank wants to share in (and profit by) an economically expanding community. In periods of economic expansion, whether local or national, the bank that finds its funds so tightly committed that it cannot meet the loan demands of its regular customers will most likely lose those customers to competitors.

Thus the nature of commercial banking is such that a bank needs a liquidity cushion both to meet emergencies caused by unfortunate events and to take advantage of opportunities brought about by favorable events. For reasons already discussed, the loan portfolio cannot be depended on as a source of liquidity. A bank simply cannot on short notice demand that existing loans be paid, either to satisfy deposit withdrawals or to make new loans to others. There remains then the investment portfolio as the only logical and practical source of liquidity.

The Investment Portfolio

It will be seen that the investment portfolio of a bank is really divided into two distinct parts—a liquidity account and an income account. The management-directed purchases for each of these accounts differ rather sharply in character. The liquidity account is sometimes referred to as the bank's *secondary reserves,* but in a way this is as much a misnomer as the term *primary reserves.* Secondary reserves implies that there is another more available source of liquidity, but, as has been indicated, primary reserves are not at all suited for this purpose.

The Liquidity Account

Assets held in the liquidity account include primarily short-term United States government securities, federal agency issues, and other top-grade debt obligations preferably having an *average* maturity of one year, with individual maturities of not more than two years. Among other investment-type assets that may properly be included in the liquidity account might be repurchase agreements, commercial paper, and bankers acceptances, provided that they meet the tests of short maturity, ready marketability, and high quality. It must be remembered, however, that the element of risk should be absolutely minimal insofar as the liquidity account is concerned.

Determining Liquidity Needs

Liquidity needs vary sharply from bank to bank, due to the many external factors over which banks have little control but which have a decided influence on both a bank's assets and liabilities. In the discussion of the establishment of loan policy, it was emphasized that each individual bank must carefully not only examine its own characteristics, but also scrutinize the characteristics of the community, the clientele it serves, and the prevailing economic climate in which it exists. Determining an individual bank's liquidity needs requires a somewhat different but no less careful study of external factors. The banker whose deposits have dropped 10 percent from the previous year finds little solace in the fact that the national level of bank deposits has actually increased. Nor can the banker whose loan demand has dried up take any comfort from the news that large banks in

New York City are faced with unprecedented loan demand. Each bank has its own unique problems, and the determination of liquidity needs, like all management decisions, must be based on an analysis of those problems rather than on abstract theory.

Liquidity for Deposit Declines

As has been stressed, the most important need for liquidity is to have the ability to meet sudden and unexpected withdrawal demands of depositors. Obviously, if a bank dishonors a check because of insufficient funds, it must be because of insufficient funds in the depositor's account and not because of insufficient funds on the part of the bank.

By tracing the behavior of the bank's deposits over a period of several years, bank management can get a fairly good idea of the general trend of deposits and how special circumstances might affect that trend. Deposits are volatile and do not move evenly in any one direction. They move up and down from week to week, from month to month, and from year to year. A simple chart comparing quarterly fluctuations over a five-year period should reveal some sort of pattern. Significant external events that may have influenced the trend in any particular period can be footnoted on the chart. If no great changes in the bank's operating environment have occurred, it should be possible to predict fairly accurately the normal upward and downward swings in deposit levels and thus be prepared to meet them. The next step is to estimate a minimum "floor" beneath which deposits are unlikely to decline in the next year or so, even if unfavorable external developments should occur. Both predicted deposit levels and the estimated floor should be reappraised quarterly or even more frequently if actual data indicate that projections have been wide of the mark. Essentially, the liquidity needed to meet deposit fluctuations is the spread between the current deposit level and the floor. (See Exhibit 15, Total Deposits and Estimated Deposit Floor.)

Liquidity for Loan Expansion

Liquidity as a means of meeting unexpectedly sharp declines in the deposit level is of course the most important consideration. But as indicated earlier, there is another good reason for adequate liquidity. Just as a banker is concerned about his ability to meet deposit withdrawals, he must also be concerned about his ability to satisfy legitimate demands for loans in his community. The inability of a poorly managed bank to satisfy the loan demands of regular or prospective depositors forces the applicant to seek the services of competing insti-

Exhibit 15. Total Deposits and Estimated Deposit Floor

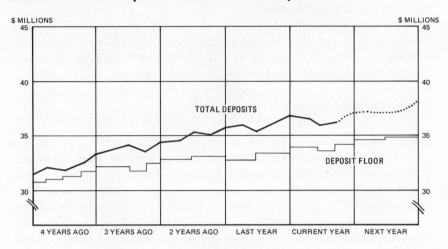

Solid heavy line = actual deposits
Solid light line = estimated
Dotted line = current projection

Exhibit 16. Total Loans and Loan Ceiling

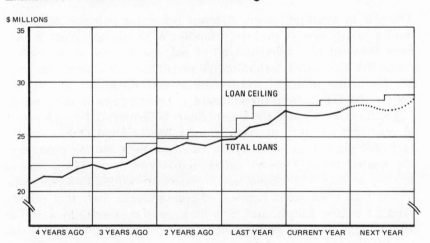

Solid heavy line = actual loans
Solid light line = estimated
Dotted line = current projection

tutions and frequently results in the loss of an account or the failure to obtain a desirable account.

A similar approach is followed in estimating liquidity needs for loan expansion, except that instead of the floor for deposits, a ceiling for loans is estimated, based on the possibility of a stronger than projected loan demand. (See Exhibit 16, Total Loans and Loan Ceiling.)

Total Liquidity Needs

Total liquidity needs are estimated by adding together the amount needed for deposit withdrawals and that needed for loan expansion. There is no formula to predict liquidity needs exactly, but a close approximation can be made by utilizing the available tools. This determination is not made once and for all, for liquidity needs are constantly changing. In the same way that a sailor must adjust his rudder and sails to adapt to changes in the wind and tides, so must the bank adjust its liquidity account to meet circumstances as they change. The objective, though, is always the same: to have enough liquidity but not too much.

Market Risk vs. Credit Risk

The sale of nonliquid assets at prices below the purchase price does not necessarily involve the credit standing of the debtor. What is most often involved is a different kind of risk; *market risk* as opposed to *credit risk*. Credit risk focuses on the possibility that a debtor may not be able to pay principal and interest as they come due. By contrast, market risk results from the influence of interest rates on bond prices.

To illustrate, suppose the United States government, during a period of relatively low interest rates, issues a 20-year bond with a coupon rate of 4 percent. In other words, based on then existing conditions, the United States Treasury agrees to pay purchasers $40 a year in interest on each $1000 bond, and investors are willing to accept those terms. Five years later, however, the government finds that interest rates have risen sharply, and in order to market successfully a similar 20-year bond, it must set the coupon rate at 6 percent. Obviously this would cause the older 4 percent bond to drop in price, as no one would pay $1000 for a bond paying $40 per year in interest when for the same amount they can purchase a bond of the same debtor paying $60 per year in interest. Actually, the 4 percent bond would be worth only about $700 to an investor in order to produce a yield to maturity approximating that of the 6 percent bond ($40 in interest plus $20 average yearly increment in value for 15 years—$300 divided by 15).

Note that there is no question of credit risk. Both bonds are certain to be paid by the United States government in full at maturity. The difference in market price is accounted for by the fact that when interest rates move upward, the market price of outstanding bonds falls, and when interest rates fall, bond prices fall. This is what is known as market risk.

Insufficient or Excess Liquidity

If a bank has insufficient liquidity, it will not *necessarily* have to close its doors and go out of business, provided that it has other disposable (but less liquid) assets. A bank that runs out of short-term "liquidity account" assets can make up the difference by selling longer-term investments. However, the circumstances which force a bank to dispose of long-term assets invariably place other banks and investors in the same position, and they too are trying to sell long-term assets. Selling pressure causes market prices to drop and consequently the bank may have to sell at bargain basement prices.

The penalty for insufficient liquidity is at best a probable substantial *capital loss* on the sale of nonliquid (long-term) assets at prices far below those at which they were purchased. Alternatively, the bank that cannot satisfy legitimate loan demand because it lacks liquidity and is unwilling or incapable of absorbing a capital chargeoff, suffers not only the loss of potential income but also an even more harmful loss of prestige and customer goodwill.

The penalty for having excess liquidity is also a loss in income. The bank could achieve 100 percent liquidity by maintaining all of its assets in cash. But if it did, it would not have any earnings. Maintenance of an excessively liquid position usually involves foregoing some potential earning power, since assets held for liquidity purposes carry relatively low yields. In satisfying liquidity needs, then, the banker tries to strike a happy medium between the extremes of having idle funds on hand and running the risk of being forced to sell longer-term assets on a soft market.

The Income Account

As our priority schedule indicates, although the income section (longer-term securities) of the investment portfolio is the last to be considered, there are certain minimum needs in this area. The income account is composed of securities (bonds, notes, or other evidences of debt having a maturity of more than two years, principally United States governments and municipals, that is, obligations of state and local governments), although some banks might include federal agency issues or top-grade corporate bonds. Thus, the income account includes all investment securities other than those in the liquidity account.

There are several good reasons for keeping a reasonable portfolio of long-term, higher yielding bonds in the investment portfolio. Mention has been made of the necessity of pledging eligible securities in connection with deposits of public funds which frequently become available coincident with tax payment dates, or as collateral for temporary loans. Another good reason is to provide diversification of risk, to balance possible concentrations in the loan portfolio. This is especially important for smaller banks whose opportunity for loan portfolio diversification is limited geographically as well as by a lack of variety of borrowers. Even larger banks, which normally have greater loan diversification because of their broad range of regional and national borrowing customers, can often use the income account to compensate for loan concentrations.

Risk Assumption

Normally, a commercial bank should take most of its credit risks in the loan portfolio. Bank lending officers are professional specialists, and an intimate relationship and personal contact between a bank and its borrowing customers provide ample opportunities for careful analysis of the creditworthiness of a loan application. There is risk involved, for most commercial bank loans, in terms of numbers, are made to small and medium-sized businesses that lack the financial resources of giant corporations. The experienced bank lending officer is well-equipped to gauge the risk and serves both his community and his bank by assuming justified credit risks.

Conversely, it can be argued that a bank should avoid credit risks as much as possible in its investment portfolio. This is certainly true of the liquidity account, but there may be room for a *degree* of credit risk in the income account. As the name indicates, one of the purposes of the income account is to provide satisfactory earnings. Income yield varies with the risk involved. The greater the risk the higher the yield. If it is felt that credit risk in the loan portfolio is well diversified and not excessive, more risk might be assumed in the income account. This is not to suggest that a commercial bank can safely acquire anything but high-quality investments. But, federal agency bonds, municipal bonds (due to their federal tax exemption), and high-grade corporate bonds generally yield a greater return than U. S. Treasury bonds and notes of comparable maturity. If the overall risk exposure is favorable, a higher proportion of such securities could be safely purchased.

Under normal circumstances, long-term investments yield more than short-term investments, and the longer the term to maturity, the greater the yield. This might suggest that the income account should consist solely of 20- to 25-year maturities, which would not be wise, because market risk is greatest when the term to maturity is longest. Should unforeseen events, accompanied by rising interest rates, compel the sale of such long-term assets, the capital loss might be more than the bank's ability to absorb. Even U. S. government bonds issued with low coupon rates have been known to sell at 70 percent or less of face value in a period of rapidly escalating interest rates.

Ideally, the income account should consist of well spaced maturities which would result in a satisfactory average rate of return. In addition, as maturities in income account investments come within a two-year span, they can be transferred to the liquidity account.

Liability Management

For many years, the managers of commercial bank funds concentrated their efforts on the asset side of the balance sheet. Within the last decade or so, there has been an increasing appreciation of the fact that the liability side also offers opportunities for management skills. Relatively recent developments in banking regulations and banking practices have enhanced these opportunities.

On a short-term basis, the introduction of the negotiable certificate of deposit literally permitted banks to buy deposits as a means of satisfying liquidity needs. Bank certificates of deposit, however, must compete with a variety of other short-term money market instruments, and at times the competition is quite keen. Nevertheless, if a bank is willing to raise its rates to an attractive level, it should have no difficulty in increasing its deposit liabilities in this manner. In addition to this source of deposits, banks can also attract short-term funds through various forms of borrowing, including the purchase of federal funds, borrowing from correspondents, or, if a member bank, borrowing from its Federal Reserve bank.

Attracting funds for liquidity needs on a short-term basis requires considerable skill and judgment because of the danger of placing the bank too deeply in the position of "borrowing short and lending long." Short-term investor-type deposits mature with annoying regularity, and the source of replacement funds could dry up suddenly, particularly if investors become willing to take greater risks to obtain yields beyond a bank's competitive capabilities. Similarly, short-term lenders are inclined to become concerned when "temporary" loans, however well secured, take on an air of permanency.

Capital Funds

Capital funds consist of all monies the bank has received through the sale of stock or borrowed through the sale of notes or debentures, plus earnings retained in the business.

Funds raised through the sale of securities can consist of two distinctly different types: (1) equity securities such as common or preferred stock which represent, not an obligation in the sense of a debt to be paid, but shares of ownership in the business, and (2) capital obligations such as notes or debentures, which are debts due and payable on a specified future date. All capital accounts, except for *capital obligations,* represent the net worth of the bank or the excess of assets over actual liabilities. This is the equity interest of the shareholders. On the other hand, holders of capital obligations, who may or may not be shareholders, are creditors and not owners of an equity interest.

The difference between the holder of a capital obligation and a depositor is significant. Depositors are protected by deposit insurance and in addition they are preferred creditors in liquidation, that is, all deposits must be paid before the claims of general creditors are considered. By contrast, holders of capital obligations are not protected by deposit insurance, and they rank with other *general* creditors in that their claims are subordinated to the claims of depositors.

Federal and many state regulations have been liberalized since the early 1960s and now give the banks wide latitude with respect to methods of attracting longer-term capital funds through the sale of senior securities. At one time it was felt that banks should raise capital only through the sale of one class of equity securities, namely capital (common) stock, and the issuance of senior securities, such as preferred stock or capital notes, was interpreted as a sign of weakness. Now, there is no stigma attached to the issuance by banks of preferred stock, capital notes, convertible debentures, or variable interest obligations. The ability to raise long-term capital funds in this manner not only provides an opportunity to adjust a bank's liquidity position but also provides a base for long-term expansion of both deposit liabilities and earning assets.

The management of capital funds also requires skill and sound judgment, as indeed do all other phases of bank management. For instance, the sale of debentures places a mortgage of a fixed amount on future bank earnings, for unlike the dividends on capital (common) stock, the interest on capital obligations must be paid when due to avoid bankruptcy. In relation to total earnings, however, the interest "mortgage" would probably be quite small, and the sale could prove most beneficial. But if expected growth does not materialize, if net earnings decline and interest rates in general fall sharply, the "mortgage" could become rather burdensome.

The management of bank assets requires careful consideration of three basic objectives: safety, liquidity, and income.

The investment portfolio offers the most practical means of satisfying liquidity needs. The nature of the relationship between a commercial bank and its borrowing customers makes it impractical to regard the loan portfolio as a source of asset liquidity. By contrast, in the purchase and sale of investment securities, banks generally deal with markets rather than directly with borrowers.

There is also ample opportunity for employment of banking skills in liability management. Deposits can be purchased through the use of negotiable certificates of deposit. In addition, longer term capital funds can be raised through the sale of both common and preferred stock or by the sale of capital obligations such as capital notes and debentures.

The prudent management of both commercial bank assets and liabilities involves heavy responsibilities which demand the utmost in bank management skills.

Questions Based on This Chapter:

1. What are the three objectives of bank asset management?

2. Why is the loan portfolio regarded as a poor source of asset liquidity?

3. What is meant by the term *primary reserves?*

4. Distinguish between the purposes of the *liquidity* and *income* sections of a bank's investment portfolio.

Chapter 16

Other Banking Services

Part I: Trust Services—International Service

Purposes of This Chapter:

1. To discuss some of the many services offered by banks as fiduciaries or agents.

2. To explain the major underlying principles applicable to the conduct of trust institutions.

3. To describe some of the problems peculiar to international financial transactions.

4. To examine the important role played by bank-issued letters of credit in international trade.

In addition to the basic commercial banking functions (the deposit, payments, and lending functions), banks offer to their customers other traditional services which have long been considered logical adjuncts to banking. In this and the following chapter special consideration will be given to three such services, which have been so frequently utilized by banking customers that they are today expected by the public as

248

standard features of commercial bank facilities: trust or fiduciary services, international services, and safe deposit services. A number of other services currently offered will be treated briefly and in less depth. The number and variety of specialized services have mushroomed so rapidly in recent years as to render any other approach somewhat impractical.

Trust Services

Although some companies have been organized in the past for the exclusive purpose of offering trust or fiduciary services, most such functions are carried out today by the trust department of commercial banks. A fiduciary is an individual or trust institution charged with the responsibility of activity for the benefit of others.

Bank fiduciary services fall under five main headings: (1) settling estates, (2) administering trusts and guardianships, (3) performing agencies, (4) acting as trustee under corporate indenture, and (5) cooperating with attorneys, accountants, and life underwriters in planning estates.

Settling Estates

Settling the estates of deceased persons is perhaps the best known of all trust services rendered by banks. When a property owner dies, his estate must be administered according to law; that is, his assets must be inventoried, his debts and taxes must be paid, and any assets remaining must be disposed of properly. Except in those cases where a deceased person's possessions are limited to bearer items, such as cash and personal effects, it is necessary to form an estate in order to transfer legally ownership of assets to others.

A great many people leave specific written instructions as to the disposition of their possessions after death. Such a document is known as the *last will and testament* of the deceased, and the person who leaves a will is known as a *testator*. On the other hand, perhaps a greater number do not leave such a document, in which case they are said to die *intestate*. Whether or not a will exists, the settlement of an estate and the distribution of remaining assets falls within the purview and control of a court of jurisdiction in the area in which the deceased person was domiciled.

If the decedent left a will, the document must first be probated, that is, filed with the court with acceptable proof of its authenticity. A testator may name a specific person or an institutional fiduciary to settle the estate. A person or institution so named is known as the *executor* of the estate. However, the executor (or co-executors, if more than one is named) must appear before the court to be qualified and formally appointed. Unless there are compelling reasons why it should not do so, the court will usually qualify and appoint the executor (s) named in a will.

If the executor named in the will is unable to serve or refuses to serve or if the court declines to appoint the executor named in the will, the court must appoint some other individual or institution to settle the estate in accordance with the terms of the will. The fiduciary so appointed is known as the administrator with the will annexed, or *administrator c.t.a.* (*cum testamento annexo*). On the other hand, if a property owner dies *intestate,* that is, without having made a valid will, the court appoints a qualified person to settle the estate; the one so appointed is simply known as the *administrator.*

The duties of a bank as executor or as administrator are to take possession of the property of the deceased person, to pay the debts and other charges against his estate, and to distribute the remainder of the property as directed by the will if there is a will, or as provided by law if there is no will. An administrator (other than an administrator c.t.a.) has only the power given him by the law; an executor has the same power given him by law plus any additional powers the will may confer upon him.

Administering Trust and Guardianships

Administering trusts and guardianships is the second main branch of trust services rendered by banks.

1. *Trusts.* A trust exists when one person holds the legal title to property and another person is entitled to the benefits derived from the property. The person who provides property to create a trust is called the *trustor or settlor;* the person holding the legal title is known as the *trustee;* and the person who derives the benefits from the property is known as the *beneficiary.* It sometimes is said that the trustee is the legal owner while the beneficiary is the equitable or beneficial owner of the property. The terms of a trust may provide for more than one trustee (co-trustees) and more than one beneficiary (beneficiaries).

A trust may be created by a will, by agreement, by declaration, or by court order. Some of the best known types of trusts administered by banks are: (1) trusts under wills, often called testamentary trusts, (2) insurance trusts, where the property represents the death benefit value of life insurance policies, (3) living trusts, (4) employees' trusts, (5) institutional trusts, and (6) community trusts.

A trust under a will or a testamentary trust is created when a testator directs that certain specific property or all or part of the residual estate, be held in trust and administered for the benefit of one or more beneficiaries. Since a testamentary trust is created by a will, it becomes effective upon the death of the testator, or as soon thereafter as the executor of the estate is in a position to deliver the trust property to the trustee.

An insurance trust is created when a trustor makes his life insurance policies made payable to a trustee, and by agreement directs the trustee as to the manner in which the proceeds are to be handled and distributed. For example, the trustor may authorize the trustee to invest the proceeds and to pay all income received to his widow during her lifetime, and upon her death, to distribute the principal amount to their children. In an arrangement of this kind, the widow is usually referred to as a *life tenant* and the children as *remaindermen*. If the trustor continues to pay the premiums on the policies, the trust is known as an *unfunded* insurance trust. On the other hand, if the trustor transfers additional property to the trust and the income (rents, dividends, interest, etc.) from that property is sufficient to pay the insurance premiums, and the trustee is then charged with the responsibility of paying the premiums, the trust is known as a *funded* insurance trust. An insurance trust of this kind also becomes effective on the death of the insured (trustor) when the life insurance policies become payable.

A living trust becomes effective during the lifetime of the trustor and might possibly continue in effect long after his death. An almost infinite variety of terms and conditions of living trusts is possible depending on the wishes of the trustor. The following examples illustrate two possible arrangements. Suppose a trustor transfers title to and delivers certain property to his bank (trustee) under an agreement according to the terms of which the trustee is directed to pay all income from the trust property to the trustor during his lifetime; and after his death to pay the income to his widow during her lifetime (should she survive him) ; and upon the death of both husband and his wife to pay the principal to surviving children in equal shares. In this case, the trust could remain operative long after the original trustor's death. By contrast, a philanthropic trustor frequently places property in trust with instructions to pay all income to him during his lifetime, and upon his death to liquidate the property and pay the proceeds to his favorite charity. In this case, the trust would terminate with the trustor's death.

Employee's trusts are typified by the pension trust and by the profit-sharing trust. Under the terms of a pension trust the employer (and possibly his employees) contributes under a predetermined plan to a fund that is held in trust by a bank to purchase annuity contracts or to make payments directly to employees as they reach retirement age.

If the employees make payments into the fund, the pension plan is known as a *contributory plan* and the trust is a contributory pension trust; if the employees make no payments to the fund, then the plan and the trust are *noncontributory.*

Under the terms of a profit-sharing trust an employer contributes, under a predetermined plan, a portion of his profits to a fund that is held in trust by a bank for distribution to the employees of the business upon their reaching retirement age, or upon termination of the plan.

A college or university often transfers cash, stocks, and bonds, which it owns outright, to a bank to hold in trust, and to invest, manage, and administer for the benefit of the college. Such a trust is an *institutional trust.*

Various citizens of a community may, from time to time during their lifetime or by will, leave property with a bank to hold in trust and administer under the terms of a single declaration of trust for the benefit of the people of the community as directed by a committee of citizens. This type of trust is known as a *community trust.*

2. *Guardianships.* Banks serve as guardians of the property of minors and incompetents. A minor is a person under legal age, according to the laws of the state of residence. An incompetent is a person who, regardless of age, is regarded by the law as being incapable of taking care of his property. Incompetents include not only persons who are mentally defective but also, in some states, those who are unable for other reasons to manage their own property. Although the guardian may be recommended by the family, the appointment must be made by the court.

There are two main types of guardians: one of the property and the other of the person. The *guardian of the property* takes care of the property of the ward, while the *guardian of the person* takes care of the person of the ward, that is, looks after his or her home, food, clothing, schooling, and the like. The guardian of the person stands in the place of a parent as far as the upbringing or protection of the ward is concerned. A bank seldom is appointed guardian of the person, but frequently, where there is no guardian of the person, the bank as guardian of the property performs many personal services for the ward.

Terminology and practices are not uniform in all states, and the individual or bank appointed by the court to take care of the property of an incompetent is sometimes known as a conservator rather than a guardian. In others, a committee may be appointed to perform the function of a guardian.

The usual duties of a bank as guardian are fundamentally the same as its duties as a trustee. These duties are to receive, hold, and manage property for the benefit of the beneficiary in the case of a trust and for the benefit of the ward in the case of a guardianship. However, the duties of the bank as trustee cover a much wider range than those it exercises as guardian. As trustee, the work of the bank may range all the way from the mere holding of title to the property, with no active duties whatever, to management of the property as fully and completely as would an absolute owner. In the case of a guardianship, whether a minor or of an incompetent, the duties of the bank are for the most part defined and limited by law.

Performing Agencies

The third main branch of trust services rendered by banks is performing agencies for individuals and business organizations, as well as practically every kind of institution, association, or group enterprise having need for the type of expertise a bank trust department can offer.

The term *agent,* in its broadest sense, includes any person who acts for another by the authority of the latter. The person granting the authority is known as the principal, the person receiving the authority as the agent, and the relationship as an agency. The fundamental difference between a trust and an agency is that in a trust the trustee has the legal title to all the property but in an agency the title to the property remains with the principal.

Some of the more typical agency services rendered by banks are:

1. Safekeeping agent. As safekeeping agent, the bank receives, holds, and delivers property upon the order of the principal; it has no other active duties. Unlike the renting of safe deposit boxes, as safekeeping agent, the bank actually holds and has a record of the property delivered to it for safekeeping. For the most part, such property usually consists of stock certificates, bonds, and other securities.

2. Custodian. As custodian, the bank performs the duties of a safekeeping agent and other active duties, such as collecting and paying out income and buying, selling, receiving, and delivering securities on the order of the principal. A custodian may also undertake to keep the principal informed with respect to pertinent published information regarding securities held, such as notices of tender offers, stock splits, and called bonds.

3. Managing agent. As managing agent, the bank performs all the usual duties of a custodian; in addition, to the extent specified in the agency agreement, it engages in the active management of the property. For example, as managing agent of a securities portfolio, the bank may analyze and review the holdings in the account and may recommend changes, or in some cases may make changes on its own initiative. As managing agent of real property, the bank may rent, lease, or some-

times operate the property for the principal. For practical purposes the basic difference between a custodian and a managing agent is that the custodian waits for and carries out the orders of the principal, whereas the managing agent makes recommendations as to and participates in the active management of the property.

4. Escrow agent. Banks are sometimes called upon to act as escrow agents. This service greatly facilitates real property transactions. An escrow agent may be described as an impartial stakeholder who receives and holds property under an agreement with two other parties pending the unfolding of certain future events. The agent delivers the property held in escrow to one or the other of the parties as stipulated in the agreement, depending upon the occurrence and the nature of the awaited events. For example, Brown owns a house which White is ready to buy and pay for as soon as the title is clear. Brown executes a deed and delivers it to a bank. White pays over the purchase money to the bank. The bank is instructed to deliver the deed to White and the purchase money to Brown as soon as it receives a satisfactory certificate of title from a designated attorney. If the certificate of title is not received or is unacceptable for some reason, the money is returned to White and the deed to Brown.

5. Transfer agent or registrar. As transfer agent the bank serves as agent for a corporation in the transfer of its shares of stock or registered bonds from one owner to another. The transfer agent issues new share certificates or registered bonds in the name of the new owner and is responsible for the legality of the transfers.

As registrar, the bank is the agent of and serves both the corporation and the stockholders by keeping a record of the number of shares of stock cancelled and reissued in order to prevent an overissuance of securities beyond the duly authorized quantities.

Should a bank serve in both capacities in connection with the same issue, as registrar it would be checking on its own work as transfer agent—an arrangement that should be avoided or strengthened with some additional controls.

6. Paying agent or dividend disbursing agent. The bank frequently serves as the agent of a corporation for the payment of dividends on its stock and for the payment of interest on and principal of its bonds.

7. Depository. The bank serves as depository in connection with corporate reorganizations and changes in the capital structure, and in many cases in which there is need for an impartial and trustworthy stakeholder to hold cash or securities while financial transactions are being worked out.

The above list is by no means exclusive. To an increasing extent, banks are serving as agents for educational institutions, charitable organizations, churches, schools, hospitals, and political units such as cities, counties, and townships. The services are many and varied and range from custody and management of endowed property and investment portfolios to making bookkeeping entries and keeping accounting records for the treasurers of such organizations.

Not infrequently a bank may perform agency services for other fiduciaries. For instance, a nonbank executor, administrator, or trustee might employ a bank to act as agent in connection with the administration of the estate or trust, delegating to the bank one or more of the ministerial duties of the individual fiduciary, such as custody of securities, collection of income and principal, the making of disbursements directed by the fiduciary, and the keeping of records of receipts and disbursements. The discretionary duties of the individual fiduciary cannot be delegated, however, and a bank cannot perform such duties for an individual fiduciary. Through an arrangement of this sort, an individual who has undertaken to act as a fiduciary may relieve himself of many of the burdensome features of his undertaking with the assurance that the duties he has delegated to the bank will have the attention of its trained specialists.

Trustee Under Corporate Indenture

A bank acts as trustee under an indenture when a corporation wishes to borrow money by the sale of its bonds. The agreement or indenture for a publicly offered bond issue must meet certain minimum standards in defining the obligations of the borrower and the rights of the bondholder. One of the trustees under an indenture must be a bank or a trust company. The duty of the trustee is to serve as intermediary between the borrower and the lenders. The trustee authenticates each bond as part of the authorized issue and may operate a sinking fund to retire part of the bonds before maturity. The trustee handles the redemption, conversion, and payments of the bonds, and the destruction of all cancelled bonds. In the event of default, the trustee takes such action as it feels will best protect the interest of the bondholders.

Planning Estates

The impact of taxes on estates of even relatively modest size has made estate planning imperative for the property owner. In recent years trust departments, in cooperation with attorneys, accountants, and life underwriters, have played an increasingly important role in helping to analyze all kinds of property in an individual's estate. This analysis leads to an estate plan to accomplish the purposes of the owner. The plan may involve the drawing of a will, the creation of one or more trusts or agencies, or immediate dispositions of property. Since trust departments are not permitted to practice law, the drawing of a will and other legal work is done by the person's attorney.

All of the foregoing is illustrative in nature and is intended only to give the reader an overall view of the tremendous range and variety of trust department services. For those interested in more detailed coverage of the subject, the Institute's textbooks and related courses are recommended.

Principles of Trust Institutions

The underlying principles of trust institutions have been set forth clearly by the Trust Division of the American Bankers Association in *A Statement of Principles of Trust Institutions*. At least four of these statements should be common knowledge to students of commercial banking as well as to students specializing in trust business.

The Duty to Exercise Care

It is the duty of a trustee, in administering the trust, to exericse the care a prudent man familiar with such matters would exercise as trustee of the property of others.

This principle differs from the usual standard of care applied to a trustee, which is that of a man of ordinary prudence administering his own property under similar circumstances. Thus, the trust institutions of the United States have set for themselves a higher standard, from that of a prudent man handling *his own* property to that of a prudent man handling *other people's* property. The practical difference between the two standards lies in the fact that a prudent man might be justified in taking chances with his own property that he would not be justified in taking with the property of others. The point here is that trust institutions have set for themselves a higher standard of care than the law imposes.

The Duty to Keep Trust Property Separate

The properties of each trust should be kept separate from those of all other trusts and separate also from the properties of the trust institution itself.

The legal penalty for the mingling of trust property with the property of the bank is that, if any loss to the beneficiaries results from such mingling, the bank itself must stand the loss, whereas if any profit results, the bank must account for it to the beneficiaries. The practical effect of this separation is that the fate of any one trust account is not involved in the fate of the bank or in the fate of any other trust account. The failure of the bank would not jeopardize the trust property, nor would the termination or depletion of any one trust account affect any other trust account.

The mingling of the property of different trusts, other than that resulting from the operation of a duly authorized collective investment fund, should be neither permitted nor practiced by any trust institution.

The Duty to Exercise Skill

A trust institution should devote to its trust investments all the care and skill that it has or can reasonably acquire.

It is the phrase "can reasonably acquire" that is the main point in this principle. It may be taken for granted that a trust institution devotes to its trust investments and, in fact, to all its trust work all the skill that it has, or else it would not be living up to the standard of the prudent man. But should it go further and try to acquire additional skill and apply its ever-increasing skill to the execution of its trust work? The trust departments of our nation's banks have given an affirmative answer to this question.

Upon this principle of self-improvement are founded the trust educational programs of the American Institute of Banking and of The National Trust School, as well as the internal training courses of trust institutions.

The Duty to Avoid Self-Dealing

A trustee should not have any personal financial interest, direct or indirect, in the trust investments, bought for or sold to the trust of which it is trustee, and it should not purchase for itself any securities or other property from any of its trusts.

This principle applies with equal force to every phase of trust administration, and it rules out all dealings between the bank itself, its affiliated or subsidiary organizations or its directors, officers, or employees and its trust accounts.

Those who offer their services as fiduciaries assume a heavy mantle of responsibility. The management of wealth of any kind, whether it be in the form of real estate, commodities, stocks, bonds, or other personal assets, has grown more complicated due to the multiplicity of laws, regulations, and tax technicalities. Nevertheless, our courts have always (and properly so) taken a dim view not only of a deliberate breach of trust on the part of a fiduciary, but also of inept handling of trust assets, faulty judgment, acts of commission or omission, or any other action by a fiduciary, however well-intentioned, that proves harmful to the interests of the beneficiaries. The reason for this is simply that most fiduciary arrangements are established because the beneficiaries, who may be minor children, elderly persons, incompetents, persons not familiar with business and financial matters, or others who are incapable of acting for themselves or may not be in a position to do so. The very purpose of appointing a fiduciary is to obtain the skill and experience needed to protect and preserve the interests of the beneficiaries.

Although there are many individuals who are quite competent to serve effectively as fiduciaries, human beings have inherent shortcomings that have led to increasing use of institutional fiduciaries. Unfortunately, humans are prone to die, suffer heart attacks or strokes, become senile, or for other personal reasons are unavailable at a time when they are most needed. By contrast, the trust department of a bank has the advantages of continuous existence, continuous capacity, accessibility, collective information, specialization, group judgment, adaptability, government supervision, and substantial financial responsibility.

International Financial Services

The success of any bank can be influenced to a considerable degree by the extent of mutual support offered by its many service departments. The foreign or international service section of a bank is just another of the many areas of specialization which, when used in conjunction with the more familiar domestic banking functions, allows a commercial bank to offer a more complete spectrum of services to its customers.

While international commerce is certainly nothing new, there can be little doubt that improved communications and transportation, together with modern international banking facilities, are likely to increase the volume of all kinds of international transactions in the years ahead. There can be little doubt also that this is a highly specialized field requiring very special technical abilities. Even in our own country, differences in the laws of our several states have posed problems, resulting in continuous efforts over the years to achieve an acceptable degree of uniformity with respect to commercial and financial transactions. But domestic problems pale into insignificance when one considers the much more complex problems involved in foreign commercial dealings. The international banker is confronted with differences in languages, in currencies, exchange rates, in financial and commercial practices, and in the inevitable laws and regulations imposing taxes, duties, quotas, or other restrictions on imports and exports designed by governments to protect their own political, economic, or financial interests. It has often been said that an international department exists as a separate bank within a bank, and this is true in a very real sense.

Of course, not all of our approximately 14,000 independent banks can afford the luxury of a competent, fully staffed international department, nor would all banks have the need for such facilities. But every bank can provide such services as its customers may require by enlisting the aid and cooperation of the international department of a major correspondent bank.

The importance of domestic correspondent bank relationships is well-known, but even more important, with respect to international transactions, is the foreign correspondent bank network. In the absence of their own branch network abroad, American banks that have international departments must rely heavily on the facilities of foreign correspondent banks located in all the major trading countries of the world. Naturally, the relationship is reciprocal, as the foreign banks have a similar need for the services of our domestic banks, in order to serve importers and exporters abroad who trade with their counterparts in this country.

Not all of the problems encountered in international trade are financial in nature. Finding markets, that is, locating sources of products an importer wishes to buy or purchasers for goods an exporter wishes to sell, is considerably more difficult on a worldwide scale than on the domestic scene. In this area, the combined efforts of domestic and foreign banks can be useful. Even when a buyer or seller has been located, there are other things to be considered. Participants in international commerce are separated by great distances. Because of the distances and the longer time element associated with foreign commerce, reliable information as to character, financial standing, and business reputation of importers is of considerable importance before the actual transaction can be closed. Somewhat similar to the network of agencies and banks that exchange credit information in this country, there are comparable channels utilized by foreign correspondent banks that practically cover the entire globe, which again emphasizes the importance of correspondent bank relationships in foreign trade.

The receipt of a favorable credit report by an exporter justifies closing the deal and taking the necessary preparatory steps (purchasing raw materials, adjusting production schedules, etc.), but there still remains the question of the importer's ultimate ability to pay for the goods. Can an exporter afford to ship merchandise to an importer located perhaps 5,000 or 10,000 miles away and run the risk that the buyer will not be able to pay, because of some unforseeable event? In such an unfortunate event, the hapless exporter would be faced with the alternatives of a "distress" sale of his merchandise in a foreign country (assuming that a buyer can be found) or ordering the merchandise returned, thereby suffering additional sizable transportation costs.

For this reason, in foreign commerce, as contrasted with domestic trade, a seller must have more positive assurance that the buyer's commitment will be honored. Such assurance can be had by use of a document known as a *letter of credit*.

The Letter of Credit

In simple terms, a *commercial letter of credit* may be defined as a written document whereby a bank substitutes its credit, which is both good and well-known, for a buyer's credit, which may be as good but is not as well-known. Although a buyer of goods always agrees, tacitly or otherwise, to pay the seller for the goods, under a letter of credit a more responsible third party, a commercial bank, assures the seller that if he ships the goods according to the conditions set forth by the buyer, the bank will guarantee payment.

A bank letter of credit is a very versatile document that can be adapted to facilitate any transaction in which the primary parties must deal at arm's length, either because they are separated by wide geographical distances or because the normal time required to complete the transactions would unreasonably delay financial settlement or because a close personal relationship between the parties is lacking. Letters of credit, however, are by no means limited to this type of transaction. They are frequently used in connection with domestic commercial trade, and the parties involved need not necessarily be buyers and sellers. In, fact, there is an increasing tendency to use such instruments simply as a bank guarantee of the contractual obligations of its customer. Standby Letters of Credit (as they are called) guarantee the satisfactory fulfillment of a wide variety of obligations of the customer, including performance as well as financial obligations.

However, the most common and perhaps the most important use of the letter of credit is in the area of foreign trade—the purchase and sale of merchandise and commodities between private citizens in different countries. An illustration of how a letter of credit is used in this type of transaction should serve to reveal as well the immense potential of this useful document.

Let us suppose that the Ajax Specialty Company, a domestic importer, has made contact with the Nagoya Trading Company, a Japa-

Exhibit 17. An Irrevocable Import Letter of Credit

	INSTITUTE NATIONAL BANK EREHWON, ILL.	ORIGINAL
INTERNATIONAL DIVISION	CABLE ADDRESS: **INSTIBANK**	

IRREVOCABLE DOCUMENTARY CREDIT		OUR CREDIT NO.	CREDIT NO. – ADVISING BANK	DATE
ADVISED VIA ☒ AIRMAIL ☐ SHORT CABLE		90115		MAR 31, 19—

ADVISING BANK	APPLICANT
The Wadai Bank Kobe, Japan	Ajax Specialty Company North & South Streets Centerville, USA

BENEFICIARY	AMOUNT
Nagoya Trading Company 15 Nigashi-Ku Nagoya, Japan	US $10,475.00 Ten Thousand Four Hundred Seventy-Five and 00/100 US DOLLARS
	EXPIRY DATE FOR NEGOTIATION April 18, 19—

Gentlemen:

We hereby issue in your favor this Documentary Credit which is available by your drafts at   sight drawn on ourselves bearing the clause: "Drawn under Documentary Credit No.   **90115**   of the Institute National Bank," accompanied by the following documents:

1) Commercial Invoice in triplicate.

2) U.S. Special Customs Form # 5515.

3) Insurance Policy Certificate @150% of CIF value covering all risks.

4) Full set clean on board ocean Bills of Lading issued or endorsed to the Order of The Institute National Bank, notify applicant and notify John Charles Co., 115 Apple Street, Centerville, marked "Freight Prepaid."

Covering: General merchandise, CIF Centerville, USA

DISPATCH/SHIPMENT FROM Japan TO Centerville USA	PARTIAL SHIPMENTS are not permitted	TRANSHIPMENTS are not permitted

SPECIAL CONDITIONS:

All Bank Charges outside USA are for account of Beneficiary.

The Negotiating Bank Must Forward All Documents To Us In One Registered Airmail.

We hereby engage with drawers and/or bona fide holders that drafts drawn and negotiated in conformity with the terms of this credit will be duly honored on presentation. The amount of each draft must be endorsed on the reverse of this credit by the negotiating bank.	ADVISING BANK'S NOTIFICATION
AUTHORIZED SIGNATURE	PLACE, DATE, NAME AND SIGNATURE OF THE ADVISING BANK

EXCEPT SO FAR, AS OTHERWISE EXPRESSLY STATED, THIS DOCUMENTARY CREDIT IS SUBJECT TO THE "UNIFORM CUSTOMS AND PRACTICE FOR DOCUMENTARY CREDITS" (1962 REVISION), INTERNATIONAL CHAMBER OF COMMERCE, BROCHURE NO. 222.

nese exporter, and Ajax has agreed to buy and Nagoya has agreed to sell general merchandise valued at $10,475 (U.S. dollars). Terms are arranged and a purchase order specifically describing the merchandise is executed.

Ajax discusses the transaction with the international department of his American bank and applies for a letter of credit. Ajax is a regular customer in good standing and the bank readily agrees to issue the letter of credit and finance the transaction. Exhibit 17 illustrates the type of letter of credit the bank would issue. More specifically now, an import letter of credit can be defined as an instrument issued by a bank on behalf of one of its customers (the importer) authorizing an individual or firm (the exporter) to draw drafts on the bank in the amount and under the conditions stipulated in the letter of credit. It will be noted that the draft must be accompanied by specific documents, such as (1) a commercial invoice in triplicate, (2) a consular invoice (U.S. Special Customs Form #5515), (3) an insurance policy certificate, and (4) bills of lading (title documents) issued or endorsed to the issuing bank.

In most cases, the letter is forwarded (in duplicate) to an "advising bank," which may be the exporter's bank or a correspondent of the issuing bank. The advising bank retains its copy of the letter and forwards the original to the beneficiary. Upon receipt of the letter of credit, Nagoya produces the merchandise, packs or crates it, delivers it to the steamship company, assembles the necessary documents, and draws a draft on the issuing American bank. The draft with the accompanying documents are then presented to the advising Japanese bank where they are thoroughly examined. After finding that the draft and documents are in compliance with the terms and conditions of the letter of credit, the Japanese bank pays Nagoya the amount of the draft, less its commission for "negotiating" the draft and documents. The Japanese bank will recover its payment from the American bank, which in turn looks to Ajax for reimbursement. It should be emphasized that the commitment of the American bank to honor drafts presented to it in conformity with the terms of the credit is *unqualified and irrevocable.* Neiher the issuing bank nor its customer (the importer) can revoke the letter of credit without the consent of all parties involved.

If the importer (Ajax) does not require financing, the bank is simply instructed to charge its account for the amount of drafts honored under the letter of credit. However, importers as well as exporters frequently need financial support, which can be arranged in several ways. If the bank is willing to extend unsecured credit, it may offset drafts paid by setting up a loan (to Ajax) on its books and surrendering control of the merchandise by delivering the title documents to

Ajax. Or it may cause the merchandise to be delivered to a warehouse and retain the warehouse receipts as collateral to the loan. This would enable the bank to make partial deliveries of merchandise to Ajax as the loan is reduced. A third alternative would be to deliver the merchandise to Ajax under trust receipts, thus enabling Ajax to have physical possession while the bank legally retains title to the merchandise as security for its loan.

There is an important difference to be noted between the usual international purchase and sale transaction and the normal domestic transaction. As previously stated, letters of credit can be used for domestic transactions whenever a seller prefers to have a bank guarantee that the buyer will honor his commitment to pay for the merchandise. However, because of the generally closer contacts, as well as shorter distances and time elements, most sellers are content to deal directly with the buyer. For example, if a merchant in Chicago, Illinois, sells merchandise to a buyer in Richmond, Virginia, he may simply attach shipping documents to a draft drawn on the buyer and deposit the draft with his bank *as a collection item,* with instructions to deliver the title documents *only* upon receipt of irrevocable payment of the amount of the draft. While the bank is under obligation to observe the depositor's instructions, it enters the transaction only as a collection agent. By contrast, in an international transaction supported by a letter of credit, two banks become active financing participants in the deal, and control of the merchandise moves from the exporter to his bank (or an advising bank), from that bank to the issuing bank, and finally from the importer's bank to the importer.

Naturally, an international letter of credit is prepared by knowledgeable personnel in the international department of the issuing bank, and its terms and provisions are intended to reflect accurately the agreement between the principal trading partners. It is of the utmost importance, both for the importer and the exporter, to be familiar with and to understand the conditions specified in the letter. For instance, the letter may permit or specifically prohibit partial shipments, a matter which could be extremely important to both parties. On the other hand, letters of credit can be by their terms revocable or irrevocable. A revocable letter of credit can be revoked by the issuing bank with or without notice at any time it sees fit to do so, which affords questionable protection for the exporter. For this reason revocable letters are seldom acceptable to an exporter and are rarely used.

Other Documents Used in International Transactions

In the foregoing pages, mention was made of certain other documents commonly used in connection with letters of credit. Actually, many of the documents employed in international transactions have their counterparts in domestic commerce. However, a few are so specialized in nature that they are rarely encountered except in connection with foreign trade. At any rate, it would be instructive at this point to describe some of these documents and explain in what respects, if any, they differ from similar domestic documents.

1. Drafts or Bills of Exchange

A demand for payment under the terms of a letter of credit is invariably made by drawing a draft or bill of exchange on the issuing bank. The terms *draft* and *bill of exchange* are synonymous—both are claims to a specific sum of money made by one party against another party—but the latter is more frequently encountered in international circles.

Drafts drawn under letters of credit may be payable on demand (at sight, that is, on presentation) or they may be payable at a future date if so provided in the letter of credit.

Technically, a sight draft drawn under a letter of credit is a check, since it is a demand draft drawn on a bank. Checks are normally drawn against demand deposit balances by the depositor himself or his duly appointed attorney-in-fact, but under certain types of revolving credit agreements, checks drawn in excess of deposit balances may be paid by the bank by automatically creating a loan to the depositor. Similarly, where an importer requires financing, the issuing bank honoring a draft drawn under a letter of credit reimburses itself by simultaneously creating a loan to the importer. On the other hand, if the importer does not require financing, a sight draft may be simply treated as a check and charged against the importer's demand deposit balance.

2. Banker's Acceptances

If the draft drawn under a letter of credit is a time draft, that is, payable at a future date instead of at sight, it is called a "usance" draft. Assuming that the instrument was properly drawn in accordance with the terms of the letter of credit, the drawee bank must guarantee to pay the draft at maturity. To accomplish this, the drawee bank stamps the word "accepted" across the face of the instrument, indicates the date and place payable, and adds an authorized signature. This transforms the draft, a drawer's order to pay, into an acceptance, which becomes a drawee's promise to pay. A draft accepted by a bank is called a *banker's acceptance*. A draft accepted by nonbank drawee (a firm or corporation) is called a *trade acceptance*.

Banker's acceptances are ordinarily payable in six months or less from the date of presentation. There is a ready market for these short-term, highly liquid instruments since they represent not merely an ordinary claim to money, but an officially signed promise to pay, backed by the resources of a well-known commercial bank. Banker's acceptances are normally sold on a discount basis, and daily quoted rates are available from dealers in short-term, high quality money market instruments. After acceptance by the drawee bank, the instrument is returned to the holder who has the option of selling it on the market, thus immediately receiving the face amount less the discount, or of holding it for payment in full at maturity.

3. Commercial and Consular Invoices

A commercial invoice is a descriptive document supporting a transaction between a buyer and a seller of goods, which contains an itemized list of goods shipped and usually specifies the price and the terms of the sale.

A consular invoice is similar in content to a regular commercial invoice except that it is usually printed in the language spoken in the country to which the goods are being shipped and is attested to by the shipper at the foreign consulate of the country receiving the shipment. The primary objective of a consular invoice is to obtain assurance in advance, by an official representative of the country destined to receive the shipment, that the transaction does not violate any laws or trade restrictions (import quotas, and so forth) of the importing country. Both commercial invoices and consular invoices are invariably included among the documents required to be attached to drafts drawn under letters of credit. The penalty for making false or misleading statements in consular invoices is severe, and their preparation should be entrusted to those familiar with their use.

4. Trust Receipts

A trust receipt is an instrument that enables a bank to retain legal title to merchandise as security for a loan while giving physical possession of the goods to the borrower. Very often the borrowing customer may need possession of the product or material for further processing or for display or demonstration purposes prior to sale. When the customer signs the trust receipts, he agrees to hold the merchandise as *trustee* for the benefit of the legal owner (the bank), and further agrees not to dispose of either the merchandise or the proceeds from the sale thereof without first satisfying the legal owner's interest therein. Banks using trust receipts should be thoroughly familiar with state laws, which for the protection of other creditors generally limit the time within which they are effective and require the filing of financing statements as public notice of the arrangement.

Other International Services

In addition to facilitating and financing foreign trade, an international department can perform many other services useful to individuals as well as businessmen.

Collections and Remittances

Many citizens of this country are constantly receiving and making payments to persons residing in foreign countries. As can well be imagined, in addition to governmental transfers of funds, there is a steady stream of checks, drafts, and other financial instruments flowing between countries.

Through its correspondent relationships, the international department can collect or redeem financial instruments payable anywhere in the world, whether payable in U. S. dollars or any foreign currency and, in the latter case, convert the foreign money at current exchange rates into domestic currency. Similarly, citizens of this country desiring to make payments to relatives, friends, or business representatives abroad can obtain drafts drawn on foreign banks payable in foreign currencies if they choose, instead of sending a check payable in U. S. dollars. Where the element of time is important, payments of funds can be made by cable transfers, which are similar to the wire transfers used domestically.

Services for Travelers

An international department can be helpful to travelers in many ways. For instance, a person contemplating a trip abroad can protect himself from fluctuating exchange rates by purchasing in advance foreign currency from the international department of his bank. Obviously, goods and services purchased abroad will have to be paid for in the currency of the country to be visited. Or if the sum involved is large, the traveler can obtain either a travelers letter of credit or travelers checks.

A travelers letter of credit is somewhat similar to a commercial letter of credit. The purchaser deposits with his bank the maximum sum of money intended to be spent abroad. The bank then issues a letter of credit guaranteeing payment of withdrawals up to the dollar amount limit specified in the letter. When the traveler arrives in the foreign country, he presents the letter to a correspondent of the issuing bank and identifies himself. Usually the letter of credit will bear a specimen signature of the traveler verified by the issuing bank. The reverse side of the typical letter of credit is printed with lines providing space for the indorsement by foreign banks of the dollar amount of credit extended, which is then converted into local (foreign) currency. Thus any foreign banker called upon to honor the letter of credit can determine the remaining amount available to the traveler by deducting the amounts indorsed from the aggregate amount stated in the letter. As a rule, the foreign bank compensates itself by charging the account of the issuing bank and mailing an advice stating the date and amount of the charge.

Travelers checks are check-sized documents, serially numbered and issued in such denominations as $10, $20, $50, and $100. They are more easily negotiated than a personal check because they have printed on them a guarantee that there are sufficient funds on deposit at the issuing bank, express company, or well-known travel agency to repay those who cash them. The purchaser signs each check in the presence of an employee of the issuer or a selling agency and also provides a specimen signature for the seller's files. When the purchaser wishes to cash a check, it is signed again in the presence of the cashing party. Normally, the only identification required is provided by a comparison of the two signatures on the item. If the purchaser should lose traveler's checks before cashing them, a claim for the loss is filed with the issuing company through one of its selling agents. Since the most attractive features of traveler's checks are their international acceptance and their protection against loss, a great majority of loss claims are settled in favor of the purchaser.

In some respects, travelers checks resemble a series of small denomination, individual letters of credit, with repayment for funds advanced to the presenter guaranteed by the credit of a large internationally known bank or issuing company.

Letters of Introduction

Traveling businessmen and tourists sometimes encounter problems or require assistance in non-financial matters. The ability of the bank's international department to furnish its customers with letters of introduction addressed to foreign correspondents is a most valuable service which can be especially beneficial when unforeseen and unexpected situations develop. As in domestic banking, international correspondent relationships are reciprocal in nature. Many a bank customer has been spared a great deal of inconvenience and trouble because of the on-the-scene presence of a friendly correspondent banker who is in a position to make local contacts, open doors, and in many other ways extend a helping hand to a stranger away from home.

———————

Trust services and international banking services have long been regarded as natural complements of commercial banking. Through their trust divisions, banks act as fiduciaries and as financial agents in performing a wide variety of services. Without the services of international bankers, it would be much more difficult if not a practical impossibility for the nation's producers, manufacturers, and merchants to conduct and finance foreign trade. Both fields are highly specialized and require the expertise of well-trained and experienced personnel.

Questions Based on This Chapter:

1. What is the difference between a trustee and an agent?

2. What inherent advantages are found in institutional fiduciaries that are not necessarily found in individual fiduciaries?

3. What special problems confront international bankers that do not apply to domestic banking?

4. How can a letter of credit assist an American importer in making purchases of goods produced in foreign countries?

Chapter 17

Other Banking Services

Part II: Safe Deposit—Specialized Services

Purposes of This Chapter:
1. To describe the nature of safe deposit services.
2. To emphasize the importance of strict adherence to sound procedures when granting access to boxes.
3. To discuss briefly the transition from pure commercial banking to "full service" banking.
4. To call attention to the prospect of an even broader expansion of bank services and the possible restrictive effect of regulatory decisions.

Safe Deposit Services

Providing facilities for the safe storage of gold, jewels, precious possessions, and other articles of value was one of the earliest forms of banking. From the outset, banking was built on the twin cornerstones of *trust* and *protection*. People trusted the early temple banks and looked to them for protection of material things that meant a great deal to them. Sometimes overlooked today is the fact that *protection* of assets ranks high among the services people desperately need and banks can offer.

For instance, banks very effectively protect the bulk of our current medium of exchange (checkbook money) in the modern demand deposit account. The advantages as well as the protection afforded to those who make payments by check are well-known, and it will be recalled that much of the protection is based on the clear responsibility of the drawee bank to carry out faithfully the specific instructions of the depositor. Even clearer, however, is the responsibility of the bank that offers and rents safe deposit boxes, a service that is intended to provide nothing but the safeguarding and protection of items of value and ready access to such items as required.

The Nature of Safe Deposit Service

There is a significant difference between the nature of the service rendered by a bank to its depositors and the service offered to the renter of a safe deposit box. The person who deposits $100 in cash in his checking account does not expect to withdraw the identical coin and currency. It is understood that the cash will be commingled with other cash deposits received by the bank and that the bank's responsibility is simply to repay $100 in whatever denominations of coin or currency the depositor may require or to transfer all or part of the deposit credit to someone else in accordance with the depositor's instructions. All deposited items become bank assets, offset by an equal dollar amount of deposit liability. Except for the equivalent value, no relationship whatsoever exists between what was originally deposited and what is ultimately withdrawn.

On the other hand, the person who rents a safe deposit box and places in it an insurance policy or a diamond ring expects to retrieve, when he so desires, the same identical insurance policy and the same identical diamond ring. Items placed in a safe deposit box remain the exclusive property of the renter. There is no debtor-creditor relationship; all the bank does is provide a private section of vault space for the exclusive use of the renter, and under normal circumstances, the bank should have no knowledge of what is placed in or withdrawn from the box.

Physical Protection

In offering safe deposit facilities, the bank is essentially selling protection, and it is morally as well as legally bound to provide adequate protection. Safe deposit boxes should be housed in a bank vault built in accordance with acceptable *and appropriate* construction specifications.

For example, the Bank Protection Act of 1968 prescribes certain minimum standards for bank vault construction. But there is a strong temptation to offset rising construction costs by accepting minimum standards as the norm. Those responsible for the construction of banking offices should consider many factors, particularly in the case of branch offices. Specifications that might be suitable for a free-standing structure would not necessarily apply to rented quarters in a building or in a shopping center where relatively thin walls separate banking quarters from other rented areas. The nature of the community served and the size and number of boxes to be offered are also factors to be considered.

Breaking and entering bank vaults and the rifling of safe deposit boxes is unfortunately not without precedent. The ensuing claims of the renters of looted boxes would be astronomical in any event, but if a successful burglary can be attributed to inadequate protection in any particular set of circumstances, the result would be disastrous. It is both logical and equitable to expect that those who offer to sell protection will be held accountable for failure to take whatever reasonable steps may be required to provide adequate protection.

Safe Deposit Contracts

Safe deposit services are based on a written contract. The legal nature of the contract depends on applicable state law. For instance, some states maintain that the relationship between the bank and the customer is that of bailor and bailee. A bailor is one who delivers property to another (the bailee) for a specific purpose. Other jurisdictions declare the relationship to be that of landlord and tenant, on the theory that the bank (landlord) merely rents private vault space to the customer (tenant), and what may be properly deposited in the space is of no concern to the bank. There is some logic to both contentions, but in any event the customer pays an annual fee for the service.

From the bank's point of view, the procedures for entering into a safe deposit contract are quite similar to the steps taken to enter into a deposit account contract, except that the safe deposit contract invariably is and should be in writing, whereas many deposit-account contracts are not. Safe deposit services are offered to individuals, either singly or jointly, to corporations, partnerships, fiduciaries, or to any legal person having contractual capacity. The renter of safe deposit facilities may confer on specific individuals the right of access to the box or vault space, and those so authorized are generally known as deputies. Establishing the identity of individuals or determining the authority of deputies or others granted powers to act in other than their individual capacity is no less important in connection with a safe deposit box than in the case of a deposit account. In the former case, however, the authority refers to the right of access to the box, rather than to the privilege of signing orders for the withdrawal of funds.

It is obvious that a bank must investigate very carefully before entering into banking relationships with those having unsavory reputations or known criminal backgrounds. In the safe deposit department this rule is of particular importance. For the few dollars necessary to rent a box, a criminal would have the privilege for an entire year of frequently visiting the bank's safe deposit area, perhaps observing the habits of an intended victim, while at the same time making careful notes of the bank's procedures and the diligence of the bank's employees in following such procedures.

Actually, banks that offer safe deposit facilities do so primarily for the purpose of providing a full range of services for their regular customers. Renting boxes is hardly one of the most profitable areas of banking service, and many banks are taking a closer look at the transient box-renter, whose motives might be less than friendly. The relatively small annual fee does not justify the risk of potential fraud or expensive vandalism. When a prospective safe deposit renter is not a regular customer of the bank and is otherwise a complete stranger, such banks insist on investigating the prospect's background carefully before actually renting the box to him.

The Bank's Responsibility

Once a safe deposit contract has been signed, the bank's chief responsibility centers on the right of access to the box. In this respect, the contract is similar to the one entered into when a deposit account is opened in an individual name. The depositor and the depositor alone is authorized to withdraw funds from the account, unless someone else (an attorney-in-fact) is duly authorized to act on the depositor's behalf. Similarly, a safe deposit contract permits the renter alone to have access to the box unless someone else (a deputy) is duly authorized to have access on the renter's behalf. In either case, the bank is fully responsible if it permits the withdrawal of deposited funds or access to a safe deposit box by unauthorized persons.

While the bank can and must take positive steps to eliminate the possibility of unauthorized access, it can do little to avoid occasional allegations by renters that items of value have been removed from a safe deposit box without the knowledge or authority of the renter. Since the bank has no record of what was placed in or removed from a box, it is in no position to offer direct evidence to refute such a claim.

Situations that pit the word of a safe deposit customer against the word of the bank's employees are often difficult for a court to decide. Invariably, some extraneous bit of evidence persuades a judge or jury to place more credence in the testimony of one side than in the testimony of the other. If the bank has established a carefully designed procedure that provides maximum protection for its safe deposit customers and if the evidence shows that this procedure has been meticulously followed, it is most unlikely that the depositor's testimony will prevail. If there is any evidence, however, that the bank's procedures have not been carefully designed and that loopholes exist that provide opportunities for either bank personnel or other unauthorized persons to gain access to safe deposit boxes, or if there is testimony to the effect that, although the procedures are sound, bank personnel do not always follow these procedures or are careless in the execution of their duties, then there is an excellent chance that the court will decide in favor of the claimant, the safe deposit customer.

When a customer claims that the contents of his box have been disturbed, the bank can only say in its own defense, "This is highly improbable, because our procedures are specifically designed to prevent such an event, and our employees follow them faithfully." If the bank can make that statement without fear of refutation, its risk is minimal and the claimant must assume a heavy burden of proof. On the other hand, any evidence that tends to weaken the bank's defense could be disastrous, as a judge or jury might conclude that since the alleged incident *could* have happened, it probably did.

For these reasons, the importance of sound access procedures, thoroughly understood by safe deposit department personnel and meticulously followed at all times, cannot be overemphasized.

Access Procedures

Naturally, the safe deposit contract must clearly identify those who are to have access to the contents of the safe deposit receptacle, which is normally limited to individual renters and their duly appointed deputies, or where the renter is a legal entity such as a corporation, specifically identified representatives. In some cases access may require the presence of two such individuals or representatives. Specimen signatures of those having the right of access are usually obtained on the contract itself, but in any event are kept in departmental files, readily available for comparison. Identification of individuals seeking access to bank deposit boxes is extremely important, and some banks, to aid in the identification process, are using photographs, as well as specimen signatures of those authorized to have access.

The following paragraphs describe some of the more common procedural steps that are designed to provide maximum protection for the customer. However, there is no intention here to prescribe definite rules of procedure for any given safe deposit department. In the first place, the legal concepts involved are not uniform in all states, and in the second place, procedures must necessarily conform to the physical properties of the available facilities. While this should be borne in mind by the reader, it is urged that the steps listed below be given serious consideration.

The outer door to the receptacle in which the safe deposit box is housed normally has two cylindrical cores, each of which is operated by a separate key. One is for the customer's key; the other is for the bank's preparatory or guard key. Both keys are required to open the outer door; neither the customer's key nor the bank's preparatory key alone can provide access to the safe deposit box.

In granting access to a safe deposit box, the average bank might proceed substantially as follows:

1. The person desiring access is required to sign an access slip or similar record on which the date and time of the request is noted. Except in cases where there is *absolutely no question as to identity,* the signature on the access record should be compared with the specimen on file. The possession of a customer's key is not in itself evidence that the possessor has the right or the authority to use that key.

2. The person to whom access is granted should always retain physical possession of the customer's key, except momentarily, when a bank custodian or attendant may accept the customer's key at the outer door of the receptable for the purpose of opening the outer door to withdraw the box or to replace the box and lock the outer door. This should be done *in the presence* of the person granted access, and the customer's key should be *immediately* returned following its use.

3. When a box is removed from its receptacle, the outer door should never be left unattended with keys inserted. The door should either be *locked shut* or *locked open* and both the preparatory key and the customer's key promptly removed.

4. After receiving the safe deposit box, the customer should be immediately escorted to private quarters, such as a room, a booth, or a stall. The opening of a box in exposed areas should not be permitted.

5. If a bank employee carries the box, as a courtesy or because of its weight, to or from the vault and such private quarters as are available, the box must always be kept in full view of the customer.

6. Private facilities utilized by customers should be searched after each occupancy to ensure that valuable articles have not been left behind inadvertently.

Safe Deposit Keys

Mention has been made of the fact that the bank's guard key (or preparatory key) must be used in conjunction with the customer's key in order to open the receptacle in which a safe deposit box is housed. For this reason, it is important to see that no bank employee having access to the guard key is also placed in the position of possessing a customer's key unobserved. Obviously, this would admit the possibility that a duplicate key might have been made, thus permitting the employee alone to obtain access to a customer's safe deposit box.

Therefore, with respect to keys, a bank should consider two important points:

1. Whatever system is used, no employee of the bank should have sole control of an unissued customer key before the safe deposit box is rented. Some banks meet this situation by changing lock tumblers after each box is surrendered and receiving all keys from their locksmith in sealed envelopes to be opened only by the new renter. When keys are not in sealed envelopes, some form of dual control should be utilized before the keys are delivered to a new customer.

2. After a safe deposit box is rented, it would be most unwise for any bank employee or officer to accept control of a customer's key. Occasionally a key may be lost by a customer while he is in the safe deposit area. Effective procedure requires that such keys must be turned over immediately to the auditor of the bank or to an officer, if the bank has not designated someone as auditor. The customer should be notified immediately, and when he calls to claim his key, the bank should insist that he open the box and make an immediate and complete inventory of its contents to avoid the possibility of a claim at a later date.

On occasion a customer will mail his keys to the bank, state that the safe deposit box is empty, and request that his lease be canceled. In such circumstances, the box should always be opened in the presence of the bank's auditor or at least two other employees. If the box is found to be empty, the customer can be so notified and the lease canceled. If, on the other hand, the box is found to have contents, the box should be immediately closed and locked and the keys returned to the sender by registered mail with a request that he appear to remove the contents.

When two keys are issued, the customer is requested to separate the keys and provide a different location for each. The obvious reason is to minimize the chance of losing *both* keys, in which case the vault cannot be opened *except* by drilling, usually at the customer's expense.

Death or Incompetency

It would be futile to attempt to discuss in detail the effect of death or incompetency of a safe deposit customer since local laws could have a considerable bearing on the procedures to be followed. In the case of death particularly, state inheritance tax laws frequently specify the manner in which a decedent's box is to be opened and the contents inventoried.

In the case of joint renters, the bank's form of contract (co-lessee) may or may not give sole right of access to the survivor. This would depend on stipulations as to access by the parties themselves as well as local laws and possible inheritance tax restrictions. It must be remembered, however, that the right of access by a survivor does not imply that title to property in the box passes to the survivor upon the death of a co-lessee. This is a matter to be settled between the survivor and the executor or administrator of the decedent's estate or by a court of law if the parties at interest cannot agree.

Personnel

When the volume of business is sufficient to require full-time personnel, the personnel so selected should be efficient, careful, and capable of exercising mature judgment. There is no substitute for adequate training in this specialized field and full cognizance of the responsibility of the safe deposit attendant. The ability to recognize situations in which snap judgment cannot be exercised and in which it is advisable to confer with officers, and possibly counsel, is essential. Decisions with respect to a non-routine request for access must be carefully made. When consultation is desirable, a request for access can be deferred rather than refused. When circumstances do not permit the designation of a full-time safe deposit attendant and this responsibility is shared by a number of employees, all of those involved in vault operations should meet these requirements.

Other Services

It is safe to say that the American public—businessmen as well as private citizens—is well aware of the fact that the so-called traditional banking functions and services by no means represent the full spectrum of available commercial bank services. Indeed, the number and variety of such other services range from the relatively uncomplicated Christmas and vacation clubs to highly specialized data processing services.

While much can be done by imaginative men to create and even stimulate a demand for new services, in the final analysis, it is the public itself that determines what services it wants and will accept and pay for. This is true of all products as well as services, and the principle applies to all businesses, including banking.

In the early days of this nation, life was rugged but relatively simple. A great many of our nation's citizens were self-sufficient and had little need for sophisticated services. There was little demand for banking services by the average citizen. It was natural, therefore, that early banking services were designed exclusively for and offered to the more affluent citizens and to businessmen whose needs for such services were most urgent.

For almost a full century, the most pressing need of our young nation was for a dependable and reliable monetary system. Specie or hard metallic money was scarce, and much of it was imported from older countries. Early banks tried hard to supply this need by providing paper currency in the form of banknotes, but too few bankers understood the basics of sound money or appreciated the necessity of instilling and sustaining the public's confidence in its ability to redeem paper money for value. It wasn't until the passage of the National Bank Act (1864) that a reasonably sound and effective banknote system became available.

About that time, however, a drastic change was taking place in our monetary system with increasing momentum, that is, the substitution of demand deposits (checkbook money) for coin and currency as our principal medium of exchange. The full impact of this significant event was yet to be felt, but commercial banks were forced to adapt to the change and to develop new operating techniques to handle a radically different payments system. However, it is probable that very few bankers could visualize the extent to which the public would accept the idea of using checks as a means of payment and the extent to which this practice would eventually broaden the potential market for banking services.

Nevertheless, through the first two decades of the twentieth century, banking services were still largely limited to business customers and a small clientele of more wealthy citizens. Many bankers took pride in the fact that their institutions were exclusively commercial in nature; they concentrated on service to business, industry, and commerce and made no effort to cater to the needs of the average citizen. To be sure, following World War I some of the smaller banks, whose access to commercial deposits was somewhat limited, began to solicit individual accounts, to offer savings accounts, and even began to experiment with consumer loans. The severe depression and bank troubles of the 1930s, however, temporarily ended further attempts to expand bank services.

Following World War II, however, the situation began to change rapidly. The pent-up demand for consumer goods caused by years of shortages and deprivation during the war stimulated an unprecedented demand, and factories began to produce an avalanche of automobiles, refrigerators, gas and electric ranges, small household appliances, in fact, all sorts of consumer goods, in an effort to satisfy the hungry demand. Banks not only furnished working capital to the manufacturers and dealers, but also began on a large scale to make direct loans to consumers. Bankers that formerly extolled the exclusively commercial nature of their business, began actively to cultivate the image of the "full-service" bank that offered a wide range of services to every class of business and every type of citizen. Consumer credit, mortgage loans, trust services, savings accounts, safe deposit boxes, night depositories, and other individual-oriented services once thought of as foreign to the business of commercial banking sprang up everywhere, even in the largest banks. Somewhat reluctantly but inevitably the pure commercial bank became a creature of a bygone age.

But the most sensational proliferation of new specialized services was yet to come. If anything good can be said of wars, it has to be the forceful stimulus such catastrophes give to scientific and technological advances. The development of the electronic computer to the stage of commercial usefulness, as well as other such marvels as television and nuclear fission, undoubtedly came several decades earlier than could have been possible without wartime experimentation. In the business world the digital computer opened the door to a vast array of additional services to business and industry based on mass data-processing techniques. In banking the computer was warmly welcomed as a means of modernizing operating techniques to cope with the pressing problems that resulted from an ever-increasing volume of paper transactions. But more imaginative bankers quickly seized on the unique opportunity to expand greatly the range of banking services that could now be offered to their customers. The high cost of computers provided a strong incentive in this respect as new computer services could produce income and spread the cost by utilization of all available computer time. A wide variety of novel and useful services were conceived and developed, many of which were eagerly accepted by customers anxious to participate in the new electronic age.

In developing new services, however, commercial bankers face a special problem not shared by most private enterprises. Because of the critical role played by the commercial banking system in monetary affairs and as private allocators of credit, regulatory authorities have a special interest in banking activities. There are many who firmly believe that in order to avoid harmful conflicts of interest commercial banks should confine their activities to the banking business only and not engage in extraneous or unrelated fields. While there is much logical support for this position, some perplexing questions arise. "In precise terms, what is the banking business and what if any are the limits of its proper sphere of activity?"

The Board of Governors of the Federal Reserve System has stated that any activity that is "so closely related to banking or managing or controlling banks as to be a proper incident thereto" is a permitted activity. But such imprecise terms as "closely related" and "proper incident thereto" require interpretation. Efforts in this direction have been made, but it is probably safe to say that for some time to come, Congress, the regulatory bodies, and bankers will be devoting much time and effort to resolving the inevitable (and natural) differences of opinion with respect to these terms.

Some of the special services described in the following pages have been made possible by or depend heavily on sophisticated accounting machinery. Other services exist solely because of customer need and can be profitably rendered by banks using more conventional equipment or even by manual effort. But all of them have one thing in common, in that they represent a singular departure from older concepts of commercial banking functions.

Account Reconcilement

One of the first of the modern business services offered by banks was account reconcilement for active commercial accounts. The company furnishes the bank with daily input data including the amount and check number of all items issued in machine-readable form. such as punched cards or magnetic tape. At the end of each statement period the company receives a listing by serial number of all checks paid and a similar listing of checks issued but unpaid (outstanding). This information, coupled with data relating to deposits made during the period, permits a quick and relatively simple reconcilement of the balance shown on the bank statement with that shown on the company's books.

Accounts Payable Services

A logical extension of account reconcilement services is the assumption by the bank of the paper work, including accounting reports, related to the accounts payable function. In addition to check serial numbers and accounts, the company furnishes more complete input information with respect to the purpose of the payment, the product or services purchased, and the particular function, operation, or account to which the payment relates. The bank can then furnish a complete cash disbursements register, distributive reports, and controls of purchasing and procurement activity. If desired, the service can also include the preparation of the checks.

Payroll Services

There are few disbursements that demand more accuracy and accumulation of detailed data than the payment of salaries and wages. Many banks offer payroll services, some quite simple but others quite complex. For instance, in some cases the service begins with the acceptance of raw input data, such as hourly rates and hours worked, from which the bank computes the payrolls, deducts federal and local withholding taxes, renders related reports to the government, the employer, and the employees and makes the actual payment to the employees. In the latter connection, the bank may issue a check to each employee or may credit accounts opened for the employees, who are permitted to withdraw the entire amount immediately without being subject to any charge. Not to be ignored, however, is the opportunity for the bank to attract the banking business of a substantial number of the employees.

Accounts Receivable

Whenever an account is opened, the bank automatically becomes involved in both the deposit and the withdrawal of funds, and there is no reason why specialized services should be confined to only one of these functions. Deposits consist of funds received, and where merchandise or services are sold on a credit basis, deposits represent the liquidation of accounts receivable. Many businesses, in order to meet current operating expenses, pledge their accounts receivable as collateral for bank loans. In additional to financing accounts receivable, many banks are in a position to render a valuable accounting service as well by maintaining a ledger record for each debtor from input supplied by the customer, by preparing a cash receipts register, and by preparing trial balances for settlement purposes as well as periodic statements and "aging" reports showing accounts past due for 30, 60, or 90 days.

Billing and Collection Services

A logical extension of the financing and accounting services rendered in connection with accounts receivable is the actual billing or preparation and mailing of the debtors statements. This type of service is especially useful to utility companies. Input data might consist of beginning and ending meter readings together with the company's rate structure, from which the customer's bill is computed and mailed by the bank.

At this point another logical step suggests itself. There is no valid reason why the company must handle each customer's remittance check. Eventually they must be handled and collected by the bank, so why not bypass the company and have the checks mailed directly to the bank through a post office box to which the bank has access or have them paid in person by the customer at a banking office? This procedure not only reduces unnecessary paper handling, but it also results in an increased volume of available funds. Moreover, the bank can render an accounts receivable report in whatever form is most suitable for the company's purposes.

Lock Box Banking

In connection with remittances, another popular service has proved most rewarding to customers through speedier conversion of checks to usable funds. This service appeals particularly to businesses operating on a nationwide basis who serve customers located many miles from the company's main office. To illustrate the point, consider the time lost in transportation when West Coast buyers mail remittance checks to an East Coast vendor, who deposits the checks in his East Coast bank. In the collection process, the checks must then retrace their steps to be presented to the West Coast drawee banks. Depending on the sales volume, the dollar volume of funds immobilized while remittance checks take round-trip tours of the country can reach substantial proportions.

By designating "lock box banks" as collecting agents in those areas where an appreciable number of remittances originate, the vending company can save several days float and receive the tangible benefits of increased available funds. Remittance checks are simply mailed by the customers to a local post office lock box, where the agent bank picks them up at regular intervals. Thus the collection process starts at or near the point of origin where the drawee banks are located. In many cases the checks may not travel outside the city or county in which the customer resides. As soon as they become available, the lock-box bank wires the funds to the vendor's East Coast bank and furnishes regular reports or other evidence of remittances received to the company for accounts receivable posting.

Providing a safe place for the protection of items of value has long been regarded as a normal extension of banking service. Despite the existence of systems designed to prevent unauthorized access to a safe deposit box by a bank employee or anyone else, allegations are sometimes made by renters that contents have been wrongly removed. The only defense available to a bank in such circumstances is the assertion that access procedures are sound and are meticulously observed.

The foregoing pages only briefly describe a few of the newer special services offered by many banks today. Any attempt to catalog fully all such services or even to describe any of them in detail would be futile, for at this point in time, the situation is quite fluid. Some services presently offered might conceivably be discontinued due to lack of demand or of profitability. More certain is the fact that innovative services will be developed continuously as time goes on. Clarification by Congress and regulatory bodies of activities considered to be "a proper incident" to banking will undoubtedly have an effect on the future services. If history proves anything, it is that few fields of human endeavor remain static for long, and banking is no exception as the 200-year record of banking in the United States amply demonstrates.

The rapid proliferation of related banking services since World War II and the adoption by banks of electronic data processing systems make it difficult to catalog such services with any degree of precision. The only conclusion that seems justified is the probability that the full range of services "incident to" the business of banking is yet to be explored.

Questions Based on This Chapter:

1. In what respects does safe deposit service differ from demand deposit service?

2. What defense can a bank offer if a safe deposit customer claims that the contents of his box have been removed without authority?

3. Describe some specialized banking services that are closely related to the traditional *payment* and *receiving* functions.

4. What is "lock-box" banking? Explain the advantages to users of this banking service?

Chapter 18

Bank
Accounting

Purposes of This Chapter:
1. To emphasize the need for a system of bank accounting capable of producing accurate and informative financial reports whenever required.
2. To explain the principles and objectives of double-entry bookkeeping.
3. To illustrate and review the details of certain basic bank financial reports.
4. To explain the general purpose of cost accounting and its application to account analysis.

Bank accounting is the art of systematically recording, presenting, and interpreting the accumulated result of many thousands of individual transactions handled daily by even the smallest of banks.

Transactions must be recorded in a manner to permit isolation and identification of individual transactions long after the event and also to provide summarizations of transactions by type to reveal the overall impact on the bank's financial picture. In addition, the manner of recording must readily supply the specific data required for regulatory reports, such as call reports, statistical reports, income and dividend reports, and tax returns.

The accumulated data must be presented in a report that is acceptable, informative, and understandable to those who receive it. Thus the mode of presentation may vary with respect to supervisory reports and management reports as compared with stockholder reports and published reports, in which technical terminology must be avoided wherever possible.

Interpreting deals with the explanation of reports. A single isolated financial report as of a certain recent date or covering the most recent period of time does reveal important current information. But of greater importance perhaps is the need to uncover established longer-term trends that indicate the direction in which the bank is moving. Is its financial position improving, is it remaining static, or is there evidence of deterioration? To be fully meaningful, current financial reports must be compared with similar reports as of a previous date or comparable previous periods. Many accounting reports now offer five-year comparisons of similar reports in order to give readers a broader view, encompassing a longer period of time. For instance, suppose a particular bank statement shows net operating earnings for the year just ended of $2.70 per share. In itself, this indicates little more than the fact that the bank is operating profitably. But if for the previous year, the same bank reported net operating earnings of $3.00 per share, with the same number of shares outstanding, it would be understandable if stockholders showed some concern about a 10-percent drop in net earnings. On the other hand, there would be much less concern if an explanatory footnote revealed that the $2.70 figure represented the second highest per share earnings in the bank's history. In connection with comparative reports, unusual or otherwise significant differences between comparable figures should be discussed in an explanatory footnote. Very often external forces beyond the bank's control may account for such differences.

Accounting Records

Three types of records are common to bank accounting: temporary records, semi-permanent records, and permanent records.

Temporary records are helpful in the day-to-day operations of a bank. Almost all temporary records (such as tape listings) relate to the balancing of transactions and lose their value as the work flows through the bank and data are recorded on more permanent types of records.

Semi-permanent records may be summaries of temporary records or may be the originals or reproductions of source documents, such as deposit slips and checks. Banks are required by law to keep such records for at least five years, although individual bank policy may dictate longer retention for reference purposes.

Permanent records usually are ledgers and, in some instances, journals. Even these records, with the normal exception of the general ledger, are not retained indefinitely but are kept only as long as the bank's record retention policies and the legal requirements of the state dictate.

Journals and Ledgers

A *journal* is a record of original entry. Normally each processing department of a bank will have its own journal record. Each transaction is recorded in the journal in chronological order, as it is received and processed.

A *ledger* is a record of final entry. In conventional systems, every journal entry is ultimately transcribed and posted (individually or in groups) to the particular ledger account affected. For instance, every on-us check received during the course of a day will be recorded originally in a journal-type record. In most cases, this would be a proof department journal. Eventually, however, all on-us checks must be sorted (classified) by account number, and each check must be posted against the ledger account of the depositor who issued it. Ordinarily each individual check is posted separately, but in the case of active accounts, sizable groups of checks drawn by the same depositor may be listed and posted as a single amount (list posting).

In the older conventional accounting systems, the original journal posting and the subsequent classified ledger posting were handled as two distinct and separate operational steps. In some newer systems, the use of multi-copy forms permits the simultaneous preparation of loose-leaf journal and ledger records. In the more modern electronic systems, raw data are fed into a computer in almost any order and can be printed out in journal form or ledger form or in practically any other manner in which the information is desired. It should be noted, however, that modern methods have not diminished the usefulness or the importance of journals and ledgers. They have only made unnecessary the preparation of these two records as separate physical operations.

Types of Ledger Records

Because of the tremendous volume of daily transactions and the fact that most transactions are concentrated in specific areas or functions, it has been found necessary as well as convenient to create two classes of ledger records: (1) general ledger records and (2) subsidiary ledgers.

The general ledger department maintains and controls the essential data relating to the bank's financial condition, such as income, expense, asset, liability, and capital accounts. General ledger records supply the data used to compile and publish the necessary financial reports. However, some of these accounts are so subdivided and so tremendously active that it would be highly impractical to attempt to record there the details of all related transactions. For instance, the general ledger liability account Demand Deposits is affected every day by all the deposits received and all the checks paid and the resulting changes in the credit balances of many thousands of checking account customers. For the purposes of the general ledger and to facilitate the preparation of financial reports, all that needs to be recorded in the Demand Deposits account is the *total* of deposits received and the *total* of checks paid during the day, without reference to the accounts affected. The details, which of course must be recorded fully and accurately, are posted in a subsidiary ledger.

The purpose of a subsidiary ledger is to maintain the detailed records and, as its name implies, to support the summarized data shown in the general ledger account. In the example given above, the subsidiary ledger is variously known as *Bookkeeping*, the *Individual Ledger*, or the *Demand Deposit Accounting* (DDA) *Ledger*. The general ledger account (Demand Deposits) is the control account, and after all deposits (and other credits) and checks (and other debits) have been posted to the subsidiary ledger, the total of all demand deposit accounts should settle with the general ledger control account.

Not all general ledger accounts need to be supported by a subsidiary ledger. For instance, transactions affecting capital accounts are relatively infrequent and can be posted directly to the general ledger account affected.

The more common types of subsidiary ledgers found necessary in most banks are:

1. Bookkeeping, individual ledgers, or **DDA** ledgers (for checking account customers) ;

2. Savings ledgers (for savings account depositors) ;

3. Loan ledgers (individual borrowers' records, often called liability ledgers) ;

4. Stockholders ledgers (showing individual holdings of bank stock) ;

5. Property ledgers (for fixed assets owned).

A bank may have more than one general ledger. For example, in a branch banking system each branch might maintain its own records rather than having them maintained at the main office. When a bank has more than one general ledger, the information in each general ledger must be combined or consolidated before financial statements can be rendered or information given relative to the bank as a whole. The number of general ledgers depends upon each bank's particular recording methods.

Double-Entry Recordkeeping

Banking transactions are recorded by a system of accounting known as double-entry bookkeeping, a system that makes use of the general scientific principle that for every *action* that takes place, there is an equal and opposing *reaction*. In double-entry bookkeeping, transactions are recorded by means of debits and credits, and application of the above principle means that every debit must be balanced by an equal offsetting credit. In recording some transactions one or more debits may be offset by one or more credits, but in any event, the sum of the debits must equal in dollar amount the sum of the credits. Debits always appear on the lefthand side of a statement, journal, or ledger, while credits appear on the righthand side. If every transaction is properly recorded as indicated above, the total of all debits will equal the total of all credits, and the books of the entire bank will always be in balance.

Double-entry bookkeeping is simply a balanced system of accounting. The objective is to present the bank's financial position in balanced form and to maintain that balance as additional transactions are processed—an objective that is especially important in bank accounting. Unless the bank is insolvent, its assets (what is owned by or owed to the bank) will exceed its liabilities (what is owed to creditors). The difference (the excess of asset dollars over liability dollars) is the net worth of the bank or the equity of its owners (shareholders). In bank accounting, the net worth is represented by Capital Stock, Surplus, and Undivided Profits. Thus the financial position of a bank as of a given date might be expressed in simplified form as follows:

December 31, 19___
(in thousands)

Assets		*Liabilities*	
Cash	$ 3,500	Demand Deposits	$15,400
Loans	20,500	Time Deposits	16,400
Investments	10,900	Other Liabilities	1,100
Other Assets	700	(Net Worth)	
		Capital	500
		Surplus	1,500
		Undivided Profits	700
	$35,600		$35,600

287

It will be noticed that the assets (debit balance accounts) appear on the lefthand side of the statement, and the liabilities and the net worth or equity (credit balance accounts) appear on the righthand side, and that both sides are in balance. This form of financial report is known as a *Statement of Condition or a Balance Sheet,* and it illustrates the accounting equation:

Assets = Liability plus Net Worth

In terms of photography, a statement of condition resembles a snap-shot since it reflects the financial condition of the bank as of a *precise moment,* usually at the close of business on a given day.

Like any other business organization, a bank is an ongoing enterprise, and it is simultaneously *earning income* from the financial services it renders and *incurring the expenses* necessary to provide those services. Therefore, the bookkeeping system must include another group of debit balance accounts (expense accounts) and another group of credit balance accounts (income accounts). In order to reflect the results of the bank's activities, a second important financial report is required—an *Income Statement.* This report summarizes all items of income and expense and shows the net profit (or loss) for a period of time. Unlike the statement of condition, an income statement might be likened to a time-exposure since it shows operating results for a period of time between two specific dates.

In double-entry bookkeeping, balance is maintained because debits and credits have certain uniform characteristics:

A debit posting *increases* an asset account or an expense account.

A credit posting *increases* a liability account, an income account, or a capital account.

The converse is also true:

A debit posting *decreases* a liability account, an income account, or a capital account.

A credit posting *decreases* an asset account or an expense account.

Recording Typical Transactions

By applying the double-entry principle to some common banking transactions, the always-in-balance characteristic of the system is clearly revealed. Note that each transaction is recorded by means of a balanced set of entries (a debit or debits offset by an equal corresponding credit or credits)

1. A customer makes a deposit of coin and currency in his checking account. This transaction would be recorded by the following:

Debit—Cash $150
    Credit—Demand Deposits $150

The transaction has a direct effect on the balance sheet. Cash is an asset account; Demand Deposits is a liability account. The debit *increases* the asset Cash while the credit *increases* the liability Demand Deposits. Both sides of the balance sheet rise by the amount of the deposit, and therefore remain in balance.

2. The bank purchases investment securities at a cost of $10,000 and pays for them by means of a check drawn on its demand deposit with a correspondent bank. The transaction would be recorded as follows:

Debit—Investments $10,000
    Credit—Cash and Due from Banks $10,000

The debit *increases* the asset Investments and the credit *decreases* the asset Due from Banks by the same amount. The two entries offset each other so that Total Assets remains unchanged. The transaction does not affect any account on the liability side, and therefore the two sides remain in balance.

3. When a bank certifies a check for a depositor, the transaction is recorded as follows:

Debit—Demand Deposits $1,000
    Credit—Other Liabilities (Certified $1,000
    Checks Outstanding)

The debit *decreases* the liability account Demand Deposits, but the credit *increases* another liability account. In this case no asset account is affected, and therefore both sides of the statement remain in balance.

Transactions that affect income and expense accounts are handled in somewhat different manner and do not necessarily have an immediate direct effect on the Balance Sheet. It will be recalled that an income statement lists summaries of all items of income and expense over a period of time, and reports *net income* (where income credits exceed expense debits) or a *net loss* (where expense debits exceed income credits). Periodically, a *net* income credit is added to Undivided Profits or, in the event of a *net* loss, the amount is deducted from Undivided Profits. How often a bank nets out its income and expense accounts depends on its own particular needs. It can be done daily or monthly or quarterly, as desired.

For the sake of illustration, the ultimate impact on the bank's Balance Sheet will be shown in the following examples:

The bank replenishes its supply of paper clips and rubber bands and makes payment by issuing its cashier's or treasurer's check. Actually, the transaction would be recorded as follows:

Debit—Office Supplies (Expense Account) $55
    Credit—Official Checks Outstanding $55
    (Liability Account)

At this point, the balance sheet will not be in balance. The increase in a liability account is offset by an increase in an expense account, which is not a balance sheet account.

Eventually, however, the official check will be presented by the supplier's bank and paid, and the expense account (Office Supplies) will be consolidated with other income and expense accounts and result in a net credit (or debit) to Undivided Profits. But if we isolate this transaction and disregard the procedural time-lag, the *ultimate* effect of the purchase on the Balance Sheet would be:

Debit—Undivided Profits $75

    Credit—Cash and Due from Banks $75

The debit to Undivided Profits has the effect of *reducing* the liability side, while the credit to Cash *reduces* the asset side, and the Balance Sheet remains in balance.

To summarize, double entry bookkeeping is a balanced system of accounting that aids in isolating errors on settlement sheets as the many thousands of daily entries are processed. If each transaction is correctly recorded by a balanced set of entries, (debit or debits equal credit or credits), then the bank's books will always be in balance. This system is especially useful in banking where accurate settlements, particularly where customers' deposit balances are concerned, are of tremendous importance. A bank's accounting system should be able to produce, at almost any given time, an Income Statement and an accurate Statement of Condition (Balance Sheet). For instance, a Call Report is a demand by regulatory authorities for complete financial information. Banks receive requests for Call Reports four times a year, roughly on a quarterly basis. For statistical purposes, such reports are generally made as of June 30 and December 31 each year. But in order to prevent window dressing, the interim reports are usually called for as of a *past* date. That is, a bank will receive, say, on April 3, a demand for a Call Report as of March 25; or will receive on October 11 a demand for financial data as of October 2, and it must be in a position to furnish figures as of the past dates.

Cash and Accrual Accounting

There are two basic systems of accounting, cash basis accounting and accrual accounting.

In cash basis accounting, entries are generated by the movement of cash, whether received as income or paid out as expense. Very few if any banks follow a strict cash basis system, for to do so could result in severe distortions of *net* income of the bank for any particular period of time. A few examples should illustrate the inherent weaknesses of restricting income and expense accounting to cash movements.

1. Banks credit interest to the accounts of their savings depositors on a quarterly, semi-annual or annual basis. In the case of a bank that credits interest annually on the last day of the year, an Income Statement for the month of December or even for the last calendar quarter would show, on a cash basis, a huge operating loss, while statements for the first 11 months, or the first three-quarters, would reflect unrealistically inflated profits. For the bank with sizable savings deposits, interest payable is a substantial operating expense, and it is incurred and payable to depositors throughout the entire year.

2. Another relatively large expense item is the insurance premium paid on Bankers Blanket Bonds, which most banks carry. In many cases, such insurance is renewable on a three-year basis, with the premium payable in advance. It takes little imagination to visualize the distorted Income Statement that would result, on a cash basis, for the month or quarter in which the three-year premium is paid. Actually, each of the 36 months during which the insurance is effective should bear $\frac{1}{36}$ of the premium cost, and this is precisely what accrual accounting accomplishes.

Accrual accounting records expenses as they are incurred, regardless of when they are actually paid and takes income into consideration as it is earned, regardless of when it is received. Like everything else, accrual accounting can be carried to extremes. Many banks accrue only those major items of income and expense that would most seriously distort operating results if handled on a cash basis, such as interest income on loans and investments, interest expense due to savings and time depositors, income taxes, real estate taxes, and large pre-paid expenses such as insurance premiums. On the other hand, the accuracy of income statements varies in direct proportion to the number of income and expense accounts on an accrual basis.

Accrual accounting is not difficult to put into practice. The first step is to establish certain additional general ledger accounts, such as the following:

1. Accrued Income Receivable   (Asset)
2. Prepaid Expense   (Asset)
3. Accrued Liabilities   (Liability)
4. Unearned Income   (Liability)

These are broad classifications, which may be subdivided or supported by subsidiary accounts. For instance, Accrued Income Receivable may be subsidivided into interest on loans, interest on investments, or any other situations where income has been earned but not collected. The three-year insurance premium is one example of a prepaid expense item. Accrued Liabilities would include interest payable on savings and time deposits, taxes, salaries, and other items where the expense has

291

been incurred but not yet paid or is not yet payable. Unearned Income is income collected but not yet earned, such as discount (interest collected in advance) on loans.

A simple example should illustrate the mechanics of accrual accounting. For example, suppose a bank makes a loan on March 1 and agrees to collect the interest by charging the borrower's account on a quarterly basis. Thus on May 31 it would collect the interest earned during March, April, and May. Assuming that the bank accrues interest on loans monthly, on March 31, April 30, and May 31 it makes the following entries, each representing the interest earned in that month:

Debit—Accrued Interest Receivable $30.00
       Credit—Interest on Loans $90.00

Then on May 31 when it charges the borrower's account to collect interest for the three-month period, it wipes out the accumulation in the accrual account as follows:

Debit—Demand Deposits $90.00
       Credit—Accrued Interest Receivable $90.00

For purposes of illustration, the above entries isolate one particular loan. Actually, a single debit or credit to accrued interest receivable would cover a substantial block of loans.

Accounting Reports

Mention has already been made of two principal accounting reports, the Balance Sheet (a Statement of Condition) and the Income Statement. To these should be added a third basic report, a Statement of Changes in Capital Accounts. Typical examples of these reports are illustrated in Exhibits 18, 19, and 20. Many banks, of course, might include much more detail in financial reports, but the illustrations, although somewhat simplified, show the most important account categories.

The Statement of Condition

Assets

CASH:

On hand. This category represents all of the money held in the bank, including the reserve cash held in the vault.

Due from banks. This category represents cash balances due from other banks that are or will be withdrawable on demand.

INVESTMENTS:

United States government obligations. It is common practice to show United States government obligations as a separate item on the state-

Exhibit 18: Comparative Statement of Condition

INSTITUTE NATIONAL BANK

December 31, 19— and December 31, 19—.
(in thousands)

Assets	*Current Year*	*Previous Year*	*Increase (Decrease)*
Cash on Hand and Due from Banks	$ 27,995	$ 29,320	$ (1,325)
Investments:			
U. S. Government Obligations	$ 21,619	$ 19,582	$ 2,037
State, County, and Municipal Bonds	10,848	9,410	1,438
Other Securities	6,868	6,509	359
Total Investments	$ 39,335	$ 35,501	$ 3,834
Loans: (net of reserve for loan losses)			
Commercial Loans	$ 58,724	$ 55,337	$ 3,387
Instalment Loans	30,145	28,704	1,441
Mortgage Loans	22,710	23,890	(1,180)
	$111,579	$107,931	$ 3,648
Premises and Equipment			
(less accumulated depreciation)	$ 6,356	$ 6,209	$ 147
Other Assets	$ 9,312	$ 8,920	$ 392
TOTAL ASSETS	$194,577	$187,881	$ 6,696

Liabilities			
Deposits:			
Demand Deposits	$ 78,724	$ 79,566	$ (842)
Savings Deposits	40,506	37,911	2,595
Other Time Deposits and Certificates	37,750	38,280	(530)
Total Deposits	$156,980	$155,757	$ 1,223
Other Liabilities:			
Short-Term Funds Borrowed	$ 15,200	$ 10,500	$ 4,700
Dividends Payable	175	158	17
Accrued Taxes and Expenses	846	820	26
Unearned Income	205	195	10
Other Obligations	317	353	(36)
Total Other Liabilities	$ 16,743	$ 12,026	$ 4,717
Capital Funds:			
Capital Debentures, 5% due 7/1/92	$ 10,000	$ 10,000	—
Equity Capital:			
Capital (common) Stock $10.00 par	3,500	3,500	—
Surplus	6,500	6,000	500
Undivided Profits	854	598	256
TOTAL LIABILITIES	$194,577	$187,881	$ 6,696

A Comparative Statement of Condition. The above illustration should not be considered a standard pattern. The detail shown in the Statement of Condition (or balance sheet) of a particular bank depends upon its size and scope of activities.

ment. This category usually includes United States Treasury bonds, notes and bills, and any government guaranteed agency bonds.

State, county, and municipal bonds. These bonds are usually classified as a separate item because of differences in risk, marketability, yield, and tax status of income.

LOANS:

Loans normally represent the largest asset appearing on the statement of condition. A reasonable breakdown by major types of loans is desirable because of differences in yield and maturity. The categories of commercial, instalment, and real estate loans may be detailed. They are usually shown net of the accumulated reserve for estimated loan losses.

Other securities. This category includes all other bonds and stocks not applicable to the above categories and includes stock in the Federal Reserve bank. Stock, if any, of corporations owning bank premises is excluded.

FIXED ASSETS:

This category includes all of the premises used for banking purposes as well as those owned for possible expansion, plus the furniture and equipment necessary for the business. Since these assets (except for land) gradually deteriorate with time, they are subject to depreciation. The depreciation factor is recognized by periodic charges to expense and a credit to a depreciation reserve account or accounts. Although such accounts reflect a credit balance, they are shown in the statement of financial position as a deduction from the related fixed assets.

OTHER ASSETS:

The classification of items in the category Other Assets varies widely among banks and includes all of the assets that do not properly belong in the other categories, including accrued interest receivable (for accrual basis banks), prepaid expenses, and many other small items too numerous to mention.

Liabilities

DEPOSITS:

Deposits can be subdivided in many ways, but the usual classifications are:

Demand deposits. Regular checking accounts. If the amounts are substantial, the accounts of other banks (Due to Banks) and United States and local government deposits might be shown separately.

Savings accounts. Regular savings accounts of individuals, non-profit organizations, and others eligible to open savings accounts, and savings certificates.

Other time deposits. This category would include time deposits—open account and regular (negotiable or non-negotiable) certificates of deposit.

OTHER LIABILITIES:

Official checks. This classification includes outstanding items in all categories of checks drawn by the bank against itself—cashier's checks (treasurer's checks), dividend checks, expense checks, and so forth—as well as any customers' checks that have been certified by the bank.

Accrued items. Accrued federal taxes. This item is usually large enough to be shown separately. Unless the statement is very detailed, accrued expenses are generally lumped in one item, although accrued interest on savings and time deposits may be shown separately.

Unearned income. This category represents the difference between the face amount of a discounted loan and the amount actually disbursed. For example, assume a one-year loan of $100 discounted at an interest rate of 6 percent. The amount disbursed, say, in the form of an official check, would be $94. The transaction would be reflected as follows:

Debit—Loans	$100	
Credit—Official Checks		$94
Credit—Unearned Income		6

The unearned income account is shown on the Balance Sheet as a liability, because if the borrower repays the loan before maturity, the amount of interest not actually earned would be refunded to the borrower. Banking regulations generally require banks to handle unearned income on an accrual basis even if the bank is otherwise a cash basis bank. The unearned interest account is reduced periodically with each accrual period, as the interest is actually earned. The entries would be:

Debit—Unearned Income
    Credit—Interest on loans

Capital Accounts

This section of the Balance Sheet contains the liability of the bank to holders of capital obligations, and the equity of shareholders.

Debentures and Capital Notes. Unsecured obligations of the bank that have been sold for the purpose of raising temporary capital funds. They normally have a stated rate of interest and maturities ranging from several years to as many as 25 or 30 years. Such obligations are not a part of shareholder's equity capital, since the purchasers are general creditors of the bank, whose claims are subordinated to those of depositors but are superior to the claims of shareholders. Debentures and Capital Notes are debt obligations that must be paid or refunded at maturity.

All other capital accounts represent the equity of shareholders. Shareholders are not general creditors, they are owners. Shares of stock do not represent obligations in the sense of a debt that must be paid at some future date. Except in the case of insolvency or liquidation, a shareholder has no enforceable claim against the bank, and if he wishes to liquidate his investment, his only course is to sell his shares to someone else.

Preferred stock. A preferred shareholder, although also an owner, enjoys special rights over the holders of common (Capital) stock. Preferred shares carry a stated dividend rate, and in most cases dividends on preferred stock must be fully paid and current before dividends can be declared on common stock shares. In liquidation, the preferred shareholders' claims are superior to those of common shareholders.

Common stock. At one time, banks were permitted to issue only one class of stock, and for this reason common shares are often simply described as Capital Stock. As the basic owners, common shareholders assume the greatest financial risk. In liquidation, they are the last in line and share only in remaining equity after all depositors, general creditors, and preferred shareholders have been paid in full. However, common shareholders have voting control of the bank.

Surplus. The surplus account represents funds derived from two sources: (1) contributions by the stockholders (paid-in surplus) and (2) transfers to surplus from the undivided profits account (earned surplus).

Undivided profits. This account consists of retained earnings derived from operations and other activities, less dividends paid and transfers, if any, to surplus and reserves. Transfers are sometimes made to the common stock account by issuance of stock dividends.

Reserve for contingencies. This account represents amounts set aside for a condition that may but is not certain to occur. Unlike accrued expenses or other liabilities, this account does not provide for any known or estimable losses. Since this account should not be used to absorb routine losses, it is merely a segregation of undivided profits and should be returned to that account when no longer required.

Income Statement

As previously indicated, the income statement tells the story of a bank's operations for a *period of time,* usually one year. It sets forth the sources and dollar values of revenue, the types and amount of expenses, and the resulting net income (or loss) for the accounting period.

Revenues of a bank consist primarily of interest on loans, interest and dividends on securities, various service charges, trust department fees, and gains (or losses) on the sale of securities. The major expenses are salaries and wages paid to officers and employees and interest expense on time and savings deposits. These items are usually shown on the income statement in the order of dollar importance, with the exception of gains or losses on the sale of securities, which are normally shown at the bottom of the statement as an addition to or deduction from operating income.

Exhibit 19: Comparative Statement of Income

INSTITUTE NATIONAL BANK
Calendar Years 19 - - and 19 - -

(in thousands)

	Current Year	Previous Year	Increase (Decrease)
Income:			
Interest on Loans	$ 9,534	$ 8,590	$ 944
Interest on U. S. Government Obligations	1,260	1,004	256
Other Interest and Dividends	961	743	218
Services Charges, Commissions and Fees	278	151	127
Trust Department Income	1,599	1,380	219
Other Income	182	151	31
Total Operating Income	$13,814	$12,019	$1,795
Expense:			
Salaries, Wages and Personnel Expense	$ 3,873	$ 3,590	$ 283
Interest on Savings and Time Deposits	2,729	2,750	(21)
Interest on Borrowed Funds	1,240	845	395
Occupancy Expense	852	729	123
Provision for Loan Losses	1,500	1,000	500
Other Expenses	612	575	37
Total Operating Expenses	$10,806	$ 9,489	$1,317
Net Income from Operations Before Federal Income Taxes	$ 3,008	$ 2,530	$ 478
Less: Federal Income Taxes	702	778	(76)
Net Income from Operations	$ 2,306	$ 1,752	$ 554
Other Credits (Charges) Net Gain (Loss) on Securities (net of tax effect)	$ (850)	$ (450)	$ (400)
Net Income Transferred to Undivided Profits	$ 1,456	$ 1,302	$ 154

Statement of Changes in Capital Accounts

This statement, frequently called a Reconciliation of Capital Accounts, normally shows the balance in both the Surplus account and Undivided Profits account at the beginning of an accounting period, debits, credits, and any transfers affecting these accounts, and the balance as of the end of the accounting period. Less frequently, the reconciliation would reflect the sale or redemption of debentures, capital notes, or preferred stock, and dividends paid in common stock.

Exhibit 20: Reconcilement of Capital Accounts

INSTITUTE NATIONAL BANK
(in thousands)

	Current Year	Previous Year	Increase (Decrease)
Capital Debentures 5% due 7/1/92	$10,000	$10,000	—
Capital Stock	$ 3,500	$ 3,500	—
Authorized. 400,000 shares			
(Issued and Outstanding: 350,000 shares)			
Surplus Account:			
Balance on January 1,	$ 6,000	$ 5,500	$ 500
Add: Transfer from Undivided Profits	500	500	—
Balance on December 31,	$ 6,500	$ 6,000	$ 500
Undivided Profits Account			
Balance on January 1,	$ 598	$ 426	$ 172
Add: Net Income, Period ending Dec. 31,	1,456	1,302	154
Deduct: Dividends Paid	(700)	(630)	70
Transfer to Surplus Account	(500)	(500)	—
Balance on December 31,	$ 854	598	256
Total Capital Funds	$20,854	$20,598	256

Cost Accounting

A bank is in business to make a profit. In fact, it can be said that an unprofitable bank, more so than other private enterprises, is a potential menace to the community it serves. In periods of economic depression or in the event of some unforeseen disaster, even a well-managed bank might be compelled to report an operating loss for a period of time. But the bank that is constantly faced with the problem of reporting operating losses or of reaching for ways to compensate for such losses not only endangers the investment of its shareholders and the welfare of its employees, but also threatens to impound the cash assets of its depositors (temporarily at least) and precipitously cut off a needed source of credit to the community.

Unlike many businesses that have a tangible product to sell, banks deal mainly in services, and it is extremely important for the bank to know the cost of the various services it performs. In some cases, a bank may not charge enough to cover the cost of a particular service, or it may not even charge at all. If this is the result of a deliberate management decision based on reasonably accurate data, because the service in question holds promise of producing collateral benefits of a tangible nature, the intended result might well justify the means. But where there is a complete lack of knowledge of the true costs of the service as well as inability to appraise adequately the value of the expected collateral benefits, the soundness of the strategy is at least questionable.

Commercial banking has undergone many changes over the years, and each change produces a new challenge to the managers of banks. Perhaps the most serious challenges are those thrust on banks because of the changing habits, practices, and needs of those who use banking services. For instance, there was a time when operating profits came rather easily. Businesses as well as individuals looked to banks primarily for safety, and relatively inactive accounts with substantial balances were fairly common. The profits from such accounts often served to hide the losses on smaller, more active accounts. The banker had little cause for concern as long as the net results represented satisfactory profits.

Money management is not a new art, but it is one that is more widely practiced today than ever before. Bank depositors, from the treasurer of the largest corporation to the average wage earner, are well aware of the fact that money can be productive. Today, high-quality investment opportunities are more abundant than ever before, and many of them, such as interest-bearing accounts in commercial banks, savings banks, savings and loan associations, and credit unions are guaranteed by government agencies. For the most part, depositors are quite willing to compensate banks for the valuable services they offer, but are not so anxious to pay more than the service is reasonably worth.

In simple terms, bankers deal in money; they acquire funds at a cost in terms of interest paid or services rendered, and they lend or invest funds at a price. The spread between the cost paid and the price received must be sufficient to cover all of a bank's operating expenses plus the reasonable profit that justifies its existence in a free enterprise system.

The gross income a bank receives for its loans and investments, as well as the interest it pays for deposits or borrowed funds, is easily determined. More difficult is determining the individual cost of the many services it renders, such as handling deposit credits, collecting checks, paying checks, certifying checks, handling return items, money transfers, Christmas clubs, vacation clubs, collection items, rendering statements, and standing ready to serve by manning tellers' stations, drive-in windows, providing automatic teller equipment and night depository services, to say nothing of insurance, protection, management and overhead costs related to each of these services.

How can these costs be determined with reasonable accuracy? The answer has been known in industry for many years and more recently in many banks. It is an accounting system that can relate all direct and indirect costs and expenses to the specific function performed—a system known as *cost accounting*.

Almost every function in the bank can be classified either as one that provides funds or one that uses funds. Without a system of cost accounting the functions that use funds appear to be those that provide a large profit to the bank, while the functions that provide funds for use by other departments give the initial impression of losing money. An example of a funds-using function is the instalment loan department. Since money must be given to the borrowing customers, this function is said to use funds. The money that is loaned to those customers had to come from somewhere, and this somewhere could be, for example, the savings department. Customers deposit surplus money in their savings accounts, so the savings department is a funds-providing function. Since interest must be paid on savings accounts, and no direct income is received from these accounts, it might appear that the savings department must operate at a loss, while the instalment loan department surely must make a large profit. Cost accounting puts the entire picture into proper perspective.

Cost Accounting Procedures

The first step involved in a simple cost accounting system is to allocate all of the bank's expenses to the various departments. Some of these allocations, such as the salaries of the people working in the department and the depreciation on the equipment used, are relatively simple. Allocating indirect expenses, however, can be quite complicated, since certain items of overhead, such as the president's salary, the rent or depreciation on the bank building, the cost of fuel to heat the building, and other similar items must be prorated on an equitable and uniform basis to all departments in the bank.

Not only must expenses be allocated, but income as well. These income allocations must include not only direct income, but also a realistic credit for any funds provided to other departments. Naturally this credit should be offset by debits to the departments that use the funds, such as the loan and investment departments.

Apportioning the various items of income and expense to the various departments and then to the major functions in the bank will give an overall picture of whether or not an entire function is operating at a profit or loss. When this has been done, work still remains to find the cost of handling a specific transaction or rendering a specific service within each major function. This latter process is called the determination of unit (or per item) costs.

Unit costs

In order to calculate unit costs it is necessary to know how many work units are involved in a particular activity. For example, the book-keeping department handles checks drawn against the various checking accounts, deposits to those accounts, returned items, and overdrafts. Not only must the bank know how many there are of each of these items during the period being studied, but it also must know approximately how long it takes to process each type of item. By relating these and other factors with the income and expense of the department, it becomes possible to calculate the cost of posting a check or of posting a deposit, as well as the overall cost of maintaining the account each month.

Although this description of cost accounting has been greatly over-simplified, it should be clear that the costs of most bank services can be determined with reasonable accuracy and need not be left to vague impressions or pure guesswork. However, this knowledge can be obtained only by the expenditure of a certain amount of effort and additional costs. Banks that have installed good cost accounting systems obviously feel that the results are well worth the additional effort and expense.

There is another very practical benefit that even a modified system of cost analysis can produce. What better way can be found to measure the efficiency of a bank's operating methods? For instance, if analysis indicates that it costs a bank ten cents to handle a certain type of transaction while its competitors claim to be able to handle the same transaction for five cents, the situation should be carefully investigated. All the other competing banks could be wrong, of course, but a more probable alternative is that the high-cost bank is employing an out-moded and needlessly expensive operating procedure.

Account Analysis

The purpose of account analysis is to determine whether the total cost of rendering banking services to a particular account can be recovered by bank utilization of the depositor's residual balance. If the servicing costs exceed the calculated amount that can be earned on the available balance, then the bank is justified in making a service charge to recover the difference, plus a reasonable profit. The justification is based on the logical premise that in a free-enterprise economy, those that market products, goods, or services are entitled to and indeed must receive some profit compensation as an incentive for continued efforts. This is not to say, however, that bankers as well as businessmen may not decide, for good and sufficient reasons, to forego the profit element in certain circumstances.

Complete or Full Analysis

In essence, account analysis involves two basic steps: (1) calculating the costs of servicing the account; and (2) offsetting against those costs a figure representing the extent to which balances maintained contribute to the bank's earnings.

Under present laws, banks are not permitted to pay interest on demand deposits. Nevertheless, for analysis purposes, it is common practice to allow the depositor a theoretical earnings credit based on the average investable balance maintained. Despite the active nature of balances subject to withdrawal by check, a substantial portion of total demand deposits can be utilized profitably by the bank. In theory, every account, regardless of how small, contributes in some measure to the bank's earnings. Obviously, some accounts contribute more than others and, conversely, some accounts require more banking services than others. From the depositor's viewpoint, however, it would not be fair to consider only the negative cost factors while ignoring the positive contribution-to-earnings factor.

Normally accounts are analyzed on a monthly basis. A full analysis requires at a minimum consideration of the following:

1. *Average daily balance.* The most accurate way to determine the average ledger balance is to add the closing balance for each day in the month and divide the result by the number of days in the month. In earlier days this was done manually—admittedly a laborious and costly project. For this reason, many banks used a more practical but less accurate method, such as adding the closing balances of the 10th, the 20th and the 30th days of the month and dividing the result by three. Modern computerized analysis systems, however, can perform the more accurate process with ease.

2. *Average daily float.* Float is the term to describe the amount of uncollected funds in a ledger balance. Since cash item deposits are immediately credited on the ledger record as of the day received, it is evident that the average daily ledger balance can be quite misleading. The amount of uncollected funds in a given account balance varies with the number and dollar amount of deposited items. It is quite pos-

302

sible, when deposit activity is high, for the amount of uncollected funds to exceed at times the posted ledger balance, in which case the account would be technically overdrawn. Uncollected funds have no value to the bank as far as earnings are concerned, and in account analysis it is customary and logical to deduct a figure representing float from the daily average ledger balance.

With a computerized analysis system, it is possible to calculate a reasonably accurate float figure for each individual account. Most banks, however, are satisfied to use for analysis purposes an average period of collection for all deposited items, based on a careful study of the type of items normally received. Coin, currency, and on-us items are of course immediately available funds to the bank, while certain items collected through the Federal Reserve System would be available in two days. Other items might take three or more days to collect. Nevertheless, the use of an average time outstanding is reasonably fair to all concerned. If all deposits made during the month total $10,000, total float for the month (based on an average collection period of one and a half days) would be $15,000, which divided by 30 (the number of days in the month) would produce an average daily float figure of $500.

3. *Reserves*. In addition to the legal reserves required by law, banks must also set aside a proportion of demand deposit balances as practical reserves in order to function properly in serving their customers. Practical reserves consist of inventory coin and currency (vault cash and tellers' till money) and demand deposit balances with correspondent banks. Banks that are members of the Federal Reserve System must keep reserves in non-interest-bearing balances with a Federal Reserve bank, although vault cash (also nonproductive) may be counted as part of the legal requirements. The extent to which legal reserves cannot be used to produce income depends on the applicable regulations, since state-chartered nonmember banks have some leeway in this respect. In account analysis, it is customary to deduct a percentage of the average collected balance to compensate for unproductive legal and practical reserves. A reasonable figure for some member banks would be 20 percent to cover each account's proportionate share of legal reserves, vault cash, and correspondent bank balances. Obviously, in some cases the percentage would be higher, in others lower.

4. *Earnings credit*. Deducting the float and reserve factors from the average ledger balance leaves the daily average investable balance, which is the amount the bank can use to increase earnings. The earnings credit is usually expressed as an annual percentage and represents the *net* return or the spread between gross interest income and applicable costs, such as the expenses allocated to the loan and investment divisions.

5. *Maintenance and activity charges.* Some expense is always involved in handling an account, even though the customer draws no checks and makes no deposits during the month. Such expenses include unallocated overhead (a bank must provide facilities, equipment, and staff sufficient to serve all depositors properly whenever they choose to avail themselves of banking services), and certain direct expenses, such as balancing of ledgers, preparing and mailing of statements, and insurance costs based on total dollar volume or the number of checking accounts. Many banks prorate such costs among all accounts on the bank's books and make a uniform flat maintenance charge each month, which has no relationship to account activity.

The most common activity charges are based on the number of deposit credits received, the number of deposited items handled, and the number of checks drawn and paid during the month. Depending on the type of service rendered in particular cases, an account analysis may include activity charges for bulk cash deposits, collection items, coupons collected, payrolls prepared, regular requests for rolled coin, and other services normally offered to checking account customers. As previously indicated, the rates charged for the various transactions may result from a cost accounting system and determination of actual unit costs (to which a nominal profit is usually added). In many cases, however, actual unit costs may be adjusted or the rates arbitrarily fixed by management for competitive reasons.

A Typical Account Analysis

With this discussion of the principal elements of a complete account analysis, it is now possible to put the pieces together and present a visual picture of the analysis of a hypothetical account. For the sake of brevity, the example given includes only the more common activity charges. A full analysis for an active business account would in many cases include charges for one or more of the routine but less frequently utilized services described above. The rates and percentages used are for illustrative purposes only and are not to be construed as representative of current practice and certainly not as suggestions.

In a situation such as that shown opposite, the action taken would depend on bank policy. Some banks would make the charge shown; some banks have a minimum service charge of one dollar; others waive analysis charges of under one dollar.

It should be obvious that the full or complete analysis method should not be applied to all accounts. It is most appropriate when applied to large corporate accounts, active business accounts, or any accounts where float is a significant factor because a substantial number

Example of a Full Account Analysis
X Y Z COMPANY
March 19—

Average Daily (Ledger) Balance	$5,600.00
Less: Average Daily Float	950.00
Average Daily. Collected Balance	4,650.00
Less: Reserves (20%)	930.00
Investable Balance	3,720.00
Earnings Credit (4% annual rate)	12.40
Activity Charges:	
Maintenance Charge (flat amount)	1.00
16 Deposit Credits @ 15¢	2.40
196 Deposited Items @ 3¢	5.88
49 Checks Paid @ 8¢	3.92
Total Charges	13.20
Less: Earnings Credit	12.40
Service Charge for Month	$ .80

of out-of-town checks are deposited, where a great many checks are issued, or where other banking services are regularly used.

Some types of charges are partially punitive in nature, and it is common practice in such cases to make a direct charge against the depositor's account rather than to include them in account analysis. For
instance, if a bank finds it necessary to dishonor a check drawn against
insufficient or uncollected funds, the special and prompt handling of
such an item to meet a return item deadline is both time-consuming
and costly. Many banks make a substantial direct charge for dishonored on-us checks primarily to discourage the indiscriminate drawing
of checks against inadequate balances. The abuse of a normal banking
privilege, such as the frequent and excessive use of stop-payment orders, which places an unreasonable burden on the bank, frequently results in a punitive direct charge against the account.

Analysis of Personal Accounts

For the average individual who maintains a checking account for
purely personal use, a complicated analysis system would be somewhat
self-defeating. The average wage earner or salaried worker whose deposits consist almost entirely of paychecks drawn on local banks is certainly not going to create a float problem for his bank. In all probability, checks drawn would not exceed 25 or 30 per month, and rarely if
ever would such a depositor demand rolled coin, ask for certification of
a check, issue a stop-payment order, or submit a documentary draft for
collection.

Most banks analyze personal checking accounts, if at all, in a very uncomplicated manner. It would be fruitless to attempt to describe any specific simplified analysis method, for there are almost as many different methods as there are banks. Float, reserves, and earnings credits are background considerations but are ignored as specific factors. Probably most personal account analysis methods are on a so-called metered basis. For instance, balances may be divided into round units of $100, and the depositor is allowed so many items of activity for each unit of balance. No distinction is made between a deposited item and a check drawn, and a charge is made for excess activity. A direct charge is made for other than purely routine checking account service. This description is not necessarily typical, for there are many variations of personal account analysis currently used by our 14,000 independent banks.

There is a growing tendency in some areas to waive service charges on personal accounts entirely. The philosophy seems to be that personal account balances, however small individually, have definite value to the bank in the aggregate, while the net profit after deducting the cost of calculating and collecting thousands of relatively small service charges is overshadowed by expanded opportunities to cross-sell other banking services.

Over the past half-century or so, the attitude of commercial bankers toward service charges has blown alternately hot and cold. But there is a good reason for this. The ever-changing trend of interest rates has a decided impact on commercial banking strategy. In periods of low interest rates, bankers are somewhat less aggressive in soliciting deposits and are more concerned with the cost of servicing them. It is difficult today to conceive of an economic climate where the Federal Reserve discount rate is $1\frac{1}{2}$ percent, federal funds sell at a fraction of 1 percent, long-term U.S. Treasury bonds sell at prices that yield less than $2\frac{1}{2}$ percent, and the prime rate hovers around 3 percent with a noticeable lack of interested borrowers. Yet such conditions have actually existed. It is not difficult to understand why commercial bankers would suddenly exhibit a keen interest in service charges in such circumstances. The converse is true during periods of high interest rates, when bankers are inclined to compete fiercely for the funds of smaller depositors and to pay more to attract deposits in the form of higher interest rates on savings accounts or in the form of free banking services.

As usual, the future will unfold with tantalizing slowness in its own good time. None of us can pierce the veil, but of one thing we can be sure: neither economic conditions nor banking practices, including account analysis and service charges, will remain static forever.

Few businesses have as great a need for effective accounting systems as do our nation's banks. All regulated industries face somewhat similar problems, but the unique position of commercial banks as custodians of the bulk of our money supply exerts additional pressure on the bank accounting function. Call reports, as well as unannounced bank examinations, require bank records to be current and up-to-date at all times. The fact that banks deal primarily with money belonging to the public places a high premium on accuracy, especially with respect to details of their deposit liabilities.

Like all other profit-making enterprises, banks must be able to obtain fairly accurate data as to the true costs of their services in order to ensure that equitable and just compensation is received.

Questions Based on This Chapter

1. What is meant by the interpretation of financial reports and to whom is this function especially important?

2. Briefly explain the objective of double-entry bookkeeping.

3. How does accrual accounting differ from cash basis accounting and what is its significant advantage?

4. Distinguish between a Statement of Condition and an Income Statement.

5. What is the purpose of cost accounting?

Chapter 19

Marketing
of
Bank Services

Purposes of This Chapter:

1. *To enumerate some of the many facets of the marketing function.*
2. *To explain why marketing must be viewed as a team effort involving the entire organization.*
3. *To describe the basic elements of bank marketing.*
4. *To emphasize the fact that bank marketing must necessarily deal with two kinds of "profits."*

There is an all too frequent tendency to associate *marketing* exclusively with sales efforts, the art of persuading, enticing, or cajoling people to purchase a product by means of advertising, promotions, and special inducements such as premiums, discounts, prizes, and other forms of giveaways and gimmicks. In a sense, the term *marketing* is misleading because a *market* to most people means a place where things are sold and rarely calls to mind the many steps that must take place before those things reach the marketplace.

Among other things, marketing involves research, planning, and product development as well as public relations, advertising, and sales training—all, however, with the ultimate objective of selling the institution and its services to the public. As Peter Drucker has expressed the whole marketing concept: "Marketing is the identification or creation of customer needs, and then the motivation and coordinated use of all functions within a business that can fill those needs with benefit to the buyer and seller."

Books have been written on the subject of bank marketing, providing more than enough material for a separate course of study. The objective here is to present bank marketing in somewhat skeletal form, with just enough meat on the bones to demonstrate how vital this function is to the success of a banking institution. It is not the purpose of this chapter to offer an in-depth treatise on this highly specialized activity.

Perhaps the most imaginative phase of bank marketing lies in the area of research and product development, the creation of new banking services, or the conception and introduction of extensions or improvements to existing services to make them more attractive and useful. In the following pages, this aspect of bank marketing will be treated first and emphasized more than others for illustrative purposes, but not for the purpose of de-emphasizing other aspects, for all basic elements of marketing are important.

In simple terms, marketing means keeping a close touch with people, finding out what they need, what they want, and what they probably would like to have, and then determining how best to satisfy those needs, wants, and desires profitably, as befits any private commercial enterprise.

Marketing is actually a scientific process beginning with study and research that leads to developing ideas; testing the soundness of ideas, not by guesswork, but by methodical, orderly processes; determining that an idea can be converted into a product or a service that will be useful, desired, and acceptable; exploring the depth of acceptances and the number and type of people for whom the product or service will fill a need; making sure that realization of the envisioned product or service is within the capabilities of the producing organization; being satisfied after serious cost studies that the product or service can be sold competitively at a profit; completing definite plans for refining, shaping, and packaging the product or service; and, *finally,* offering the result to the public by advertising, promotion, and other sales techniques. Sounds complicated? Actually, it is.

In this context, marketing cannot be the exclusive function of a marketing officer and his staff. Marketing involves the entire organization, and successful marketing requires close cooperation between all functions, departments, and personnel. The marketing specialist supervises and directs the overall complex process, but the talents of many different specialists must contribute to the end result.

An imaginative mind comes up with new ideas and new thoughts, but a more methodical mind conducts demographic and psychographic studies; an inquiring mind probes the potential of consumer acceptance by means of surveys or perhaps random sampling of public opinion; the experience-hardened mind of the operations specialist examines the practical aspects of producing the product or offering the service; the pencil-sharp mind of an accountant calculates the costs involved and the minimum selling price required to produce a profit; an impartial mind must consider possible social or legal implications; a promotion-oriented mind develops the most effective ways to present the idea to the public; and, finally, all public-contact elements of the staff, having convinced themselves of the value of the product or service, must contribute to the sales efforts.

Rarely if ever are all of the requisite viewpoints needed to conceive, explore, develop, and finalize a successful marketing project found in one man. Devil's advocates must be found or invented, rather than discouraged. Imaginative, innovative ideas and the services or products they envision are sharpened, honed, and perfected on the stones of constructive criticism. Objections must be raised and overcome, either by the force of reason or, as is more often the case, by modification and improvement of the concept. Marketing is a team effort through all of its complex stages, or put another way, marketing involves the entire organization.

To achieve optimum performance, any organization must be market-oriented. Conversely and equally important, marketing techniques and strategy must be organization-oriented. Marketing is a vital part of the organization it serves. But essentially it is the handmaiden of the organization rather than the other way around.

To illustrate this point, it is obvious that the marketing programs that successfully sell crunchy potato chips would not necessarily apply to the promotion and sale of diesel locomotives. The widespread distribution of "10¢-off coupons" may promote coffee sales or detergents and win new customers who are tempted to purchase the product. But this strategy would hardly apply to the sale of nuclear reactors. Similarly, the marketing of consumer products differs from the marketing of services. Quality is a necessary ingredient of both products and services, but those who sell services have a more personal and intimate contact with their customers. A food processing company doesn't keep a list of all those who purchase its cake mixes. To the supermarket chain, if the hordes of shoppers who wait on themselves and pass in endless lines through the checkout aisles wore halloween masks, it wouldn't make any difference. It is how many and how much that matters, not who.

Bankers sell services. Moreover, they sell professional services, highly personal and confidential in nature. The most satisfying and productive banking contacts are those of long duration, and they are based on mutual trust and confidence. A bank must be concerned with the identity and the character of the customers it serves. Customers are impressed with honest straightforward dealings that inspire confidence, and they rightfully expect efficient and accurate service. Nothing will disturb a depositor more than discourtesy, indifference, or an inaccurate bank statement.

Essential Elements of Bank Marketing

1. *Research.* A good start in any undertaking is to find out what the ball game is all about. It is rarely possible to build constructively on inadequate or inaccurate information. Research is aimed at the discovery and interpretation of factual data. The marketing specialist wants and needs to know a lot about the bank's customers as well as those who are not customers—in other words, the entire community that the bank serves. This involves obtaining and analyzing demographic information—vital statistics concerning population size, density and distribution, income levels, age groupings, family size, proportion of married to unmarried residents, as well as ethnic and religious characteristics. He will also want to know something about the lifestyle of the people, as a whole or in groups, their saving habits, their spending habits, and their financial stability. Not to be neglected are similar data with respect to the business elements of the community—the number, sizes, and types of retail outlets, whether they are locally owned or branches of foreign (to the community) corporations, and the number and sizes of manufacturing or other industries, together with current information with respect to annual sales volume, net profits, number of employees, and so on.

Also important are the physical characteristics of the community, the nature and extent of land use, its stage of development, economic status, and future potential. What all of this boils down to is best expressed in the words of a familiar song: "Getting to know you, getting to know all about you."

The factual data gathered through research techniques must then be pulled together, analyzed, and interpreted. Such information should suggest ideas for the present as well as for longer-range market planning for the future.

2. *Product Development.* Product development is the creative stage of marketing, but it also is a very pragmatic stage. The intimate

311

knowledge of the community, its people, and their living habits gathered through research is bound to stimulate imaginative thinking. Marketing begins to ask itself questions. In terms of financial services, is this community and its people being adequately served? Are there any additional services that the community could use advantageously? How can the bank make existing services more attractive or more easily available? These questions call for introspective analysis—a careful review of the nature and quality of existing services. Precisely how and in what ways is the bank serving the community? Is innovation needed, such as an entirely new service? Or do existing services need renovation in the form of refinements and improvements?

An idea (or several ideas) is generated, discussed, and carefully considered. One or more of the ideas is determined to have definite potential. Now comes the pragmatic stage as the idea is discussed with the operating staff. Will the new service or the extension of an existing service pose any serious practical problems? What will be the impact on personnel or equipment? Are there any legal problems—possible violations of existing laws or applicable regulations? Will the new service expose the bank unreasonably to potential losses? Does it conform with generally accepted, *sound* banking principles? (A dispute in this area might necessitate a management decision. What was considered unsound yesterday might be perfectly acceptable in the world of today.)

Few of these questions have easy and obvious answers. Rampant enthusiasm cannot run roughshod over valid practical objections; yet inertia and a stodgy affection for status quo cannot be permitted to stand in the way of progress toward better banking. When the questions have been answered and the differences if any have been resolved, attention is turned to other things.

At this point the services of a good accountant with a sharp and accurate pencil are needed. Is the new or improved service to be rendered gratis? If so, what will be the impact on earnings, and is the potential of new business or an improved competitive stance sufficient to offset any adverse impact? If the new product is saleable, what will it cost, how will it be priced, and can it be sold at a profit? While banks are in business to make a profit, this fact does not rule out the possibility of a management decision to offer a specific service at less than cost or even at no cost. It goes without saying that such decisions are not made lightly and only after careful consideration and in justifiable circumstances.

While these practical factors are being considered, the marketing group is not idle. The length, breadth, and depth of the potential market for the new service must be thoroughly explored. Whether it is to be offered gratis or sold at a price, if the service has appeal to only a very limited number of prospects, it may not be worth the trouble. A bank may feel that people *should* want a new service, but people have a way of deciding for themselves what they want and what they don't want.

To be successful, a new or improved product must have a broad-based appeal, and a competent marketing specialist has many ways of testing the depth of the potential market. In some cases, there may be little cause to doubt widespread acceptance of the service, for instance, where a similar promotion by banks in other areas has met with considerable success. In other cases, it may be necessary to conduct a random-sampling test of public opinion. Platform personnel can be enlisted to test the reaction of regular customers.

In any event, product development is much more than hit-or-miss experimentation. A creative, imaginative idea for a banking service, like the vision in an artist's mind, must eventually be materialized through a technological procedure. The artist's vision doesn't miraculously appear on the canvas; it must be reproduced with professional skill by means of such practical tools as pigments, solvents, and brushes. Similarly, a banking service must be rendered with professional skill through equipment, operating methods, records, and most important, people. Few things could be more damaging to a bank than an ill-conceived idea, inadequately tested, hastily and improperly developed, and introduced with great fanfare, only to plummet like a lead balloon for want of acceptance by the public.

3. *Public Relations.* Public relations deals with the creation of a positive and favorable image of the bank in the mind of the public. Continuity is basic to effective public relations, for a bank's image is not created overnight, nor once created does it last forever. This means constant and unceasing communication with many segments of the community, including people and businesses that do business with the bank as well as those that don't.

Effective communication can take many forms. A communication can be directed to the community at large by means of institutional advertising, or it can be directed to a specific group, such as in the reports to stockholders or in statement stuffers that go to depositors. Another effective form of communication is the press release concerning a bank-sponsored community action program or contributions in dollars or manpower to local charities.

Public relations tends to be viewed as an external exercise—messages emanating from within the bank to the world outside. But internal communication is no less important. Why? Because the bank staff must be made aware that there *is* a world outside, a world which does not hesitate to convey to the bank its reaction to the quality of bank services. It is not enough to *tell* the world how good you are; the staff must prove it, and the performance and actions of bank personnel speak much louder than words.

There are many ways to communicate internally, but the preparation and distribution of a house-organ, a periodic "just-about-us" publication, can be especially effective. One way of stimulating employee consciousness of customer reaction might be by featuring staff members whose courtesy, efficiency, or service beyond mere duty has evoked a favorable comment from a satisfied customer.

4. *Advertising and Promotion.* Advertising is a form of communication and therefore is an integral part of a public relations program.

There are two general types of advertising. The first is institutional advertising, the objective of which is to keep the name of the bank before the public, to create and sustain visibility. Institutional advertising expresses itself in general terms and usually associates the institution with some favorable characteristics such as a "friendly" bank, a "convenient" bank, or a "full service" bank, capable of serving all of the banking needs of people and business organizations. The second type is specifically aimed at the promotion of a particular service.

In addition, there are two differing techniques that can be applied to both types, that is, the broadside (or shotgun) approach or the rifle shot aimed at a specific target. Institutional advertising generally (but not necessarily) employs the former approach, while advertising designed to promote a specific service is often (but not always) directed toward a specific segment of the community. Determining the best technique depends on many factors, not the least of which is cost. When promoting a specific service, the criterion is the number of "sales" produced per advertising dollar spent.

As a part of its public relations program, a bank must engage in a continuous advertising program, intermixing different methods (shotgun vs. broadside), different media (television, radio, newspapers, statement stuffers, and so on), and with different objectives in mind (promotion of the institution or promotion of a specific service).

Most important is the advertising and promotion campaign that introduces a new service or a special improvement of an existing service. The advertised service must be fairly and honestly described. Exaggerated claims or restrictive features hidden in fine print are dangerous and can do much to destroy a previously enjoyed favorable image. The best advertising campaign can backfire dangerously if the advertised service is not provided as described, or if follow-through performance of the bank's staff is slipshod.

5. *Staff Training.* It is not surprising that bank customers are most apt to characterize a bank in terms of the staff members with whom they come in contact. Bricks, mortar, and glass can be artistically fused

to form an impressive, attractive, and inviting banking office, but it takes people to make it come alive and give it character. People—from the bank president down through the ranks to the behind-the-scenes file clerk—do more to shape the image of bank than a battery of public relations experts. Occasionally, platform personnel become well-acquainted with the difficulty of placating a customer whose statement reflects debits for which the bank cannot produce the related cancelled checks, because of a filing error.

A good in-house training program can encompass many areas. First and foremost is competent training in duties and responsibilities of the work assigned to each employee, with emphasis on the fact that customers are more than names and numbers, but are real people who are personally affected when errors are made in handling their transactions.

Some part of employee training should include knowledge about the bank as an institution: how long it has served the community, what it stands for, its basic policies, its record of growth, its plans for future growth. In short, creating an image in the minds of employees is as important as creating an image in the public mind. Officers and employees alike do a better job when they are proud of *their* bank, and such pride must be based on knowledge of what the bank is doing and why. Too often this type of education is disposed of in a single short orientation session for new employees. Staff meetings should be held regularly and should include mention of current bank-wide developments in addition to the problems of the particular department or division involved.

All members of the staff should have a fairly complete understanding of the range of the bank's services and should be kept abreast of any new or expanded services. This is particularly important for those who have personal contact with the public, such as tellers, platform personnel, and customer representatives. But those who do not normally have such contacts should be reasonably well-informed too, for anyone who works in a bank can be questioned by family, friends, and neighbors.

Knowledgeable employees who are proud of their work and the institution they work for can be the best salespersons the bank has. An effective training program needs only to add to this knowledge and pride some instruction in sales techniques. For instance, courtesy and friendliness leads to conversation, and conversation leads to information about a customer, which in turn frequently creates opportunities to cross-sell other bank services that the customer is not presently using.

A word of caution is in order. Pride, product knowledge and sales techniques are important and should be elements of staff training. But, as indicated earlier, employees must be competent in what they do. First and foremost, a teller must be a well-trained teller. The most courteous, polite, and personable employee, who smilingly fouls up a customer's transaction, who shortchanges or overpays a customer or otherwise reveals incompetence, is more likely to "sell" an unfavorable image than other services.

In-house training, as important as it is, should be supplemented by employee attendance at schools sponsored by the industry (the American Bankers Association) including the many AIB courses.

6. *Sales*. Effective marketing culminates in profitable *sales*. This is the objective—the reason for the existence of a bank or any other free enterprise institution.

There are two kinds of profits, however, and marketing is concerned with both. First of all, there is the bottom line, the net profit from operations. A second kind of profit is the impact of a bank's overall performance in promoting community growth and prosperity. As a corporate citizen, a bank has a dual responsibility to its community. It must be strong and healthy and as competent as it can be in the field of banking and also must be aware of and accept its social responsibilities.

Bank marketing cannot be concerned only with profits measured in per-share earnings. It must also be concerned with the health of the community and be responsive to the community's social needs to ensure that the need for the bank and its services will continue to exist.

Profits and social responsiveness go hand in hand; they are mutually interdependent. Thus, to act in the public interest is often the best form of self-interest.

Marketing is a highly complicated, scientific process that involves a great deal more than sales efforts. It is a function that demands the coordinated efforts of many specialists throughout the entire organization.

The ultimate objective of bank marketing is, of course, the profitable sale of banking services. But the objective cannot be achieved solely by heaps of self-praise liberally sprinkled with smiles and charming manners. The process starts with careful research and study, which leads to ideas for new services or the improvement of existing services. The public is made aware of a new or improved service by means of effective advertising and promotion techniques. Finally, the product is placed on the counter, so to speak, by a competent and well-trained staff. These are the steps that lead to profitable sales.

Questions Based on This Chapter

1. What is the ultimate objective of bank marketing?
2. Why must the marketing function involve the entire organization?
3. Name at least four essential elements of the marketing function.
4. Explain why staff training plays an important role in the selling of bank services.

Chapter 20

The Evolution of American Banking

"Those who cannot remember the past are condemned to repeat it."
George Santayana

Purposes of This Chapter:

1. To describe briefly the circumstances and events that shaped America's unique banking system.

2. To discuss some of the critical questions that have troubled Americans through the years.

3. To explain how major pieces of banking legislation sought answers to these questions.

4. To offer tentative answers to the most controversial of those questions.

The American banking system was not patterned after any existing banking system. It is peculiarly and uniquely American, and there is no better way to describe its development than to term it an evolution.

The system as it is known today was not suddenly inspired or created. It developed gradually and was shaped and reshaped by the growing pains of a new nation, torn by conflicting ideologies and buffeted by booms and busts, periods of complacency and panic, successes and failures.

When Francis Scott Key wrote about the "land of the free" he was reflecting the dominant spirit of a new nation. Many of the early settlers risked their lives in this beautiful but dangerous wilderness in order to escape the shackles of oppression and persecution that characterized some of the older civilizations. The early settlers were tough and self-sufficient—they had to be to survive. They became fiercely independent and proudly individualistic. They learned to prize freedom above anything else and proved their dedication by their willingness to fight and die for the right to shape their own destiny unhampered by traditional social, religious, or autocratic restrictions. It was perhaps inevitable that the colonists would eventually shake off the yoke of the British crown.

But the spirit of freedom, like all other personal rights, can be exploited and pushed too far. In a viable society, even individual freedom must have its limitations—a basic principle of life that many Americans are still unwilling to accept.

It was natural that early American banking should reflect the spirit and the philosophy of the times. Freedom in banking was as richly prized as freedom in any other area of human endeavor, and early bankers stubbornly refused to accept anything that sought to control or restrain what they considered to be their inalienable right to conduct business as they saw fit. These individualistic views were reflected in the attitude of the 13 original colonies toward the new federal government. While all agreed that there should be some sort of federation or union of the colonies to protect their common interests, they were most begrudging when it came to surrendering any of their sovereign powers to a central organization. To these 13 units, later to be called states, freedom meant the right to exercise full control of individual activity within their borders, with no interference from any external source of power.

This was the atmosphere in which American banking first saw the light of day. Due to unhappy experiences in colonial days, there were some who distrusted and hated banks and who would have been glad to do without them, but this was not possible. The currency situation in the colonies had been particularly chaotic. The young nation was fast developing an economy of its own, but money in some form, a readily accepted medium of exchange, is the lubricant without which business, industry, and trade cannot flourish. America desperately needed a monetary system, and banks had the means of providing such a system by supplementing the inadequate supply of specie (gold and silver money) with banknotes redeemable in specie. At least this was the basis of monetary systems in other countries.

Banking service and banknote currency were not entirely unfamiliar. Prior to the Revolution, English banks were active in the colonies, principally for the purpose of financing foreign trade. The new country could have modeled its banking system along the lines of the English system or the French or the German or any of the familiar European systems. In one respect, however, the old world systems were somewhat alike. In each there was one dominant bank closely associated with the government. In England there was the Bank of England, founded in 1694. The Old Lady of Threadneedle Street (as it is affectionately called) had its predecessors, such as the Bank of Sweden, which had issued banknotes as early as 1661, and the Bank of Amsterdam. Germany had its Reichsbank and France the Banque de France. At first these banks operated as independent commercial banks, competing with the few other banks that were permitted to be formed. Gradually, however, it was realized that such government-dominated banks (later to be called central banks) had a role to play in national affairs and had an obligation to do what they could to prevent or mitigate national commercial crises.

Thus America could have formed a central bank to exercise some control over the monetary affairs of the nation. But the spirit of freedom and the reluctance of the several states to yield any of what they considered their sovereign rights to the federal government resisted any such attempts. At a very early stage following the Revolution, some basic banking issues surfaced and were hotly debated. There were sharp differences of opinion, especially between the "states' righters" and those who favored a stronger federal government. Strange as it may seem, some of these issues are still unresolved and are the subject of current differences of opinion. Among the questions that troubled our forefathers were:

1. Is commercial banking just another free enterprise? Is there any reason why a citizen may not open and operate a bank just as easily as he opens and operates a foundry? Should not everyone be permitted a free choice of vocation?

2. Is it necessary to exercise some form of control over banking activities?

3. If control is necessary, should it be, in this country, a state function or a federal function?

4. Must all commercial banks be cast in the same mold? Is there no freedom of choice?

319

5. Should the amount of money created by banks (banknotes and later demand deposits) be controlled in the interest of the nation as a whole?

These questions are necessarily stated in broad terms. In the following brief history of the American banking system, reference will be made from time to time to these crucial points. At the end of the chapter, an attempt will be made to offer the answers that temporarily have been accepted. It is quite likely—and this point must be kept in mind —that the final answers have not yet been fully crystalized. Like Topsy, our banking system just grew—and its present form was shaped more by the unplanned pressures of wars, depressions, and crises than by deliberate careful planning.

The Colonial and Post-Revolution Period

In the colonial days domestic banking was virtually nonexistent and what banking services were offered by private lenders and land banks were woefully inadequate. The currency situation in the colonies was particularly chaotic. Hard money (specie) was not available in sufficient quantity, and gold and silver tended to flow out of the country to pay for much needed manufactured goods. After the Revolution, a number of commercial banks were established, beginning with the Bank of North America in Philadelphia in 1791. The Bank of North America and several other banks issued notes of high quality which were redeemable in specie, but they were the exception. In general, the colonial and post-revolutionary periods were characterized by depreciated currencies in which the populace had little faith—and all too frequent bank failures.

The Bank of the United States

There was a growing feeling, in some quarters at least, that banking was unlike other free areas of private enterprise. People were becoming painfully aware of the fact that a sound monetary system was essential to the health of the nation's economy. In the absence of sufficient quantities of gold and silver money, a monetary system had to be devised with some form of circulating medium, whether in the form of paper money, wooden money, lightweight coins, or whatever. Moreover, regardless of its form, people had to have confidence in the circulating medium. Paper money was acceptable only to the extent that people believed it actually was worth its equivalent value in specie and could be redeemed upon request. If everyone shared that confidence, paper money would not necessarily be redeemed but would pass freely from hand to hand at its face value.

Largely due to the efforts of Alexander Hamilton, the Congress in 1791 chartered the first Bank of the United States. This federally-chartered bank had a number of duties assigned to it, not the least of which was a deliberate attempt to restore the almost destroyed public confidence in private banknote issues.

The Bank of the United States issued its own paper currency up to the amount of its capital, $10 million. It made loans to the federal government and aided in the collection of taxes and also made loans to and accepted deposits from the public. Most important, it instituted a system of policing the note issues of other banks. During the course of a day's business, it would take all banknotes received, sort them, and promptly send them to the issuing banks for redemption in hard money or specie. As a result, over the 20 years of the bank's existence, the quality of the nation's banknotes improved appreciably, and the number of failures of over-extended banks was reduced.

In spite of this impressive record, the private independent bankers didn't like the "policeman." To them, freedom of enterprise meant the absence of oppressive controls and restrictions. The several states which granted their charters placed few if any restrictions on the size of their note issues, and they saw no reason why the federal government should interfere with their freedom to conduct their bank's business as they saw fit. Despite its accomplishments, there was a great deal of grass-roots' political opposition to the bank, and when its charter expired in 1811, the first Bank of the United States expired with it.

The Aftermath

During the next five years (1811-1816) the monetary situation deteriorated rapidly. Admittedly, federal government financing of the War of 1812 had a lot to do with it. In any event, the period was marked by a tremendous inflation of state banknote issues. There was a huge demand for circulating currency, and state banks, no longer fearing insistent presentment of notes for redemption by the former "policeman," readily accommodated that demand. The number of banks increased from 88 to 246 in that brief period, and the face value of banknotes outstanding nearly tripled. Specie redemption often had to be suspended, resulting in a renewed lack of confidence in the principal circulating medium.

The Second Bank of the United States

The proponents of banking control were able to say "We told you so," and it was difficult to deny the facts. In 1816, the Congress was persuaded to charter a second Bank of the United States.

The second federal bank had much the same duties as its predecessor, and it immediately reinstituted the practice of presenting promptly state banknotes to the issuing bank for redemption in hard money. But the individualistic state bankers took no more kindly to the second federal bank than they did to the first. If anything, they more strongly resented what they considered to be unwarranted federal interference in the affairs of the sovereign states. They argued that this country did not want and did not need a dominant government bank after the pattern of European banking systems. They contended that the states alone should have the power to regulate all commercial activities, including banking, within their respective borders. They were joined by a liberal group of easy money advocates who felt that prompt redemption of banknotes restricted the free growth of bank credit and therefore was a form of control that tended to raise interest rates and stifle economic growth. The issue of hard money vs. easy money has cropped up again and again in our nation's history as it has elsewhere in the world, and it remains a highly controversial question even to this day.

The 20-year life of the second Bank of the United States was hardly a tranquil existence. Like its predecessor, it was successful in bringing about substantial improvements in commercial banking practices throughout the nation. But this did not satisfy an ever-growing army of free banking advocates, and the hotly contested issue became a major plank in Andrew Jackson's presidential campaign platform. Andrew Jackson was elected president in 1832 in considerable measure because of his vigorous and outspoken opposition to the Bank of the United States. No one was surprised when President Jackson promptly vetoed a bill to renew the bank's charter. His veto was sustained; the second bank expired with its charter in 1836, and a second attempt to provide some form of national regulation of banking practices was soundly rejected.

State Control

The demise of the second Bank of the United States again placed commercial banking under the sole control of the several states. By this time, however, some of the states were becoming aware of the fact that there were inherent dangers in a completely unrestricted banking system.

The New York Free Banking Act of 1838 was a bold attempt to retain freedom of entry into the banking business, while at the same time seeking to control the more serious hazards.

Prior to that time, each bank in the country had to be chartered by a special act of a state legislature. This procedure made possible all kinds of political abuse, and bank lobbyists and politicians were quick to take advantage. The legislators arranged to obtain charters for their personal friends and supporters, while they denied applications for charters by potential competitors. Most charters resulted from political deals involving some form of compensation to the state government and often to the legislators personally.

In order to eliminate the political abuses, the New York Free Banking Act permitted almost any group of citizens to obtain a charter to start a bank. At the same time, recognizing the danger of completely unrestricted and uncontrolled banking activities, the Act sought to impose some regulations as to how banks were to be operated. This was the beginning of efforts to exercise some measure of state control.

The basic principles behind the new law were sound enough, and the pattern of the New York Act was copied by a number of states. In practice, however, the sensible objectives proved illusive. Individual bankers were still unwilling to submit to strong controls and wanted no fetters to control the way they conducted their business. They had considerable political influence and, consequently, state legislatures were unable or unwilling to impose effective restrictions on banking operations. In spite of the good intentions of the free banking laws, almost anyone, however poorly qualified, could choose to become a banker and was free to conduct his business with few legal restrictions.

Wildcat Banking

The story of American banking under free banking laws (1838-1863) was certainly not one of commendable progress and glorious achievement. On the other hand, it was a period that would have placed considerable stress on any banking system. The fledgling nation was spreading its wings and was rapidly expanding both physically and economically. Its western borders were being rolled back to the Pacific; canals and railroads were opening up new markets, and business was booming. There was money to be made in all types of business, given the necessary financing. Everyone needed money and, naturally, banking shared generously in the boom.

The free banking laws made it easy to start new banks, and the frantic demand for credit made it very profitable to do so. The number of banks soared—and so did the number of banknotes in circulation. No longer subject to the restraining influence of the second Bank of the United States, banks issued banknotes with accommodating abundance. Any bank that even attempted to maintain a reasonable relationship between its note issue and its supply of gold and silver sharply restricted its ability to make loans and thus to make profits. Instead of making any pretense as to ability to redeem banknotes in specie, many banks openly discouraged redemption in every possible way. One ingenious method was to permit redemption only at the head office of the bank, and then to locate the head office in an inaccessible forest or swamp where only wildcats lived, a practice which gave the period its name.

For every speculative boom there is a bust. Many of the banks that had overextended themselves in the 1830s failed at the first sign that the boom was over. Failures continued throughout the 1840s and 1850s. These failures had many causes: excessive note issue and inadequate reserves, risky loans, inadequate capital, and, not infrequently, fraud or embezzlement. No matter what the causes, the effects were the same in most cases: worthless banknotes, loss of depositors' savings, confusion, and the disruption of business and trade.

An old problem—counterfeiting—worsened with the proliferation of banks that followed the free banking laws. Each bank could issue notes of its own design in many denominations. Many notes were poorly engraved and printed on low quality paper. The situation was a counterfeiter's paradise. It was easy even for amateurs to copy notes, raise denominations on genuine notes, or even print notes on fictitious banks. *Nicholas' Bank Note Reporter*, published in 1858, gave 5,400 separate descriptions of fraudulent notes in circulation. Only about 7,000 different kinds of genuine notes were in use at the time.

By no means were all banks mismanaged during the period of wildcat banking. Indeed, many banks served their communities well and jealously guarded their depositors' money, particularly those in Boston and New York City. But serious abuses were common enough to bring discredit to the banking industry in general. Public cries for reform were heard with increasing frequency in the years prior to the Civil War. Massachusetts, New York, and Louisiana did enact laws to promote sounder banking, but these were the exception rather than the rule.

The National Banking System

It is a well-known fact that such catastrophes as wars, panics, or severe depressions give birth to the most drastic reform legislation. Our Civil War was no exception. By 1863 the Union government had all but exhausted its ready sources of credit, and this critical problem was seized upon as a golden opportunity not only to provide funds for the government but also at the same time to revamp thoroughly the banking and currency system.

Congress passed the National Currency Act of 1863, which was revised by the National Banking Act of 1864, with two objectives in mind. One objective was to replace the hopeless hodge-podge of 7,000 different kinds of state banknotes with a more sound and dependable currency system. The other objective, to solve the most pressing problem of the moment, was to create a captive market for federal government bonds in order to finance the Union war effort. The two objectives were achieved simultaneously by what can only be described as a stroke of legislative genius. The soundness of the new paper currency was brought about by requiring each issuing bank to pledge collateral with the Comptroller of the Currency in the form of government bonds. Thus, the U. S. Treasury stood ready to redeem promptly the outstanding notes of a failing bank by cancelling the pledged bonds. In addition, a greatly expanded market for such bonds was thereby assured.

The main features of the National Banking Act provided for—

1. *A system of national banks.* These banks were to be chartered by the federal government rather than by the several states, and the Act provided for a series of uniform regulations governing their operations. New banks were free to apply for national charters, and existing banks could renounce their state charters and join the national system if they chose to do so. Both the new and existing state banks had to meet relatively high standards in order to obtain national charters.

2. *A national currency.* The Act restricted national banks to issuing banknotes of a *uniform design.* Thus, except for identification of the issuing bank, all national banknotes presented the same appearance. As noted above, in order to make these notes perfectly sound, the Congress required national banks to pledge government bonds against the amount outstanding. Thus national banks were forced to buy huge quantities of government bonds. In this manner, the government obtained a vast new source of funds, and the public got a uniform, easy-to-recognize, hard-to-counterfeit, safe form of paper currency, which practically ended about 80 years of almost constant state banknote troubles.

3. *Reserves against deposits.* National banks were required to maintain cash reserves based on a percentage of deposit liabilities. The percentage varied depending on the location of the bank. Higher reserves were required for banks located in cities designated as reserve cities, or central reserve cities. Part of the cash reserve had to be held in the bank's vault and part could be deposited with correspondent banks.

4. *Supervision.* The Act also created a new office in the United States Treasury to supervise national banks, which was called the Office of the Comptroller of the Currency. The Comptroller of the Currency was responsible for determining that banks applying for national charters met the required standards. For instance, there were minimum capital requirements related to the population of the cities or towns in which the banks were to operate.

The Comptroller of the Currency also ensured that national banks conformed to all requirements of the Act, such as legal reserve requirements and restrictions on certain types of loans, and was authorized to establish a force of bank examiners to carry out these functions.

The Office of the Comptroller of the Currency still exists today, and its basic functions of supervision and examination of national banks remain essentially the same.

The Dual Banking System

Prior to the passage of the National Banking Act, there was much opposition by the banking fraternity to some of its features. While the Act did not establish a single dominant central bank, to which there continued to be strong vigorous objection, many viewed with suspicion a widespread chain of competitive, federally-chartered institutions supervised by a unit of the United States Treasury department.

At first, a disappointingly small number of banks elected to join the national system. Most bankers naturally preferred the more permissive state charters with which they were more familiar. But the tenseness of the prevailing wartime atmosphere demanded that the new legislation be made effective, and the Congress acted promptly by levying a tax of 10 percent on all notes issued by state-chartered banks.

Actually, this prohibitive tax should have sounded the death knell for state banking systems, and this was probably the intent. A bank that could not pay the proceeds of loans and discounts by issuing its bank notes had little prospects for profitable operation. For a while it seemed that state-chartered banks would become a relic of the past, but then an almost miraculously timed and unexpected development saved the day. Although checks or orders for the payment of deposited funds were not new, this payment device had not been utilized to any great extent prior to the Civil War. But the use of checks drawn against bank deposits had been gradually growing, and the practice began to accelerate rapidly following the War. As a result, banks could operate profitably without issuing notes by crediting the proceeds of loans to accounts subject to withdrawal by check. Thus the state banking systems received a new lease on life, and the dual banking system became a fixture in American banking. To this day banks have the option of operating under a national charter or a state charter, as they see fit.

Weaknesses of the National Banking Act

Every major piece of reform legislation is optimistically expected to solve problems for all time to come. But experience teaches us that this is seldom the case. On the whole, the National Banking Act achieved its major purposes very well. In time, it did provide a means of replenishing the federal Treasury at moderate costs; it brought higher standards to bank operations; it provided a much needed overhaul of the currency system and in so doing restored faith and confidence not only in the nation's circulating medium but also in the banking business. But conditions have a way of changing faster than laws can be changed, and by 1900 the national banking system was creaking with several major defects. To do justice to the framers of the Act, it would have taken extraordinarily clear vision to have foreseen these defects from the viewpoint of war-torn 1863 and 1864.

The major defects were three in number:

1. *An inflexible currency.* It will be recalled that there were two purposes for requiring national banks to pledge United States government bonds as collateral for their note issues. Both of these purposes (a market for government bonds and a safe currency) were successfully achieved. But a circulating medium has to have another quality—the ability to expand and contract as required by the needs of the economy. When business is good more money is needed to finance a greater volume of commercial transactions. Conversely, when business slackens, the volume of money ideally should contract accordingly. The requirements of the National Banking Act tied the volume of national banknotes—the major form of currency—to the available supply of government bonds rather than to the needs of the economy. Actually, the supply of government bonds and the demand for money and credit tended to move in opposite directions. Thus, when business conditions were good, the Treasury often ran a budget surplus and retired some of its bonds. Consequently, national banks were unable to increase the volume of banknotes; in some cases they were forced to reduce the volume of their outstanding notes because of inability to obtain the required collateral. National bank currency, therefore, which was made safe and which restored confidence in paper money, proved in the long run to be inflexible and unable to respond to economic needs.

2. *No provision for efficient check collection.* That the National Banking Act made no provision for a systematic method of collecting checks is not surprising, since in 1864 there were hardly enough checks being circulated to cause a problem of national concern. As indicated earlier, however, the use of checks accelerated rapidly in the years following the Civil War, and by the turn of the century the problem of check collection was becoming more and more serious. Local checks were normally collected quickly and easily through local clearinghouse arrangements, but collection of out-of-town checks was an entirely different matter. At that time the only available facility for presenting and collecting out-of-town checks was through correspondent banks, whereby funds could be transferred and settlements made through a

network of account relationships. There was no systematic method of getting a check from the bank in which it was deposited to the bank on which it was drawn, and more often than not the check would travel an aimless circuitous route. For instance, if a check drawn on a bank in Lexington, Kentucky was deposited in a New England bank, it might be sent first to a Boston bank. The Boston bank, not having a Kentucky correspondent, might send the item to its Philadelphia correspondent, which in turn might send it to a Chicago correspondent, which might send it to a Cincinnati correspondent, which *might* be able to send it to the drawee in Lexington. The journey could take weeks.

With checks becoming a more and more common means of making payments, the clumsy, snail-paced collection procedure was daily becoming more unbearable.

3. *Pyramiding Reserves.* National banks were permitted to deposit a portion of their cash reserves (against deposits) with correspondent banks, and since such deposits could draw interest, they had a strong incentive to do so to the extent allowed. For instance, country banks could deposit up to two-fifths of their cash reserves in reserve city banks. The reserve city banks in turn could keep up to one-half of their cash reserves in central reserve cities.[1] Thus cash reserves tended to move from smaller cities to larger cities and from larger cities to the central reserve cities, with the bulk of these reserves concentrated in New York City, the nation's principal money center. In order to employ these funds profitably, the New York City banks invested heavily in short-term loans to stockbrokers and dealers.

The system worked well enough as long as things went smoothly, but a few sharp shocks often caused difficulties. When the country banks needed an unusually large amount of currency, they would withdraw their deposits from the reserve city banks which then would be forced to reduce their own deposits in the central reserve city banks. The pressure on reserve city banks, particularly New York City banks, would build up rapidly. In order to cope with the severe drain of deposits, these banks would be forced to call their loans to stockbrokers and dealers, who in turn would be forced to sell the securities that the loans had financed. Naturally, these forced sales would depress market prices, and as the market sagged, investors would panic and sell out, and prices would tumble faster and faster.

These money panics fed on themselves and often led to a decline in general business activity, as the pressure to liquidate assets reverberated

---

1. New York City was designated a central reserve city in 1864, but Chicago and St. Louis were also so designated in 1887. At that time there were about 49 reserve cities, in addition to the three central reserve cities.

throughout the banking system. Not only reserve city banks, but also all banks would find it difficult to make loans or even maintain existing loans to other customers. Before long the entire nation would be mired in recession or depression.

The Federal Reserve System

After nearly a half century of experience under the National Banking Act, some definite thoughts had crystallized. For one thing, there were very few observers who still clung to the belief that commercial banking was no different than any other private enterprise. It was being recognized that the commercial banks of the nation played an important role in the monetary system as creators as well as the holders of the bulk of our money supply (demand deposits), and as issuers of much of the currency. They served and facilitated the nation's payments mechanism by which most business transactions and a growing number of personal transactions were settled; and they were the principal mobilizers and allocators of credit. The federal government had no choice but to concern itself with the soundness and stability of commercial bank operations in order to ensure the safety of depositors' money and the effectiveness of our monetary system.

Something had to be done about improving the check collection system; the inability of the Office of the Comptroller of the Currency to control the nation's money supply and to make it responsive to the needs of the economy was interfering with the smooth processing of business transactions; and the tendency of the cash reserves of banks to concentrate and pyramid in large money centers was contributing to sporadic and disturbing money panics.

The old issues and some corollary questions came to the fore again. Was it necessary to have some authority empowered to control the volume of currency and demand deposits in the interest of national economic stability? If so, should the authority be centralized in the hands of a federal government agency or should it be decentralized and perhaps left for the several states to exercise? If the former, would this not mean another attempt to establish a central bank, such as the first or second Bank of the United States? (This thought was still unacceptable to those who feared a resurgence of federal interference in state affairs.) On the other hand, could decentralized authority give proper weight to the interests of the nation as a whole?

If the National Banking Act could be considered a stroke of genius in its time, the Federal Reserve Act, enacted into law in 1913, was a masterpiece of compromise. It provided for regional (decentralized) control for local affairs and centralized control at the federal level for matters of national concern. It provided for private ownership, as opposed to government ownership, but severely limited the extent of private control, and it devised a means of insulating the system from political pressures and the pressures of private financial interests. It also provided for a sort of central bank, but in a form quite different from those in other countries, in that it was constituted as an independent agency within the structure of the federal government, but insulated to a considerable extent from political control by either the Congress or the executive branch. In addition, the Act addressed itself specifically to the major weaknesses of the national bank system and was quite successful in correcting those defects.

Under the Federal Reserve System, the country was divided into 12 districts based on trade and economic considerations rather than along state lines. Thus two or more whole states or even parts of states might comprise a single district. A Federal Reserve bank was located in a principal city of each district, and branches of the district bank were located in other cities depending on the geographic expanse and the need for such branches. All but two of the districts felt it desirable to establish branches.

Each Federal Reserve bank was constituted as a semi-independent organization with a board of directors, a chairman, a vice-chairman, a president, and other executive officers. Since each district bank would be most familiar with conditions and needs in its own area, its board of directors was given a substantial measure of authority with respect to local matters.

Instead of a single central bank, a body called the Federal Reserve Board (later renamed the Board of Governors of the Federal Reserve System) was superimposed on the regional or district system and was authorized to provide overall direction in matters of national importance. Thus the 12 district banks were free to act as they pleased in serving the interests of their own areas, subject only to the authority of the Federal Reserve Board as that body discharged its responsibility to provide coordinated, system-wide economic and monetary policies for the nation as whole.

The Federal Reserve Act did not attempt to disturb the dual banking system, which gave bankers the choice of operating under a state charter or a national charter. On the contrary, it created a new classification of banks. National banks were required to become members of the System, automatically placing them under the jurisdiction of a district Federal Reserve bank or branch and making them subject to the regulations of the Federal Reserve Board. But state banks were given a choice. They could become members of the System or not, as they saw fit. Furthermore, if a state-chartered bank joined the System, it could choose to withdraw at any time. In addition to state banks and national banks, therefore, two other categories were added: member banks and nonmember banks. This was pleasing to the independent-minded bankers who still cherished the freedom to decide for themselves whether they would or would not submit to federal control and regulation.

Ownership of the System

The question of ownership of the System was considered a knotty problem. The thought of private ownership raised the old fear of domination by powerful financial interests, while government ownership suggested political control and the fear that Federal Reserve policy might be based more on vote-getting appeal than the ultimate effect on the nation's welfare. Whether the problem was real or fancied, it was solved in an ingenious manner.

Member banks were required to buy stock in the Federal Reserve bank of the district in an amount based on the member bank's capital and surplus. Thus, individual banks are technically the legal owners of the 12 Federal Reserve banks and their branches. But stock ownership brought the member banks very little control and only a partial voice in the operation of the district bank.

For instance, member banks elect six of the nine directors of each district bank, three of whom must be bankers, and three of whom must be chosen from other fields. The remaining three are appointed by the Board of Governors in Washington, D.C. which designates one of these three as chairman and another as vice-chairman. In addition, the Board of Governors must approve the appointment of the president and first vice-president of each bank. While the member banks elect a majority (six out of nine) of the board of directors of each district bank, it is clear that the minority appointed by the Board of Governors could indeed exert a powerful influence. In this case, ownership proved to be a far cry from effective control, as was intended.

The Board of Governors

In the framing of the Federal Reserve Act, perhaps the knottiest problem of all was how to make the System independent to the extent that it could conscientiously serve the nation free of undue influence from the legislative or executive branch of government or susceptible to the influence of private banking interests. The solution to this problem was amazingly simple, yet it has proved rather effective in practice.

The seven members of the Board of Governors are appointed by the President of the United States with the advice and consent of the Senate. They are appointed to serve *14-year terms*, and the terms are staggered so that one term expires every two years. The significance of this arrangement should be readily apparent. In the absence of deaths or voluntary retirements, it would take any president two full four-year terms in office to appoint a hand-picked majority to the Board of Governors.

Congress intended to make the System independent within the government, and in this it succeeded. While the Congress can amend or even repeal the Act whenever it chooses, it is clear that drastic action would be required to destroy that independence. Thus, neither the president nor the Congress is in a position to dictate policy or procedure to the Board of Governors.

Curing the Defects of the National Banking System

1. *Inflexible Currency*. It will be recalled that the supply of national banknotes depended on the availability of U.S. government bonds, which banks were required to deposit with the Comptroller's Office as collateral for their note issues. When business activity stimulated the demand for more currency, the banks frequently found it difficult if not impossible to obtain the necessary bonds. Thus the volume of paper money tended to shrink just when the demand was increasing.

Again, the solution to this problem was rather simple. The Act authorized the Federal Reserve banks to issue their own banknotes, but directed that collateral should consist of *eligible commercial paper* and gold, rather than U.S. government bonds. *Eligible commercial paper* refers to the promissory notes banks receive as they make loans for commercial, industrial, or agricultural purposes. When business activity expands, the demand for such loans increases as borrowers seek funds to purchase raw materials, add workers to their payrolls, step up production schedules, and build inventories in order to meet the demands of the expanding economy.

With certain limitations, banks could discount "eligible" notes with the district Federal Reserve bank to obtain additional reserve funds, and the Federal Reserve System could automatically meet the demand for an increased volume of circulating paper money. In this way the System was able to relate the volume of its Federal Reserve notes to the needs of the economy for currency.

At the present time, the collateral for Federal Reserve notes consists almost entirely of government securities. The former requirements for gold reserves have been dropped completely. Thus, Federal Reserve notes again resemble the national banknotes, but with the great difference that they can be issued in any quantity demanded by the public. National banks continued to issue banknotes for two decades after the passage of the Federal Reserve Act, when their authority to do so was withdrawn. The United States Treasury has for all practical purposes discontinued issuing Treasury currency.

2. *Eliminating the Pyramid.* The Federal Reserve Act provided that each member bank had to maintain its reserves against deposit liabilities with the district bank or branch serving its area. In this manner, the System created 36 regional pools of reserves to replace the tottering financial pyramid with New York City as the apex. The reserve banks were also given the power to create reserves and to lend them to member banks whenever legitimate needs arose. Whenever a single bank, all the banks in a city, or even the entire banking system needs money in a hurry, the Federal Reserve System, as the lender of last resort, stands ready to make it available. Thus the fear of recurring money panics was at last laid to rest.

3. *Providing a Check Collection System.* The 12 districts provided an excellent basis for an efficient check collection system. When a check is deposited in any Federal Reserve bank or branch, it is sent directly to the district in which the drawee bank is located.

Checks drawn on out-of-town banks simply move from the district of deposit to the district of payment and thence directly to the drawee bank, instead of being subjected to the somewhat aimless routing frequently resorted to by correspondent banks. Even checks deposited and payable within the same district stand a better chance of speedier collection through the Federal Reserve collection system.

As a matter of fact, the improved check collection system had a beneficial side effect. Correspondent banks were not about to lose the balances carried with them by banks that depended on them for services other than check collection. Large correspondent banks felt compelled to improve their own collection methods, which they did by widening their contacts to establish more direct sending points. Obviously, when a depository bank has a correspondent relationship with the drawee bank, direct presentation is possible without involving intermediate collecting banks. Direct presentation, therefore, can be even faster than collection through the Federal Reserve System, as Federal Reserve banks normally serve as intermediate banks. The ultimate result has been a general overall improvement in check collections and a healthy competitive atmosphere. Nevertheless, the greatest number of checks by far is collected through the Federal Reserve System.

The Banking Acts of 1933-35

If the Federal Reserve Act eliminated the danger of sporadic money panics, it certainly did not end banking troubles in the nation. Individual banks have the choice, under the dual banking concept, of organizing under state laws. There was a brief period, following passage of the National Banking Act in 1864, when national banks outnumbered state-chartered institutions by better than five to one. However, the growing use of demand deposits as our principal medium of exchange gave state banks a new lease on life. Given the choice, bankers increasingly favored the less restrictive state laws, and, by the turn of the century, state-chartered banks again outnumbered national banks. In the next two decades (1900-1920) over 17,000 new banks were organized, more than 75 percent of them under state charters. Although certain minimum standards had to be met under both federal and state laws, it was not difficult to obtain a charter, and any individual or group of individuals wishing to enter the banking business was relatively free to do so, and many did. As a result there were far too many banks in existence in 1920—many of them small unit banks located in rural areas. From 1921 to 1930 more than 5,000 banks had to suspend operations.

The economic collapse following the stock market crash in 1929 all but destroyed the banking system. Commercial bankruptcies soared as did the rate of unemployment. Borrowers could not pay their debts, and from 1930 to 1933 nearly 9,000 more banks failed. A glance at the balance sheet of the average bank reveals how vulnerable such institutions are in periods of severe financial stress. They are firmly committed to pay a substantial percentage of their liabilities *in cash, on demand,* or on very short notice, with little possibility of liquidating the assets supporting those liabilities, however basically sound, at anywhere near the same pace. The weaker, poorly-managed banks had no chance at all, and even sound, well-managed banks had to struggle for survival.

It was a foregone conclusion that the virtual collapse of the nation's banks would lead to forced-draft legislation designed to reform and strengthen the banking system. The Banking Act of 1933 and, subsequently, the Banking Act of 1935 had this in mind. Regulations covering the chartering and operation of national banks were tightened, and many state legislatures followed suit. Significant additional regulatory powers were given to the Board of Governors of the Federal Reserve System, and its monetary powers were expanded and strengthened.

The Federal Deposit Insurance Corporation

One of the most important features of the Act of 1933 was the creation of a new federal agency, the Federal Deposit Insurance Corporation. The immediate objective of the FDIC was to reestablish confidence in the nation's badly shaken banking system. All Federal Reserve member banks were required to become FDIC insured, and nonmember banks were invited to participate if they could qualify. Again, there was a choice for the individual state-chartered bank—it could accept or decline the invitation. Most nonmember banks wisely decided that they should avail themselves of this means of protecting their depositors.

The framers of the Act realized that the power to grant or withhold deposit insurance protection would give the new agency considerable influence on bank operations. The FDIC therefore was used as a lever to compel upgrading of the standards of the banking industry. It was empowered to prescribe certain minimum operative requirements that a bank had to meet in order to qualify for insurance. Furthermore, on the theory that an insuring agency should be able at any time to inspect its risks, the agency was authorized to examine any insured bank and to hire a staff of examiners for this purpose.

Insured banks pay to the FDIC an assessment of one-twelfth of 1 percent [2] of their aggregate yearly deposit liabilities, although accounts are insured only up to a maximum figure. The original Act of 1933 insured deposits up to $2,500 for a single ownership. This was increased to $5,000 by the Act of 1935 and has since been increased in successive stages so that the present maximum stands at $40,000 per account or per single ownership if more than one account is maintained by an owner in the same bank.

In a psychological sense the mere existence of the Federal Deposit Insurance Corporation has done much to reduce the need for it. When the mass of depositors are secure in the knowledge that their money is protected, they no longer make the hasty, panicky withdrawals that can cause so many otherwise sound banks to close their doors.

Bank Holding Companies

The story of the evolution of American banking would not be complete without mention of the rapid expansion of banking activities made possible in recent years by means of holding companies. A bank holding company may be defined as a separate nonbank corporate organization that owns or controls one or more banks.

Although bank holding companies have been in existence for a long time, they were not considered to be a significant factor in banking until fairly recently. For the most part, holding companies were originally used as a means of circumventing restrictive branching laws. For instance, the holding company device permitted the operation of a number of banking offices under centralized control but as separate corporate entities rather than as branch offices. This had been known as *group banking*—a practice that flourished briefly at the turn of the century and again in the 1920s and the early 1950s. Another such de-

---

2. When FDIC reserves are considered sufficient a portion of the assessment is refunded to the insured banks.

vice was known as *chain banking*, where control was exercised by individuals rather than by a (holding company) corporation.

The "Banking Only" Concept

Because of the special nature of commercial banking, particularly in view of its role as allocator of credit, there has been a rather strong feeling in Congress that banks should be engaged *only* in the banking business and should not be financially involved through ownership and control of other forms of commercial enterprises, in order to avoid harmful conflicts of interest.

The Banking Act of 1933 endorsed this concept to an extent, since it forbade banks from engaging in the underwriting and distribution of securities, except for obligations of the United States and its instrumentalities and the obligations of states and their political subdivisions. In the 1920s when there was a tremendous increase in investor interest in stocks and bonds, a number of expansion-minded metropolitan banks began to deal quite actively in securities. The collapse of the financial boom in 1929 brought to light some evidence of self-dealing between the commercial banking area and the security-dealing unit of the same institution. For instance, if a bank, through a securities affiliate, participated in the underwriting of a bond issue that did not sell well, there might be a strong temptation to sell the bonds to the bank's trust accounts. Not all banks engaged in such practices, but enough abuses were found to convince the Congress that it was necessary to remove the potential conflict of interests by prohibiting banks from engaging in the underwriting or distribution of securities.

The Bank Holding Company Act of 1956

The "banking only" concept was plainly in the minds of the framers of the Bank Holding Company Act of 1956. The purpose of this legislation was not to ban bank holding companies, but to provide for regulation and control of their formation and expansion. Significantly, however, it specifically required bank holding companies to divest themselves of all nonbanking interests. The Board of Governors of the Federal Reserve System was made the sole regulatory authority for bank holding companies at the federal level and therefore the judge of what constituted a "nonbanking" interest.

At the time the 1956 legislation was being discussed, the use of the holding company device in banking was viewed by the authorities primarily as a means of expansion via the multi-office route in order to avoid existing branching restrictions. Therefore, although in retrospect it seems strange, the Act specifically defined bank holding companies subject to its provisions as those owning or controlling 25 percent or more of the voting shares of *two or more banks,* thus exempting companies holding control of only *one bank.* There were a number of one-bank holding companies in existence, but for the most part they controlled relatively small, diversified family interests, and the banks they controlled were usually quite small and were located in rural areas. There seemed to be no compelling reason to bring such companies within the purview of the Act, and suggestions that one-bank holding companies be excluded were unopposed and consequently adopted.

But larger banks, anxious to expand and diversify their activities, were quick to take advantage of the loophole provided by the exemption. Actually, bank holding companies formed for the purpose of multi-office banking did not present very serious problems with respect to nonbanking activities. But the obvious purpose of a sudden rush to form one-bank holding companies during the 1960s was to expand areas of activity by establishing or acquiring units engaged in what might or might not be construed to be "nonbanking" enterprises.

The Bank Holding Company Act Amendments of 1970 sought to bring the one-bank holding companies under control, and it made the Board of Governors responsible for interpreting such generalizations as "so closely related to banking" and "a proper incident thereto," by refusing to spell out specific activities deemed to be proper functions for bank holding company affiliates. However, the amendments clarified the language of the 1956 Act by directing the Board to consider such factors as benefits to the public in terms of convenience, increased competition, or gains in efficiency, and the extent to which such benefits might outweigh adverse factors such as undue concentration, decreased competition, and conflicts of interest. Congress therefore established broad guidelines, but the Board of Governors, in applying the law and the guidelines to specific cases, is expected ultimately to define rather precisely the full range and scope as well as the limitations of the business of commercial banking. Some progress has been made in this direction, but it is too early yet to tell just where the outer boundaries of banking and activities properly incident thereto will be set or even whether they will ever be set on a permanent basis.

Present holding-company legislation offers some interesting opportunities for banking expansion. For instance, the 1970 amendments permit a one-bank holding company to become a multi-bank holding company if it so desires. At the present time, other bank acquisitions are limited to state lines, and the extent of multi-office banking is considered a matter for the states to decide. On the other hand, bank-related activities conducted by affiliates of the holding company are not so restricted, and unless prohibited by specific legislation will probably enjoy a much broader geographic area of operations without regard to state lines.

The opportunities for a more sophisticated banking industry, offering a still broader range of services beneficial to the public, are abundant. It is to be hoped that the enthusiasm of bankers in seizing on these opportunities will be tempered by the exercise of sound judgment and much discretion. The extreme importance of the basic banking functions has been emphasized over and over again in these pages, and bankers can never lose sight of the obligation they owe to the nation—the maintenance of a sound banking system. The possibility of serious conflicts of interest between *bank-related functions* and *pure banking functions* most certainly exists, and it would be unfortunate if the former in any way served to sap the strength and vigor of the latter.

The foregoing brief sketch of the story of American banking touches only the highlights. Some of the questions that troubled our forebearers were spelled out earlier. For the present at least, some answers appear to have been found, not in books or in the lives of others, but in the fiery crucible of our own sometimes painful experience.

1. Commercial banking is not "just another free enterprise." It bears the responsibility of a significant difference. While freemen should be able to choose their life's pursuit, there are certain fields of endeavor that touch so intimately on the lives of others that society is fully justified in demanding the right to inspect qualifications and to set minimum standards to ensure competent performance. Freedom of action must always be limited to that point where the exercise of freedom by any person or persons endangers the freedom or well-being of others. The disastrous effects of incompetence in commercial banking that must be suffered by the entire populace makes the difference.

2. While any form of control impinges to some extent on personal freedom, those who choose to enter the business of commercial banking must be prepared to submit to rather rigid controls. This nation has valiantly tried to live with completely free, uncontrolled, and unregulated banking. The repeated failures cannot be ignored.

3. This nation has experimented both with state control and national control, and the evidence is unmistakable that in certain respects unified control at the federal level is necessary. Yet in areas that do not appear to endanger national interest, substantial controls have been left to the several states. Thus the conclusion seems to be that a combination of local and national controls is the most desirable answer.

4. Our banking laws have avoided compulsion wherever possible. After two hundred years of experience, a substantial degree of freedom of choice remains. Thus those that seek to enter the field of commercial banking can elect to organize state banks or national banks (dual banking) ; there is no compulsion to join the Federal Reserve System,

and they can be member banks or nonmembers; and they can choose to accept or reject the benefits of federal deposit insurance. It is easy to defend the broad principle of freedom, but it is not so easy to defend the resulting maze of overlapping regulatory authorities. Yet a cooperative spirit among the several authorities has seemed to minimize the disadvantages thus far.

5. Commercial banks have the power to create money. Our experience, as well as that of other nations, teaches that uncontrolled and unjustified expansion of a nation's medium of exchange debases that medium and if carried far enough produces the ravages of runaway inflation. There is little doubt that the money supply must be controlled in the interests of the nation as a whole. A more difficult question might be: In whose hands should this control be placed? American banking produced its own unique answer by creating an *independent* government agency to exercise such control—the Board of Governors of the Federal Reserve System—and by insulating it as far as possible from self-serving political and private pressures.

From the very beginning, our forefathers were determined to devise a banking system best suited to the ideals and philosophies of the new nation. By refusing to adopt the pattern of older banking systems, they chose to set sail in uncharted waters. The journey has been long and often difficult.

After 200 years of banking history, it would be foolhardy to assume that all of the right answers have been found. Banking has changed drastically during those years, and there seems to be no reason to believe that the future will be any different. Laws will be changed, regulations will be loosened or tightened, and the banking fraternity will always press for more freedom of operation.

In any event, American banking has come a long way. It is certainly not perfect—it may not even be the best banking system. But it is safe to say that American banking serves more people in more ways than any other banking system in the world. In this respect, American bankers can be proud of their heritage—as long as they never permit themselves to think that the millennium has been reached.

Questions Based on This Chapter

1. Discuss the first attempt in this country to form a "central" bank and explain why its charter was not renewed.

2. Describe the principal provisions of the National Banking Act.

3. How did the Federal Reserve System deal with the weaknesses of the national banking system?

4. What is meant by the "dual banking system"?

Chapter 21

External
Regulation

Purposes of This Chapter:

1. To describe the complex nature of the external regulation of American banks.

2. To discuss the nature and purpose of bank examinations.

3. To mention some of the ways in which bank operations are regulated.

4. To explain how the Board of Governors of the Federal Reserve System exercises a measure of control over the nation's money supply.

Commercial banking in this country is subject to more forms of external regulation than in any other country in the world. Our regulatory system is far more complicated than that of other countries, for a number of different regulatory agencies are involved and, since the lines of authority between some of the agencies have not been precisely drawn, they sometimes overlap.

It is somewhat paradoxical to consider that a country that prized freedom of enterprise so intensely should eventually find itself with a system of banking regulation more complex than that of other nations that did not or could not share our vigorous quest for freedom. It was precisely the spirit and vigorous pursuit of free enterprise that led to the present somewhat unwieldy structure. As our history of banking demonstrates, external control at the federal level was always strongly resisted, and the more drastic banking legislation usually resulted from a major crisis of some kind. In each case a certain degree of compromise was necessary. Those who wanted freedom got at least a little of it, while those who favored strict controls got a little more each time. Thus there was a little "give" in each new piece of legislation. The National Banking Act did not insist that every bank had to have a national charter; the Federal Reserve Act did not insist that all banks had to join the system; and the 1933 Banking Act did not require that all banks be federally insured. The freedom of choice on the part of individual bankers created different categories of banks and, naturally, there had to be an agency with responsibility for each category.

The regulatory agencies at the federal level are the Office of the Comptroller of the Currency, the Federal Reserve System, and the Federal Deposit Insurance Corporation. At the state level there is the state department of banking.

The categories and the agencies exercising some degree of regulatory control over the banks in each category are:

National banks. National banks are chartered and directly supervised by the Office of the Comptroller of the Currency. Since they must be members of the Federal Reserve System, they are also subject to the regulations of the district Federal Reserve bank and the regulations of the Board of Governors. National banks must also be federally insured and thus are subject also to the regulations of the Federal Deposit Insurance Corporation.

State member banks. State member banks are chartered by and subject to state laws and the regulations of the state banking department. Since these banks have chosen to become members of the Federal Reserve System, they are also subject to regulations of their district Federal Reserve bank and the regulations of the Board of Governors. Since all members banks are required to participate in federal deposit insurance, they are also subject to regulations of the Federal Deposit Insurance Corporation.

State nonmember banks. State nonmember banks are chartered by and are subject to state laws and regulations of the state banking department. They need not be insured, but if they are, they are subject to the regulations of the Federal Deposit Insurance Corporation. A nonmember, noninsured bank is subject only to state laws and regulations of the state banking department.

The regulatory controls listed here refer only to *banking* regulatory agencies. Banks in all categories are subject to regulations of certain nonbanking agencies, which will be discussed later.

Bank Charters

External control of banks begins naturally enough at the beginning. Persons wishing to enter the commercial banking business have the choice of applying for either a federal charter or a state charter.

Those applying for a federal charter are required to file an "Application to Organize a National Bank" with the Regional Administrator of National Banks (a branch of the Office of the Comptroller of the Currency) of the area in which the bank will be situated. The application is then investigated thoroughly, and the following questions are considered:

1. Is the proposed amount of capital adequate?
2. What are the prospects for profitable operation?
3. Is the proposed management capable and of good character?
4. Does the community really need another bank?

Since a national charter automatically carries with it membership in the Federal Reserve System and the Federal Deposit Insurance Corporation, the Comptroller asks these two agencies for their recommendations with respect to the application. The Comptroller of the Currency makes the final decision and issues the charter only when convinced that the proposed bank will be entirely safe and soundly managed.

Applications for state charters are made to the department or division of the state government charged with responsibility for banking institutions within its borders. Although the chartering requirements of the several states vary considerably, any variation is rarely significant, except in the unlikely situation where a new state bank decides to forego the benefits of federal deposit insurance, in which case only the requirements of the state's banking laws would have to be met. While the Federal Reserve System and the FDIC are not chartering agencies, they do have the authority to approve or reject applications for participation in their respective organizations. In arriving at a decision both agencies consider substantially the same factors as the Comptroller's Office does in granting a new federal charter, and they are not necessarily bound by the provisions of the laws of the state involved. Thus, for all practical purposes, it can be said that the requirements for both state and federal charters are much the same.

Once a bank receives its charter and commences to do business, it will become acutely conscious of the external controls—practically on a day-to-day basis.

Financial Reports

The most basic regulatory tool, perhaps, is the authority to require the filing of detailed financial reports at regular and sometimes irregular intervals. The principal reports are the Report of Condition (a balance sheet) and the Report of Income (an income statement). At the federal level, the Comptroller of the Currency obtains these reports from national banks; the Federal Reserve from state-chartered member banks; and the FDIC from insured but nonmember state banks. The three federal agencies have collaborated in the design of the report forms so that the data received by each agency are comparable with those received by the other agencies.

In order to prevent "window dressing" by banks in anticipation of a report date, the Report of Condition may be called for at any time, and may require balance sheet information as of a date prior to the time of the call. *Call reports,* as they are commonly known, are made four times a year. Although not required to, the federal agencies usually call for a Report of Condition as of June 30 and December 31 of each year (or as of the last business day of those two months) for statistical purposes. However, the other two reports usually contain an element of surprise. They are made either before or after the end of the first and third calendar quarters and call for a report as of a date prior to the date on which the call is announced.

For their own purposes, state banking authorities also issue call reports which invariably are timed to coincide with the federal agency reports.

Bank Examinations

One of the chief purposes of bank examinations is to assemble and analyze facts that will reveal a bank's true financial condition. Bank examinations are never announced in advance, and in this case the usual financial reports are prepared in the examiner's presence; the examiner ensures that the financial data are accurately transcribed from the bank's books.

At first glance, the examining authority of the three federal agencies presents a confusing picture of overlapping activity. For example, national banks are subject to examination by the Comptroller's Office. But national banks are also members of the Federal Reserve System and therefore are also subject to examination by the district Federal Reserve bank. Furthermore, all national banks must be insured by FDIC, and that agency—with some limitations—has the authority to examine any insured bank. Fortunately the three agencies have cooperated by working out a mutually satisfactory arrangement that provides for a relatively free exchange of information between them and avoids unnecessary duplication of examining effort. As a result, the Federal Reserve banks limit their examinations to state-chartered member banks, and the FDIC examines only those insured banks that are not members of the Federal Reserve System.

In the same vein, the federal agencies that examine state-chartered banks have cooperated with state bank examiners to avoid the trouble and inconvenience to banks that would result from frequent, separately conducted examinations. In many cases, the federal and state examiners work together to produce a joint report. If this is not possible, they schedule examinations so that both can work in a bank at the same time, even though they prepare and sign separate reports.

The purpose of bank examinations is by no means limited to analysis and appraisal of financial reports. Examiners also appraise the quality and effectiveness of management; they appraise the quality of loans and investments; they comment on the adequacy of the bank's capital, its liquidity position, and its operating performance. And, of course, examiners make sure that all statutory and regulatory provisions that apply to the bank's operation are being properly observed.

The above comments should make clear the difference between a bank examiner and an internal bank auditor. While the authority conferred on an auditor may vary considerably among different banks, it is generally limited to verification and does not include appraisals. For instance, an auditor verifies the total of loans listed in the general ledger, makes sure that the bank has notes or valid debt obligations for all loans, and by direct verification with borrowers may determine that all obligations are genuine. But he is rarely if ever authorized to second-guess the lending officers by appraising the quality of the credits.

Similarly, the auditor verifies the amount and the existence of all bank investments and determines that the bank has clear and clean title thereto; but he does not review the work of the investment division by appraising the quality or the appropriateness of the bank's investments. This is not to say that the auditor in his reports to the board of directors would not or should not comment on such functions, but this would be done only in extremely extenuating circumstances. Thus, in general, the bank examiner is more an appraiser than a verifier, while the opposite is true of the auditor.

Regulation of Banking Operations

Banking operations are regulated to some extent by statutes but mostly by regulations established by the agencies under the authority given them by the law.

The Banking Act of 1933 itself, for example, prohibited banks from paying interest on demand deposits, required banks to divest themselves of security affiliates, and prohibited them from otherwise engaging in the underwriting and distribution of securities, except for obligations of the United States and its instrumentalities and the general obligations of states and their political subdivisions. In addition, the Act prohibited interlocking directorates between banks and security houses.

On the other hand, the 1933 Act gave to the Board of Governors the power to regulate interest rates on savings and time deposits, to define such accounts, and to limit their availability to certain classes of depositors. In general, profit-making organizations are not permitted to open savings accounts; however, they can enter into contracts to open interest-bearing time accounts under more strict rules with respect to withdrawing such deposits than those applicable to savings accounts.

There are also regulations governing bank lending activities, most of them designed to prevent banks from indulging in unsound banking practices. For instance, to avoid an undue concentration of risk, all banks are limited as to the size of loans that they make to any one borrower. Although there are variations, the usual limit is 10 percent of the bank's combined capital and surplus accounts. Most banks are also restricted as to the size and maturity of real estate loans. In some cases the aggregate amount of real estate loans may not exceed a certain percentage of a bank's savings deposits. With the objective of controlling the use of bank credit for stock market speculation, the Board of Governors regulates the amount banks can lend on stock market collateral when the proceeds are to be used for the purpose of purchasing or carrying securities listed on a national exchange as well as certain unlisted securities.

With respect to investments, both national banks and federally-regulated state banks are limited to the purchase of debt obligations for investment purposes and are prohibited from including equity issues (shares of stock representing ownership) in their investment portfolios. This rule does not prevent a bank from owning all or a controlling interest in the stock of a legally permitted subsidiary corporation. But where a bank acquires equity shares in connection with the settlement of a defaulted loan, for example, it is obliged to dispose of such shares within a reasonable length of time.

Banks are also required to observe certain other statutes, such as the Truth-in-Lending and the Fair Credit Reporting Acts, which apply also to other lenders and organizations supplying credit information. In addition, there are other federal bodies not directly concerned with banking whose regulations in some measure may restrict banking practices, such as the Federal Trade Commission, the Department of Health, Education and Welfare, the Department of Labor, and the Department of Housing and Urban Development.

The Department of Justice has a measure of control over banks wherever there are indications of monopolistic tendencies, anticompetiveness, or combinations in restraint of trade. The Securities and Exchange Commission has jurisdiction over any corporation that issues and sells securities to the public, including banks and bank holding companies.

While no attempt has been made to spell out all of the many regulatory provisions that tend to restrict or control banking operations and practices, the foregoing should provide a general idea of the expansive scope and degree of federal regulation.

Regulating the Volume of Bank Credit

There is one other area of regulatory control that goes beyond concern with the soundness of individual banks or the propriety of their operations. Congress has given to the Board of Governors of the Federal Reserve System the responsibility for managing the nation's money supply. The Board's activities in discharging this responsibility have a definite effect on the abilty of banks to make loans.

Money is much like fire. Under control it is very useful, but running wild, it can do great harm. Who gets money and how they spend it is determined by the American free-enterprise system, in which millions of people make their own decisions. The Federal Reserve deals in totals only; it attempts to make sure that the overall amount of money in circulation is about right. Too much money can make prices rise; too little money can cause recession and unemployment.

When banks make loans they create money and add to the total money supply. In order to exercise control over the extension of bank credit and thus the amount of money banks create, the Board of Governors must take steps that affect the ability of banks to make loans.

The Federal Reserve System has the power to create reserves and pump them into the banking system. This action enables banks to make more loans if they wish to. Or the Federal Reserve can withdraw reserves from the banking system and cause banks to refrain from making new loans or even to reduce the volume of existing loans.

The Board of Governors accomplishes its purposes by means of what are called the three "tools of monetary management." They are:

1. *Open Market Operations.* The System owns huge amounts of United States government securities. These securities draw interest, and thus the Federal Reserve obtains the income to finance its various functions. At any time the System can buy more securities or sell some of

those it has on hand. Transactions are made in the open market in New York, which gives this tool its name. The Open Market Committee makes the basic decisions and directs the Federal Reserve Bank of New York to execute them.

When securities are sold by the Reserve bank, they leave its vaults and go into the hands of private owners. When the purchasers pay for the securities, the checks they draw have the effect of reducing the reserve accounts of the banks on which the checks are drawn. In other words, the Federal Reserve has exchanged the securities for cash which comes out of bank reserves, and with less reserves, the banking system can make fewer loans. The Open Market Committee generally decides to sell securities because it wants to reduce bank credit, normally at a time when there seems to be too much spending and prices are rising.

When the Federal Reserve Bank of New York buys government securities, the dealer who sells the securities deposits the check representing the proceeds in his bank. The bank puts these funds in its reserve account, and with this increase in its reserves, the bank can make more loans. The Committee generally buys securities because it feels that there is not enough spending in the market for goods and services.

2. *The Discount Rate.* The Federal Reserve banks lend reserves to member banks and charge interest on these loans, called the discount rate. The discount rate is the second tool of monetary management. When the Federal Reserve wants to encourage banks to borrow reserves (and thus be able to make more loans), it lowers the discount rate, thus making it less costly for a bank to add to its reserve. On the other hand, should the Federal Reserve want to discourage bank borrowing, it raises the discount rate. The directors of each Reserve bank set their own rate, which must be approved by the Board of Governors of the Federal Reserve System.

3. *Reserve Requirements.* Changing reserve requirements is the third method by which the System may influence bank reserves. The Federal Reserve can require that member banks keep a higher or lower percentage of reserves against their deposits. Suppose the reserve requirement is 20 percent, meaning that banks must keep $20 of reserves for each $100 of deposits. If the System lowers the reserve requirement to 10 percent, the same $20 of reserves will now support $200 of deposits, and since loans create deposits, banks can make more loans. The Federal Reserve lowers the required reserve percentage when it wants to increase spending and raises the percentage when it wants to cut down on spending.

It would seem that the use of these three tools of monetary management would make it relatively easy to produce precise increases or decreases in money supply, as desired. But the problems faced by the

Board of Governors are much more complex, since the process of regulating money supply also requires the ability to forecast rather accurately certain actions taken independently by the private sector.

For example, there are several ways in which money supply can be defined, depending on which components are included in any particular definition. The most commonly used indicator of the volume of money supply is a relatively narrow definition that includes only private demand deposits and coin and currency in circulation.

In this definition, savings and time deposits are excluded. Therefore, if the Board of Governors fails to anticipate an unusual shift of funds from demand deposits to savings deposits (or vice versa), a planned change in the volume of money supply might be completely negated.

Furthermore, when commercial banks make loans they create new money, which adds to the volume of money supply. Conversely, when borrowers repay commercial bank loans, the volume of money supply decreases. So the Board of Governors must also be able to forecast and take into consideration the future behavior of those who borrow from banks.

Nevertheless, despite these and other complicating factors, it is possible, over a period of time, to exercise rather effective control.

It is clear that this important responsibility of the Board of Governors must be discharged in the interest of the economic health of the nation as a whole rather than in the interest of the banking system. It is equally clear that the power to manipulate bank reserves by the methods described exerts a powerful influence on the activities of individual banks.

The regulation of commercial banking in this country is admittedly complicated. But the major complications exist more through a desire to give banks a degree of freedom of choice than because of an attempt to inhibit their activities. The fact that banks can choose for themselves whether they want a federal charter or a state charter, whether they want to join the Federal Reserve System or not, and whether they want to quality for deposit insurance or not, accounts for the several overlapping regulatory agencies.

In addition to the regulation of individual banks, the banking system as a whole must also be controlled to some extent because of the fact that commercial bank lending and investing *creates* money. Obviously, the national interest requires some control over the nation's money supply, but the exercise of such control affects the ability of banks to make loans and investments.

Questions Based on This Chapter:

1. Name the principal federal agencies that regulate the nation's banks.

2. In what respects do the responsibilities of bank examiners differ from those of internal auditors?

3. Identify at least three nonbanking federal agencies that exercise a degree of control over banks.

4. What are the three tools of monetary management employed by the Board of Governors of the Federal Reserve System? How are they used to affect the volume of money supply, and how do they affect bank operations?

Chapter 22

Internal Controls

Purposes of This Chapter:

1. *To classify and describe the various types of internal controls.*
2. *To discuss the three most important principles of audit control.*
3. *To describe briefly the general features of bank insurance programs.*
4. *To emphasize the importance of personnel training as a factor in loss prevention.*

Banks are known as quasi-public institutions. They fall somewhere between purely public utilities and completely private institutions. Unlike a public utility, a bank does not acquire a monopoly by franchise; on the contrary, competition is a very important factor in banking. Nevertheless, banks do not and should not enjoy the same degree of complete freedom of action as other segments of private enterprise. The availability and continuity of complete banking services is of tremendous importance to every individual and every community in the country, because banks are the arteries through which flows the economic and financial lifeblood of the nation. Banks are also the custodians of much of the liquid wealth of the people and the medium through which commonplace but vital everyday business affairs are transacted. For these reasons a considerable degree of external control is exercised over banking by regulatory authorities created by banking laws on both the federal and state levels. But laws, regulations, and bank examinations are only the safety valves. A safe and sound banking system must be effectively controlled and policed from within.

The primary responsibility for internal controls rests with the board of directors of a bank. This responsibility is defined by statute and by common law. Directors are charged with the responsibility for prudent and positive action with respect to the affairs of the bank, including the custody and protection of depositors' funds. To discharge this responsibility they must actually direct the affairs of the bank. The directors cannot perform in a perfunctory manner, following the path of least resistance, for they are responsible not only for improper action, but also for failure to take prudent action when it is required.

The board of directors elects officers and delegates to them the active executive control of the bank. Working together, the board and top management devise, adopt, and constantly revise policies designed to create a sound organization in a healthy atmosphere. The soundness of the organization depends to a considerable extent on the quality and effectiveness of its internal controls.

Obviously the board of directors can do little more than *provide* for an efficient system of controls. The board must delegate to others the maintenance of controls and the constant checking necessary to ensure that the controls are faithfully observed and are effective. The board may delegate this responsibility and authority, but it cannot delegate its accountability.

In like manner, although senior management of a bank is more actively engaged in the daily operation of the bank than are members of the board, it too must delegate to others responsibility for internal controls. It cannot be expected that the president of the bank should personally wind the time clocks and close the vault door each night. Internal controls play such a vital part in the daily operation of so many departments and divisions of the bank that practically everyone—junior officers, department heads, supervisors, and operating personnel—must share some of the responsibility for the safe operation of the institution.

Internal controls cover a much wider area than is generally realized. They involve every conceivable means of protecting the bank from losses, whether they be caused by the robbery, larceny, and fraud from without, or by faulty management, embezzlement, inefficiency, carelessness, or thoughtlessness within the organization. They range from broad management policies to such simple routine procedures as locking important filing cabinets. They are the product of many years of experience in banking and business that have pinpointed an ever increasing number of areas of exposure to loss, as the size and complexity of our commercial organizations have increased.

In general terms, internal controls may be roughly classified as follows:

1. Managerial policies
2. Operating safeguards
3. Efficiency controls
4. Audit control
5. Security standards and devices
6. Insurance
7. Personnel training

Managerial Policies

As indicated earlier, a sound system of internal controls must start from the top. The best protection a bank (and its depositors) can have is a well-organized, thoroughly trained, efficient, and competent staff of employees. This is an elusive goal, but management policies can do a great deal toward developing an atmosphere where all employees know their jobs, are aware of their responsibilities, and take pride in their work. Sound personnel policies constitute the best insurance against poor morale, which leads to dissatisfaction, unrest, sloppy performance, and even dishonesty. Hiring policy must be designed to ensure high standards of employment while offering equal opportunity to all qualified applicants. Salary administration and promotion policies must be fair and equitable. A policy with respect to employee loans should be accompanied by positive steps to encourage discussion of financial problems with superiors.

Managerial policies reach in other directions too; in fact, they can support and make more effective all other areas of internal controls.

Operating Safeguards

Operating safeguards are often based on definite management policies and are primarily designed as loss prevention measures.

All employees tend to fall into routine habits in the handling of their daily tasks. A well-managed bank sees that these habits are developed by design rather than by accident, by establishing approved procedures, preferably in writing in the form of procedural manuals.

Rotation of duties is desirable whenever practical, not only as a control measure but also as a means of personnel development. When a person knows that he may be assigned to other duties with little if any prior notice, he is more likely to keep all records current and in proper form. Moreover, bank personnel who become acquainted with as many operations and functions as possible not only provide for flexibility in personnel management, but also are more valuable as individuals.

Segregation of duties (sometimes called separation of duties or division of duties) is an important operating safeguard. Based on the principle that no single transaction within a bank should be fully controlled throughout by one person, segregation of duties provides for at least two persons to be involved in every transaction. Simple illustrations of this internal safeguard are: the person who originates the transaction should not post the related records; a person who handles cash should not also be the bookkeeper.

A closely related control measure is that of providing dual control for certain transactions. In dual control a second person is involved, either to approve the transaction or to act as a party to it. A common illustration is the officer who signs an official check that has been prepared by a teller or clerk. Joint custody provides a more rigid example of dual control: two or more persons must act together in handling bank assets or valuables belonging to customers. For example, reserve cash, portfolio securities, negotiable collateral, and trust securities are invariably placed in the custody of a specified group of persons, at least two of whom must act jointly to handle a transaction. This safeguard is usually enforced by placing such valuables in safe or vault compartments with two combinations, split combinations, or combination and key controls.

Other forms of internal control are available to the control-minded management. The accounting system can be designed to provide clear, traceable records. For instance, all entries can be adequately described when placed on the records. The use of pre-numbered multicopy forms can be incorporated into an effective control device. Through the simple expedient of accounting for all numbers, whether used or voided, a definite degree of transaction control can be established.

Frequently the equipment used in daily operations can be provided with built-in internal controls as, for example, certain types of window-posting machines. In many cases these locked-in controls are accessible only to persons not directly connected with the transactions being processed. In a sense these machine controls are a form of dual control, because a second, disinterested person verifies the volume of transactions processed through the equipment.

Efficiency Controls

Paradoxically, the most effective thief in many banks is not the embezzler, but plain, ordinary operating inefficiencies. Carelessly planned operating methods and poor work habits bleed operating profits on a daily basis, and the cumulative effect over a period of a year can be devastating. Recognizing this fact, an aggressive management will employ some form of systems review, work measurement, and production goals as an integral part of internal control.

Periodic systems reviews should be conducted to ensure that the most modern techniques and equipment are utilized whenever feasible. Work measurement programs for the larger banks can represent a highly scientific undertaking. For the average bank it need not. Careful observation and study of work processes combined with regular recording of work hours and volume data should enable management to arrive at a reasonable standard of the man-hours required to process a given volume of items, transactions, and postings. Comparison of standards with those of other institutions or with average standards is rarely difficult and is extremely helpful. Work measurements and resulting work standards make it possible for management to set reasonable production goals. Once the standards have been adopted, the individual production of personnel can be measured, and overall production of a department can be compared with a production goal established for that department. By reviewing the activity, production records, and work hours consumed by a given department, management can readily determine whether the department's personnel quota is correct or whether a problem of overstaffing or understaffing needs attention.

Another area of efficiency control concerns the daily accumulation of bank records. In the normal course of business, banks generate huge masses of paper records. Many of these records require preservation, since it is often both necessary and desirable to trace and produce evidence of past transactions.

The records produced can also become quite a storage problem. Many banks microfilm some of their records, thus permitting destruction of the more cumbersome original data. In this manner the bank retains relatively small rolls of film and is able to dispense with many storage cartons, freeing considerable floor space for more productive purposes.

The establishment and maintenance of a records control program is essential for every bank. Each individual type of record produced must be analyzed as to its importance, legal aspects, whether it should be retained, and, if so, for how long. This study should result in a definite record retention schedule.

Closely related to records control is *forms control*, which involves periodic updating of all forms used in the bank. With procedures followed similar to those used in records control, each form should be reviewed and analyzed for possible revision or discontinuance. Very frequently forms or extra copies become obsolete because of procedural changes or other factors. In some cases a slight revision or a different weight of paper will make a form more efficient or economical. In a large bank forms control can be an important economic consideration. The elimination of one useless form can pay handsome dividends, when it is considered that the cost of the form itself is relatively minor compared to the time and effort of completing it, processing it, and subsequently storing or destroying it.

Audit Control

Bank auditing as a separate and distinct control function was adopted by the largest banks of this country around the turn of the century. As banks continued to grow in size and complexity, the directors realized that they were not in a position to continue to conduct a periodic personal check into the affairs of the bank, as most boards had been doing. As an alternative in the large banks, boards of directors began to designate a specific person to represent the directors in certain areas of internal control. In effect, this person was a special agent of the board, and in most cases was given the title of "auditor." Naturally, as an agent of the board, the auditor should make his periodic reports directly to the board, rather than through those responsible for daily operations, the managing executives. To assure the auditor the necessary degree of independence, the scope of his activities and his reporting responsibilities should be spelled out in the bylaws of the bank or in a special resolution of the board of directors. It would also be advisable for management, in a policy statement, to express its belief in and support of the reporting procedure.

The auditor should have a thorough understanding of the bank operations and a good working knowledge of accounting. Although it is not necessary that the auditor be a certified public accountant, he should have a thorough understanding of auditing and accounting principles. If the bank's operations are computerized, the auditor must have on his staff a competent assistant or assistants well versed in both computer operations and programming. The auditor himself must be familiar with the special techniques required to audit a computer operation effectively. Obviously, the auditor should not become involved in routine operations. He should not have authority to make or disburse the proceeds of loans, receive deposits, disburse cash, originate entries, or sign official bank checks or official bank drafts.

An auditor has many duties and responsibilities, but primarily he is responsible for determining that all assets and all liabilities are properly stated. He must be satisfied that all income is being accounted for and that the expenses are proper. In addition, as agent of the board, he is in the best position to see that operating safeguards and operating controls, as well as prescribed procedures, are being maintained. An early concept of the auditing function limited it to double-checking entries and maintaining a duplicate set of books. The shortcoming of this narrow approach is that it not only becomes increasingly expensive as the bank grows, but it is entirely ineffective in the broader area of internal control.

It is also the responsibility of the auditor to reply to requests for verification of certain data, such as account balances, items held in safekeeping, and collateral pledged to secure loans. Such inquiries are regularly received from outside accountants, other financial institutions, regulatory agencies, and others entitled to receive such information.

Many small banks are not able to afford the services of a full-time auditor. To have a person spend his entire time auditing the work of 10 or 15 bank officers and employees would be difficult to justify. In a small bank the auditor may perform a number of nonoperating functions, such as the preparation of accounting and supervisory reports, public relations duties, personnel duties, or the purchasing duties provided they are checked by another officer of the bank. Numerous other duties can be performed by the auditor in smaller institutions, but he should not originate entries, control transactions, or post records that require auditing.

The Audit Program

Like everyone else, an auditor can function best when a definite program is planned in advance. It is probably safe to say that every auditor feels that he is faced with a vast expanse of territory to cover and an inadequate staff to do the job properly. Whether or not this feeling is justified in any particular case, the fact remains that opportunities for verifying the accuracy and the manner of handling banking transactions are probably endless. Total verification is not only unnecessary but unthinkable in terms of manpower and expense.

The best that any auditor can do is to plan a definite program designed to provide for periodic audits of the head office and all branches, periodic audits of operating departments and divisions, with particular attention at all times to vital accounting areas. It would be futile to attempt to say specifically how an audit should be conducted. That is for the auditor to decide. More important is that the direction and emphasis of audits should be varied from time to time. A department or branch office audit should not be confined to the verification of numbers and amounts. The auditor should be familiar with procedural controls applicable to the function involved and should see that they are being properly observed.

A chief concern of a bank auditor is the accuracy of the financial reports prepared from the bank's general ledgers. This requires devoting considerable time to the verification of the five categories of accounts found on the general books.

1. Verification of assets. The audit should verify the existence and safety of all bank assets and of all property left in the bank's custody by others. It is essential that the assets be accounted for and that they be reflected on the bank's books at their proper value.

2. Verification of liabilities. The audit of liabilities should include all liabilities whether real or contingent and, in either case, should determine that they are properly reflected on the bank's records.

3. Verification of income. All items of income should be verified and proved to the various income accounts of the bank. The audit should also determine that the bank has received all the income to which it is entitled and that such income is reflected in the accounting records.

4. Verification of expense. All expenses incurred should be verified. The auditor should make certain that they are paid and distributed to their proper designations and captions in the accounting records, that they are properly authorized and are made for legitimate purposes, that value is received therefor, and that funds are properly disbursed and are paid to the proper parties.

5. Verification of net worth. The net worth of the bank should be proved by verifying the fact that the capital accounts, including capital stock, surplus, undivided profits, and reserves are properly stated and that proper increases, decreases, and allocations have been made.

Many effective techniques are employed to verify the accuracy of accounting records without undertaking the laborious task of checking or duplicating every single transaction. Generally speaking, verification audits within a bank fall into three categories: statement of condition audits, spot audits, and continuous audits. The latter two verification audits are often used in conjunction with the first.

1. Statement of condition audits. Statement of condition audits consist of verifying the assets and liabilities and proving net worth as of one certain day. This type of audit is used by the examining authorities and occasionally by the auditing staff.

2. Spot audits. A spot audit is a method of verifying an account by testing a limited number of posted entries, selected at random. While a spot audit is not a complete audit, it is an effective technique and is commonly used. Naturally there is an element of risk involved, for there is always a chance that incorrect or irregular entries may be over-

looked. However, the development of statistical sampling now enables the auditor to select sample transactions on a mathematical basis, which minimizes the element of risk.

3. Continuous audits. Continuous audits are, as the name indicates, a constant audit of a particular account. The procedure requires the daily audit control of all entries made to these accounts.

Direct Verification

In addition to verification by means of auditing the bank's accounting records, in many instances it is possible to verify accounts by direct contact with the bank's debtors or creditors. This method, known as direct verification, is becoming an increasingly important adjunct to an audit program. After ledger accounts are proved, the auditor prepares a notice that is sent directly to the customer. In the notice the customer is requested to verify his checking or savings account balance. In the case of loans, the customer is requested to verify the loan balance as well as the kind of collateral pledged, if any. The value of this procedure can be appreciated when it is realized that a complete audit of a bank may show no irregularities in the records of the institution, despite the fact that false or manipulated entries have been introduced as posting media.

Auditing and proving the bank's records in conjunction with securing confirmations from customers afford rather convincing proof that the records correctly state the true facts. Although direct verification alone does not afford complete internal control, it deserves an important place in every bank's audit program.

Direct verification notices may be of two types:

1. Positive verification. This type of notice contains a request for the customer's signature and the return of the notice to the auditor, whether or not the data shown agree with the customer's records.

2. Negative verification. This type of notice asks for a response from the bank's customer *only* in the event that the balance or verification shown does not agree with the customer's records.

Naturally, the positive type assures maximum results as it supplies tangible evidence of the correctness of the accounts, but it is much more costly and time-consuming because it is necessary to follow up those who do not reply, for otherwise the superiority of the positive verification over negative verification is lost.

Auditing Principles

Although auditing techniques may vary considerably from bank to bank, depending on the size, complexity, and other characteristics of the institution involved, certain basic audit principles should form the backbone of any audit program. The most important of these principles are (1) independence, (2) control, (3) surprise.

Audit independence is a basic necessity. The auditor should be assured of his freedom to examine anything and everything within the scope of his function, where and when he pleases. Any curtailment of this independence limits the value of the auditor to the organization and renders his program considerably less effective.

Unless the auditor can obtain complete control of the department or function being audited, his work will be of little significant value. Meeting this requirement calls for a high degree of cooperation between the auditing staff and operating personnel because, unless the audit is made after regular working hours, the daily routine of the department or function must be performed with a minimum of inconvenience. Very frequently, the required control is obtained by placing gummed labels or stickers on safes and vaults containing valuables and on files containing the pertinent records. In this manner, the auditor is assured that access thereto must come under the scrutiny of his staff.

To be effective, an audit must come as a complete surprise to the bank personnel involved. An auditor may present his program for an entire year in advance to the board of directors, but his detailed time schedule should be classified top secret and made known to no one except, perhaps, his most trusted assistants. It should be obvious that knowledge of an impending audit by a department or branch would render the entire operation a useless gesture.

Security Standards and Devices

Alarmed by the sharp increase in the number of holdups and burglaries of bank premises, and the coincident escalation of losses sustained, Congress decided that positive action had to be taken and passed the Bank Protection Act of 1968. While this legislation can be considered an external control, in effect it provides guidelines for those responsible for internal control.

The banking fraternity can take little comfort in the well-publicized conditions that led to this particular piece of legislation. Protection, in all of its many aspects, is such an inherent and pervading element of banking that one would be inclined to regard professional bankers as the acknowledged experts in this important area. In view of the shocking statistics, it would be hard to deny that there was a need for the legislation. But the fact that it was necessary might cause some bankers to re-think their priorities.

In essence, the Act establishes "minimum standards with respect to the installation, maintenance and operation of security devices and procedures to discourage robberies, burglaries and larcenies and to assist in the identification and apprehension of persons who commit such acts."

The Act requires the board of directors of each bank to designate an officer or other employee as "security officer" with responsibility not only for the installation, maintenance, and operation of security devices, but also for the development and administration of a security program. The legislation makes it clear that the directors are considered primarily responsible for protection and security. The board, rather than top managing officers, has the duty of supervising and directing the activities of the "security officer," who must put his security program in writing and have it approved by the board of directors.

The security program is specifically required to include such obvious routine duties as:

1. Seeing that devices are tested and kept in working order.
2. Limiting cash kept in branch offices.
3. Limiting cash kept at individual teller stations.
4. Keeping "bait" money at tellers' stations and requiring a second employee to verify the teller's record of denominations, serial numbers, etc.
5. Requiring all currency, negotiable securities and other valuables to be locked in a vault or safe during nonbanking hours.
6. Designating a person or persons to see that security devices are turned on and operating when intended to be in use.
7. Establishing opening and closing routines.

All of these are sound and sensible safeguards, and it is difficult to believe that a majority of bankers was not observing most of them before the Bank Protection Act was passed. Yet the fact that such specifics are included in the legislation offers damaging evidence to the contrary.

The original Act prescribes minimum construction standards and specifications for vaults, safes, and night depository units as well as such devices as surveillance systems and robbery and burglary alarm systems. An amendment to the Act, effective November 1, 1973, added minimum standards for automatic paying and receiving machines.

Insurance

While no bank can afford to be without adequate insurance coverage, this is in the long run the least effective of internal controls. Insurance offers protection against a wide range of losses, but insurance should not be considered an alternative to loss prevention programs.

The real value of insurance lies in the protection it affords against large catastrophic losses. Even the best managed bank faces this contingency—a sizable, perhaps unavoidable loss that, unless covered by adequate insurance, might well in one stroke plunge the bank into insolvency. The use of insurance as a means of recovering the nagging but *relatively* smaller losses due to fraud, embezzlement, petty thievery, and the operations of swindlers, confidence men, and so-called "paper-hangers," can be self-defeating. The more claims made for such losses, the higher the premium rate charged for renewal, due to an experience rating plan used by insurance companies in setting premiums. Wherever feasible, loss prevention programs afford the most effective defense against such losses.

Bankers Blanket Bonds

The most comprehensive insurance available for banks is the especially designed bankers blanket bond, which affords in one policy specific protection in five areas.

- *Fidelity.* This section covers embezzlement and other losses caused by employee dishonesty.
- *Premises.* This section in general covers the loss of property on banking premises through breaking and entering (burglary), holdups (robbery), mysterious disappearance, or vandalism.
- *Loss in Transit.* This clause covers loss of bank or customers' property while in transit, that is, off bank premises.
- *Forgery.* This section covers losses due to forgery or alteration on checks, drafts, notes, and certain other instruments.
- *Forgery.* This separate section covers losses due to forged or fraudulent securities.

The above is a very brief description of the general features and should not be taken as a complete description of this form of multi-peril insurance especially designed for banks, nor does it cover available optional endorsements for other types of losses. However, it does indicate the principal areas in which a bank may be exposed to sizable losses.

There are many areas where banks can obtain and should have insurance coverage. For instance, the bank that offers safe deposit services should have adequate protection against both successful suits alleging unauthorized withdrawal of contents, and losses due to claims following a successful burglary and rifling of the safe deposit boxes. Such losses are generally wholly or partially excluded in the standard blanket bonds, and protection is available through separate insurance policies. Coverage is generally limited to losses which the insured is *legally obligated* to pay. Banks operating trust departments might wish to consider an "Errors and Omissions" policy, or insurable risks in connection with real estate handled in the administration of trusts and estates, or a fiduciary public liability policy.

Other specific risks which can be covered are too numerous to mention. Bankers should seek competent counsel to aid in the development of a comprehensive insurance program. The Insurance and Protection Division of the American Bankers Association is a source of very helpful information.

The Deductible Clause

Most casualty insurance policies (including Bankers Blanket Bonds) may contain what is called a *deductible clause,* the purpose of which is to spare the insurance company (and the insured) the expense involved in handling and processing a huge volume of trifling claims. If a policy does not contain such a clause, the insured theoretically could claim reimbursement for any recoverable loss even in an amount as low as *one dollar.* On the other hand, if the policy provides for a deductible of $1,000, then the insured would be required to absorb losses resulting *from any one incident* up to that amount. For instance, if a bank sustained a coverable loss of $1,500, it would be obliged to absorb the first $1,000 of the loss, and could claim only the excess ($500) over the deductible from the insurance company.

There is reason to believe that first dollar coverage (no deductible clause) may soon become unavailable in Blanket Bonds for the larger banks. Loss experience in recent years has not been favorable. Indeed, for a while some major carriers were reluctant to renew or write new Bankers Blanket Bonds. In many metropolitan areas, larger banks are compelled to accept a substantial deductible clause, ranging from a few thousand dollars to as much as $1,000,000, depending on the size of the bank.

A deductible clause is, of course, a form of self-insurance. In areas where a bank is self-insured, whether by choice or of necessity, an effective loss prevention program is of prime importance.

Personnel Training

Loss prevention programs depend on the competence and cooperation of a well-trained bank staff. There are some areas of bank exposure (holdup and burglary, for instance) where bank employees are in a rather helpless position. They cannot and should not be expected to risk their lives when facing a bandit's gun, and they are usually not involved in burglaries. But there are other areas of exposure where the competence and good judgment of an employee are often deciding factors. In recent years, fraudulent crimes perpetrated by swindlers, confidence men, imposters, and forgers ("paper-hangers") have soared to the extent that losses suffered by banks and merchants alike are almost unbelievable. Statistics indicate that banks have suffered larger losses through these activities than through the *combined losses* of the more violent crimes of holdups, robberies, and burglaries added together.

Many bank employees, particularly tellers and platform personnel, personally confront such swindlers regularly in the course of discharging their responsibilities. The crook is usually intelligent, resourceful, experienced, and well-acquainted with banking procedures. It is neither sensible nor fair to expect inadequately trained employees to face such formidable opponents.

In former days banks did not have formal training programs, and they relied on years of experience to qualify personnel for teller or platform assignments. It was not uncommon for some banks to require ten years of clerical experience before allowing a person to serve at a teller's station. Today, banks have formal training programs, improved methods and techniques such as programmed instruction, and yet the facts indicate that in certain respects, formal training programs are not producing the desired result. In most cases, the fault lies in the training program rather than in the trainee. At any rate, the swindler seems to be winning the battle of wits.

Some banks have attempted to meet this situation by "de-skilling" certain positions involving public contact, as an example, severely limiting the authority of tellers to carry through any but strictly routine transactions. Whether this is the proper solution remains to be seen, but customer service is bound to suffer to some extent.

In any event, it is difficult to see how a bank can go wrong in spending much time and effort in the training of its personnel. Banking is a highly technical business, and many staff positions are very demanding in terms of experience, mature judgement, and knowledge of financial transactions. Moreover, the opportunities for education and training are better than ever. In addition to in-house programs, there are the many courses offered by the American Institute of Banking, state banking schools, workshops, seminars, and discussion groups.

In the final analysis, a well-trained, competent staff is the best insurance against all kinds of losses, including many not covered by insurance policies. The "image" that many customers have of their bank is the image projected by personnel, through personal contact and through contacts made via telephone or correspondence. There is no insurance available that covers the cost or the difficulty of repairing a fractured image.

Internal controls are of special importance to the banking industry, mainly because banks handle money, which for the most part, belongs to the public.

Primary responsibility for internal controls rests with the board of directors, but of necessity, the supervisory staff of the bank must share some of the responsibility. However, this does not relieve the board of its duty to provide for an efficient program of internal control and to delegate such authority and responsibility as may be necesary to see that the controls are observed and are effectively handled.

Those to whom significant areas of responsibility are assigned, such as auditors and security officers, should be required to make periodic reports directly to the board of directors.

It is also the responsibility of the board to see that the bank has an adequate insurance program, which essentially is a means of controlling the devastating effects of unpredictable and unforeseen catastrophies. But, insurance programs should be supplemented with well-planned loss prevention programs, in which personnel training plays a vital role.

Questions Based on This Chapter:

1. In your own words, explain why a safe and sound banking system must be controlled and policed from within.

2. Name and briefly describe at least three specific areas of internal control.

3. What are the three most important principles of an audit program?

4. Why is it considered unrewarding for a bank to rely on insurance as protection against relatively small petty losses, and what alternative is available?

Chapter 23

Banking
and
Public Services

Purposes of This Chapter:

1. To discuss the human side of the banking business.

2. To stress the particularly close relationship between the banker and his customers and the community at large.

3. To describe the attractive and challenging aspects of a banking career.

4. To mention some of the essential qualifications of a banker.

Among those who read this last chapter, there are many who are seriously interested in a banking career and some who are destined to become top managing executives in individual banks and perhaps national leaders in the banking industry. It is to those serious students that this chapter is dedicated.

The preceding pages have been largely devoted to the everyday operating problems that banks face and the manner in which they discharge their obligations in the *world of practical finance*. But careerminded people must be exposed to another extremely important view of banking. This chapter deals with the problems banks encounter and the manner in which they must discharge their obligations in *a world of human beings.*

Modern society is a highly complex organism that operates smoothly only when all of its component parts are functioning properly. One of the most important components of a well-organized society is a sound banking system, and the foremost duty of banks and bankers is to perform vital banking services with the greatest possible degree of competence. Not to be ignored, however, is the fact that every member of society—individuals and business organizations alike—has a fundamental duty to contribute to society as well as to extract a living from it. Thus all elements of society, including banks and bankers, must also be keenly aware of their social as well as their economic responsibilities.

It is important to place these two duties in proper perspective, for both are important and to some extent interdependent. The bank that is poorly managed, that indulges in unsound practices, that performs its basic functions and renders its essential services carelessly and inaccurately, and that is forever explaining why something or other went wrong, is not likely to be a respected influence in its community. It is hoped that the preceding pages have amply demonstrated the importance of a sound and efficient banking system and, conversely, the hazards inherent in irresponsible or careless banking. Only by first achieving professional competence can a bank effectively discharge its social obligations. But a bank must work through people; thus it is the individuals who aspire to positions of responsibility in our nation's banks who must constantly strive for professional excellence.

A banker can and should be a trusted confidant, an advisor, and a respected leader in the community. But respect does not automatically go with the position—it must be earned. Therefore the first duty of all bank employees is to learn all they can about their jobs, their bank, and the services it renders. Whether a bank is friendly, useful, and respected depends on its performance—the job done by the entire staff in and out of banking hours.

On the other hand, no bank can afford to direct all of its thinking inwardly, completely disregarding any considerations of the people and the community that provide the very reason for its existence. An intelligent banker knows that his bank cannot prosper in a community that is stagnant or slowly deteriorating for lack of interest or leadership. If a bank is to grow and develop, it must do its best to see that the community it serves grows and develops. The bank must take an interest in community problems and offer its fair share of financial support in efforts to solve those problems.

The Banker and Bank Customers

A very close relationship frequently exists between a bank and its depositors. The nature of banking is such that it cannot very well thrive on transient trade. The best relationships between banks and their customers, from the standpoint of both, are those of long duration. Ranking high among the afflictions that plague the average individual and household are those resulting from financial mismangement, which accounts for a sizeable proportion of the incredibly long annual list of personal as well as business bankruptcies.

The banker who knows his customers is usually well aware of their financial problems. If they need help, he is in an excellent position to advise them and aid them in achieving the peace of mind that springs from successful financial management. In the field of finance, the banker can be an indispensable counselor, a source of strength, and, whenever possible, of practical assistance to those experiencing financial difficulties. When people have confidence in and respect for a banker, they seek advice on many matters beyond merely asking how to indorse a check. People often want and need help on family budgeting; they may wonder whether to buy a new home, and how much they can afford to pay for it; whether they should pay off an existing mortgage or let it run to maturity; how to invest safely money set aside for the education of children; or, in applying for a loan, they may ask whether or not they should borrow for the purpose intended. A good banker looks at a loan from the borrower's point of view as well as from that of the bank and will never make a loan that would jeopardize the financial well-being of his customer, however well-protected the bank may be.

The Banker and the Community

The banker's relationship to the community is no less close. He knows its people, its businesses, its strengths and weaknesses, its beauties and where they exist, its ugly spots. Here, too, the banker can be a tower of strength, a confidant, an advisor, and an ever-present help in many ways. Indeed, the community aspect of banking holds the greatest appeal for many bankers and deserves the thoughtful consideration of every student of banking.

Opportunities for community service are often created by the banker's familiarity with money matters. A banker is frequently called upon to serve as treasurer of the community fund or other charitable or civic organizations. He may be a member of the school board, the local chamber of commerce, or the municipal finance committee.

The alert banker constantly searches for new ways to serve people, not only through routine banking services but also through constructive community activities. Sometimes he may go to the local school to talk to the senior class about the fundamentals of banking or economics or the merits of thrift. He might also talk about good citizenship or the advantages of continuing one's education.

Banks frequently sponsor junior achievement companies that teach young people the ways of the business world. The banker-counselor shows the young industrialists how to keep accounts and how to merchandise their product. Many banks sponsor forums for young businessmen, women, investors, or pensioners and retirees. A bank officer may talk at these sessions, or the bank may obtain outside specialists in a particular area to address such a gathering.

In addition to such educational efforts, a bank must also share in the more pressing social problems of the community. It must be involved in housing problems, in the rehabilitation of slum areas, if any exist, in educational and training programs for the underprivileged; in short, it must be concerned with any efforts to improve the quality of life in the community. The bank that fails to fulfill its social responsibilities also fails to reach its own maximum potential, not only in service but also in profits.

Obviously there are countless ways in which to engage in community activities, but it should be equally obvious that no single bank or banker can effectively take an active interest in everything. Each bank must decide for itself the most productive area for its efforts.

The Banker and the Nation

The commercial banking system in the United States is composed of more than 14,000 separate and independent banks. The contribution the banking system as a whole makes to the larger community of the nation is just as important as the contribution the individual bank makes to the local community it serves. Each individual bank is an integral part of the banking system, and it has an obligation to act in the best interests of the system, just as any member of a group must respect the interests of the whole. Nevertheless, America's banks have a considerable degree of independence and they cannot nor would they be permitted to act collectively in a manner that could be construed as anticompetitive or in restraint of trade. Americans have long been proud of the fact that our banking system is basically a *competitive free enterprise* system.

The system itself has being; it takes on a definite form, shape, and substance and, indeed, possesses a voice. This entity has been created through the formation of national and statewide bankers associations, which offer their members an opportunity for a unified approach to mutual problems and an active role in shaping the concepts and principles of the industry as a whole.

Bankers associations, at the state or national level, have become responsible for representing the industry when the enactment of banking laws is being considered. Association spokesmen confer with legislators in an attempt to create laws and regulations that will serve the public but which at the same time will strengthen rather than weaken the effectiveness of the banking system.

Technological Advancement

No less important than technological research and development itself is the necessary industry-wide coordination of these efforts. Whenever the individual parts of an entity are interdependent, a minimum level of uniformity is necessary to ensure coordinated operation. Imagine the chaos that would have resulted if all banks had installed automatic sorter-reader equipment, but each individual bank had decided to choose its own style of magnetic ink characters. The work of one bank would have been hopelessly incompatible with that of any other, and countless hours of experimentation in the fascinating field of automation would have ended in a costly and fruitless fiasco.

During the past few years the development of more sophisticated machinery and equipment has been a source of pride to the banking industry. Yet these results were not the work of one man or one bank or one manufacturer; they were the product of the combined efforts of many interested people working together in search of a common solution.

Not all recent improvements in operational functions have been related to machinery. Among other studies, improved check clearing, systems studies, work flow management, and personnel administration have been scrutinized by banking associations, and the resulting benefits have been made available to all banks.

The achievements of industry associations become more understandable when consideration is given to the tremendous resources represented by the members as a group. Association contacts reveal that most problems are mutual problems. When an individual bank combines its particular talents with the complementary talents of other banks, satisfactory solutions are much more readily obtained. Joint efforts produce mutual benefits that far exceed anything that could be accomplished on an individual basis.

A Banking Career

Banking is one of the few occupations generally thought of as being a "profession" that does not have any formal educational requirements prerequisite to its practice. One might think, therefore, that banking should be an easy career in which to become established, but quite the opposite is true. Years of on-the-job training and self-education take the place of the formal schooling required in other professions. Anyone who is self-educated knows that this path is more difficult to follow than one in which an academic curriculum is established and well-defined. For instance, this text was prepared for use in only the *first* of a series of courses of study, designed to prepare students for a banking career. Its main purpose is to provide an overall view of the business of banking with the hope that it will stimulate interest in more advanced and specialized courses of study.

The fact is that individual education is a never-ending process. The banker with 20 years of experience will readily confess that something new is learned almost every day. The only difference is that the motivation of an experienced person to find out the what and why of something new must come from within; the need to inquire, to study, and to find out is no longer fired by the need to obtain a passing grade.

American Institute of Banking

As early as 1900 it was realized that the education of a good banker is never-ending. In that year, the establishment of the American Institute of Banking marked the first formalized attempt to improve the professional skills of bankers in this country. From its inauspicious beginning, the Institute has grown until it now has about 140,000 students enrolled each year. The courses offered by the Institute are made available to every employee who works for a bank that is a member or is eligible for membership in the American Bankers Association. Every weeknight of almost every week, the Institute, the school without a campus, offers its services to bankers across the country. Thousands of qualified instructors impart the benefits of their experience to students who use their new knowledge to do a bigger job in a better way.

Graduate Schools

For the student who desires further banking education, graduate schools of banking are conducted at universities across the country. Probably the best known of these schools is The Stonier Graduate School of Banking sponsored by the American Bankers Association at Rutgers University in New Jersey. In addition, the Pacific Coast Banking School at the University of Washington, the Southwestern Graduate School of Banking at Southern Methodist University, the Graduate School of Banking at the University of Wisconsin, and several other graduate schools offer the banker an opportunity for higher education. In addition, there are specialized schools for financial public relations experts, trustmen, auditors and comptrollers, consumer credit personnel, and other specialists.

Also of interest to the banking student is the rich variety of instruction available within many banks. Seminars, lectures, and conferences supplement on-the-job training and in-house American Institute of Banking courses in an increasing number of banks, and some banks regularly send qualified personnel to local colleges and universities for extra study.

Bankers associations are numerous; in fact, there are almost as many varieties of them as there are banking interests, and they function at several geographical levels: National and state organizations, county, district, and regional associations. Many other associations are organized on a functional basis, such as operations, auditing, savings, credits, investments, mortgages, marketing, and public relations. All of these associations contribute materially to increased banking competence and better banking service.

Through banking associations other forms of education are offered that should not be overlooked. Personal contacts and frank discussions of banking theory and practices with bankers from other areas are rewarding experiences. Although these opportunities come mostly to bankers whose experience has advanced them to positions of leadership, the possibilities are there for all. A more extensive review of "organized banking" will increase awareness of the many opportunities available for personal contacts.

The opportunities for education through these organizations are boundless. Many of these associations sponsor their own educational programs. Few enterprises offer wider or more comprehensive opportunities for education, study, and self-development than banking—and for *all* bankers, from the brand new employee to the president of the bank.

The Challenge

There are few fields of human endeavor that can offer as exciting a challenge as does the banking business. Consider the following:

Modern banking is relatively new

Banking is almost as old as the history of mankind, but what a difference between the money-changer that plied his trade on a bench in front of a temple, and the modern full-service bank. Banking in the United States is only 200 years old. Yet the changes that have taken place in that relatively short span have been little short of sensational.

The business of banking is expanding rapidly

Banks are no longer confined to the boundaries of a local community as were the independent unit banks of long ago. No longer does banking serve only the businessman, the industrialist, and the wealthy. Banking services have been brought within the reach of every household and individual. Banking touches on the lives of every man, woman and child in America, whether or not they are direct customers of a bank. Not only has the range of banking services been expanded sharply, but so has the geographic expanse of the markets that the modern bank reaches. To the extent permitted by law, large and small banks alike have dotted the country with branches, while large banks continue to establish branches abroad or purchase interests in foreign banking institutions. The development of bank holding companies has enabled many banks to extend their services to many bank-related areas. Even the unit banks (one-office institutions) that still exist in considerable numbers have expanded the range of their services and the markets they serve.

The business of banking is still developing

Lest anyone think that banking has at last stabilized and will remain for long as it exists today, it should be pointed out that changes now in sight hint at even more drastic changes, perhaps in the near future. The modern check may soon become a relic of the past, as electronic transfer systems now actively considered are developed and placed in operation. The approximately 26-billion checks currently being issued annually will not disappear overnight, but the handwriting is on the wall. The law of negotiable instruments, which is so important today, may lose much of its relevance in days to come. Current banking regulations are certain to be revoked, amended, or replaced with new regulations as the mechanics of money transfers change in the future. The entire complex structure of external regulation may be replaced with a more simplified, better coordinated system. The lines that separate the functions of present financial institutions (commercial banks, savings banks, savings and loan associations, and so forth) grow more fuzzy every day, and undoubtedly these lines will either be sharpened or eliminated altogether in the future.

As we have learned from our own history, novel and drastic changes do not always work out according to plan. Bankers and legislators both will play an important role in shaping the course of our banking and monetary systems in the days ahead. Because of the importance of a sound and efficient banking system to the welfare of the nation, the need for statesman-like qualities in the country's leading bankers is vital. Ill-considered, hasty, and impulsive changes can produce chaotic results. The banking system must be designed to serve the nation and not simply the individual interests of banks or bankers.

Qualifications of a Banker

Not everyone is cut out to be a cowboy or a tightrope walker. Both of these occupations require certain personality traits, certain physical abilities, and certain personal preferences. For the same reasons, not everyone is cut out to be a banker. Most people adapt more easily and more naturally to one type of job than to another.

To be a good banker, a person must be willing to devote many years of his or her life to acquiring certain required skills. Although some individual banking functions—even very technical ones—can be learned in a short time, mastering one or even several of these functions does not make a person a banker.

A good banker must develop a feel for this challenging profession: a special awareness of and a sense of pride in banking's peculiar potential for service both to the individual citizen and to the nation as a whole. The banker must have a firm concept of banking: broad enough to permit him to be receptive to the inevitable changes of the future, but solid enough to give him the courage to resist the temptations that would undermine the nation's financial structure, the soundness of his own institution, or his personal, unique position of trust. The young man on the flying trapeze can afford to be daring. He risks only his own life and limbs. The banker must be more cautious. Excessive daring on his part can jeopardize the welfare of others and violate the confidence and trust placed in him. A good banker must be well aware of the obligations his profession owes to the public at large. He must be more objective and unselfish than most businessmen, because the soundness of his bank and the banking system must always take precedence over the immediate lure of prospective earnings.

In short, a good banker must be more than a businessman, a merchant, or a promoter. He must have the objective qualities of a statesman and a high sense of the ethics of his profession.

To the young man or woman seeking an exciting and challenging career, what field of endeavor offers more? A business deeply involved in human relationships and dedicated to public service, a vibrant force in community life; a business that is ever-changing and challenging, new in many respects, but as old as the history of human association; a business with an unexplored potential; a business that is so vital and essential that our nation's financial well-being depends heavily on its sound and efficient performance.

The challenge is there, the opportunities are abundant. Upon the quality, dedication, and devotion of those who accept the challenge and seize the opportunity depend not only the future of banking, but that of the nation as well.

The selection of a career is probably one of the most important decisions ever faced by most persons. Unfortunately, a poor decision can have permanent and unpleasant effects since the natural inertia of many human beings makes it extremely difficult to correct the error.

In this particular world it is necessary for almost everyone to make some contribution to society in order to "make a living." But how different are the lives of those fortunate enough to find satisfaction and a sense of achievement in what they do, as opposed to those to whom each day promises nothing better than a dreary uninspiring rerun.

If the field of endeavor a person chooses as his life's work, whatever it may be, does not stimulate the imagination, does not challenge one to do today's job well and tomorrow's job better, and fails to engender a feeling of contributing to something important rather than simply taking what one can, then the selection has missed the target.

Banking is an old and honorable profession. It is a vital service industry, since every society desperately needs a sound banking system. A banking career has much to offer—to those willing to dedicate themselves to a profession, those willing to serve people, the community and the nation, those willing to accept responsibility and the challenges of the future. Banking needs people who have the qualifications described in this chapter, and it offers in return what people need most: a satisfying, rewarding, and fulfilling career.

Questions Based on This Chapter

1. Why is it especially necessary for a banker to be concerned with community problems?

2. Describe some of the ways in which bankers can participate effectively in community affairs.

3. Name at least three bankers' schools sponsored by the American Bankers Association.

4. What are some of the essential qualifications of a "good" banker?

Glossary

Acceptance: A time draft (bill of exchange) on the face of which the drawee has written the word "accepted," the date it is payable, usually the place where it is payable, and his signature. Thus an acceptance is an obligation that the drawee has agreed to pay at maturity. After accepting the draft, the drawee is known as the acceptor. *See also* BANK ACCEPTANCE, TRADE ACCEPTANCE and CERTIFIED CHECK.

Accommodation Party: An indorser or comaker who has no direct interest in the instrument, but who indorses or signs it for the purpose of lending his name to a party who is directly at interest.

Account Analysis: The process of determining the profit or loss to a bank in handling a given account for a specific period, by analyzing the activity involved, determining the cost of servicing the account by applying unit and other costs, and comparing such costs with estimated earnings on average investable balances maintained during that period.

Accounts Receivable: The accounts receivable of a business enterprise represent money owed by customers for merchandise or services sold to them on open account, that is, without the giving of a note or other evidence of debt.

Accrual Accounting: The recording of earnings and expenses as they are earned or are incurred, without regard to the actual date of collection or payment.

Accrued Interest: Interest earned but not yet paid or collected. On a bank statement, Accrued Interest Payable represents interest earned by depositors on interest-bearing accounts, but not as yet paid by the bank. Accrued Interest Receivable represents interest earned by the bank on loans, but not as yet collected from the borrowers.

Administrator: A person or an institution appointed by a court to settle an estate when (1) the decedent has left no will; (2) no executor is named in a will; or (3) a named executor is unwilling or unable to serve.

Administrator c.t.a.: An individual or bank appointed to settle a decedent's estate in accordance with terms of the will.

Advice: The term *advice* is applied to several types of forms used in the banking field. Generally speaking, an advice is a written acknowledgement or notification of certain activity with regard to a depositor's relations with a bank. Examples are: credit advice, debit advice, advice of payment, advice of execution, and so forth.

Agent: Any person who acts for another by the authority of the latter. The party granting the authority is known as the principal.

Agency: The relationship between an agent and his principal.

Altered Check: One on which the date, payee, or amount, or which in some other respect has been materially changed. A bank is responsible for paying a check as it is originally drawn; consequently, it pays a check that has been altered at its peril and may be liable to the drawer for any injury suffered thereby.

American Bankers Association: The American Bankers Association (ABA), founded in 1875, is the voice of organized banking. Its purpose is to keep its members abreast of the rapidly changing needs for banking services, to develop and maintain educated and competent personnel for banks, to spread knowledge and understanding of economic problems, and to elevate the standards of bank management and service.

ABA Numerical System: The system of bank numbers whereby each bank in the United States and its territories is provided with an individual identifying number. *See* ABA TRANSIT NUMBER.

ABA Transit Number: A numerical code indicating the name and location of a specific drawee bank under the national numerical system. The transit number has two parts separated by a hyphen: the first part designates the city, state, or territory in which the bank is located, and the second part identifies the particular bank. The transit number appears on checks today as the numerator of a fraction, the denominator of which is the routing symbol.

American Institute of Banking: The American Institute of Banking (A.I.B.), a section of the American Bankers Association, was founded in 1900 for the purpose of providing an educational program for bank employees. Since the turn of the century hundreds of thousands of bankers have taken courses through the Institute. In addition, about 140,000 persons have earned one or more of the certificates awarded by the Institute. No other industry has matched the efforts of the American Bankers Association in the educational developments of career employees. The Institute's activities are carried on through numerous chapters and study groups in many cities and towns. In addition to its regular classes, the Institute conducts correspondence courses. Membership and enrollment is open to employees and officers of ABA member institutions.

Asset: Anything owned by a business or by an individual which has commercial or exchange value. Assets may consist of specific property or of claims against others, in contrast to obligations due to others (liabilities).

Auditor: In banking, an officer of a bank who is in charge of all "audit functions." In most banks he is responsible to and reports directly to the Board of Directors.

Availability Schedule: A schedule of time limits or closing hours for the receipt of deposits of various types of cash items, according to where they are payable and the period of time required before specific items deposited are considered as available funds. Availability schedules are published by Federal Reserve banks and many correspondent banks.

Average Daily Balance: For analysis purposes, the average amount of money kept on deposit by a customer, determined variously by adding all or selected daily balances and dividing by the number of balances taken.

Average Daily Float: That part of the average daily balance considered to be in the process of collection. Many banks use averages to calculate this figure. For instance, if the average collection time for all items (on-us checks, local items, and out-of-town items) is two days, the total of all deposits made is multiplied by 2 and the result divided by the number of days studied, to give an average daily float figure.

Balance Sheet: A detailed listing of assets, liabilities, and equity capital accounts (net worth) showing the financial condition of a company on a given date. Thus, a balance sheet illustrates the accounting equation: assets = liabilities plus net worth. The balance sheet of a bank is generally referred to as *statement of condition.*

Bank Acceptance: A time draft drawn on a bank and accepted by the bank. *See also* ACCEPTANCE.

Bank Check: (Also called cashier's check, treasurer's check, or official check.) A check drawn by a bank on itself. Since drawer and drawee are identical, acceptance is considered automatic and such instruments have been held legally to be promises to pay.

Bank Draft: A check drawn by a bank against funds deposited to its account in another bank.

Bank Examination: An examination conducted by representatives of a federal or state bank supervisory authority, to make certain that a bank is solvent and is operating in conformity with banking laws and sound banking principles.

Bank Examiner: A person who as the representative of a federal or state bank supervisory authority examines the banks under its jurisdiction with respect to their financial condition, management, and policies.

Bank Funds: This term includes all direct bank obligations, such as cashier's checks, treasurer's checks, bank drafts, bank acceptances, certified checks, and negotiable certificates of deposit.

Bank Holding Company: A separate nonbank corporate organization that owns or controls one or more banks.

Bank Statement: A statement of a customer's checking account issued by the bank periodically, usually monthly. It shows the balance at the beginning of the period, all deposits and other credits, and all checks and other debits posted to the account, and the balance at the end of the period. Cancelled checks and debits are usually returned to the depositor with the statement. In many cases, banks also issue statements to savings account depositors. *See* No Passbook Savings.

Bankers Blanket Bond: A broad coverage insurance policy, especially designed for banks, which affords protection against certain hazards to which those engaging in the banking business are particularly exposed, such as embezzlement, burglary, robbery, mysterious disappearance, forgery, and fraud.

Batch: A group of deposits or incoming clearings assembled as a unit for proof purposes. A batch may consist of from 100 to 1,500 checks. The term *block* is also sometimes used.

Bearer: The person in possession of an instrument, document of title, or security payable to bearer or indorsed in blank.

Beneficiary: (1) The person in whose favor a letter of credit is issued. (2) The person who is to receive the proceeds of or benefits accruing under an insurance policy or annuity. (3) A third party who is to receive all or a share of the benefits arising from an arrangement between two other parties, one of whom holds title to money or property in a fiduciary capacity.

Bill of Exchange: *See* Draft.

Bill of Lading: A receipt issued by a common carrier for merchandise to be delivered to a person at some distant point. Bills of lading are issued in two forms: (1) an "order bill of lading," which provides for the delivery of goods to a named person or to his order but only on proper endorsement and surrender of the bill of lading to the carrier or his agents; and (2) a "straight bill of lading," which provides for the delivery of the goods only to the person named in the bill of lading. In this case, the bill of lading may or may not be surrendered, but the carrier or his agents must ensure that the person receiving the goods is actually the person named in the bill.

Board of Governors of the Federal Reserve System: A board of *seven* members appointed by the President of the United States and confirmed by the Senate. The Board of Governors of the Federal Reserve System supervises, coordinates, and formulates monetary policy of the Federal Reserve System, and has regulatory powers with respect to member banks.

Bond: An interest-bearing debt certificate under seal which promises that the issuer (a government, a corporation, or other legal entity) will pay a certain sum of money to the holder of the bond at a specified date. In effect, it is a long-term loan by the bondholder (lender) to the issuer (borrower).

Bond of Indemnity: A written instrument under seal by which the signer, together with his surety or bondsman, guarantees to protect another against loss. In banking, such instruments are often required to protect the bank when (1) a depositor requests that payment be stopped on a certified check; (2) a savings depositor reports a lost passbook and requests issuance of a new one; or (3) any similar situations that might expose the bank to third-party claims. Such an agreement without sureties and not under seal is called an *indemnity agreement.*

Bookkeeping Department: The department or unit of a bank that maintains complete, accurate, and current records of the accounts of all demand depositors. Alternately called *Individual Ledger Department* or *Demand Deposit Accounting Department.*

Branch Bank: A bank that has a head office and one or more branch offices.

Bulk Cash: Rolled or bagged coin or banded currency.

Cable Transfer: The transfer of funds to or from a foreign country through instructions sent by cable.

Call Report: A sworn statement of a bank's condition as of certain dates, submitted in response to demand made by supervisory authorities.

Capital: In an accounting sense, the excess of assets over liabilities. *See* Equity Capital and Capital Obligations.

Capital Funds: Consists of all money the bank has received through the sale of stock (equity capital), or borrowed through the sale of notes or debentures (capital obligations), plus earnings retained in the business.

Capital Loan: A loan, the proceeds of which are invested in capital assets, in contrast to a loan, for example, to purchase merchandise, the sale of which will provide funds to repay the loan.

Capital Obligations: Funds raised through the sale of long-term evidences of debt such as bonds, debentures, or capital notes. *See also* EQUITY CAPITAL.

Cash Basis Accounting: An accounting system in which income and expenses are recorded when actual payment is received or payment is made regardless of when the income is earned or the expense incurred.

Cash Items: Items (commonly checks and other items payable on demand) that a bank accepts for immediate credit to depositors' accounts.

Cash Letter: An interbank transmittal letter that accompanies cash items sent from one bank to another.

Cash Surrender Value: The amount that an insurance company will pay the insured upon the cancellation of a policy.

Cashier's Check: *See* BANK CHECK.

Certificate of Deposit: A formal receipt for funds left with a bank as a special deposit. Such deposits may bear interest, in which case they are payable at a definite date in the future or after a specified minimum notice of intention to withdraw; or they may be noninterest-bearing, in which case they may be payable on demand or at a future date. They are issued either in negotiable or non-negotiable form. These deposits are payable only upon surrender of the formal receipt properly endorsed, and they are carried on the general ledger of the bank under the heading "Certificates of Deposit" rather than on the individual ledgers under the name of the person to whom the certificate was originally issued.

Certified Check: A depositor's check across the face of which an officer of the bank or some other authorized person has stamped the word "certified" and then has signed his name on behalf of the bank. By its certification the bank guarantees that sufficient funds have been set aside from the depositor's account to pay the check when payment is demanded. In legal effect, certification of a check is similar to acceptance of a draft, and therefore the instrument becomes the bank's promise to pay.

Charter: A document issued by a federal or state supervisory agency granting a bank the right to do business. The terms and conditions under which the bank may operate are enumerated in the charter. As a general rule, state charters permit more latitude in the banking field than do federal (national bank) charters.

Chattel: Any article of personal property.

Check: A draft drawn upon a bank by a depositor and payable on demand.

Check Digit: A suffix digit that a computer, by means of a programmed mathematical formula, can use to test the validity of the account number.

Check Routing Symbol: A device to facilitate the handling and routing of transit items drawn on banks that remit at par throughout the United States. The check routing symbol is the denominator of a fraction, with the numerator the ABA transit number assigned to the drawee bank. The entire fraction is located in the upper right corner of the check above the figure amount line. The check routing symbol (denominator of the fraction) is composed of three or four digits. The first digit in a three-figure number or the first two digits in a four-figure number number identify the Federal Reserve district in which the drawee bank is located. The next to the last digit designates the Federal Reserve bank head office or branch through which the item should be cleared and also any special clearing arrangement. (The head office is indicated by the figure "1." Branches, if any, arranged alphabetically are indicated by figures "2" to "5." Figures "6" to "9" are used to designate special collection arrangements.) The last digit serves two purposes: (1) It shows whether the item is acceptable for immediate or deferred credit. (Figure "0" designates items which are receivable for immediate credit. All other numbers, "1" to "9" inclusive, designate items which are acceptable for deferred credit, but the numbers do not indicate the number of days of deferred availability.) (2) The last number when other than "0" also designates the state in alphabetical progression in which the drawee bank is located.

Checking Account: A bank demand deposit account against which checks may be drawn.

City Collections: *See* COUNTRY COLLECTIONS.

Clearing: A bank term referring to the interbank presentment of checks, the offsetting of counterclaims, and the settlement of resulting balances. The term may be used in a purely local operation, a regional operation, or on a nationwide basis.

Clearing Credit: The total amount of checks presented by a clearinghouse bank drawn on the other participating banks.

Clearing Debit: The total amount of checks presented to a clearinghouse bank by the other participating banks.

Clearinghouse: A place where representatives of the banks in the same locality meet each day at an agreed time to exchange checks, drafts, and similar items drawn on each other and to settle the resulting balances.

Clearinghouse Association: A voluntary association of banks in the same locality for the purpose of maintaining a clearinghouse arrangement and, in some cases, for the purpose of discussing matters of common interest.

Coin: In banking terminology, coin refers to metallic money only.

Collateral: Specific property that a borrower pledges as security for the repayment of a loan and agrees that the lender shall have the right to sell the collateral to liquidate the debt if the borrower fails to repay the loan at maturity or otherwise defaults under the terms of the loan agreement.

Collateral Note: A promissory note secured by the pledge of specific property.

Collecting Bank: Collecting bank means any bank handling the item for collection except the payor bank.

Collection Items: Items (drafts, notes, acceptances, and so forth) that are accepted by a bank against receipt, for which actual payment must be received before the proceeds will be credited to the depositor's account (as distinguished from a cash item). Collection items are usually subject to special instructions and in most banks are subject to a special fee for handling, which is a collection charge.) Also termed *collections*.

Collection Number: A number assigned by the processing bank to each collection item it handles.

Commercial Bank: A bank that accepts demand deposits subject to check and makes short-term loans to business enterprises, regardless of the scope of its other services.

Commercial Invoice: A descriptive document supporting a transaction between a buyer and seller of goods, which contains an itemized list of goods shipped and usually specifies the price and terms of the sale.

Commercial Letter of Credit: An instrument by which a bank lends its credit to a customer to enable him to finance the purchase (importation) of goods. Addressed to the seller, it authorizes him to draw drafts on the bank under the terms stated in the letter. Letters of credit may also be used to finance the sale (exportation) of goods, and they are sometimes used to finance domestic commercial transactions.

Commercial Loan: A short-term loan made by a bank to a business enterprise for use in the production, manufacture, or distribution of goods or in the financing of related services.

Commercial Paper: Short-term negotiable notes, drafts, bills of exchange, and acceptances that arise from transactions involving the production, manufacture, or distribution of goods.

Common Stock: The class of capital stock that represents the last claim on the earnings and assets of a corporation, in other words, the ownership not allocated to other classes of stock. Dividends cannot be paid on common stock until interest on all bonds and other debt and dividends on preferred stock issues have been paid. On the other hand, common stock generally carries superior voting rights as compared with other classes of stock.

Comptroller of the Currency: An appointed official in the United States Treasury Department who is responsible for the chartering, supervision, and liquidation of national banks.

Conditional Indorsement: An indorsement that subjects the transfer of an instrument to a specific condition.

Consular Invoice: A copy of an invoice for merchandise shipped from one country to another, prepared by the shipper and certified at the shipping point by a consul of the country of destination. The consul's certification applies to the value of the merchandise, the port of shipment, the destination, and, in certain cases, the place of origin of the merchandise. A primary purpose of consular invoices is to ensure that the transaction does not violate any laws or trade restrictions of the importing country.

Consumer Credit (Loans): Credit granted to an individual to purchase consumer goods.

Continuous Audit: A constant audit of all entries affecting a particular account.

Contributory Pension Trust: A trust in which the employees make payments into the fund.

Control Account: An account in the general ledger used to carry the aggregate total of accounts carried in a subsidiary ledger. Whenever a subsidiary account is affected, the posting will be reflected in the control account total.

Control Total: A figure obtained by a process in which all transactions, or balances of a given type are included in a single total, so that the accuracy of their recording may be proved.

Conversion of Funds: Appropriating, dealing with, or using funds belonging to another without right or consent as though funds were one's own.

Corporate Indenture: When a corporation borrows money by means of a publicly offered bond issue, a bank is selected to act as trustee under an indenture (agreement to act as intermediary between the borrower and the lenders). It is the trustee's duty to protect the interests of the lenders (bondholders).

Correspondent Bank: A bank that maintains an account relationship with another bank or engages in an exchange of services with another bank.

Cost Accounting: An accounting system that relates all direct and indirect costs and expenses to the specific function performed.

Counterfeit Money: Spurious currency and specie coins that have been made to appear genuine. The act of creating counterfeit money is a felony under law, and the conspirators making and distributing counterfeit money are subject to long prison terms and heavy fines. The United States Secret Service, a bureau of the Treasury Department, is responsible for tracking the criminals who traffic in counterfeit money.

Country Collections: A term describing all items that are being sent outside the city in which the sending bank is located. A banker will speak of *city collections,* which are items drawn on or payable by banks and business houses within the city of the bank's location; and *country collections,* which are sent out of a city to the bank's correspondents for collection and payment.

Coupon: One of a series of promissory notes of consecutive maturities attached to a bond or other debt certificate and intended to be detached and presented on their respective due dates for payment of interest.

Credit: An advance of cash, merchandise, or other commodity in the present in exchange for a promise to pay a definite sum at a future date, with interest if so agreed.

Credit Department: A department in a bank where credit information is obtained, assembled, and retained for reference purposes. Credit applications for loans are presented to this department by a loan officer. The credit department gathers all available information on the customer and prepares it for the confidential use of the loan officer. Working with the findings of the credit department, which will make an analysis of the credit information, the loan officer is in a position to make a decision as to whether the customer is entitled to the credit requested or whether the loan application should be rejected. The credit department also obtains information and answers credit inquiries for its customers and bank correspondents, who may have a business transaction pending that will involve credit knowledge on a local business.

Credit Risk: The possibility that a debtor may not be able to pay principal and interest as they come due. *See* MARKET RISK.

Creditor: One who is due money from another.

Currency: Technically, any form of money that serves as a circulating medium including both paper money and metallic money (coins). In banking terminology, however, the term generally refers to paper money only.

Custodian: As custodian, a bank performs the duties of a safekeeping agent and other active duties such as collecting and paying out income, and buying, selling, receiving, and delivering securities on the order of the principal.

Debenture: An intermediate or long-term obligation that is not secured by specific lien on property. As the term is generally employed, a debenture is an unsecured note of a corporation, usually issued in a distinctive printed form similar to a bond.

Decedent: A person who has died. The term is used in connection with inheritances, estates, wills, and so forth. A decedent who had made no will is called an *intestate decedent;* one who had made a will is called a *testator.*

Decedent's Estate: The entire group of assets owned by an individual at the time of his death. The estate includes all funds, personal effects, interests in business enterprises, titles to real and personal property, and evidences of ownership or debt obligations, such as stocks, bonds, mortgages, notes receivable, etc. All claims against an estate must be duly filed with the "executor" or "administrator" of the estate.

Deed: A written document that transfers the title to real property from the seller to the buyer.

Demand Deposits: Deposits payable on demand, which are usually made by presentation of depositors' check. Prior notice of the depositor's intention to withdraw all or any part of a demand deposit balance is not required. *See also* CHECKING ACCOUNTS.

Demand Draft: A draft that is payable on demand. Also called sight draft, which is payable upon presentation.

Demand Loan: A loan that is payable on demand.

Deposit: In a banking sense, a deposit consists of funds (cash, checks, drafts, and so on) left with a bank to be used according to banking practice. A deposit balance in a bank is merely a credit; it represents the depositor's right to receive an equivalent sum of money from the bank.

Deposit Function: A banking function whereby paper financial instruments are converted into usable money. Deposit credits may be placed in demand deposit accounts subject to withdrawal by check, or in savings or other interest-bearing time accounts.

Depositor: Any person, firm, corporation, or association that has placed funds in a bank to be placed to the credit of his or its account.

Deposit Slip: An itemized memorandum of the cash and other funds that a customer (depositor) presents to the receiving teller for credit to his account (also called *deposit ticket* and *deposit tag*).

Deposit Receipt: A printed receipt for the deposit that may be a part of a multicopy form bearing a teller's acknowledgement stamp, a machine-issued receipt, or an entry in a savings account passbook. The depositor keeps deposit receipts until the bank statement has been received. After verifying the statement for accuracy of entry of all deposits, the receipts can be destroyed if the deposits have been properly credited by the bank as evidenced on the statement.

Depository: A bank serves as depository in connection with corporate reorganizations and changes in the capital structure, and in many other cases in which there is a need for an impartial and trustworthy stakeholder to hold cash or securities while financial transactions are being worked out.

Depositary Bank: Depositary bank means the first bank to which an item is transferred for collection even though it is also the payor bank.

Direct Verification: A audit procedure whereby accounts are verified by direct contact with the bank's debtors or creditors.

Discount: (1) The amount of interest withheld when a note or draft is purchased. (2) A note on which the interest is paid in advance. (3) The process of making a loan by requiring a note larger by the agreed interest charge than the amount paid to the borrower or credited to his account (sometimes referred to as an *add-on discount*). A discount is distinguished from a loan by the fact that interest on a loan is collected at the time the note is paid or at regular intervals during the term of the loan, as in case of a demand loan. (4) The process by which a Federal Reserve or other bank discounts for a member or customer bank the notes, drafts, or acceptances that the member or customer bank has already discounted for its customers.

Discount Rate: The term applied to the interest rate charged by the Federal Reserve banks on loans to member banks.

Discount Register: A book of original entry that provides a daily record of all loan department transactions for settlement and control purposes.

Dishonor: As applied to financial instruments, dishonor means: (1) The refusal of the drawee to accept or to pay a check, draft, or bill of exchange when it is presented to him for acceptance or for payment, as the case may be. (2) The refusal of the maker to pay a note when it is presented to him for payment. Strictly speaking, an instrument is dishonored when payment is refused because of some deficiency attributable to or caused by a drawee, drawer, acceptor or maker. For example, a check refused for "not sufficient funds" is dishonored. A check, payment of which is refused because of a missing indorsement or because it is post-dated, is "returned" but not "dishonored."

Document-Handlers. Equipment designed to handle MICR-encoded documents. Also called *sorter-readers.*

Documentary Draft: A documentary draft is a negotiable or non-negotiable draft with accompanying documents, securities, or other papers to be delivered against payment or acceptance of the draft.

Dormant Account: An account that has shown no activity, either by increase through deposits or decrease through withdrawals, over a period of time. In the case of savings accounts the crediting of interest in the depositor's passbook is considered activity. States have escheat laws limiting the period in which a bank can hold dormant accounts. The bank is required to publish the names of all dormant account depositors for a specified period of time, after which the funds are transferred to the state for disposition.

Double-Entry Bookkeeping: A balanced system of accounting in which all transactions are recorded by a set of entries where a debit (or debits) is balanced by a credit (or credits) of equal amount.

Draft: A signed written order addressed by one person (the drawer) to another person (the drawee) directing the latter to pay a specified sum of money to the order of a third person (the payee). In international banking, a draft is often referred to as a *bill of exchange.*

Drawee: The party who is directed to pay the sum specified in a check, draft, or bill of exchange. In the case of a check, the drawee is a bank.

Drawer: The person who makes and signs an order (check, draft, or bill of exchange) for the payment of money.

Dual Banking System: In this country, individual banks have the choice of being state banks or national banks, that is, they may operate under a charter issued by the state in which they are domiciled, or under a charter issued by the federal government through the Office of the Comptroller of the Currency. The choice creates what is known as a *dual banking system.*

Dual Posting: A term used to describe the manner of posting accounts. It applies to any system where the posting media is posted twice, each time by a different person. Although the system requires double handling of all items, a high degree of accuracy is achieved.

Equity: (1) An interest of an ownership nature, as distinguished from an interest of a creditor. (2) The value of collateral over and above the obligation it is pledged to secure. To the owner of the collateral (borrower), this is his equity. To the holder of the collateral (lender), this is his margin of safety.

Equity Capital: Funds raised through the sale of certificates of ownership, such as common and preferred stock, plus retained earnings.

Equity Securities: Shares of stock, either common or preferred, which represent a share in the ownership of a corporation. Unlike holders of debt obligations, such as bonds or notes, a shareholder is not a creditor. Except in liquidation, a shareholder has no claim against the corporation and can only recover his investment by selling his shares to someone else.

Escrow: A written agreement between three parties that sets forth the terms under which funds, securities, or other property are deposited by one party called the *grantor* to a third party, called the *escrow agent,* for the eventual benefit of the second party, called the *grantee.* The escrow agent holds the deposit until certain conditions have been met. The grantor cannot recover the deposit unless the grantee fails to comply with the terms of the contract, nor can the grantee receive the deposit until the conditions have been met.

Estate: See DECEDENT'S ESTATE. The term is also used to describe the assets of a legal entity (firm, corporation, etc.) which has been placed in bankruptcy.

Exchange Charge: In domestic banking, the term *exchange charge* generally refers to a remittance charge made by nonpar banks when paying checks drawn on themselves, presented by mail from out-of-town points.

Executor: A person or an institution named by an individual in his will to settle his estate in accordance with the terms of his will. Executors must appear before a court to be qualified and formally appointed.

Federal Reserve Banks: Federal banking corporations that deal principally with their member banks and with the government. They deal with the general public only to a limited extent.

Federal Reserve Note: A noninterest-bearing demand promissory note of a Federal Reserve bank issued for general circulation as money and designated as legal tender for all public and private debts.

Federal Reserve System: The central banking system of the United States, created by an act of Congress (Federal Reserve Act) in 1913. It consists of regional bankers' banks (twelve Federal Reserve banks and their branches), and all national and state member banks. A Board of Governors located in Washington, D.C. exercises general control of the System.

Fiduciary: An individual, corporation, or association, such as a bank or trust company, to whom certain property is given to hold in trust, according to the terms of a trust agreement. The property may be utilized, managed or invested for the benefit of the property owner or designated beneficiaries to the best ability of the fiduciary. Administrators and executors of estates and trustees under wills, declarations, or deeds of trust are common examples of fiduciaries. Investments of trust funds, unless otherwise specified in the trust indenture, are usually restricted by law.

Financial Institutions: This term embraces a wide variety of service organizations, such as commercial banks, savings banks, savings and loan associations, consumer finance companies, and mortgage companies.

Financial Instrument: Any writing having monetary value or evidencing a monetary transaction.

Float: A term used to describe that portion of a bank's total deposits that represents cash items in the process of collection. The amount of float in a specific depositor's account is known as uncollected funds.

Forged Check: This term generally refers to a check on which the drawer's signature has been forged.

Forgery: The alteration of any document or instrument with the intent to defraud or prejudice any individual constitutes forgery, which is a statutory crime punishable by imprisonment. The most common concept of forgery is a false signature placed on an instrument. However, raising the amount, altering the payee, changing the number, writing a true signature to an instrument known to be false, or changing an entry in a deposit passbook constitutes forgery.

Formal Trusts: A trust supported by formal documentary evidence, which in many cases is filed as a matter of public record.

Funded Insurance Trust: A trust in which additional property is transferred to the trust and the income from that property is sufficient to pay the insurance premium. The trustee is then charged with the responsibility of paying the premiums.

General Ledger: A bank's general book of accounts, the functions of which are: (1) To provide in summary form a record of changes in a bank's financial status; (2) to provide control accounts for the detailed subsidiary ledger records maintained by various operating units of the bank (Bookkeeping, Loans and Discounts, and so on); (3) to provide a basis for the preparation of statements of condition and other financial reports for the bank's management, supervisory authorities, stockholders, and the public.

Guardian: (1) An individual appointed by a court to manage the property or person (or both) of a minor or a mentally incompetent individual; (2) a corporation appointed by a court to manage the property of a minor or a mentally incompetent person.

Hard Money: Metallic money as distinguished from paper money.

Hold: A restriction that freezes the entire balance or a specific part of a bank account, or in some other manner restricts payments from the account.

Holder in Due Course: As defined in the Uniform Commercial Code: A holder in due course is a holder who takes the instrument (1) for value; and (2) in good faith; and (3) without notice that it is overdue or has been dishonored or of any defense against or claim to it on the part of any person.

Immediate Parties: Persons who are normally named on the face of a negotiable instrument.

Income Statement: *See* PROFIT AND LOSS STATEMENT.

Individual Account: An account in the name of one individual, as contrasted with an account of a corporation, a partnership, or an account in two or more names.

Indorsement (Also **Endorsement**): The signature plus any other writing or other authorized inscription on an instrument by which the holder transfers his rights therein to someone else. An indorser usually signs on the reverse side of an instrument, but a signature on the face of an instrument not designated as that of a maker, drawer, drawee, or payee is construed to be an indorsement.

Indorsement in Blank (General Indorsement): The indorser's signature on the reverse side of the instrument.

Indorsee: The holder of a negotiable instrument to whom it has been transferred by indorsement.

Indorser: A person who signs his name or causes his name to be inscribed on a negotiable instrument, such as a check, draft, or promissory note, for the purpose of transferring his title to the instrument or for the purpose of guaranteeing payment. *See* Accommodation Party.

Informal Trusts: A trust that is not court supervised or governed. An informal trust is established when one or more individuals deposit a sum of money in a bank account and the bank is simply notified by the suggested title of the account that the money is being held in trust for one or more named beneficiaries.

Institutional Trusts: When a college or university transfers cash, stocks, bonds, which it owns, to a bank to hold in trust and to invest, manage, and administer for the benefit of the college.

Insufficient Funds: (Sometimes abbreviated **N.S.F.**, not sufficient funds). A term used by a bank to indicate that the drawer's deposit balance is smaller than the amount of a check presented for payment.

Insurance Trust: Is created when a trustor makes his life insurance policies made payable to a trustee and by agreement directs the trustee as to the manner in which the proceeds are to be handled and distributed.

Insured Bank: A bank that subscribes to the deposit insurance plan of the Federal Deposit Insurance Corporation. National banks and members of the Federal Reserve System must subscribe to the plan. A state banking instiution which does not subscribe to this plan is referred to as a *noninsured bank*.

Interest: The price paid for the use of money or credit. Interest is computed on a per centum rate of the principal borrowed for a given period of time.

Inventory Financing: A form of credit extended by a lender to a dealer to carry on an adequate supply of goods for display and sales purposes. Also called *flooring, floor planning, wholesale floor plan.*

Investment: The exchange of money *either* for a promise to repay at a later date or for an ownership share in a business venture that carries the right to share in profits or in the liquidated value of assets, but with no definite obligation by the recipient to repay the amount invested.

Investment Portfolio: The list of securities owned by a bank, an individual, or a business enterprise. In banks the investment portfolio is a title given to the complete list of securities held by the

bank for investment purposes. In the general ledger, the investment account is a control account supported by a subsidiary
ledger, which contains the title and complete description of each
investment held by the bank.

Involuntary Bankruptcy: If a debtor is unable to pay his creditors,
three or more creditors can petition a court of jurisdiction to
place the debtor in involuntary bankruptcy.

Joint Account: An account in the names of two or more persons,
usually supported by a written agreement that specifies the manner in which funds are to be withdrawn. Sometimes called an *al-
ternate account* or, if consistent with the terms of the agreement,
a *survivorship account.*

Journal: An accounting record of original entry in which transactions
are listed and described in chronological sequence.

Ledger: The accounting record of final entry, on which transactions
are entered according to the accounts they affect. The ledger
may be posted from a journal, which is the book of original
entry. In modern accounting systems, loose-leaf journal or ledger
records are prepared simultaneously. Computer systems reproduce raw data in either journal (chronological) or ledger (classified) form.

Legal Entity: A legal person as opposed to a natural person; legal entities are created by law or court action, and as such they can be
sued by other parties or bring suit against other parties.

Legal Reserves: A bank's legal reserve is the portion of its deposits
(both demand deposits and time deposits), which it is required
by law to maintain in the form of cash, readily available balances, or certain eligible securities, for the protection of depositors. Members of the Federal Reserve System must keep their
legal reserves in cash on deposit with the Federal Reserve banks
of their respective districts, but vault cash may be counted as a
part of reserve requirements. The amount and composition of
the reserves of nonmember banks are determined by the laws of
the respective states.

Lending Function: In commercial banking, the function of supplying
money or credit to borrowers, either through making loans or
purchasing investments. Through this function, commercial
banks have the power to create additions to our money supply.

Letter of Credit: An instrument issued by a bank on behalf of an individual, or corporation by means of which the bank substitutes
its own credit for that of the individual or corporation. *See also*
COMMERCIAL LETTER OF CREDIT and TRAVELER'S LETTER OF
CREDIT.

Liabilities: In banking parlance, the liabilities are the funds a bank owes. By far the largest item on the liability side of a bank's financial statement is its deposit liabilities. The indebtedness of a bank to other than depositors is usually relatively small in total and represents obligations that are to be paid on a certain future date, including such items as accrued expenses and taxes. Capital Stock, Surplus and Undivided Profits are listed in bank statements as liabilities, but these accounts represent the net worth of the bank, or the equity interest of stockholders. They are not liabilities in the sense of debts that must be paid at a definite time. However, the equity interest of stockholders does not include capital obligations such as capital notes or capital debentures, which are definite debts that must be paid or refunded at maturity.

Liability Ledger: A most important bank loan accounting record is the liability ledger. This ledger shows all outstanding loans made by the bank to every borrower. Each borrower has an individual ledger card, wherein is recorded all loans made, loan payments, and the total outstanding indebtedness. Most banks maintain several liability ledgers according to types of loans, such as commercial loans, consumer loans, and mortgage loans. Liabiltiy ledgers are subsidiary ledgers, which settle with control accounts on the general ledger.

Line of Credit: An agreement between a bank and a customer whereby the bank agrees to lend the customer funds up to an agreed maximum amount. The bank can withdraw from the agreement if the financial status of the borrower changes or if the borrower fails to live up to any conditions stipulated in the agreement.

Liquidity: The quality that renders an asset easily convertible into cash on short notice with minimum risk of loss, by virtue of the fact that the asset is callable or redeemable on demand, can be quickly sold on an open market, or is readily acceptable for discount by established lending agencies.

Liquidity Account: That portion of a bank's investment portfolio, which includes primarily short-term U.S. government securities, federal agency issues, and other top-grade debt obligations preferably having an average maturity of one year, with individual maturities of not more than two years.

Living Trust: A trust that becomes effective during the lifetime of the trustor.

Loan: A business contract wherein one party, known as the *lender,* agrees to "rent" funds to the second party, known as the *borrower.* The borrower's obligation to return the fund is represented by a promissory note or some similar debt obligation. The funds may be "rented" with or without a fee, which is called *interest* or *discount* in banking circles. Loans may be demand or time loams, depending upon the agreement as to maturity. They may also be secured or unsecured within the above categories.

Loan Participations: Two or more banks sharing or participating with each other in loan transactions.

Magnetic Ink Character Recognition (MICR): Magnetic Ink Character Recognition is the standards program developed by the American Bankers Association to permit the automatic handling of documents, such as bank checks, by electronically reading precoded, standardized characters printed on the documents in special magnetic ink.

Maker (Promissor): The party who signs and issues a promissory note or a depository bank that engages to repay a certificate of deposit in accordance with its terms.

Market Risk: The special risk involved in the purchase of investments bearing a fixed rate of return. When interest rates rise, the market value of such investments falls. Unlike credit risk, market risk is not related to the debtor's financial strength.

Maturity: The date on which a note, draft, acecptance, bond, or other instrument becomes due and payable.

Maturity Tickler: In banking, a file maintained by due dates in order to ensure that notes are properly presented for payment when they fall due.

Medium of Exchange: Any commodity (commonly money) that is widely accepted in payment of goods and services and in settlement of debts and is recognized as representing a standard of value.

Member Bank: The term applied to any bank, either national or state, that is a member of the Federal Reserve System. A state bank that is not a member of the system is termed a *nonmember bank.*

Money: Any form of coin or currency declared by a government to be legal tender, which passes freely as a medium of exchange.

Money Supply: Amount of money in public hands immediately available for spending. There are several ways in which money supply is defined, but the most commonly accepted definition includes only demand deposits (excluding U.S. government and domestic interbank deposits) and coin and currency in circulation (which excludes that held in bank vaults) .

Mortgage: An instrument by which the borrower (mortgagor) gives the lender (mortgagee) a lien on real estate as security for a loan. The borrower continues to use the property, and when the loan loan is repaid, the lien is removed or satisfied.

Mortgage Loan: A loan secured by a mortgage on real estate. Also called a *real estate loan.*

Mutual Savings Bank: A bank that is owned by the depositors and managed for them by a self-perpetuating board of trustees. It has no capital stock and therefore no stockholders. The profits, net after deducting all necessary expenses for conducting the business, accrue wholly to the benefit of the depositors.

National Bank: A corporation organized under a federal banking law (National Banking Act) and authorized to do a general or commercial banking business, that is, to receive deposits subject to check and to make loans. It usually also performs a variety of other functions. A national bank must have the word "national" in its corporate title or the initials NBA or NA (National Banking Association or National Association) following its title.

National Numerical System (Numerical Transit System): The plan under which every bank in the United States and its territories has a distinctive number, which is usually printed below or beside the bank name on all forms in external use, including checks. The identifying number is used in listing checks on deposit slips and transit letters and in many other ways. The system is some times referred to as the *ABA numerical system. See also* TRANSIT NUMBER.

Negotiable Instrument: An unconditional written order or promise to pay money, which can be transferred by one person to another free from many defenses available to original parties. The law sets forth certain standards with which an instrument must conform in order to be negotiable.

Negotiation: The transfer of a holder's title to and rights in a negotiable instrument, which is accomplished by indorsement (except in the case of bearer instruments) and delivery to the transferee.

Net Worth: The excess of assets over liabilities *including* capital obligations. Net worth is the equity of shareholders, which in a bank is its capital stock, surplus, and undivided profits.

Nonpar Items: Items for which the drawee bank (called a *nonpar bank*) deducts an exchange charge before remitting to a collecting bank.

No Passbook Savings Account (Also called **Statement Savings Account**): Such accounts are similar to regular savings accounts except that instead of recording deposits and withdrawals in a passbook, the bank renders periodic detailed statements to the depositor.

N.S.F.: *See* INSUFFICIENT FUNDS.

Numerical Transit System: Same as national numerical system.

Official Check: *See* BANK CHECK.

On-Us Checks: A term applied to checks by the bank on which they are drawn.

Overdraft: The amount by which the total sum of checks paid against an account exceeds the applicable balance on deposit in the account.

Par Bank: A bank that honors checks drawn on it at full face (par) value, no matter by whom presented.

Par Item: Items which the drawee bank will honor at face value, remitting the full amount thereof to a collecting bank without charge.

Par Value: The principal or nominal value appearing on a bond, note, coupon, or other instrument calling for payment of money.

Passbook: In general, a book supplied by a bank to a depositor for record purposes. A savings passbook contains a complete record of the customer's account, showing deposits and withdrawals as well as the interest credited at regular periods; it must be presented to the bank for proper entry of these transactions.

Payee: The person named in an instrument calling for the payment of money as the one to whom or to whose order payment is to be made.

Paying Agent: A bank serving as the agent of a corporation for the payment of dividends on its stock and for the payment of interest on and principal of its bonds or promissory notes.

Paying Teller: A representative of the bank who is responsible for the proper paying or cashing of checks presented at the window. *See also* UNIT TELLER.

Payor Bank: A bank by which an item is payable as drawn or accepted.

Postdated Check: A check dated ahead. It is not an effective order on the drawee bank until the future date is reached.

Power of Attorney: A document, usually acknowledged before a public officer or witnessed, authorizing a named person to perform certain acts on behalf of the signer. It is void on the death of the signer. The person so authorized is known as an "attorney-in-fact."

Preferred Stock: Stock which usually has a right to receive a specified share of the profits of a corporation before any distribution can be made on the common stock. In liquidation, it is usually entitled to share in the assets ahead of the common stock.

Presenting Bank: Presenting bank means any bank presenting an item except a payor bank.

Presentment: The physical presentation of a financial instrument coupled with a demand for payment made upon the maker, acceptor, drawee, or other payor, or a demand for acceptance made upon the drawee of a time draft on or before the date payable.

Prime Rate: The lowest rate charged by banks to their most creditworthy borowers.

Principal: (1) The sum of money stated in a contract, account, or financial instrument as distinguished from the sum actually to be paid, which might include interest or other charges; (2) a person who appoints another person to act for him as agent or attorney-in-fact.

Profit and Loss Statement: A record of income and expense relating to the operations of a business; a summary of transactions resulting from the sales of goods or services. *Operating statement* and *income statement* are other terms that are sometimes applied to this accounting record.

Promissory Note: A written promise made by one person (the maker) to pay a sum certain in money to another person (the payee), or to his order, on demand or at a determinable future date.

Proof: A process for testing the accuracy of a previous operation, as relisting the checks and adding their amounts to determine the accuracy of the total shown on a deposit slip. Proof is generally effected when a total agrees with another total of the same items arrived in a different manner; it is then said to be in balance.

Proof Department: A department of a bank charged with the responsibility of sorting, distributing, and proving all transactions arising from the commercial operations of the bank. The proof function involves the creation of adequate records of all transactions, showing the source and proper distribution of all items going to other departments for further processing, and proof of the correctness of all transactions passing through the bank. Proof is accomplished by balancing and adjusting differences between source totals and control totals established for processing departments.

Proof Machine: A machine designed to facilitate the processing of large groups of items by simultaneously performing the following: (1) verifying the accuracy of source totals; (2) sorting the items for further processing; (3) establishing a control total for each sorted group of items.

Protest: A written statement under seal by a notary public or other authorized person for the purpose of giving formal notice to parties secondarily liable that a properly presented instrument has been dishonored, either by refusal to accept or by refusal to make payment. In practice, protest is generally limited to items of $1,000 or over that on their face appear to be drawn or payable outside the states and territories of the United States in which they are payable.

Public Funds: Money deposited by the U.S. Treasury, a federal agency, a state, county, city, or any political subdivision or municipality.

Qualified Indorsement: An indorsement including the words "without recourse" or words similar thereto, intended to limit the liability of the indorser.

Raised Check: One on which the amount has been fraudulently increased.

Real Estate Loans: *See* MORTGAGE LOANS.

Receiving Teller: A representative of the bank who receives and verifies deposits and issues receipts for them. *See also* UNIT TELLER.

Registrar: A bank or a trust company that has been appointed by a corporation to keep an accurate record of its shares of stock and to see that the number of shares issued does not exceed the total amount authorized.

Repurchase Agreement: An agreement between a seller and buyer that stipulates the seller will buy back the items sold, (usually securities) at an agreed price at the expiration of a period of time. In effect, a repurchase agreement is a short-term secured loan, the seller being the borrower and the buyer being the lender.

Reserve: A portion of a bank's funds that has been set aside as (1) legal reserve required by law (*see* LEGAL RESERVE) ; (2) reserves for specific known expenses that must be paid in the future (such as taxes); (3) reserves for loan losses; or (4) reserves for unknown contingencies, set aside as a matter of prudence.

Restrictive Indorsement: Restricts the transferee in some manner, such as by naming the specific purpose of the transfer or imposing a condition on the transferee.

Return Items: An item returned unpaid by a drawee or payor bank.

Routing Symbol: *See* CHECK ROUTING SYMBOL.

Safe Deposit Box Service: A traditional banking service wherein a bank grants the customer exclusive access to a box housed in a private section of its vault, for the storage and protection of personal items of value. The bank keeps a record of the time and date of each access, but has no record of what is deposited in or withdrawn from the box.

Safekeeping Agent: As safekeeping agent, the bank receives, holds, and delivers property upon the order of the principal. Unlike safe deposit box service, the bank keeps a complete record of all property delivered it.

Savings Account: A special kind of time deposit that a depositor may use to accumulate gradually a fund from earnings or income, and on which the bank pays interest. Although member banks are required to *reserve the right* to require at least 30 days notice of intention to make withdrawals, it is customary for banks to waive (on a non-discriminatory basis) their right to such notice.

Savings Bank: A corporation chartered by the state to receive savings deposits primarily from people of moderate means. It invests those deposits for the most part in securities (bonds) and real estate mortgages.

Savings Certificate: A type of savings deposit where the bank issues a negotiable or non-negotiable certificate which indicates the name of the depositor, the rate of interest, and the maturity or conditions under which the deposit is returnable. The certificate must be surrendered before the deposit can be withdrawn.

Security Officer: A bank officer or employee who is responsible not only for the installation, maintenance, and operation of security devices, but also for the development and administration of a security program.

Service Charge: A charge made by a bank for the cost of handling a depositor's account.

Sight Draft: A draft payable upon delivery and presentation to the drawee, or "upon sight."

Sorter-Reader: *See* DOCUMENT HANDLERS.

Special Indorsement: An indorsement that names the person to whom the instrument is being negotiated.

Signature Card: A card signed by each depositor and customer of the bank. The primary use of the signature card is that of identification of the depositor. Signature cards are generally made out in at least two sets. One set is for the signature file department, where all signatures are held for ready reference; the other set is for a file at the teller's window.

Split-Deposit: A deposit usually consisting of a single check, where the depositor requests that part of the amount be credited to his account and the balance paid to him in cash. Also called a *cash-back deposit.*

Spot Audit: A method of verifying an account by selecting at random for testing, a limited number of the entries that have been posted to the account.

Stale Check: One that has been held an unreasonable long time after issue before being presented for payment to the bank on which it is drawn. Subject to individual bank policy (and sometimes depositor's instructions), checks may be considered stale if presented more than 30 days, 90 days, or 6 months after the indicated date of issue.

State Banks: A corporation organized under the general banking laws of a state and authorized to do a commercial banking business, that is, receive deposits subject to check and make loans. It usually performs a variety of other functions as well. In a broader sense, a state bank is any bank chartered by the state.

Statement of Condition: A detailed listing of a bank's resources, liabilities, and capital accounts showing its condition on a given date. On requests (calls) by supervisory authorities several times a year, banks are required to submit sworn statements of condition. In general accounting, this type of financial report is known as a *balance sheet*.

Statement of Condition Audits: Consists of verifying the assets and liabilities and proving net worth as of one certain day.

Statement Savings Account: *See* No Passbook Savings Account.

Stop Payment Order: An order issued by a depositor instructing his bank to refuse payment of a specific check drawn by the depositor. A stop payment order must be received by the bank in reasonable time to act on it.

Subsidiary Ledger: Its purpose it to maintain detailed records and to support the summarized data shown in the general ledger account.

Surplus: In banking, a surplus account is required by law, primarily for the protection of depositors and also to absorb unusual losses to prevent impairment of capital stock. Surplus funds are derived from two sources: Paid-in surplus represents an amount paid by stockholders over and above capital stock subscriptions at the time of organization. Earned surplus represents accumulated earnings not paid out as dividends, but added to capital funds.

Right of Survivorship (Survivorship Account): An account in the names of two or more persons, supported by a signed agreement covering the withdrawal of funds and specifying that the survivor or survivors shall be the sole owner or owners of the balance in the account on the death of the other or others.

Teller: A bank representative who, in one capacity or another, transacts routine over-the-counter business with customers.

Tenant: Depositors who share a joint account are known as tenants.

Testamentary Trust: A trust under will, created when a testator directs that certain specific property or all or part of the residual estate be held in trust and administered for the benefit of beneficiaries.

Testator: A decreased person who has left a will instructing his executor or administrator as to the distribution of his residual estate (after payment of all debts and taxes).

Time Certificate of Deposit: A definite contract between a depositor and a bank evidenced by a formal certificate delivered to the depositor rather than an individual ledger record on the bank's books. Time certificates may be issued in negotiable or non-negotiable form. If negotiable, there must be a definite engagement on the part of the bank to repay the deposit, and the certificate must bear a maturity date.

Time Deposit-Open Account: An interest-bearing deposit evidenced by the usual individual ledger record. The deposit must be supported by a written contract, specifying a definite maturity date or providing for written notice (not less than 30 days) of the depositor's intention to withdraw the deposit.

Time Draft: A draft that is payable at a fixed or determinable future time.

Time Loan: A loan that is payable at some specified future date.

Title: The right to ownership of property. Legal title to certain kinds of property is often represented by a title certificate, a deed, a bill of lading, or a warehouse receipt.

Trade Acceptance: A time draft drawn by the seller of goods on the buyer and accepted by the buyer before maturity. On its face there often appears a statement indicating that the acceptor's obligation arises out of the purchase of goods from the drawer of the draft. *See also* ACCEPTANCE.

Trade Name (also called **Trade Style**): A fictitious name assumed for trade or business purposes. In most states, persons wishing to do business under a trade name must register or file the name with state authorities and with local county officials.

Transfer Drafts: An instrument employed mainly by corporations for the purpose of transferring funds from one bank to another. As a rule, the drafts are drawn on secondary banks and are deposited in the corporation's home office bank account. Because the transfer does not involve a change in ownership of the funds, an official manual signature on such drafts is normally not required.

Travelers Checks: Special checks sold to tourists, vacationers, and other travelers, preprinted in convenient denominations, such as $10, $20, $50, and $100, which bear a guarantee that there are sufficient funds on deposit at the issuing bank, express company, or well-known travel agency to repay those who cash them. For identification purposes, they are signed by the purchaser in the presence of the issuing agent, and again in the presence of the party requested to cash them.

Traveler's Letter of Credit: A letter of credit issued by a bank to a customer preparing for an extended business or pleasure trip. The bank furnishes a list of correspondent banks where drafts drawn against the letter of credit can be negotiated and unconditionally guarantees that it will honor such drafts on presentation. The bank also provides a means of identification by obtaining a specimen signature of the purchaser on the folder enclosing the list of correspondent banks. Each bank that subsequently pays a draft endorses on the letter of credit the date of payment and the amount drawn against the letter of credit.

Treasurer's Check: *See* Bank Check.

Trust: A trust exists when one person (or institution) holds the legal title to property and another person is entitled to the benefits derived from the property. A trust may be created by a will, by agreement, by declaration, or by court order.

Trust Company: A corporation chartered by the state to engage in the trust business serving both individuals and business organizations. It may or may not perform banking functions as well, depending on the powers granted in its charter.

Trust Institution: Applied to both a trust company and a banking corporation (either national or state) that has the power to perform trust services, regardless of the scope of its other services.

Trustee: The person holding the legal title to property placed in trust.

Trustor or Settlor: The person who provides property to create a trust.

Trust Receipt: A trust agreement (in receipt form) between a bank and its borrower that is temporarily substituted for goods, merchandise, or other collateral securing a loan. By signing the trust receipt, the borrower agrees to hold the collateral in trust for the benefit of the bank and agrees to keep the property, as well as any funds received from its sale, separate and distinct from his own property until the loan is paid. Thus the bank, in effect, permits the borrower to take physical possession of the collateral without actually relinquishing its title thereto.

Uncollected Funds: *See* FLOAT.

Undivided Profits: Undistributed earnings available for dividends and for absorbing bad debts or special losses.

Uniform Commercial Code: This Code regulates a broad segment of the business world and is very important to bankers and to the business community in general. Specifically, its regulation apply to: bulk sales of goods; commercial paper including all negotiable instruments; bank collections; negotiable securities; title documents; and secured transactions in personal property. The Code, at least in some form, has now been adopted by all states of the union.

Uniform Fiduciaries Act: This legislation is of interest to banks opening fiduciary accounts, since it accepts the principle that it is the fiduciary and not a depositary bank on whom the primary responsibility has been placed; hence a depositary bank acting in good faith is not expected to police the actions of a fiduciary in the handling of a bank account.

Uniform Gifts to Minors Act: Provides tax relief for those who make gifts of money or other property to minor children, in that income derived from the "gift" is taxable to the minor and not to the donor. To be noted, however, is the fact that gifts made under the act are totally irrevocable.

Uniform Partnership Act: A special body of law dealing with partnership affairs.

Unit Bank: A single independent bank that conducts all of its operations at one office.

Unit Teller: An arrangement for the convenience of customers who wish to handle routine banking transactions at one place and with one person. A unit teller accepts deposits, pays and cashes checks, and may also handle savings account transactions, loan payments, mortgage payments, and so forth.

Unsecured Loan: A loan that is not secured by a specific pledge of collateral but rather is based upon the integrity of the borrower, his credit standing, and his ability to repay as evidenced by a financial statement.

Warehouse Receipt: A receipt issued by a warehouseman, a person engaged in the business of storing goods for hire. By the terms of the receipt, the warehouseman promises to keep the goods safely and to redeliver them upon the surrender of the receipt, properly indorsed, and payment of the storage charges. The receipt is also evidence that the owner or holder has title to the stored goods.

403

Will: A formal written instrument by which a person gives explicit instructions regarding the disposition to be made of his property after his death.

Wire Fate: An instruction accompanying an item sent to an out-of-town bank, requesting that the sending bank be notified by wire whether or not the item is paid.

Wire Transfer: A transaction activated by telephoned, telegraphed, or cabled instructions between banks to pay or credit a sum of money to a designated payee.

Without Right of Survivorship: Upon the death of a co-tenant, the joint tenancy is severed. The surviving tenant may claim his share of the property jointly held, but an executor or administrator may claim the deceased tenant's share.

Working Capital: (1) That portion of the capital of a business enterprise which is not invested in fixed assets but which is kept liquid to provide for day-to-day working needs; (2) in an accounting sense, the excess of current assets over current liabilities.

Writ of Attachment: A document issued by direction of a court of law which may be served on banks or anyone in possession of assets of the debtor.

Zero-Out Proof: A method of proof whereby a control figure is first entered into a machine or system, from which all posted items are then successively subtracted. When the posting run is completed, a zero balance indicates that all items included in the control total have been correctly listed and added.

INDEX

406

statement of changes in, 292, 297-8
Capital notes, 295
Cash (*see also* Bulk cash; Coin and currency; Paper money)
   control of, 88, 183-4
   shorts and overs, 190
Cash accounting, 290-2
Cash inventory, 237
   teller's station, 183-5
Cash items, 83, 84-6
   collection, 101-9
   defined, 83-5
   float, 99-100
   indorsements, 91
   presentment, 100-4
   processing, 140-3
   receipt and acceptance, 87-93
   savings deposits as, 130
Cash letters, 111, 143
Cashless society, 202-3
Casualty insurance, 361-2
Central banks
   foreign banks, 319
   historical development, 329-30
Central reserve cities, 328-9
Certification stamp, 181
Certificates of deposit, 134-6
   liquidity, 245
   savings, 132
   time, 132, 134-5
   Uniform Commercial Code, 16
Certified checks, 21, 180-2
Chain banking, 335-6
Check clearing (*see* Clearinghouse)
Check digit, 195
Check handling devices, 140-3, 145-6
Check numbers
   magnetic ink character recognition, 147-9, 199-200
   transit numbers, 144-5
Check routing symbol, 145-7
Checking account analysis, 305-6
Checks
   advantages, 47
   alteration, 45, 160, 177
   cancelled, 165-6
   as cash items, 84-6
   cashing, 174, 179-80
   certified, 21-2, 180-2
   collection, 152
   dates of, 159-60
   defined, 16
   dishonored, 30-3
   drafts distinguished, 116
   electronic data processing, 152
   examination, 158-64
   historical development, 5-7, 277
   lost or stolen, 41-5, 182-3, 267
   on us, 88, 155, 169-70, 285
   payment of, 155-64, 174-9
   postdated, 160-1
   posting, 155-6, 157-8
   return items, 169-70
   routing symbol, 145-7
   sight drafts as, 264
   signatures, 160

sorting, 141-3, 145-6, 152
stale, 177
theft, 41-5, 182-3
travelers, 267
validity tests, 159-64
City items
   collection, 101-9
Civil War period, 324-6
Clearing credit, 106
Clearing debit, 106
Clearing items, 87-8
Clearinghouse
   development of, 109
   multi-county, 109
   operation of, 103-9
   presentment through, 103-9
   regional, 109
   return items, 108-9, 169-70
   revenue to support, 108
   rules and regulations, 107-9, 170
   settlement, 104-7
Clearinghouse association, 107-9
Clearinghouse proof, 106-7
Clearinghouse settlement, 104-7
Club or social accounts, 76, 174
Coin and currency (*see also* Bulk cash; Cash; Paper money)
   bulk cash, 89
   control of, 183-4
   counterfeit, 90
   deposits, 87-90
   foreign currency, 266
   money supply, 7-8, 206-7
   as reserves, 114
   "till money", 237
   United States Treasury, 7-9
   vault cash, 237-8
Collateral
   accounts receivable as, 280
   attachment, 54-6
   for bank notes, 332
   care of, 229
   loans, 211
   securities as, 218
Collection, 99-124
   automated, 143
   bank collection number, 121
   charges, 123
   check, 143-6, 152, 333
   clearinghouse, 103-9
   correspondent banks, 333
   electronic data processing, 152
   exchange charges, 113
   Federal Reserve System, 333
   forms, 121-2
   instructions, 121, 123
   notice of payment, 120
   par system, 113
   procedures, 121-2
   records, 121-2
   reserve account, 114
   transit items, 109-15
Collection charges, 123
Collection department, 121-2
   of partner, 64-5

posting, 194-7
proof operations, 151-2
report preparation, 198-9
statement preparation, 197
teller's station, 200-1
validity tests, 176
Electronic funds transfer systems (EFTS),
202-3
Electronic sorting, 149-50
Embezzlement, 361-2
Emergency withdrawals, 136-7
Employee trusts, 251-2
Escrow
   agent, 254
   certificate of deposit, 134
Estate planning, 255-6
Estates
   administrator, 53-4, 71, 250
   bankruptcy, 54-6
   executor, 53-4, 71, 249-50
   of incompetent, 54
   preferred claims, 54
   settlement, 53-4, 249-50
   testamentary trust, 250-1
Executor, 53-4, 71, 249-50
   bank as, 249-50
   defined, 249-50
Exchange
   bill of, 12-13
Expense
   verification of, 357
Exporters
   services for, 258-63
External controls, 342-9

F

Fair Credit Reporting Act, 228
Fair credit reporting laws, 80, 228
Federal agencies
   bonds, 244-5
   external control, 342-9
Federal Deposit Insurance Corporation,
127, 334-5
Federal Reserve Act of 1913, 128, 329-31
Federal Reserve banks
   bank notes, 7-8, 332
   borrowing from, 245
   clearing facilities, 107
   computer applications, 201-3
   money supply, 7-8
   routing through, 113-15
   Schedule of Availability of Credits,
   114
   settlement with, 114
   stock of, 205
Federal Reserve Board, 330
Federal Reserve districts, 146
Federal Reserve notes, 7-8, 332
Federal Reserve System
   bank credit, regulation, 222, 346-8
   Board of Governors (see Board of
   Governors of the Federal Reserve
   System, 330-2)
   collection of transit items, 113-15
   collection system, 113-15, 333

Committee on Check Collection, 145-6
control of, 331-2
country collection items, 120
functions of, 332-3
historical development, 329-33
money supply, 222, 346-8
nonmember banks, 341-2
ownership, 331-2
par collection system, 113-14
Schedule of Availability of Credits,
114
state member banks, 341
state nonmember banks, 341-2
structure, 329-31
Treasury securities, 208
Fictitious names (see Trade name or style)
Fiduciaries (see also Trustees; Trusts)
   agency services, 252-4
   death, 75
   defined, 249
   delegation of duties, 255
   estate settlement, 249-50
   trusts and guardianships, 250-2
Fiduciary accounts, 70-73
Fiduciary services, 252-4
Financial instruments, 5-6 (see also Negotiable instruments)
Financial reports (see Accounting reports)
Financial statements
   credit investigation, 224-7
Float, 100
   average daily, 302-3
"For deposit only", 27, 177
Foreign banks (see also International
transactions)
   advising banks, 262
   central banks, 319, 329-30
   correspondent, 259-63
   drafts on, 266
Foreign currencies, 259, 266-7
Foreign collections, 266
Forgeries, 45-6
   bank's obligations, 45
   detection, 186-9
   insurance, 360-2
   reimbursement, 161
   statute of limitations, 161
Formal trusts, 71-3
Forms
   control, 354-5
   multicopy, 121-2, 353
Fraudulent schemes, 41-5, 186-9
   conversion of funds, 92-3
   deposit accounts, 41-44, 91-3
   dormant accounts, 170-1
   fictitious names, 60-1
   insurance coverage, 360-2
   personnel training, 362-3
Free banking laws, 323
"Full service" banking, 278

G

General contract of indorser, 23
General indorsement, 26
General ledger, 155, 285-7

415